ARCHEOLOGY and a Science of Man

ARCHEOLOGY
and a Science of Man

WILFRED T. NEILL

COLUMBIA UNIVERSITY PRESS

NEW YORK 1978

LIBRARY OF CONGRESS CATALOGING IN PUBLICATION DATA

Neill, Wilfred T
  Archeology and a science of man.

  Bibliography: p.
  Includes index.
  1. Archaeology—Methodology.   I. Title.
CC75.N44   930'.1   77-11038
ISBN 0-231-03661-2

COLUMBIA UNIVERSITY PRESS

New York   Guildford, Surrey

To Ripley P. Bullen

AND

Adelaide K. Bullen

Contents

Introduction

It is easy to justify the appearance of a book on archeology, which deals with past cultures; for we cannot understand modern culture without a knowledge of its antecedents. We cannot predict where man is going until we know where he has been.

It is perhaps not so easy to justify the direction I have taken in the present work. As I explain at greater length in the text, I am sure that a science of man is badly needed, and think it is in the making. In this science, a scientific archeology will play a prominent role. By a "scientific" archeology, I mean one that follows the lead of the true sciences in using the scientific method, the most elegant method ever devised for augmenting man's knowledge.

In the opening chapter I have explained what is involved with this method, although many readers may already have a good idea of what it entails. Considerably fewer readers, I suspect, will understand precisely what I mean by interactions of archeology with other disciplines. This is the principal theme of my book: that a scientific archeology would utilize data from a host of other disciplines. For if archeology becomes a full-fledged science, it will follow the lead of the preexisting sciences, and so build interdisciplinary bridges. The major scientific development of modern times has been the breaking down of barriers between disciplines formerly discrete. The breakdown has given us such new hybrids as bionics, cybernetics, biomedical engineering, communication theory, information theory, econometrics, praxeology, functional morphology, semantics, symbolic logic, mathematical biophysics, and many more, including that triumph of modern science, molecular biology. A breakdown of barriers between the social disciplines, or between the latter and the natural sciences, will prove equally fruitful.

Over the opposition of some traditionalists, archeology is beginning to employ the scientific method, and to use data from other disciplines in the elucidation of archeological problems. So far, most interactions of archeology with other disciplines could be subsumed under the heading of environmental archeology. In general, this subdiscipline turns to various environmental sciences, such as botany, zoology, and parasitology, to throw light on vanished cultures. However, my interest extends far beyond environmental archeology in the usual sense of that phrase.

Thus, in the second chapter I have shown how archeology might profitably interact with linguistics; and with ethnology, a discipline that has usually focused on the culture of preliterate peoples in historic times. The third chapter, perhaps surprisingly, explains possible archeological interactions with toponymy, the study of place-names. The fourth chapter summarizes the relation between archeology and physical anthropology, while the fifth covers paleoanthropology, a new composite of archeology, paleontology, paleoecology, geology, animal behavior, and systematic zoology.

Chapter 6 attempts to show that economics, geography, history, sociology, psychology, and several other disciplines also have much to interest archeologists. Chapter 7 reviews some of the multifarious directions that have already been taken by environmental archeology. Chapter 8 does much the same, but extends beyond published material to show how data from environmental studies might contribute toward the solution of several archeological problems. Chapter 9 is devoted much more to problem-solving than to a review of published papers. Finally, chapter 10 attacks four archeological problems from directions that might prove novel to most archeologists. My intention here has not been to solve these problems beyond peradventure, but to provide stimulating insights into methods whereby archeological puzzles might be resolved.

Several people have helped with this book, in one way or another. William C. Pasco, Jr., has facilitated the book's completion in every possible way. For assistance in excavating, I am indebted especially to Laurence Hope, Leonard Hope, Dewey and Sally Mitchell, David and Victoria Mitchell, Wayne Mitchell, W. Trammell Neill, III, and George Ferguson. William F. Grey kindly conducted me to many archeological sites, and provided a synoptic collection of Gulf coast marine shells. Leonard Herrick supplied information about mollusks. Richard

Thomas donated many important archeological specimens, and provided pleasant companionship in the field. For permission to examine sites on property in their possession or care, I am indebted especially to Jerry Allen, Ross Allen, Meredith Dobry, the late W. M. Davidson, and the late W. C. Ray. Ross Allen supported several of my excavations, even though his interest was not archeology but herpetology. All these people have my thanks.

A special indebtedness to Ripley P. Bullen and Adelaide K. Bullen is suggested by the dedication. If archeology was not a science at the time I entered it, they at least were true scientists, for whom the pursuit of truth was of paramount importance. They encouraged my entry into archeology at a time when and in a milieu where it was unfashionable to encourage newcomers of any kind.

New Port Richey, Florida   WILFRED T. NEILL

ARCHEOLOGY and a Science of Man

CHAPTER ONE

Toward a Scientific Archeology

I want to discuss scientific archeology and the role it might play in a science of man, but it might be well at the outset to define a few terms that are used frequently throughout the book.

The term "culture" is here used to encompass all human ideas, and outward expressions thereof, that are not inherited but instead are transmitted socially. This usage, common in modern anthropology, is doubtless familiar to many; but it needs explication at the outset, for other usages are often encountered. Even in anthropology there have been numerous slightly or even markedly different definitions of culture (Kroeber and Kluckhohn 1952), but in modern times these have centered around the view that cultural behavior is something that must be communicated from one person to another, and from one generation to the next; it is not encoded into the genes even though it may be the overt expression of some innate, genetic urge. Certain cultural activities, such as the use of fire and the manufacture of flint tools, were carried on by some of man's prehuman ancestors, and a few human activities are strikingly foreshadowed in the behavior of modern subhuman primates; but otherwise, cultural studies in their great volume and complexity are focused upon man, his social, religious, artistic, ideological, and technological patterns of behavior, his methods of utilizing and coping with the environment. Language, too, is a part of culture, although it is often listed (and usually studied) separately from other cultural activities.

Man lives in groups, which may be large or small. Occasionally, a number of people may be thrown together for a short while by happenstance, but in most cases a human group is an organized aggregation that persists in time; its members follow a certain way of life, and regard their aggregation as having definite limits. In anthropological parlance, a group of this kind is called a society. Between one society and the next there are barriers to the spread of ideas. A barrier may be physical, as when two societies are separated by mountain ranges, deserts, or seas that are difficult to cross; or it may be linguistic, as when two societies speak mutually unintelligible languages. But the commonest barrier is attitudinal. Members of one society generally view those of another with something less than full acceptance; and as a rule, ideas circulate much more freely within one society than between two. Accordingly, each society tends to develop its own slightly or markedly distinctive version of culture; for if two groups are separated by any kind of barrier, each is likely to produce some inventions and adaptations that remain localized, and to admit the entry of somewhat different ideas and stimuli from outside sources.

This being the case, it is anthropologically acceptable to speak not only of culture in general, but also of the culture of some particular society, which may be extant or extinct. It is in fact permissible to speak of the culture of some human group that is not a society but that somehow warrants consideration as a unit. However, the total cultural activities of a large, complex society often are designated as its civilization rather than as its culture; for a society of this kind is likely to be characterized by cultural heterogeneity.

Although cultural activities are taught by one person to another, and handed down from one generation to the next, the patterning of these activities is determined for the most part by the society to which the teacher and the bestowing generation belong. An entrant into a society, whether by birth or by immigration, is taught and comes to learn its customs. This is why culture is described as being transmitted socially, and why the adjective "sociocultural" can be used meaningfully. The description does not rule out the probability that, as time goes by, a society may give up some old cultural activities and take up some new ones. While a few societies have been remarkably static of culture, a majority have been dynamic; and one of archeology's most absorbing tasks is the demonstration and interpretation of culture change with time.

The anthropologically knowledgeable reader will see that I have dealt rather casually with terminological matters to which a great deal of thought has been given by others. The general reader will see that such words as "culture" and "society" do not have the same meaning in the anthropological disciplines (including archeology) that they have in popular speech.

Archeology is a discipline that is concerned with a major part of culture: the part that is not discoverable from the observation of extant societies or from the study of written records. In an earlier stage of development, this discipline was sometimes called prehistoric archeology, as though the archeologist and the historian had to deal with mutually exclusive time periods, respectively before and after the advent of writing. But such a view was short-sighted, partly because in many areas there was a protohistoric period during which literate peoples coexisted with non-literate ones. More importantly, early written records often are very specialized in context, dealing only with such topics as magic, religion, royal lineages or conquests, and the invoicing of goods. Indeed, well down into historic times there were literate groups that did not record much about their own social organization, subsistence activities, general environmental relations, ideologies, technologies, or items of material culture. Accordingly, in many parts of the world there is a time period that can be investigated profitably by archeologists and historians alike.

In recent times, the term "prehistoric archeology" has had connotations more of methodology than of time period. That is to say, the phrase has been used to emphasize a distinctive approach to the study of the past, an approach more or less aloof from the concerns of the historian or the antiquarian. Certainly, human affairs are complex enough to warrant investigation from many different directions. But it is important to remember that from its inception culture has formed a continuum; in fact, it is the cumulative nature of culture that so conspicuously distinguishes it from whatever learned behavior may exist among lower animals. Thus, culture will not be fully understood if the earliest segment of the continuum is studied wholly from one direction, a somewhat later segment from a very different direction, and so on up to the present.

The temporal span to be covered by archeological studies might reasonably begin with the advent of culture, and in any particular region might extend down to a time when questions about some past culture could be answered more readily through a study of written records than through excavation. By this view and in the light of present knowledge, the span to be studied begins at least two million years ago, when a subhuman primate of East Africa was chipping out rude stone tools to a set pattern, and piling rocks into a large circle, perhaps to form the base of a simple shelter. Of course, in many parts of the world the span does not begin so long ago; for certain regions were never reached by man's subhuman ancestors, and others were reached by man himself only at a comparatively late date.

From the standpoint of widespread, current interest, the span ends well down into historic times, with the accumulation of written records in abundance and diversity. Records accumulated in some regions long before they did in others. In the United States, there has been a recent upsurge of interest in the archeology of historic towns, buildings, and shipwrecks. Most of these date from colonial (Spanish, French, Dutch, English) or early American times, for which written records are abundant but are not highly enlightening in some particulars. British "industrial archeology," concentrating upon sites of the Industrial Revolution, is a rough counterpart of American "historic site archeology." The British and other Europeans have also excavated many of their historic sites that were not especially related to industrialization; and just lately, in the United States, the British term "industrial archeology" is coming to be applied to excavation of old factories, mills, and other structures that were involved with the beginnings of American mass production.

A discipline, whether archeology or some other, is seldom changed very much by a critique of it; for its direction and methods are determined mostly by its practitioners, their intellectual capacities and bent, the opportunities that are open to them, the traditions that bind them. But as it happens, we have lately been promised a revolution in archeological thinking, and presumably this will reap a rich harvest of facts that eluded the older workers. True, it has lately become fashionable to reject the traditional simply because it is traditional; true, also, that idealism sometimes makes limited headway when confronted with practicality. But it seems that archeology is indeed at some kind of a turning point; and so any critical examination of it might now have a modicum of usefulness. I should like, therefore, to open with comments on archeology, from the standpoint of someone whose interests have extended from that discipline to adjoining ones in anthropology and biology.

There already exist many approaches to the study of man. Some of these are not rightly to be called sciences, for they do not use the scientific method of augmenting knowledge. But most of them have guiding principles or procedural rules, and so could be called disciplines whether or not they emphasize the scientific method. Although specialized in its aims, and therefore capable of progressing more or less independently, any one of these disciplines is likely to have some overlap with several adjoining ones, and to profit (or suffer as the case may be) from the position it traditionally occupies in a broad framework of investigations into human affairs and concerns. Accordingly, it is not amiss to begin with remarks on this framework, and proceed thence to one of its components, archeology.

At the start of such discussion, it is well to draw a distinction between science and technology. "Science" is the name given to man's vast accumulation of facts and his efforts to collect more of them, while "technology" is the application of these facts to human needs or desires. Although connected, scientific research and technological work are for the most part carried on by two different groups of people, each with its own orientation. Scientists can go only where impersonal facts lead them; but technologists cater as best they can to the wishes of the public or of some segment thereof, and as a rule they can do so only by dipping into the pool of facts previously accumulated by scientists. The general public clamors for the fruits of technology but has little knowledge of technological processes, and less of science upon which these processes must be based. Still, it is obvious even to the casual observer that science and its application have permitted man to understand and master a large part of the world around him.

Today, man easily overleaps mountain ranges, deserts, or oceans, and from orbiting satellites sends thoughts and pictures halfway around the world in a flash. He splits the atom, using its energy to supplement other power sources. He drills deep into the earth, explores the black depths of the sea, commands the biotic and physical resources of his planet, preserves or brushes aside thousands of plant and animal species. He drains or fills swamps, levels mountains, reshapes the coastal shorelines, extracts fresh water from the sea to irrigate the arid lands. He builds complex machines in never-ending diversity, from electric toothbrushes to transistor radios, from wristwatches to chain saws, movie projectors to nuclear reactors, refrigerators to television sets, bulldozers to supersonic jet planes. He even builds brain-like machines to store and manipulate data. He synthesizes the chemicals of life, transplants anatomical organs, transmutes the elements, turns out an endless variety of compounds that do not exist in nature. He explores the surface of the Moon afoot and by electric rover car, sets down robot vehicles on Mars, probes Venus and Jupiter, analyzes radiations from inconceivably distant galaxies. He unravels the mysteries of cosmic, chemical, and organic evolution.

But it is also obvious even to the casual observer that man has not amassed the facts that would permit self-knowledge and self-mastery, and has not developed the techniques that would adequately minimize painful frictions within and between societies.

Admittedly, there recently have been gains in the field of intersocietal relationships. Colonialism has nearly vanished, at least under that name. The so-called space race has proven a blessing to all mankind, for it has permitted great powers to compete fiercely but without bloodshed; and in addition, the "spinoffs"—processes and products discovered in the course of the race—have more than offset the cost of space programs. In some countries, civil rights are being extended to minority groups that were previously denied them. But these and a few other gains have come about all too slowly, while new social problems have been burgeoning. Localized wars follow one another in constant succession, and technology is turned to aggressive ends at the demand of societies or their leaders. There are revolutions, rebellions, riots, intolerance, injustice, chicanery in high places, inflation, recession. There are hostilities from the interpersonal level to the international, and widespread personality disorders resulting partly from social pressures. In one country the people starve, while in another they wonder how to dispose of food surpluses. In some lands most technological fruits have yet to be harvested, while in other lands there has been misuse of technology at the demand of the public, so that vast tracts are gutted of resources and the ecosystems destroyed for financial gains of the moment. Large cities decay and are taken over by the culturally deprived who may be lawless. Overpopulation threatens, and is not widely recognized for the manace it is. Educational systems progressively decline in several ways, as educators often chose not to lead the public but to follow its whims. Like the proverbial virtue, intellectuality and ethicality usually must be their own reward, for they command less and less in the marketplace.

Yet, all this is not to predict doom, even though it is fashionable, and I suppose saleable, to do so. For there is no problem that man cannot solve, whether it be splitting the atom or establishing peace on Earth, flying to other worlds or preserving this one, deciphering the genetic code or getting at the roots of interpersonal and intersocietal hostilities. But if complex, urgent problems are to be solved, first there must be a vigorous, effective search for the facts that bear upon them; for in the long run, factuality is considerably superior to fallacy as a basis for action. Since the physical and biological sciences have made such astounding advances, it would be well to investigate the method whereby they accumulate the facts bearing upon and permitting the solution of exceedingly intricate problems.

There is nothing mysterious about the scientific method. While it is somewhat flexible, in general it involves the explicit statement of a question or problem, and a marshalling of previously known facts that bear upon it. These facts may already fit some logical scheme, such as a classificatory one. Some facts can be stated mathematically or as measurements, but others not. When the pertinent facts have been amassed, a mental search is made for a hypothetical explanation of them, although even after having done so it remains but a tentative conjecture to be tested further. Where possible, the hypothesis is tested by direct experimentation; when this is not feasible, there are alternative procedures whereby it can be evaluated. If the hypothesis stands testing, it is elevated to the status of a theory, and is published as such. Publication usually is in a journal that is issued explicitly for the presentation of the theories that arise from research, but a theory and its documentation may also be published as an article or a book that is apart from any journal series. In any event, publication is essential; hypothesis, experimentation, and theory are as nothing without it. For the next step in the scientific method is the critical analysis of the published theory by other workers, who may oppose it, approve it, refine it, or build upon it according to their own findings. And their critiques, in turn, are published for critical review.

In the scientific method, all questions, pertinent facts, hypotheses, experimental or other evaluative procedures, theories, and critiques are stated as unequivocally as possible, always with careful attention to semantics, and often in a special terminology that minimizes misunderstanding. At all stages of investigation, effort is made to be wholly objective. If human error or personal bias creeps into one worker's published theory, it will soon be pointed out and eradicated by other workers whose findings are themselves offered up for evaluation. When an investigation has reached only a controversial stage, interpretation of findings may for a time be influenced by consensus; but there is no rigid acceptance of authority. Logical schemes, such as classificatory ones, are regarded simply as tools useful in investigation, or as "shorthand" ways of expressing concepts. They are not immutable, but are changed when facts reveal that they should be; and proposed changes of them are likewise published for review. In scientific work there is a search for regularity and causality, but no *a priori* insistence that regularities or causal relationships must exist in every case.

By the scientific method, facts are collected with maximum efficiency, taking full advantage of human ratiocinative abilities. The method permits, in fact it calls for, the continued canceling out of any errors that may have crept in as a result of human fallibility, and it continually opens pathways for further attack upon the unknown. By this approach, knowledge is augmented at an exponential rate. So much cannot be said of other approaches, which are inefficient, progressing by fits and starts, and garnering almost as much chaff as good solid grain. The advances of the twentieth century in the physical and biological sciences would not have been possible without the scientific method, which extols factuality and eschews fallacy, just as far as the human mind can distinguish the two. Use of the method has provided a vast pool of facts upon which technologists have drawn at the demand of the public or some influential segment thereof.

Although collectively called the "social sciences," most of the social disciplines have made but little use of the scientific method, and in consequence have accumulated only a comparatively small pool of facts. This situation exists partly because workers in the social disciplines have occasionally shared some widespread misconceptions about the scientific method, and have mistakenly regarded it as demanding a greater degree of rigor than is practical when human affairs are studied. Actually, there are sciences (for example, astronomy) whose practitioners can only observe, not experiment with, the objects that interest them. A major part of biology is founded on evolutionary theory, yet the evolution of any particular species is neither repeatable nor directly observable. Nuclear physicists live with the realization that certain characteristics of an atom must inevitably be altered simply by the act of observing it. And so on through the sciences: at times, almost any of them can only proceed obliquely. The "exact sciences" never included all the sciences, and today it is a rare scientist who would use the expression at all.

As for the individual scientist, he need not follow the steps of the scientific method in the precise order of their description. In fact, he is more likely to range back and forth through them, mentally adjusting them to one another until he arrives at a publishable conclusion; and in many of the scientific problems confronting him, most of the steps have already been taken and published by others. Only a minority of scientific research papers offer a flashing new insight. A majority of them serve principally to uphold or question a current theory, to present an observation for possible use by colleagues, to describe a promising analytic technique, to help standardize terminology, to clear up troublesome minor details of a problem that has largely been solved, or to extract a generalization from the scattered observations of others.

The various social studies have been moving from a position near the humanities to one nearer the sciences. Some branches of sociology and of psychology have in fact become quite scientific, and one branch of linguistics purposefully dubs itself scientific. An explicitly scientific approach has been urged for archeology, and there are contentions that anthropology in general could now be thought of as a science, albeit a struggling one. A new kind of history takes culture history into account, and searches for generalizations. All the social disciplines strive toward factuality, and are becoming more inclined to search for causalities and regularities. But on the whole, these disciplines still tend to accumulate their facts rather haphazardly, and all too slowly to meet the desperate needs of the modern world in which social problems are multiplying and looming ominously.

In most recent times, it has become dramatically evident that a comprehensive science of man must emerge, and speedily. By "science" I mean, of course, a discipline that employs the scientific method, which is unsurpassed as a way of providing a factual foundation for judgment and action; and I say "comprehensive" because man's cultural, social, linguistic, psychological, and physical peculiarities are all tightly interwoven, and this interweaving must be taken into account even though at times it may be practical or convenient to investigate the aforesaid peculiarities separately.

By etymological derivation, and by definition in most dictionaries, anthropology is the study of man; but in spite of recent advances, it is not the desperately needed science of man. For it often fails to employ the scientific method, it is all too limited in its scope, and the few disciplines included in it are in some cases less related to one another than they are to disciplines that are excluded from it.

The subdivisions of anthropology have sometimes been listed as physical anthropology, linguistics, ethnology (including ethnography), social anthropology, and archeology. Physical anthropology came to be grouped with linguistics and ethnography because early anthropology was oriented toward description of each society as a unit; the aim was to describe the physical characteristics, language, and customs of the people who made up each society—not every society in the world, I hasten to add. The early anthropologists were interested in Africans, American Indians, and the islanders of the Pacific and Indian oceans; and it was the direction of this interest that resulted in anthropological preoccupation with simple societies and unadvanced cultures.

Ethnography provided the raw data for ethnology, whose approach was more interpretive and cross-cultural. As for social anthropology, its original development may have reflected a concern—especially but not exclusively a European concern—with social organization and relationships as determinants of culture; but in time, it was not consistently distinguished from ethnology, and either discipline was likely to appear under the name of cultural anthropology.

Meanwhile, archeology had been growing more or less independently. Its name was once given to what we would now call ancient history. However, I am concerned here not with changing terminology but with the actual practice of studying the tangible relics of vanished societies. The practice had its roots in the Renaissance, with the first efforts to recover information about the highly admired civilizations of Classical antiquity. Archeological interest was later extended to other traces of past societies. It was easy to bracket archeology with ethnography, since they both dealt with culture.

Hence, five disciplines were subsumed under anthropology, the number often reduced to four by the equating or combining of social anthropology with ethnology. Occasionally, the anthropological disciplines were simply divided into cultural anthropology and physical anthropology. The aim of the subdivision was to distinguish cultural from biological studies, but in practice archeology was not integrated with other branches of cultural anthropology. Under the name of human evolution, the study of man's prehuman ancestors and near-human relatives was traditionally included under physical anthropology; but of late it has metamorphosed into a distinctive new discipline, sometimes called paleoanthropology. This overlaps archeology to a considerable degree.

Until quite recently, the anthropological disciplines have not expended much effort in the study of technologically advanced civilizations or highly complex societies of an essentially modern type, although the new "urban anthropology" does indeed study city neighborhoods or ethnic groups. Paleoanthropology of necessity has dealt only with very ancient skeletal remains and cultural traces. Archeology proper has rarely treated any culture more advanced than that of the early civilizations. As suggested by the names, "historic site archeology" and "industrial archeology" have been rather closely limited to investigations at or pertaining to restricted localities of historical interest. As for ethnography, from the start it was especially concerned with the customs of so-called "primitive" peoples, upon whom ethnology or social anthropology therefore came to focus. Ethnology has occasionally dealt with peoples who were culturally advanced, but in so doing has singled out small societies, or else small groupings within a society. Of the anthropological disciplines, only physical anthropology and linguistics have not concentrated strongly upon the culturally less advanced peoples of the world.

It therefore follows that a comprehensive science of man would have to include not only the disciplines that make up anthropology, but also those that deal wholly or in part with modern times, complex societies, civilizations however advanced. In other words, it would have to include, among other studies, all the social disciplines: those of anthropology, as well as history, sociology, economics, human geography, political "science," and the multifarious subdivisions of these. This is not the place to discuss whether or how all the social disciplines would metamorphose into sciences. Their scope is well known, and it is easy to see why the facts they uncover would be incorporated into a science of man.

This comprehensive science would also have to include psychology and human ecology. I shall defer discussion of human ecology until later in this chapter, but wish to say something here about psychology. Not long ago, in anthropological texts, it was customary to mention the inevitable interaction of culture, society, and human personality. The custom was a good one; and it is unfortunate that psychology, or rather a part of it, did not become more firmly linked with sociocultural studies. Psychology did not remain wholly aloof from such studies, but most of its links were with specialized aspects of sociology. Since the early 1940s, there have appeared a substantial number of works dealing with the effect of society on personality, or with the application of psychological knowledge to problems of industry, education, and advertising. Not much attention has been given to the effect of personality on society. Most of the work along this latter line has been done by ethnologists who were studying the influence of personality variants on culture change in small societies.

In the past, psychology has often been placed among the social disciplines; but it does not comfortably occupy such a position, for one of its six traditional subdivisions is animal psychology, and in several other ways it overlaps biology. Indeed, the biologically oriented branches of psychology have lately come to the fore. It is a bit ironic to see that while sociocultural factors are so important in the patterning of man's activities, the most popular recent accounts of human behavior have been essentially extrapolations from the innate, genetically controlled behavior of animals. Needless to say, popularity is no guarantee of factuality; but there are points at which the behavior of animals throws light on that of man, and these points have been considered in scholarly fashion by some. Also, there seems to be a new science of behavior in the making, combining studies from human and animal psychology, animal ethology, neurophysiology, neuroanatomy, and biochemistry.

As a matter of fact, psychology seems to be hybridizing admirably with quite an assortment of other disciplines, not just with sociocultural and biological ones but even with mathematics, electronics, and several more. In a science of man, psychology would probably hybridize more widely than ever before. (It would be especially gratifying to learn, through some psychology-history rapport, whether the historical course of a civilization is significantly altered by the personality of its leaders, or whether "the times call forth the man" who can do no more than temporarily hasten or slow an inexorable march of events.)

A science of man should embrace the entirety of every discipline that deals principally with man, and that explicitly aims to uncover facts about human (and in some cases prehuman) culture, society, language, psychology, biology, or combination thereof. Disciplines are not tangible objects, and so it might be asked just what is entailed by "inclusion" of them within a single science of man. Doubtless many practitioners of that science would continue to specialize, some in familiar directions, others in new directions as these became feasible. But with an explicit admission that the disciplines however various were all part of one science, it would be easier for narrowly specialized approaches to broaden usefully; and among the specialists there would soon be a leavening of generalists, for an interdisciplinary view would permit a higher order of generalization than is now possible. A premium would be put not only on breadth of interest but also on use of the scientific method. Those unfamiliar with this method would soon discover that it is elegant, and more readily applicable to their work than they had previously supposed. They would be encouraged to search for regularities and causalities, not to ignore them in favor of simple description and comparison.

No doubt a science of man would group its component disciplines in a new and more logical fashion, for example by admitting that archeology has more in common with history than with linguistics, and social anthropology more in common with sociology than with physical anthropology. But there is little point in speculating now about the exact nature of the new groupings, for it is already evident that wholly unanticipated avenues of investigation suddenly beckon when workers begin to ignore the traditional compartmentalizations of knowledge.

But for a long while after formal recognition of a science of man—for just as long a while after as appeared needful—the component disciplines of that science would remain recognizable. They would maintain distinctive cores, yet could interact with and illuminate one another. Whenever desirable, any component discipline could hold the center of the stage, with the others grouped around it in supporting roles. Each component could make free use not only of other disciplines that were subsumed under the science of man, but equally free use of selected studies from fields that were not so subsumed.

Whence might come the aforesaid selected studies? Some, perhaps, from the humanities although they have already been rather thoroughly picked over for fact. Even well down into the present century, the humanities were taken to include archeology, philology and grammar, history, economics, and political science; but these have since been turned into social disciplines, and today the humanities include little more than painting, sculpture, the dance, music, drama, literature, religious mythology, and some kinds of philosophy. The representational and performing arts, along with literature, may uplift, sustain, arouse an emotion, entertain, and sometimes express an opinion; but their principal concern is not the discovery of new facts. The dozen or so major religious mythologies, and the uncounted minor ones, similarly may uplift, sustain, etc.; but they are not congruent with factuality, and indeed have generally been in opposition to it, since they do not bear analysis on the factual level.

As for philosophy, some authors have regarded it as a wellspring of ideas from which the natural sciences and social disciplines have arisen. Certainly a dozen or so of the ancient Greek philosophers were science-minded. However, it seems to me that most past philosophizing was rather indifferent to fact, being more concerned with the presentation of opinions about ethics and morality. Of course, no great body of fact was available to the older philosophers. How wonderful it would be, in some way to bring them to the present; to give them a short list of words or phrases—Anti-S Protein, australopithecine man-ape, continental drift, direct probing of the limbic system, DNA, Krebs cycle, FORTRAN language, mascon, meiotic division, meson, parsec, pansynthesis, photosynthesis, principle of parity, quasar, Special Theory of Relativity, uncertainty principle, virus—and see what kind of philosophy they would write after they had studied and learned the full meaning of these terms.

Notably seminal works—for example, those of Haeckel and Darwin in biology, or of Adam Smith, Malthus, Ricardo, Mill, and Marx in the political and economic sphere—have sometimes been labeled philosophy, but I would instead place them with the disciplines to which they relate. Also labeled as philosophy are certain modern speculations on human nature and destiny, appearing in predominantly factual works, and based upon specialized knowledge within just one or a few fields such as mathematics, symbolic logic, semantics, art, psychology, or evolutionary biology. When such speculations go beyond the speculator's field of competence and specialization, they might be called philosophy, and they might occasionally include a useful insight.

Yet, all this is not to say that the humanities are to be dismissed completely by those who develop a science of man. From simple tribal societies to the most complex modern civilizations, the laity have been entertained or stirred by the representational and performing arts, and have explained the world not in terms of factuality but of fictitious schemes from some religious mythology. The humanities should therefore be studied by workers within the appropriate components of a science of man; but they should be studied objectively, from the outside, just as an ethnographer would investigate the art, dances, music, folktales, mythology, and ideology of some tribal society. This objective study of the humanities is quite a different matter from a search within them for ideas that might be incorporated into a science of man.

Although the component disciplines of a science of man might directly take but little from the humanities, they could take much from the natural sciences. One of these components, physical anthropology, could and should derive a great deal from the zoological sciences. In the past, physical anthropology has been too limited in its scope. It has been concerned mostly with man's evolution, variation, and adaptation; but it should be extended to encompass all studies on human form and function. Many of these studies currently repose in zoological sciences such as descriptive and comparative vertebrate anatomy, functional morphology, histology, cytology, embryology, physiology, genetics, endocrinology, and systematic zoology; also in the new fields of bionics, cybernetics, and molecular biology. Psychology has already drawn upon anatomy, physiology, genetics, endocrinology, animal ethology, animal psychology, and several other sciences, but has by no means exhausted the possibilities of such draft. Finally, almost all component disciplines of a science of man would find much of value in studies selected from the sciences that deal with man's physical and biotic environment. At this point I want to comment briefly on some of these studies; to describe, not over-emphasize, their pertinence to the disciplines that focus on human affairs.

Consider the field called physiography. It would not inherently be a part of the science of man, for it deals with the natural world and certain natural processes: the relation of sea to land, sedimentation, calcareous deposits of the continental shelf, deposits of the land, erosion, drainage, soils, topographic relief, land-forms, lakes, glaciation, and the subdivision of the Earth into physiographically distinctive provinces. Yet, the physiography of the Earth has had an effect on man's migrations, history, agriculture and other subsistence activities, economics, settlement patterns, political subdivisions, trade and other intersocietal contacts, transportation, and a host of lesser cultural adaptations to local conditions. Human geography already takes some note of physiography; but actually, a variety of cultural, social, and historical manifestations in any region are to be accounted for in part by its physiography. Thus, he who attempts to interpret the human activities of that region might do well to understand its physiographic possibilities and limitations.

Again, botany treats not man but plant life. Yet, man has turned to plants for food, drink, seasonings, smoking indulgences, intoxicants, stimulants, hallucinogens, hypnotics, tranquilizers, anesthetics, abortifacients, and aphrodisiacs. He has turned to them for soaps and other cleansers, paints, varnishes, gums and chewing-gum, rubber, insecticides, cosmetics, febrifuges, and vasodilators. Also for antihelminthics, antiseptics, medicinal specifics, magical potions, cathartics, emetics, blood and stomach poisons effective in man and animals, clothing, fibers with many uses—all these and more, to say nothing of wood, which is worked into an almost endless variety of objects and which is burned to supply warmth and to cook food.

To continue in this same vein, the various subdivisions of zoology that treat specific animal groups would not themselves be part of a science of man. Yet, animals of one kind or another have fallen prey to man, menaced him, been taken by him into domestication for several reasons, provided him with food and multifariously useful bones and hides. Both plants and animals have sometimes captured man's imagination, and so have figured in art, legend, and religious mythology. Quite a few organisms, some of them not strictly plant or animal, have parasitized man, occasionally to a degree significantly influencing regional population, demography, and intersocietal contact.

Accordingly, there are circumstances under which a knowledge of the biotic environment might throw light on subsistence activities, domestications, trade, settlement patterns, medical practices, economy, and other topics of much concern to the student of man.

Without pursuing the subject at length, it should be evident that some physical and biological sciences could contribute richly to a comprehensive science of man, especially by revealing the environmental challenges and opportunities to which he has responded culturally. Among these sciences are geology (with many branches), oceanography, climatology, ecology, biogeography, parasitology, botany, virology, and the zoological subsciences that deal with specific animal groups (mammalogy, ornithology, herpetology, ichthyology, malacology, etc.). To the list could be added agricultural and medical studies. It should also be recalled that man's lineage traces back to a time when his environment differed in many ways from the one we can study directly today. Man has persisted through changes in topography and climate, in the relation of sea to land, in the distribution of plants and animals. He has coexisted with giant beasts now extinct. Thus, a science of man, and especially its archeological component, could be bolstered by findings from paleoecology, paleoclimatology, paleontology, paleobotany, palynology, and other studies that throw light on the environments and organisms of the past.

Although the aforesaid physical and biological sciences treat man's past and present environment, they extend their scope to topics somewhat remote from inquiries into human affairs. They extend, for example, to geomorphological processes, the causes of climatic episodes, the fairly detailed anatomy of thousands of plant and animal species, and the physical conditions and biota of time periods far antedating the evolution of man. But even though no one of these sciences could be subsumed in toto under even the most encyclopedic study of man, each has parts that must be considered if man's story is to be unraveled fully.

It might be asked if these parts are incorporated into the presently emerging discipline called human ecology. They are not so incorporated to any great extent at the present time, even though ecology is defined as the study of living things in relation to their environment. The reasons for this situation are worth noting briefly.

About a century ago, the word "ecology" (in the form "Oekologie") was coined by Ernst Haeckel. While earlier decades had seen some work of the kind we would now characterize as ecological, the aforesaid coining marked the beginning of self-conscious ecology. Although the science burgeoned, it did not become widely known among scholars or laymen for quite a long while. However, by the 1940s it was generally evident that ecology was one of the most promising of sciences, especially since it could synthesize material from a number of formerly discrete fields. Around the early 1950s, ecologists (in the strict sense of the term) began to ask whether their science could encompass human ecology; and ecologists, sociologists, zoologists, geographers, paleoecologists, and others debated the issue. Meanwhile, human ecology texts continued to appear, and in 1952 a journal of human ecology.

In 1953, in the encyclopedic *Anthropology Today* (Kroeber, ed. 1953), Marston Bates noted that the term "human ecology" had been used to denote the epidemiology of human diseases, the study of human geography, and the study of man's general environmental relations. It had even been used, or misused, to indicate that a particular work was regarded by its author as having broad relevance to problems of human conduct. However, Bates did not enumerate all the ways in which the expression "human ecology" had been employed. Beginning around 1950, some writers on this subject began to treat what would usually be called sociology. Such treatment was easily justified, for in ecology proper, the environment of an individual was regarded as including other individuals of the same species, and ecological studies extended to the investigation of numerical, spatial, and other intragroup relationships within a population of a species. Some authors astutely realized that responses to the environment are determined innately, genetically, in plants and animals, but are for the most part determined socioculturally in man; and with such realization, human ecology automatically encroached to some degree upon what had been sociological territory. And to further confuse the issue of human ecology's scope, a few workers held economics to play the same role in the study of man that ecology played in the study of plants and animals.

A good bit of the confusion was resolved in 1956 with the appearance of *Man's Role in Changing the Face of the Earth,* a symposium dealing with the ways in which man, past and present, had regarded, utilized, and been influenced by the resources of his environment (W. L. Thomas, ed. 1956).

While all this was going on, more and more people began to see that in or at the behest of technologically advanced nations, the commercial exploitation of the environment was proceeding all too recklessly. As early as 1956, an elementary review of the social sciences devoted considerable space to such ecological or near-ecological topics as the food chain on land and in the sea, interrelationships among living things and their environment, disturbance of ecosystems by man, improvident land-use and water-use practices, pollution of ground water, plant succession and forest management, dwindling supplies of minerals, and over-population. But the latter 1950s, and more especially the 1960s, also saw a spate of pseudo-ecological pronouncements, both by those who would save what little is left of the natural world and by those who would destroy even its remnants for immediate financial gain. At least, this was true in the United States, where opinions can be expressed freely whether their basis is factual or emotional, and where controversies are rarely settled by government fiat. The word "ecology" began to appear more and more frequently in the news media, where it was progressively shorn of much of its meaning; and by the latter 1960s, the naive reader might have been led to suppose that an ecologist was a special kind of conservationist, preservationist, or social reformer.

In short, ecology itself got off to a late start, and its relation to human ecology was just coming to be defined when attention was diverted to special ecological problems, mostly those arising from man's improvident exploitation of the environment and his heedless disposal of waste products.

Of course, work also continues along some of the earlier lines that were taken by human ecology. And within this general field, a promising new line of specialization has emerged under the name of cultural ecology. This treats the adaptation of a culture to its environment, and the way the institutions of that culture are adjusted to one another as a result of that adaptation. The aim of such treatment is the discovery of forces behind culture change. Work in cultural ecology usually involves an excursion into ethnoscience and even linguistics, for it is necessary to know how the culture-bearers classify their environment.

But just now and for a long while to come, there are many selected studies that can be borrowed by the social disciplines from the sciences that describe man's physical and biotic surroundings—borrowed with little likelihood of duplicating the work that is going on in human ecology. Needless to say, cultural ecology and other aspects of human ecology would constitute an indispensable component of a science of man.

It will be seen that I urge a science of man that embraces all disciplines dealing primarily with man, that encourages all possible use of the scientific method in these disciplines, and that borrows extensively from the physical and biological sciences. It may be felt that I am impractical or visionary in so urging; but actually, events seem already to be moving in the desired direction.

Alexis Carrel, in 1935, may have been the first person explicitly to advocate a comprehensive science of man. Describing himself as a scientist and not a philosopher, he emphasized that the biological sciences and social disciplines had lagged far behind the physical sciences, but that they should and could catch up. He saw that they had been hobbled especially by religious mythology, philosophy, and outmoded intellectual frameworks. While realizing that a science of man would require the cooperative efforts of many specialists, he warned that man would never be understood solely through a variety of specialized approaches. The approaches must be linked and integrated; and at least some scientists must aim not at narrow specialization within a science of man but at a broad comprehension of it.

Like his contemporary, anthropologist Earnest A. Hooton (1937), Carrel was perturbed by the state of the world as he saw it. He was alarmed to see that man had created an artificial environment unsuited to human physical and psychological needs; that modern civilizations put little premium on imagination, intelligence, or courage; that although the United States spent vast sums on education, it produced few intellectuals; that people were unhappy, declining mentally and morally; that human virtues were giving way to the crassest commercialism. A comprehensive science of man was badly needed, Carrel concluded, to uncover the facts that would permit cure of social evils.

"In practically every country there is a decrease in the intellectual and moral calibre of those who carry the responsibility of public affairs," Carrel wrote. "It is chiefly the intellectual and moral deficiencies of the political leaders, and their ignorance, which endanger modern nations." In 1939, just four years after he published that statement, Nazi Germany invaded Poland, and in 1940 moved into Norway, Denmark, the Netherlands, Belgium, Luxemburg, and France. Also in 1940, Japan invaded French Indochina, and in 1941 attacked the United States. The whole world was at war—a war that lasted seven years, cost over a trillion dollars excluding inestimable property damage, and took over twenty million lives excluding several million Germans who were exterminated by their own countrymen on political, racial, and religious grounds. In the closing years of the war, Franklin D. Roosevelt penned a speech, his last, in which he said that mankind's most urgent need was "a science of human relations." After the Great Depression and years of World War II, even a practicing politician could see that human affairs had to be studied scientifically.

Meanwhile, anthropologists had begun to express themselves. In 1944, Clyde Kluckhohn foresaw the growth of a comprehensive science of man, with anthropology (already so diverse) at its center, but including certain aspects of psychology, medicine, human biology, economics, sociology, and human geography. And in 1945, Ralph Linton edited and contributed to a symposium called *The Science of Man in the World Crisis*. This work was intended especially to make certain important findings more widely available. Linton accepted a definition of anthropology as "the science of man and his works." His approach was optimistic, and he made but brief comment on the comparatively unscientific way in which culture had generally been studied. (But in various other writings, he opined that there should and would emerge a science that treated man's cultural, social, and psychological characteristics.) In the 1945 work he held that anthropology, not sociology, would be at the heart of a science of man; for sociology was too firmly committed to the study of Western culture, which much of the world did not share. The clash of cultures was the source of many problems, and the aforesaid science would have to use a cross-cultural approach, something more familiar to cultural anthropologists than to sociologists.

In 1948 the physicist, banker, and philosopher L. L. Whyte predicted that the next development in human history would be the emergence of "unitary man." This new man would be free from illogical ideologies both religious and political. His convictions would stem from scientifically disciplined thought, and would spread only as they met the scientific challenges that were presented them. The new man would search for a formative process in the development of physical systems, in the history of the universe and of life, in the history of man, and in contemporary world trends. He would recognize the interdependence of all elements of the world system. Concomitantly with the rise of unitary man, there would occur a social leveling that would reduce both poverty and special privilege; and the Asian nations would rapidly rise to Western standards of living.

The years have validated some of Whyte's prognostication, although I think it will be an exceedingly long while before any sizeable percentage of the human race could be described as "unitary man." Be that as it may, Whyte was predicting a new orientation of human thinking, more or less along the lines of principles that would be incorporated in or would arise from a science of man.

Biologists also commented on the desirability of the aforesaid science. I believe that in biology, much more than in the social studies, there was willingness to bring a comprehensive, scientific approach to the study of man and his affairs. This situation existed partly because biologists knew more about the possibilities of the scientific method, and realized more clearly that any kind of progress, including intellectual progress, necessitates the constant abandoning of old stands. Also, by the mid-1940s, biologists had become very willing to break down some of the traditional compartmentalizations of knowledge, for they had discovered the enormous value of an interdisciplinary approach. Carrel, in 1935, had complained that the biological sciences were lagging behind the physical ones about as badly as the social disciplines were; but just a decade later, no such charge could have been made, for biology had been revitalized especially by a new breadth of outlook in most of its fields.

By the mid-1940s, biologists were speaking of the new anatomy, the new genetics, the new systematics, the new natural history. Anatomy had expanded beyond the descriptive and comparative to consider problems of function; to reach even into structural engineering for useful concepts. In one direction, genetics had begun to consider events on the molecular level; in another direction it hybridized with ecology, demography, evolutionary theory, and mathematics to yield population genetics. Systematics, once concerned with little more than description, had begun to cast about widely, from genetics through evolutionary theory to ecology, in an effort to discover the forces behind speciation and geographic variation of living things. The new natural history combined a part of ecology (itself the epitome of scientific synthesis) with animal ethology. These developments, and comparable ones in other branches of biology, led to a variety of new disciplines.

If by the mid-1940s biologists could speak of new bottles for old wine, a decade later they had some fine new vintages to bottle. Julian Huxley, in a 1957 collection of essays, not only reviewed the progress of biology but was also stimulated thereby to map out the tasks confronting mankind. Man is to be the caretaker of the world, and will determine the direction of future evolution. To fit himself for this high office, he must find out both the possibilities and limitations of human nature. This is an immediate responsibility, for the general outlines of the physical and biological world are already fairly clear, while the exploration of human nature has scarcely begun.

It is not enough (Huxley continued) to free the world of starvation, chronic diseases, and substandard housing; for the time will come when people will protest being starved of satisfaction or condemned to substandard fulfilment. A majority of human beings are afflicted with some kind of misery, which they try to lighten by hopes and ideals; but their hopes are usually unjustified, and their ideals have little semblance to reality. What is needed is zestful, scientific exploration of human possibilities, with a view toward the realization of hopes and the promulgation of factualistic ideals. Just as control of the physical world has been made possible by the scientific approach, so would the more gloomy aspects of human existence be illuminated by knowledge and comprehension.

According to Huxley, man's pressing needs include a more favorable social environment, an admission that beauty is indispensable, efforts toward increasing the quality rather than the quantity of people, realization that true understanding is a worthwhile end in itself as well as both a tool for and relaxation from a job, and awareness that duty is to self, to society, to future generations, and to mankind as a species. The human race could and should strive to transcend its old limitations, not just individually and sporadically but en masse; and when such "transhumanistic" thinking becomes the rule rather than the exception, man will take up a new kind of existence, as remote from ours as ours is from that of the prehuman species *Homo erectus*.

I have paraphrased Huxley at some length because he seems to me to offer the very distillation of biological thinking about man, his destiny, the way he is to be regarded and studied.

In 1960, the biologist P. B. Medawar referred not to a science of man but to what he called human biology. A practitioner of human biology, he said, should know something of genetics, anthropology, demography, history, and psychology, among other fields; and should "also be a fairly reasonable sort of human being." Human biology, as conceived by Medawar, is close to what I call a science of man; and a fairly reasonable sort of human being is a likely forerunner of unitary man who thinks transhumanistically.

Admittedly, when the wounds of World War II began to heal, there was progressively less demand for a comprehensive science of man. However, sociology in particular began to grapple aggressively, scientifically, with many of the problems confronting social man; began also to widen its scope, to build bridges toward other disciplines.

Between 1947 and the present, there were studies on class, status, and power; on American social patterns, on cybernetics and society, social changes wrought by the Industrial Revolution, the social structure of Islam, the relation between sociology and religion, social psychology, the evolutionary and comparative aspects of societies, medical sociology, the sociology of professions, the structural relations of pre-modern societies. Theories of social and economic organization were put forth, and casebooks of sociological analysis. In these and many other works, sociology interacted with numerous other disciplines, including psychology, criminology, economics, political science, cultural anthropology, human ecology, cybernetics, religion, history, medicine, demography, even mathematics.

Some sociologists emphasized the importance of the scientific method. Logan Wilson and W. L. Kolb (1949) did so, although with a bow to Pitirim Sorokin's opinion that the method cannot cope with problems of "values and ultimate ends." In several works, Talcott Parsons used a good bit of terminology from the natural sciences, a terminology implying that certain human activities are rather predictable if large groups of people are involved.

In an introduction to sociology, Alex Inkeles (1964) related it to economics, political science, history, psychology, and anthropology, and discussed the use of the scientific method in the social disciplines. He suggested that anthropology would eventually vanish into sociology, or at best remain a minor sociological subdiscipline concerned with the investigation of small groups within a society. This would happen because modern civilization was spreading to all parts of the globe, so that in time there would be no uncivilized peoples of the kind anthropologists have traditionally preferred to study.

Anyone who has traveled widely in recent years will have to admit that modern civilization is spreading rapidly to many parts of the world that were regarded as remote just a few decades ago. Like spectacular wildlife and fairly natural ecosystems, the unadvanced cultures or simpler societies of the world will not survive much beyond the present century. Nevertheless, anthropology has not yet withered. To judge from a 1972 review by David Kaplan and Robert A. Manners, several parts of the discipline have lately been revitalized, and still hold much promise.

Kaplan and Manners called anthropology the "most presumptuous" of disciplines: it treated both the cultural and the biological nature of man, and its scope could legitimately encompass culture at all times and places. Although regarding anthropology as viable for a long while to come, these authors granted that all the social disciplines were becoming more interdependent in research, analysis, and application; were moving toward a new kind of holism. They did not believe that these disciplines would vanish into an all-encompassing science of man. Nevertheless, their "new kind of holism" is close to what I mean by a science of man, whose components would maintain just as much distinctiveness as was profitable.

Whatever the convergence among the social disciplines, most subdivisions of anthropology have by no means run their course. Physical anthropology is more adolescent than senescent; it could well be expanded to encompass far more studies on human form and function, and could interact more boldly with psychology. Linguistics offers a network of unexplored pathways. The ethnologist William C. Sturtevant (in Clifton 1968) sees or foresees a "new ethnology," bringing together such approaches as ethnoscience, ethnosemantics, componential analysis, and others. Culture theory searches for generalizations more aggressively than did the old ethnology, and ethnohistory is a hybrid field that has not been fully exploited. Paleoanthropology is so new as to require much more field work before it can fill the many gaps in our knowledge of man's evolution.

As for archeology, there are several reasons why it should flourish, not decline. For in spite of a willingness to consider some ancient events, sociology is strongly oriented toward the study of extant civilizations; and in spite of a new willingness to search for causalities and regularities, history is largely committed to the study of literate societies. But culture, including social usages, is at all times a heritage, a legacy from the past; and knowledge of the past provides the only guide whereby the present can draw a workable blueprint for the future. History can deal with the recent past, paleoanthropology with the remote past; but the greater part of the human story can be interpreted only by archeology, which would therefore be a major component of a science of man.

Archeology arose out of an interest in the civilizations of Classical antiquity, an interest inspired by the Renaissance. One branch of the discipline, Classical archeology, is therefore older than the others. This one, however, has been more or less interwoven with history and the humanities; and its approach often verges upon the antiquarian, emphasizing the esthetic rather than the scientific value of artifacts from archeological sites. Archeology as a full-fledged discipline, with a distinctive methodology and broad aims, was late to emerge.

Johann J. Wincklemann (1717–1768) is generally considered the father of archeology. He was interested in statuary and other artistic productions recovered through excavation at Classical sites such as Pompeii and Herculaneum. His approach was that of the art historian.

Thomas Jefferson was among the first scientifically motivated excavators of an archeological site. In 1784, he investigated an American Indian burial mound in the lowgrounds of the Rivanna River in Virginia. He noted that the burials were in different strata, and so could not all have been interred at the same time; and that the presence among them of an infant's bones ruled out the likelihood that the mound had been erected simply to cover the remains of fallen warriors. But Jefferson was a polymath, ahead of his day in many fields; and modern archeology is sometimes regarded as having begun in 1870, when Heinrich Schliemann first dug into a heap of ruins at Hissarlik, Turkey, in search of Homer's Troy. Between Jefferson's time and Schliemann's, some archeological theorizing was done, especially by Sir John Lubbock, who coined the terms "Neolithic" and "Palaeolithic," and who first gave currency to the adjective "prehistoric." Some actual archeological work was also done—for example, by Squier and Davis in the United States, Stephens in Mexico and Central America, Rhind and Mariette in Egypt, Rich and Layard in Mesopotamia; but it was Schliemann who focused attention on stratigraphy. For his site turned out to be a number of ancient cities, piled one upon another; and it became evident that if Troy of the *Iliad* was to be distinguished from earlier and later settlements on the same spot, careful consideration would have to be given to the way younger debris had accumulated atop older.

The growth of archeology need not be traced in detail, for this has been done by others (e.g. Ceram 1967). Here I want only to emphasize the comparatively late inception of the discipline. Take, for example, the situation in the United States. Except for two or three precocious investigations of little more than historical interest, archeology in the United States began to develop during the period 1860–1910. Early attention was directed especially toward the more spectacular remains of ancient American cultures: the burial mounds that dotted the eastern half of the country, the imposing pueblos of the Southwest, the great shell middens that once were so conspicuous along the Atlantic coast and drainage, the evidence of aboriginal copper mining around Lake Superior. There were also a few early studies that attempted description and sometimes geographic analysis of certain broad categories of artifacts, such as pottery or stone work. Most of the pioneering archeologists were amateurs, in the original and finest sense of that word; they were zoologists, geologists, ministers, naturalist-explorers, business men, or scions of wealth, eager to augment man's knowledge through examination of seemingly ancient sites and artifacts.

Once the Civil War was over, the United States could concentrate upon dispossessing those few American Indian tribes who had managed to retain their ancestral lands; and in 1879 the Bureau of American Ethnology was inaugurated, primarily to garner ethnographic data from the shattered tribal remnants, but secondarily to recover archeological materials also. A Mound Division of the Bureau was established, charged with the task of showing that burial, temple, effigy, and other mounds had been erected by American Indians and not (as popular belief had it) by some mysterious "lost race." The creation of this Division gave further impetus to archeology as a discipline.

The number of archeological excavations in the United States gradually mounted through the first quarter of the twentieth century. Shortly thereafter, during 1933 and 1934, some important investigations were made using Tennessee Valley Authority funds, and labor provided through the Civil Works Administration and the Federal Emergency Relief Act. These investigations, which were published in commendable detail, involved site reconnaissance and excavation in river basins that were due to be flooded by damming in various parts of the Tennessee River drainage. The Works Progress Administration, which got under way in 1935, also supported a good bit of archeological research, as well as maintenance of museums where excavated material could be preserved. Support of archeology was also coming from universities and other sources, but I mention the Federal agencies in order to emphasize that even in their well-remembered time, North American archeology was still inchoate.

World War II stimulated an enormous amount of research in the sciences—even in sciences somewhat remote from human affairs—and to a lesser degree in the social disciplines including archeology. In the latter 1940s and early 1950s, there appeared some of the first works to attempt coordination of previous archeological studies in the United States (J. B. Griffin, ed. 1951; Martin et al. 1947, Wormington 1949). In other words, not until about 1950 had sufficient excavations been made, sufficient data accumulated, to encourage the publication of preliminary archeological syntheses for the United States.

This brief history reveals, better than any flat statement, just how young archeology is in the United States. Of course, it is a bit older in Europe, but the discipline could scarcely claim maturity, or even adolescence, until it had been extended to all parts of the world that had been occupied by man in prehistoric times. I regard archeology as being of about the same age as nuclear physics and space science. All three of these fields incorporate a few ideas from Renaissance or even Classical thinking, along with a considerable body of fact resulting from planned investigations of the nineteenth and early twentieth centuries; but all three first took recognizable shape in the 1940s and after. When in this chapter I offer what may seem to be strictures on archeology, I do not overlook that the discipline has accomplished a great deal, despite its comparative youthfulness. Apparent strictures here, and in recent works by others, really mean that archeology is having "growing pains."

American archeology had scarcely gotten under way before there were objections to the direction it seemed to be taking. As early as 1938, Julian Steward and Frank M. Setzler protested the growing dichotomy between archeology and cultural studies. A decade later, there appeared Walter W. Taylor's (1948) critical study of archeology. Taking issue with earlier approaches, Taylor deplored the fragmentation of the discipline into many narrow, unrelated studies. Description and analysis were seldom comprehensive, he complained, and there was hardly any interest in the function of artifacts recovered by excavation. Investigation at any particular site did not include efforts to reconstruct the culture of the people who once lived there; instead, the emphasis was on comparison of items from one site with those from another. There was a general archeological indifference to both theory and the drawing of inferences. Emphasizing that culture was ideas rather than artifacts, Taylor suggested that archeological attention be given to an outline of cultural materials from extant societies; to the ethnography of local peoples; to quantitative analysis of excavated items; to quality standards exemplified by these items; and to the environmental relationships of past cultures.

In the following years, Taylor's work was often cited favorably, but his recommendations were infrequently acted upon. As late as 1961, Ruth V. Evans noted that cultural synthesis, of the kind Taylor urged, was still a "will o' the wisp of New World archeology." However, she spoke favorably of V. Gordon Childe (1951, 1954, 1956, 1958), whose work seemed to her a model of Old World archeological reporting. Childe's studies were impressive especially because they were set within the framework of a culture theory.

The year 1968 saw much ferment in archeological circles. David L. Clarke presented an impressively long list of analytic procedures available to modern archeologists. Robert McC. Adams granted that archeology would benefit from a scientific approach even though some problems might elude it. However, Bruce C. Trigger was inclined to view the discipline as being history-like. Sally R. Binford and Lewis R. Binford edited a symposium in which the emphasis was on archeology as a discipline that, science-like, formulated and tested general laws. Lewis Binford also contrasted the older approach to archeology with the newer, scientific approach that seemed to be emerging. In 1969 and the two succeeding years, there appeared quite a few publications revealing a widespread desire to examine archeology critically, to push it in the direction of the sciences, and to broaden its scope (Doran 1970, Fritz and Plog 1970, Hill 1970, Hole et al. 1969, Longacre, ed. 1970, Martin 1971). These publications need not be reviewed at this point, for they have lately been remarked on by Patty Jo Watson, Steven A. LeBlanc, and Charles L. Redman, in a 1971 volume significantly titled *Explanation in Archeology: An Explicitly Scientific Approach*. These three co-authors discussed the logic of science, and the way it might be employed in archeological research. I do not wish to go over ground that they have covered, but only to concur with their general conclusions, and to supplement a few of their remarks about archeology as a prospective science.

I have defined "science" as man's accumulation of facts and his efforts to collect more of them. The definition says nothing about the way facts are obtained, for in science all facts are welcome regardless of how they were brought to light. But "a science" is a discipline that garners its facts chiefly by the scientific method. Although not yet a science, archeology has certainly contributed a great deal to knowledge, and some of its practitioners have turned out studies that were as nearly scientific as possible, considering the limitations of the previous work upon which they had to build. All this being so, it might be asked how archeology is hampered by its failure to urge the scientific method upon its devotees.

In answering this question, it is useful to consult Gordon R. Willey and Philip Phillips' 1958 analysis of archeological method and theory. Although concentrating upon American archeology, these authors considered its methodology to be typical of the discipline. They did not claim archeology to be a science, but held that anthropology as a whole was more like a science than like history in its investigation of culture and society. Disagreeing with the "culturologists" who would study culture apart from the culture-bearers, Willey and Phillips thought that archeology would profit in the long run if its data were organized in terms of a real world. They regarded the discipline as operating on three levels: observation, description, and explanation. In less abstract terms, these three levels are field work, the integration of field findings in terms of culture history, and finally the interpretation or explanation of the findings in terms of processes that are widely if not universally operative in human societies. While admitting that archeology rarely attained the third level, the authors emphasized that its ultimate aim should be the discovery of regularities.

The statement of Willey and Phillips seems a fair one. It reveals archeology to be nearly a science, but to fall short thereof through the omission of one important step in the scientific method. For a characterization of this step, I can do no better than quote George W. Beadle, Nobel laureate in physiology and medicine. "In the real world of science, the investigator almost always knows what he's looking for before he starts. His observations are usually undertaken to prove the validity of an idea. . . . Scientists are more curious than most of their fellows . . . and the best of them are as creative as the best composers, poets, or painters." Speaking of the scientists who performed the momentous feat of deciphering the genetic code, Beadle said that they "did no research—as laymen understand the word. They reread all the literature. . . . But mostly they just thought" (Beadle and Beadle 1966).

Scientists are encouraged to speculate in advance of action; to put the known facts together mentally, in one pattern after another; to devise hypotheses and possible ways of testing them. In contrast, archeologists have been encouraged by the standards of their discipline to think only about already excavated materials, and are sometimes appalled to hear archeological speculation even though its purely tentative nature is emphasized. This situation may exist partly because archeologists feel that they should be exceedingly cautious in making any kind of pronouncement about man and his story. But in science, pronouncements of all kinds are regarded as provisional, and even so-called conclusions are actually looked upon as theories to be bolstered or discredited by later work. Archeologists may also have wondered how hypothesizing could be done usefully in advance of excavation. Several scientifically oriented workers have lately shown how it can be done.

At this point I should indicate an awareness that archeology has been carried on in somewhat different ways in different countries; renovation of the discipline will be a simpler matter in some regions than in others. Watson, LeBlanc, and Redman (1971) contrasted European archeology with American, suggesting that the former is more like history, the latter more like cultural anthropology. A contrast of this kind is hard to make succinctly, for in the absence of clearly enunciated procedural rules, the discipline has had more of a sprawling than a dichotomous structure. Certainly, European archeologists often write in a straightforward, narrative style reminiscent of a history text. Also, the exceptionally long and complex history of Europe naturally pervades local thinking, and it is not surprising that there has been a sort of rapport there between historians and archeologists. Such rapport has been fostered by Classical archeology, which includes elements from history and which was developed mostly by Europeans. But regardless of how Europeans write archeology, it seems to me that they have done more than their American counterparts to investigate the past cultures of their respective regions.

The European archeologists are more inclined to show how their findings will fit into the framework of some culture theory; to emphasize the social aspect of sociocultural matters; and to consider intersocietal contacts in detail. Three circumstances may account for the

Europeans' preoccupation with culture theories and social problems. First, Europe is divided into a large number of surprisingly diverse societies, most of them with a painful history of external wars and internal class struggles. Second, many of these societies have been literate for an unusually long while, and the comparative abundance of early documents has afforded an unexcelled opportunity to follow sociocultural developments through the centuries. Third, since the Industrial Revolution, Europe has produced a large number of writers whose bold speculations on politics, government, and economics led them to offer sweeping theories about society and culture.

European archeologists have also investigated a good many special problems that have been somewhat neglected in the United States. To read an account of European archeological accomplishments, such as Grahame Clark's (1957) *Archaeology and Society,* is to discover that Old World workers have considered such topics as avenues of archeological discovery, survival of archeological evidence, the spread of agriculture, the spread of metallurgy, trade routes, the ecological setting of past cultures, reconstruction of economic life, and reconstruction of social, intellectual, and spiritual life. Topics of this kind have all too seldom been considered in connection with American Indian cultures of the past.

Archeology exhibits regional differences within Europe. Russian anthropology, including archeology, predictably follows Marxist guidelines in matters of interpretation. French archeology is noted for flair and inventiveness, German for methodical progress. But here I am especially concerned with certain differences between the British approach and the American. When archeology was developing in the British Isles, a majority of the people there could regard local archeological remains as the handiwork of their own ancestors, to be cared for accordingly; and it became a mark of refinement to speculate about the original utility of ancient artifacts, and to admire the workmanship that produced them. A very different situation came about in the United States. The American Indians were extirpated from most areas; and the conquerors, principally of European descent, had no sense of personal involvement with America's prehistoric remains. Such remains were not regarded as a precious national heritage, but rather as something to be exploited at will.

During the period c. 1890–1910, a great many American Indian burial mounds were opened, and village sites dug through, not for information but for spectacular specimens, most of which ended up in private or museum collections. One has only to look at illustrations in earlier works to realize how much extraordinary archeological material was collected around the turn of the century, and hoarded away without collecting data except perhaps a reference to the county and state of origin. Later, in Depression times, desperately poor people sometimes dug into mounds in the (usually vain) hope of finding something saleable. While all this was going on, archeology was taking shape as a discipline, and American archeologists found themselves increasingly at odds with laymen over the way Indian artifacts and sites were to be regarded.

This conflict drew national attention in 1933, with the opening of the Spiro Mound near Fort Smith, Oklahoma. The mound property had been included in 1905–16 land allotments by the United States government to displaced Choctaw Indians and their Negro associates. The mound had not interested archeologists, and in 1933 its needy owner, or rather the guardian of its minor owners, asked for and received legal permission to lease it to some equally needy diggers. The site turned out to have been a center of the so-called Southern Cult (now called the Southeastern Ceremonial Complex), a set of religious beliefs that spread widely in prehistoric times, and that was expressed as an elaborate complex of iconographic objects in stone, shell, copper, ceramics, and other materials. As Cult objects from Spiro began to reach dealers, archeologists attempted to halt the digging. The resultant dispute made nation-wide headlines; the financial value of the finds was grossly exaggerated in the press, and fantastic guesses were promulgated about the identity of the mound's builders. Dealers and archeologists published opposing and sometimes acrimonious accounts of the affair.

The Spiro controversy widened the rift between American archeologists and those laymen who were interested in prehistoric remains for any reason. Some deficiencies of American archeology, recounted by Taylor and still existing, actually reflect the disinclination of so many archeologists to consider subjects that are of lay interest.

This is not to say that archeology should adopt the so-called cognitive approach, which aims to discover precisely how different peoples organize and use their own respective cultures. Entailing an excursion into psychology and linguistics, this approach is appropriate mainly to a study of the ethnographic cultures. But it is well to bear in mind a dictum of the cognitive anthropologists: the familiar ethnographic categories of culture—subsistence activities, technologies, dress and adornment, transportation, recreation, religion, kinship, war and peace, and many more—need not have counterparts in the thinking of the culture-bearers, who may organize their conceptual world in a fashion quite different from that of the investigator.

Watson, LeBlanc, and Redman (1971) predicted, I think correctly, that archeology would turn into a science even though some of its practitioners opposed the change. A small but growing number of papers have dealt with topics or utilized approaches that many American archeologists have shied away from. Once on a scientific footing, archeology would broaden its scope enormously; for the most promising new trend in science is toward the breaking down of artificial barriers that have compartmentalized knowledge unduly.

A scientific archeology would build interdisciplinary bridges, and in so doing would anchor itself all the more firmly in a science of man.

CHAPTER TWO

Interactions of Archeology with Ethnology and Linguistics

In the preceding chapter, I suggested that a scientific archeology would build some interdisciplinary bridges, and would profit thereby. In the present chapter, I want to discuss some possible interrelationships between archeology and two other disciplines, ethnology and linguistics.

First, we may consider some interactions of archeology with ethnology (including ethnography). As pointed out by Gordon R. Willey (1966), archeologists must often depend on inferences, and some of the most reliable inferences are those that can be drawn from a comparison of certain archeological specimens with their ethnographic counterparts. Thus, a sharp flint point and a smoke-blackened pot, found in an archeological context, might convincingly be identified as a weapon point and a cooking vessel; for similar points and vessels have been studied ethnographically in many parts of the world, and their function repeatedly verified.

To cite one example of a rather simple comparison between an archeological specimen and its ethnographic counterpart, I described some thoroughly mineralized bone points from Wakulla Springs and other fresh waters of Florida (Neill 1964a). For several reasons, these implements were regarded as dating from well back in Florida Paleo-Indian times; that is, from roughly 10,000 to 9000 B.C., when the great beasts of the Pleistocene still existed and the last glaciation had just begun its retreat from the northern United States. (The reasons behind the dating need not be listed here. A later chapter discusses Paleo-Indian times in Florida.) The bone implements were of several varieties, one of which was small, sharply pointed at each end, and transversely scored a little above the middle. Closely similar specimens have been used in historic times by South American Indians whose culture has been studied by ethnographers.

In South America, the bipointed bone implement is bound to the beveled end of a wooden rod, and so serves as both point and barb. The transverse scoring marks the area where the implement is bound to the rod by fiber. The wooden rod is a pencil-shaped foreshaft which is fitted into a shaft proper—fitted firmly or detachably, according to whether the weapon is an arrow or a harpoon (Metraux 1949, 237, figs. 64–65). The bow and arrow does not date back to, and wooden foreshafts would scarcely persist from, Paleo-Indian times; but harpoon foreshafts of bone or of elephant ivory are known from a putatively or unequivocally Paleo-Indian horizon in several states, including Florida. The ethnographic specimens are used primarily in the taking of freshwater vertebrates, especially fishes; and the archeological ones in all cases were recovered from the fresh waters.

If the archeological specimens are as old as I suppose them to be, they suggest that the Paleo-Indians did not subsist wholly on big game, as has sometimes been asserted; they also took small game from the fresh waters. Even if the implements are not as old as postulated, they are still quite old, as implied by their complete mineralization. Their existence reveals a specialized pointing-barbing-binding technique to have had a wide distribution in time and space. Further study would probably show a wider spatial distribution than I have noted.

To describe a more important fusion of archeological and ethnological researches, William B. Sears (1952) investigated Mound D of the Kolomoki site near Blakely, Early County, Georgia. This complex site, with several burial mounds and temple mounds, was occupied by American Indians for centuries. Mound D was regarded as representing an extension into southwestern Georgia of a mortuary ceremonialism more familiar in Florida, where it appears at scattered localities of the Gulf drainage north of the Caloosahatchee River and east of the Escambia. In Florida, this ceremonialism characterizes what has been called the Weeden Island Period or the Weeden Island Phase, although it spread somewhat independently of the secular aspects of Weeden Island culture. (The spelling "Weeden" has always been used in the archeological literature, but is incorrect. Hereafter, I use the correct spelling, "Weedon.") The Weedon Island Period is dated roughly 400 A.D. to 1300 A.D., and Mound D was constructed in the latter part of the period.

Excavation revealed a sequence of activities involved with the mound's construction. The sequence included the clearing of the ground surface down to sterile soil, the burying in the cleared area of five people in log-outlined tombs, the filling of these graves, the placing of six large logs upright on the ground surface, and the piling of earth around the logs. A primary mound having thus been completed, it was next covered loosely with rocks; and then the protruding log tops were connected with poles to form a scaffolding. A human head with a copper and pearl brow ornament was placed atop the primary mound, under the center of the scaffold. A male person was buried just off the south edge of the scaffold, in a grave lined and covered with rock slabs; and two females were buried east of the scaffold. The male was apparently the person whose death had initiated the round of ceremonial activities, for his grave was of special type, and was a center around which later activities were oriented. As this grave was filled, a litter of poles was placed upon it. Finally, the primary mound and associated graves were covered with yellow clay, which was formed into a small quadrilateral mound, steep-sided and flat-topped, a replica in miniature of a temple mound at the site. At the south end of this replica, over the grave of the paramount individual, the clay was piled higher to form a disc.

Events at Mound D, as described so far, were likened almost point for point to the mortuary ceremonialism of the historic Natchez and Taensa Indians of the lower Mississippi Valley. Natchez-type funeral rites had been summarized by the ethnologist John R. Swanton (1911). It involved a round of activities initiated by the death of a person—chief, chief's wife, or war-chief—from the top stratum of a strongly class-stratified society. While minor ceremonies were being carried on around that person's death bed, scaffolds were erected in the public square. As the body of the deceased person was being carried to its burial place on a litter, several of his close associates (retainers, relatives, wives) were ceremonially strangled to death on the scaffolds; and then they were buried in a set pattern according to their rank.

A certain event at Mound D had no close counterpart in historic

Natchez-type mortuary ceremonialism. This was the burial of many human heads ("trophy" heads in archeological parlance), bundles of human limb bones, baskets of cremated human remains, and a great amount of pottery. The last included effigy vessels made especially for mortuary deposition. "Trophy" heads, assorted human remains, and mortuary pottery are known from ethnographic sources to have been temple furnishings. It seemed likely that the paramount person buried in Mound D had been a priest-chief who was so closely identified with the villagers' religious paraphernalia that the temple was cleaned out at his death, and its contents buried with him.

At any rate, the ceremonialism of Mound D differed from the historic Natchez-type only in being more elaborate. Ethnologists had speculated that the striking burial customs of the historic Natchez and Taensa were survivals in somewhat attenuated form of a ceremonialism that had formerly been widespread among mound-building Indians of the southeastern United States. Mound D provided archeological confirmation of this view. Sears noted that some Weedon Island Period burial mounds of the Tampa Bay vicinity, in Florida, probably paralleled the Kolomoki one in having been initially constructed to inhume an important person and his wives, retainers, etc. Sears also suggested that in a broad zone from eastern Texas to Tampa Bay, a stratified social system like that of the Natchez is expressed in burial mounds of roughly the same age.

Sometimes, ethnographic comparison provides the only clue to the otherwise puzzling function of excavated artifacts. For example, digging into early historic Tairona sites of Colombia, archeologists found a curious assocation of miniature grinders with broken beads and ornaments; a jaguar skull at the main entrance of a ceremonial structure; some wing-shaped bars of polished stone, at first mistaken for ornaments; and caches of beads or pebbles that had been buried in small pots beneath house floors. As it turned out, the local Coqui Indians, descendants of the Tairona, could clarify all these finds. Miniature grinders were used by them to pulverize beads and pebbles into a "food" for ancestral spirits of deities. A ceremonial house was still dedicated to the jaguar-god Cashindúcua, and in the old days its door would have been adorned with a jaguar skull. The stone bars were musical instruments; suspended in pairs from the elbows of a dancing Coqui priest, they tinkled. When a Coqui house was built, a pot was buried ritually in its foundation, and each member of the household placed in the pot a pebble. Pebbles varied in size, color, and shape, according to certain attributes of the people who dropped them in the pot. When a child was born, the pot was dug up and a new pebble added.

Several recent workers have agreed that ethnographic studies could prove useful in the interpretation of archeological findings, but have also warned that the equating of archeological materials with their presumed ethnographic counterparts must not be done casually (Anderson 1969, Ascher 1961, 1962, L. Binford 1967, Chang 1967, Williams 1967). And of course, analogies should be drawn cautiously, on the basis of as much data as possible. But in a scientific archeology, it would be methodologically acceptable for a worker to mention any archeological-ethnographic parallel that he deemed significant; his views would be described as or automatically regarded as tentative, and would soon be bolstered or negated by other findings.

It sometimes happens that an ethnographic-archeological analogy is impressive on typological grounds but seems dubious on geographic. A case such as this should be scrutinized closely. It is hard to prove beyond peradventure that an interareal similarity of culture resulted from independent invention rather than the diffusion of ideas, but there may be a chance of demonstrating a culture contact that had previously gone unsuspected.

Culture is not just a series of discrete trait-complexes, but is an interlocking of beliefs and practices. Thus, social stratification could be involved with mortuary ceremonialism, and religious beliefs with both. Agricultural practices could reflect environmental considerations, social stratification, division of labor by sex, and religious beliefs. Or take weaponry, which is not the simple topic that it might appear to be. On the contrary, in American Indian cultures alone, weaponry has been linked with annual cycle, hunting, fishing, technology, capital, diet, ornamentation, specialization of activities by age and by sex, craft specialization, exchange transactions, travel, gaming, athletics, dancing, concepts of the supernatural, ceremonialism, crime and punishment, warfare, and military organization. All items of material culture have some involvement with the environment, if only because it is the environment that provides raw materials of plant, animal, or mineral origin.

And so on through the rubrics of culture studies: in the lives of the culture-bearers, aspects of culture are not sharply compartmentalized but are interlocked, and the members of a society do not think of their own activities as falling into a series of discrete categories. Accordingly, if an archeologist excavates a village site or other kind of settlement, he is actually investigating what was left by a community of people whose beliefs and practices were elaborately interwoven. If he turns to ethnography and ethnology to guide his archeological interpretations, he will have to admit this interweaving even though it has often been neglected in the study of prehistoric cultures; and such admission is necessary if his aim is the organization of his data in terms of a real world. Even if the archeologist cannot indulge in cognitive anthropology, he might verge upon it at times through attention to possible combinations and permutations of the rubrics.

Although the beliefs and practices of a society are interwoven, they may not be ideally integrated; there may be certain conflicts among them, perhaps because some of them persist long after they have outlined their usefulness. This situation, too, should be of great interest to the archeologist, for one theory has it that sociocultural change is brought about through an effort to resolve conflicts of the aforesaid kind. I shall discuss this theory at greater length in connection with economics; at this point it suffices to say that an archeologist could make a great contribution by drawing attention to what he regards as disharmonies in any culture that he investigates.

Now let us turn from ethnography and ethnology to linguistics. One archeologically interesting outgrowth of linguistics is glottochronology. That was developed by Morris Swadesh and associates (1954, 1964), principally through studies on Indo-European languages. Many of these languages have existed in written form for such a long while that temporal changes of several kinds can be inarguably demonstrated in them. Indeed, some of these changes can convincingly be deduced in the absence of written records, through analytic procedures that need not be described here. The glottochronologists compiled a list of about 200 words that were comparatively resistant to replacement. These words constitute what might be called a basic vocabulary. Study revealed that if a society split into two groups, and if the groups moved apart in such a way that there was no further contact between them, then about 81 per cent of this basic vocabulary would remain essentially unchanged after a lapse of 1,000 years. Or to look at the matter in reverse, if two geographically separated groups of people, speaking related languages, now have about 81 per cent of the basic vocabulary in common, then they separated from a single parent stock around 1,000 years ago. Obviously, if basic words are replaced at a fairly constant rate through the centuries, it will be possible in many instances to determine approximately how long two peoples have been separated.

The glottochronologists realized that under exceptional conditions, one society might impose much of its language upon another; but they believed that if a society was so overwhelmed as to give up a significant percentage of its basic vocabulary, it would also have been changed profoundly in many other aspects of its culture. This culture change would be identifiable archeologically even if not recorded historically. Glottochronological studies on Indo-European languages were aided by written records, but the students thought that their methods were applicable to unwritten languages also. In other words, if conclusions based on vocabularies can be tested through history, so much the better; but such testing is not indispensable to glottochronology. Some glottochronological work has been done on unwritten languages, including those of North, Central, and South America.

In general, and with a slowly growing number of exceptions, glottochronological studies do not throw a spotlight on any particular archeological site; rather, they shed a diffuse illumination over areas and periods that are of archeological concern. Nevertheless, archeologists (e.g. Willey 1966: 16–18) have expressed considerable interest in glottochronology, and have occasionally mentioned the closely related topic of proto-languages. What with this direction of archeological interest, it is not amiss to point out that several kinds of linguistic studies rival glottochronology in their archeological potentialities.

The study of cognate words has such potentialities. For present purposes, cognates may be regarded as words that now exist in different languages but that had a common origin. English "father," Dutch *vader,* German *Vater,* Latin *pater,* Spanish *padre,* French *père*— this is a familiar series of cognates, and one that could be lengthened considerably by a search through other Indo-European languages both extant and extinct. Usually, the words that make up one cognate series will all have related if not identical meanings; occasional divergences of meaning are readily explained if etymologies can be traced.

Cognates have been studied to identify the original homeland of the people who spoke Proto-Indo-European, the long-extinct unwritten tongue from which all the Indo-European languages were derived. These languages have a series of cognate words meaning snow. Accordingly, an ancestral word meaning snow must have existed in Proto-Indo-European, and the speakers of that language must have known the substance itself. The Indo-European languages also offer a series of cognates that mean winter, and another that mean freezing cold. Five additional series relate to trees (the oak, beech, willow, birch, and pine, respectively); ten to mammals (bear, wolf, otter, polecat, marten, weasel, deer, hare, beaver, and mouse); and seven to birds (eagle, hawk, owl, wild goose, wild duck, partridge, and jay). Two series pertain to reptiles (snake and turtle, respectively), three to invertebrates (crab, ant, and bee), and two to minerals (copper and iron). Evidently, then, the proto-language was spoken in a region where the aforesaid climatic manifestations, trees, mammals, birds, reptiles, invertebrates, and minerals were all known.

Unfortunately, the "beech" word did not remain attached to a single species of tree, but was transferred from one species to another as the various Indo-European groups moved into new lands. The situation is important because the beech was limited to a fairly narrow belt of deciduous forest that stretched across Europe in an east–west direction, and the exact Proto-Indo-European homeland could be identified more readily if it lay within this belt. All in all, it seems likely that this homeland was in northern Europe, not far east of the Baltic. (It may be significant that Lithuanian, now spoken along the eastern shore of the Baltic, approaches Proto-Indo-European more closely than does any other extant tongue.) But the Indo-European languages do not have a series of cognates meaning sea, and we may suppose that the speakers of Proto-Indo-European did not live directly on the Baltic.

The foregoing discussion of Proto-Indo-European was intended, of course, to do no more than show how a study of cognates has been used to help identify the original hearth of a language group whose components are now dispersed. It will be seen why I say that from the standpoint of potential usefulness in archeology, the study of proto-languages is closely related to glottochronology. Taken together, the two help determine when and whence groups of people dispersed long ago.

Cognate words can also throw light on culture, and facilitate the dating of cultural advances. For example, the Indo-European languages have a series of cognates meaning horse, a second series meaning ox, a third sheep, a fourth goat, a fifth pig, and a sixth dog. Presumably, then, the speakers of Proto-Indo-European knew all these domestic animals; or to put the matter in another way, these animals had all been domesticated and taken to northern Europe by the time groups of people began to disperse from the Proto-Indo-European homeland. Cognates also reveal that the speakers of Proto-

Indo-European knew honey, and an intoxicating drink made by fermenting it.

In the New World, studies have been made on Proto-Mixteca and Proto-Maya, and on the glottochronology of the languages that were derived from these two. The studies indicate, among other things, that Proto-Maya in 2500 B.C. had words for maize and for cotton cloth. However, in the case of unwritten (or undeciphered) languages, archeologists have sometimes chosen not to rely on cognate words for information about cultural activities in the days when some proto-language was spoken. According to one archeological view, the name for some item of culture may never have existed in a certain proto-language; instead, it may have been introduced at a later date into all the descendants of that language—introduced along with the item itself. This view is admirably cautious, but it should not lead to wholesale rejection of studies such as those on Proto-Mixteca and Proto-Maya; rather, it should be tested.

It could readily be tested, at least for early historic times, by an investigation of Indian names for items of culture received from the Spaniards. For example, the horse was introduced into the United States from Spanish settlements in Mexico and Florida. In the Mexican border country, several tribes came to call the animal by some version of its Spanish name, *caballo*. In the east, the Mikasuki did the same. (They had lived near a chain of Spanish forts and missions across northern Florida.) But the Creek, whose language was confamilial with Mikasuki, dubbed the animal "big deer." When the Shawnee of Tennessee got the horse, they called it "elk"; so did the Luiseño of California. On the other hand, the horse was likened to the dog in some areas where the latter animal was used to carry burdens. Hence, in or near the northern plains, the horse was a "big dog" (Cree), an "elk dog" (Siksika), or a "mysterious dog" (Sioux).

There is nothing unusual in the way the Spanish word *caballo* spread, or did not spread, along with the animal it named. I suggest that when an American Indian tribe borrowed both an item of material culture and a name for it, the recipient and donor groups had rather extensive dealings with each other, usually as a result of geographic proximity. By the time an introduced item reached more distant tribes, its original name had been left behind. Some peoples may have been less inclined than others to adopt a foreign word; but otherwise, such adoption was controlled not by linguistic affiliation but by the nature of the culture contact between the donor and the recipient groups. If a series of cognates, denoting some particular item of material culture, were found to run through the components of an Indian language family, the chances would be excellent that the cognates were derived from a word in the proto-language, and that the speakers of the proto-language knew the item. To argue otherwise is to assume that the components of the family, after having moved away from one another (often to very great distances), somehow all managed to make contact with a single donor culture—a contact so intimate that a word was borrowed along with the item it identified. This seems improbable in most cases.

In the preceding paragraphs, I have restricted the discussion to names for items of material culture. Words pertaining to religious concepts may have spread in a special way. At least, this possibility is suggested when attention is turned to Spanish terms that were adopted into Indian languages of the United States in early historic times. Of these terms, the only ones to attain impressively wide distribution were names of supernatural beings from the Judaeo-Christian mythology. Of course, these names were not passed from tribe to tribe, but were introduced at many separate points by far-ranging missionaries who had much to say about *Cristo* and *el Diablo*. The urge to missionize, to superimpose one's own mythology upon someone else's, has been inadequately investigated by psychologists, psychiatrists, and cultural anthropologists; I expect it first became an important cultural factor in Neolithic times. At any rate, iconography suggests that in late prehistoric North America, a certain religious belief might be carried, as though by missionaires, to a scattering of peoples who were culturally diverse and geographically well-separated from one another.

The strange little masks of the "Long-nosed God" are a case in point (Williams and Goggin 1956). Done in copper, less often in stone or shell, these masks portray a being whose face is noteworthy for a grotesque proboscis in place of a nose. This being's eyes are large and round, with a small round pupil; his mouth is a narrow slit. He wears a headband; and above the band, his forehead is deeply cleft on the midline. Around 1300 A.D., such masks appeared at seven sites, two of them in Wisconsin and one each in Missouri, Tennessee, Louisiana, Alabama, and Florida. Archeologists have begged the question of whether the snouted being of the Mississippi Valley and the southeastern United States was identical with the Long-Nosed God of the Maya pantheon. But in any event, it is hard to escape the conclusion that someone was, missionary-like, promulgating the beliefs that were reified as these masks and associated paraphernalia.

The masks provide exceptionally good but by no means unique iconographic evidence that in prehistoric America, religious beliefs and practices could be disseminated apart from most other aspects of culture. It is evident that in prehistoric times, as in historic, the arrival of a new religion was a harbinger of other new things to come, within two or three generations; then as now, missionaries were likely to be the thin edge of a cultural wedge. But this circumstance is not important here. The point is that iconography implies deities, fables, related concepts and paraphernalia; implies, too, a priestly jargon in which the mysteries were made known to the tribespeople. A word from this jargon might exist as a series of cognates in a group of related languages, yet tell us nothing about a proto-language.

Fortunately for the student, it is often possible to determine whether a series of cognates descended from a word in a proto-language, or whether they represent borrowing at some later date. Loan-words tend to run through languages independently of linguistic groupings. This is true of such words whether they pertain to religious or secular aspects of culture. *Kawayo* (from *caballo*), *uli* (from *olla,* an earthware jar), *Kilisto* and *Diavolo, Cheesus* and *Setani*—these and other loan-words are distributed through North American Indian languages in a fashion that has nothing to do with the way such languages are classified. Their distribution reflects only the particular circumstances of tribal contact with speakers of Spanish or of English.

To look at the matter in reverse, if a series of apparent cognates cuts across the boundary of a language family, the cognates should not be regarded as necessarily the descendants of an ancestral word in that family's proto-language. Suppose that someone was impressed to see that *waka* (usually spelled *huaca*) meant holiness or supernatural influence in the language of the Inca, and that *wakan* had a similar meaning in the language of the Sioux. The Incan tongue (Quechua) does not belong to the same family, or even superfamily, as the Sioux; the two are quite unrelated. The similarity of *waka* to *wakan* is more likely to be a coincidence, less likely to be an extreme example of the way religious terminology could be spread; but in any event, it provides no clue to the vocabulary of a proto-language.

In summary, when cognates are used in the attempted recovery of a parent language, the aims of both archeology and linguistics are best served when attention is devoted not just to a cluster of descendant languages, but also to some unrelated tongues of the same general region; to the testimony of archeology, history, and ethnology regarding the general way in which culture items and their names are disseminated; and to archeological, historical, and ethnographic data bearing specifically upon the items whose names are under investigation.

Although loan-words might confuse one cultural issue, they can clarify another if their borrowed nature is evident. For example, the route of the Gypsies, from northern India to the British Isles, is revealed by the foreign words that were taken into their language as they migrated.

The original homeland of the Gypsies can be placed in northern India partly because languages related to theirs are still spoken in that region by their stay-at-home kin. The Gypsies moved westward through Afghanistan into Iran, where they picked up names for silk, wool, and wax. It was in Iran that they first reached the sea, and their word for sea is a borrowing from Persian. In Byzantine Greece they adopted words for highway and market; for heaven and time; for the metal lead; for horseshoe, kettle, table, chair, hat, and shoes; for such domestic birds as the goose, dove, and peacock. One gets the impression that in Greek-speaking lands, these wanderers first became familiar with a complex civilization. At the western terminus of their trans-Eurasian migration, in the British Isles, the Gypsies adopted words from thieves' jargon and from Shelta, a collection of disguised or corrupted Gaelic terms used by the Irish tinkers. These borrowings indicate the British social stratum with which the Gypsies made contact after their arrival.

Language does not reveal the full extent of Gypsy wandering westward across Eurasia. However, it does identify a major route that was followed by these people from northern India to Wales. It might be added that if attention is turned from language to folklore, additional details of their migration can be deduced; for the Gypsies borrowed folk beliefs and tales wherever they went.

Loan-words can in fact reveal many aspects of culture contact. As an illustration, such words in Malayan throw light on past contacts of the Malayan-speaking peoples with Hindu-Buddhist, Arab, and Portuguese cultures. I have discussed this subject at length in another book (Neill 1973), and will do no more than summarize it here.

Indianization of the Malayan-speaking world began around the first century A.D., and a large number of Sanskrit words were adopted into the Malayan language. With a few unimportant exceptions, these words can be divided into seven categories of subject matter. Many of them relate to Hindu or Buddhist religious concepts and paraphernalia, to scholarship and learning, to law and legal practice, or to matters of social position and regal pomp. A lesser number pertain to agriculture and animal husbandry, to items of material culture (a saw, a chariot, glass, etc.), or to concepts of time and its formal subdivision. Thus, Sanskrit loan-words in Malayan tell quite a lot about the nature of culture contact between Hindu-Buddhist India and the Malayan-speaking world. In particular, they identify topics that Sanskrit-speakers wanted to discuss but could not express adequately in the indigenous Malayan vocabulary.

It might be added that in the Malayan-speaking area, a majority of the researches that are dubbed archeological have dealt with the period of Indianization; so here is an instance in which linguistic studies have a direct bearing on matters of prime archeological interest.

To continue, briefly, with the subject of loan-words in Malayan, it was around the fifteenth century A.D. that the Malayan-speaking world was largely converted to Islam. Then, a good many Arabic words were borrowed into Malayan. With a few exceptions, these fall into six categories. Many of them relate to religion, to law, or to concepts of time. A lesser number pertain to scholarship, to items of material culture, or to matters of social position.

In the sixteenth century, the Portuguese established a temporary hegemony over the Malayan-speaking world. Since this happened well along in historic times, it may be asked whether the topic of Portuguese contact with Malayan-speakers might be left to historians. But the Portuguese did not write much about themselves, and their period of dominance in the East Indies is known principally from the biased writings of their enemies, the Dutch. The Portuguese were established longer and more thoroughly in islands well to the east of the main Malayan-speaking region; but even so, a good many Portuguese words were borrowed into Malayan. Only two or three of these words relate to religious concepts, for Christianity never made any headway in Islamic lands, and the Malayan-speaking principalities were largely Moslem. Portuguese loan-words in Malayan denote household objects such as a ball, clock, doll, table fork, or thimble; or else they relate to simple aspects of community life. By their nature and number, these words refute certain Dutch historical sources, which portray the Portuguese as near-pirates who had little effect on trade and less on the lives of the peoples with whom they traded.

Loan-words in Malayan also draw attention to a curious fact: under the proper circumstances, inferences about culture can be drawn when attention is given to the kinds of words that were *not* borrowed in some particular contact situation. Thus, the arrival from India of Hindus and Buddhists gave great impetus and new directions to sculpture, painting, and allied representational arts in the Malayan-speaking world. Nevertheless, there was little or no borrowing into Malayan of Sanskrit words pertaining to these arts; and we might infer that the original Malayan vocabulary was adequate to express the Indian concepts.

Loan-words have seldom been studied for the light they might throw on culture contacts in prehistoric North America, but they offer many possibilities for investigation.

Let us now pass to linguistic studies of another kind. As mentioned previously, the components of a cognate series usually have about the same meaning; but occasionally, one or two members of a series will stand out because they have somehow acquired a different meaning. At times, the reasons for such a difference cannot be inferred convincingly without historical and etymological data. As an extreme example, German *Tisch* means a table, but its English cognate is "dish"; Dutch *disch* means either a table or a dish. Of course, dishes and tables have several characteristics in common; but the diversity of meanings in this cognate series is not fully explicable without knowledge that the root-word was Latin *discus,* a disc. Again, German *Zimmer,* a room, is cognate with English "timber." It is reasonable to suggest that speakers of Germanic languages, coming as they did from a heavily forested region, once saw a close connection between timbers and the dwellings that were built from them; but the suggestion remains tentative until attention is given to the courses that were taken by the "timber" word in a constellation of these languages.

Nevertheless, it is sometimes possible, even in the absence of etymological data, to hypothesize about cultural factors involved with shifts of meaning in one or several members of a cognate series. Thus, when I was compiling vocabularies of the two Florida Seminole languages (Mikasuki and Creek), my informants drew my attention to what they regarded as an amusing situation: the Mikasuki word *kona-wi* meant money, but its Creek cognate *konawa* meant beads. Search of linguistic materials revealed that the Creek Indians proper, as well as the Creek-speaking Seminole in both Florida and Oklahoma, had retained the word in its original Muskhogean sense; it was in Mikasuki, or at least in the Hitchiti group of Muskhogean languages, that the meaning had shifted from beads to money. Even in Creek, the word for money had the literal meaning of "iron beads."

Students of American Indian culture will be immediately interested to learn that the Creek, Hitchiti, and Seminole saw a connection between beads and money. As is well known to ethnologists and historians, the early European settlers of the United States discovered that certain tribes of the Atlantic seaboard had a kind of money, in other words a medium of exchange with an arbitrarily assigned value. The unit of this currency was a bead. It was cut from mollusk shell, and its value might depend on its color and finish. Nevertheless, values were so effectively fixed that, for a while, white settlers used the shell beads as money; loose or strung into standard lengths, these beads could be exchanged not only for merchandise but also for currency. Indian bead money even became a significant factor in early New England civilization, and a corruption of its Algonquian name was adopted into English as "wampum."

The use of wampum is well-documented for the New England and Middle Atlantic states. Farther south, Robert Beverley (1705) provided a detailed description of the shell bead currency on the coast of Virginia and the Carolinas. John Lawson (1714), who surveyed the latter region (and who died in the Tuscarora uprising of 1711) described the bead money of coastal North and South Carolina; and he expressed the belief that this currency was known to tribes on the Gulf of Mexico. At a somewhat later date, we hear of wampum in the Creek country, and along the Gulf coast as far west as the lower Mississippi.

Swanton (1946) was disinclined to grant any prehistoric use of bead money south of New York. Apparently, he held white traders and settlers responsible for introducing wampum into coastal Virginia and the Carolinas, and later into the Creek country and the Gulf lowlands. No doubt white men encouraged the use of wampum in areas where it was already known, and extended its use into some areas where it had previously been lacking; but the origin of this culture trait-complex is a puzzle. A true medium of exchange, having an arbitrarily fixed value, existing in a series of denominations, convenient to carry, and acceptable tender for almost any kind of purchase—this is quite an advanced concept. If in prehistoric times it was restricted to the coastal Algonquians, we might be led to wonder if these Indians had once been reached by unrecorded voyagers across the North Atlantic, voyagers from Europe where the concept of money was entrenched at an early date.

Several aspects of Algonquian culture were surprisingly European in general configuration (Wissler 1938:58–61). Algonquian pottery vessels, made of black clay and tapering to a pointed base, had a counterpart in ancient Europe. The Algonquian creation and deluge myths had so much in common with the Judaeo-Christian that the Indians regarded their own beliefs to be substantiated by those of early historic European settlers. The pictography of the Algonquians, done on birchbark or carved in wood, was the closest approach to an aboriginal written language in the United States; and the *Walum Olum,* sacred history of the Delaware, is the only prehistoric Indian "document" that survived to be translated in historic times. (Of course, Europe was not the only center from which spread the concept of keeping records by means of symbols that could be translated into speech.)

On the other hand, advanced ideas also diffused northward from the prehistoric civilizations of Mexico and Central America, spreading in complex fashion across and around the Gulf of Mexico to reach the Mississippi Valley and the southeastern United States (Ford 1969). During late prehistoric times, the Muskhogeans were important agents in this diffusion; they are thought to have introduced the type of social organization that was elaborated upon by the Algonquians, and it might be worthwhile to consider them as a possible source of the money concept in eastern North America.

It may be significant that the Muskhogeans identified money with beads. Such an identification would hardly have been made unless beads were already looked upon as a medium of exchange. In central Georgia, a sequence of culture periods (Macon Plateau through Ocmulgee Fields) represents Muskhogean occupation. Shell beads occur in sites of these periods; and it would be desirable to compare them with historic wampum beads, which had fixed attributes of size, shape, drilling, and molluscan source. Recalling that one blackish or purplish wampum bead was worth two white ones, it would be well to record the color of shell beads from putatively Muskhogean sites. (In the Southeast, prehistoric shell is often corroded and bleached by soil acids, but exceptions are noted.) Finally, shell beads from Muskhogean sites might be compared with those identified as wampum in coastal Algonquian sites of the Northeast.

And so an apparently simple matter, a diversity of meanings in one cognate series, leads to some interesting speculations which might be tested through a more detailed investigation of archeological, ethnological, and linguistic materials.

Abandoning the subject of cognates without having exhausted its possibilities, one finds other linguistic studies that could help guide archeological hypothesizing. Such studies include those on the distribution of language families.

Among American Indians, the diversity of languages was greater than among all the other peoples of the world taken together; about 2,000 mutually unintelligible languages were spoken in the Americas at the opening of historic times. It was possible, of course, to fit many New World tongues into a classificatory scheme of taxonomic levels, building up to the level of family. However, this procedure, so satisfactory in Europe, still left the North, Central, and South American languages in all too sprawling an arrangement; and it left many languages in isolated positions. Linguists therefore made an effort to discover still higher levels, at which the Indian language families and some isolates could be grouped on the basis of very broad or general similarities. Although the resulting arrangements have been duly entered into several archeological works, I doubt that American archeologists will take much profit from a study of linguistic groupings above the family level. In cases where the postulated superfamily relationships are convincing, they probably date back to such early times that nothing but vague similarities of language now hint at former connections among peoples who later became geographically and culturally remote.

But unequivocal groupings at or below the family level—these command archeological interest. A few illustrations of this point may be given.

As Indian languages of western North America were investigated, it became evident that the tongue of the Apache and Navajo had relatives scattered from northern Mexico northward to the Arctic Circle, with outliers elsewhere. This group of related languages was termed the Athapascan or Déné family. To it were eventually added the Skittagetan family, which had been erected for the sole reception of Haida; and the Koluschan family, set up to contain Tlingit. The enlarged family was called the Nadené. The Nadené languages formed a more or less continuous bloc in large parts of Alaska and western Canada, but only straggled thence southward into the southwestern United States and down the Pacific Coast. The distribution suggested that the family had entered the New World from Siberia, in the region of Bering Strait where North America and Asia are but narrowly separated. From the point of entry, the family had spread eastward across Alaska and western Canada, with just a few ramifications southward.

True, anthropologists had generally tried to derive American Indians from Siberia by a route across the Bering Strait, or across a

Pleistocene land bridge that preceded the Strait. But actual evidence of such derivation was remarkably scanty, in both North America and Siberia; and so it was gratifying to learn the way in which Nadené was distributed. The idea grew that this family represented an unusually late migration of Asians into the New World by the Bering route. It was also gratifying to learn that Edward Sapir, who wrote a short but trenchant analysis of time perspective in American Indian cultures (1916), thought Nadené might be remotely akin to the Sino-Tibetan group of Asian languages. For in spite of the postulated immigration of ancestral Indians into the New World from northeastern Asia, this was one of the very few instances in which a qualified linguist could suggest even a remote relationship between an American Indian language and some Asian family.

More recently, J. H. Greenberg (1960) held that if all New World aboriginal languages were regarded as a single great phylum to be broken down into its components, the first partitioning would erect three groups: (1) the Eskimoan family, (2) the Nadené family, and (3) all the rest. Evidently, then, some peculiarities of Nadené were not developed in what I might call the New World linguistic milieu, and the family may indeed betoken a comparatively late migration from Asia.

Wherever they went, the speakers of Nadené borrowed culture trait-complexes from their neighbors, and evolved a way of life that was adapted to the local ecology. Tundra, forest, prairie, desert, coastal waters—all were invaded by one or another group of Nadené-speakers; and neither ethnology nor archeology would lead us to suspect kinship among such diverse peoples as, say, the Apache, the Jicarilla, the Hupa, the Sarsi, and the Dogrib. Language provides most of the clues to their relationship. (I say "most" rather than "all," for physical anthropology provides some additional clues, albeit of a minor nature.)

In the case of the Eskimo, a combination of linguistic with other data solves some problems while creating fresh ones; but this is all to the good, for a science advances most rapidly when its practitioners discover the right questions to ask.

The Eskimo occupied shores and islands of the Arctic, at localities scattered from eastern Siberia eastward through Alaska and Canada to eastern Greenland, a distance of more than 5,000 miles. Yet, in spite of this vast, spotty, intercontinental distribution, all Eskimo populations spoke the same language (although with dialectal differences). Allied to the Eskimo tongue is that of the Aleut; the two make up the

Eskimoan family, which is convincingly reported to have some affinity with the Ural-Altaic of Eurasia. The Eskimo came to hold both sides of Bering Strait, but it is improbable that they did so at the time of the Nadené migration; otherwise, the Nadené-speakers and the Eskimo would not be so sharply separable on linguistic and other grounds. Thus we are led to the conclusion that the Eskimo reached the New World after the Nadené, and probably were the last Asian entrants into America by the Bering route.

In Greenland, the Melville Peninsula, the northern Yukon, some parts of Alaska, and eastern Siberia, there are long culture sequences leading up to an Eskimo Period, and the past assumption has been that Eskimo culture arose principally from these local antecedents. The assumption is not challenged by glottochronological evidence that the Eskimo and Aleut tongues divereged from Proto-Eskimoan around 2600 B.C. Some of the putatively ancestral cultures were more complex than Eskimo, more flamboyant in material expression, and more obviously influenced from Asia; but all were less specialized for exploitation of Arctic environments. In other words, Eskimo culture was supposedly developed for the most part through simplification and specialization over a wide geographic expanse.

But somewhat contrary to this view, the Eskimo language, culture, and (to a lesser degree) physical type are all rather homogeneous, as though all three had been carried by a single people who spread rapidly and at a comparatively late date across the Arctic. The glottochronological date of 2600 B.C. is too early to mark the advent of Eskimo (as opposed to proto-Eskimo) culture. To account for all the facts, one might hypothesize about as follows: Speakers of Proto-Eskimoan separated into two groups, one remaining near Bering Strait, the other moving into the Aleutian Islands. Principally as a result of exposure to American Indian and Kamchatkan influences, the Aleutian group was considerably modified physically, linguistically, and culturally. The Bering Strait group, in the meanwhile, evolved a culture that was adjusted to the rigors of the high Arctic. Comparatively few other New World cultures had invaded that region, and none had reached the Eskimo level of adaptation to far-northern environments. With Indians already holding sway over the forested sub-Arctic, but with the Arctic no more than sparsely populated, the Eskimo spread rapidly from Bering Strait eastward along the shores and islands of the Arctic Ocean, replacing earlier peoples and absorbing a few trait-complexes from them.

Once this hypothesis (or an alternative one) has been enunciated, methods of testing it will soon come to mind.

The Eskimo problem is one in which some effort has already been expended to correlate the archeological findings with the linguistic and the anthropometric. However, there exist other problems that have interested linguists almost to the exclusion of archeologists, yet that deal with events of archeological times. An illustration is the puzzle presented by the distribution of the Siouan, Algonquian, and Iroquoian families. Except for scattered outliers, Siouan tongues existed in two widely separated areas. One of these, the larger, extended (with interruptions) from the Arkansas River northward into Wisconsin and Saskatchewan; the other lay far to the east, in the Piedmont of the Carolinas and southern Virginia. This distribution is consistent with the view that the Siouan-speakers had been early on the scene, but were dispersed by the Algonquian-speakers: when Algonquian languages are mapped, they seem to form a great wedge, splitting the Siouan family into eastern and western moieties. The Algonquian area is in turn split by the Iroquoian, as though the Iroquoian-speakers arrived last and drove a wedge through the territory of their Algonquian-speaking predecessors.

This is not to say that Siouan is an older family than Algonquian, or that the latter is older than Iroquoian. We are actually dealing with cultural matters, with the territorial expansion of the Algonquians and then of the Iroquoians. No doubt Algonquian existed for millennia before its speakers had become capable of encroaching upon Siouan territory. In like fashion, Iroquoian could long have been a geographically restricted group of languages, until its speakers had reached a point where they could successfully harry the Algonquians.

The foregoing hypothesis, purporting to account for certain peculiarities in the distribution of the Siouan, Algonquian, and Iroquoian families, has little in it that would be novel to students of American Indian languages; but it has received only scant mention in the archeological literature, to which indeed it might run contrary. Still, it is useful as something to be borne in mind by archeologists working in the appropriate areas.

Linguistics might also render the new archeologists more receptive than their predecessors to the idea that there were several prehistoric routes to the New World. Until very recent times, the rank and file of North American archeologists automatically rejected any suggestion of transoceanic voyages preceding that of Columbus. The modern attitude toward the possibility of such voyages is a bit more open-minded. Thus, Ronald J. Mason (1962), in his analysis of Paleo-Indian cultural tradition, admitted that antecedents of it are not to be found in Siberia; Emerson F. Greenman (1960; in Mason 1962:253), discoverer of the major Paleo-Indian site at Clovis, New Mexico, would derive the tradition from western Europe by way of the North Atlantic; and the artifactual evidence points to the Solutrean culture of Spain and France as ancestral to the Sandia Cave culture of the New World. The studies of Betty J. Meggers, Clifford Evans, and Emilio Estrada (1965) make it clear that the Neolithic was brought to the New World by Japanese who, around 5,000 years ago, followed the Black Current from Kyushu to the Pacific coast of Ecuador. John L. Sorenson (no date) assembled an impressive list of culture trait-complexes that characterized the Near East from the Middle Bronze Age through the Iron Age, and that reappeared somewhat later in Mesoamerica (northern Central America plus the southern two-thirds of Mexico). Certain artistic styles of China, the Shang and the Late Chou, may both have influenced those of the New World (Ekholm 1950): Meggers would even derive the Olmec culture of Mexico from the Shang of China. The speakers of the Malayo-Polynesian languages carried numerous trait-complexes from an Indochina homeland to such distant lands as Madagascar, New Zealand, Easter Island, and Hawaii; and many of these complexes also cropped up in the New World, especially along the Pacific coast thereof. Gordon Ekholm (1953) postulated that the cultures of southern Mexico were influenced by Hindu-Buddhist concepts introduced around 700 A.D. by Asians, most likely from Indochina. A good many complexes of the Japanese Ainu reappeared among Indians of coastal Alaska. The Vikings' discovery of the New World, suggested by historical sources, has been demonstrated archeologically by excavations in Greenland and Newfoundland.

It is not my intention here to summarize the cultural evidence for pre-Columbian voyages to the New World; I wish only to suggest that the intellectual atmosphere of archeology is becoming conducive to scientifically dispassionate review, not automatic rejection, of linguistic studies bearing on the problem. To give an idea of the linguists' thinking, I shall briefly note some investigations into the languages of South America, a continent that offers maximum linguistic diversity.

Various authors have likened one or another South American Indian language to Basque, to Altaic speech, and to Japanese; but the suggested similarities are vague. Paul Rivet, one of the most outstanding and productive students of South American languages, continued for years (e.g. 1925) to develop the point that Chon, along with certain other distinctive languages of extreme southern South America, was somewhat related to those of Australia. Rivet postulated a movement of Australoids across the far-southern seas during the so-called Altithermal or Climatic Optimum, a postglacial period when the climate was a bit warmer than at present and the Antarctic ice cap had melted back a little beyond its present limits. With remarkable insight, he rejected the then-popular notions of Carlos and Florentino Ameghino, who wanted to regard South America as the cradle of mankind. Rivet saw four major elements in American languages. In the order of their arrival in the New World, these were: Australian; Malayo-Polynesian, especially of the Melanesian sort; Asian with a Uralian admixture, represented by Eskimo; and Sino-Tibetan, whose influence was evident in Na-Dené.

Rivet did not limit his investigations to languages, but tried to correlate data from linguistics, ethnography, archeology, and physical anthropology; and his ideas about the peopling of the New World might perhaps have been influenced by the somewhat Australoid characteristics of Indian skulls from southern South America, as well as by the physical similarity of some historic South American tribes to islanders of the Southwest Pacific. Still, it is remarkable how many linguists thought they saw Oceanic—mostly Malayo-Polynesian—affinities in New World languages. As early as 1925, Rivet suggested that there was an element of what he called Melaneso-Polynesian speech in South American Indian languages. In a series of subsequent papers, he developed this view further. José Imbelloni (1928), another outstanding student of South American tongues, noted a pointed resemblance between Quechua, which was spread by the Inca, and the Oceanic languages. Richard Dangel (1930) found similarities between Quechua and Maori, the latter a Polynesian language of New Zealand. F. W. Christian (1932), who had studied Maori language and migrations, thought he could detect Polynesian and Oceanic elements in Yunca of north coastal Peru, and in Quechua.

In more recent times, attention has centered on Hokan as the American Indian language family with the most similarities to Malayo-Polynesian speech. The largest continuous area of Hokan occupied all but the southernmost fourth of the Baja California peninsula, and extended thence over much of Arizona. Four large enclaves of Hokan also existed farther north, in parts of California and Nevada. The family reappeared in Central America as Jicaque, which in historic times was spoken in certain Carribean lowlands of Honduras; and in South America as Yurumangui, limited to a small area of Pacific coastal Colombia. J. Alden Mason (1950), in his review of South American languages, regarded Subtiaba of Nicaragua as Hokan, along with Maribichicoa, whose few speakers moved into Guatemala in historic times. He noted that enclaves of more or less Hokan-like speech existed as far south as the Gran Chaco of Paraguay and Argentina. Quechua, itself a minor enclave until spread by the conquering Inca, has been likened to Hokan by several linguists.

Even excluding languages that are merely suggestive of Hokan, the distribution of the family is extraordinary. No other family of the New World is strung out in a line more than 3,300 miles long, or involves North, Central, and South America.

The South American students apparently visualized a movement of Neolithic-level Polynesians or Melanesians across the Pacific, and it would not be surprising to find evidence of such movement on the parts of those great seafarers; but in connection with transoceanic voyages, it might be well also to consider the more advanced cultures that were developed in southeastern Asia by speakers of Malayo-Polynesian. It might also prove instructive to compare Hokan with the principal languages of the Greater Sundas, and with what little remains of Malayo-Polynesian speech in Indochina. In this connection, it is interesting to note the opinion of Betty J. Meggers (1966:93–95), apparently concurred in by Gordon R. Willey (1971:293), that the Bahía culture of the Ecuador coast was influenced by trans-oceanic voyagers from southeastern Asia. Bahía pottery house models portray a building with a saddle-shaped roof and decorated gables; similar houses, and pottery models thereof, are well known from southeastern Asia. Bahía pottery headrests, "golf tee" ear ornaments, portrayals of dragons, and tusk-shaped pendants all have prototypes in southeastern Asia, as does the Bahía pan-pipe with tubes graduated toward the center. In many ways, Bahía was set apart from surrounding cultures. It developed between 500 B.C. and 100 B.C., by which time various peoples of southeastern Asia were civilized, and were sailing the Pacific in huge vessels that could carry up to 1,000 metric tons of cargo and a crew of 600. Perhaps not coincidentally, the line of Hokan enclaves stretches northward from the Bahía locus; the latter lies about 350 miles south of the Yurumangui speech area.

There are still other ways in which archeology could profit from linguistic studies. Thus, Marion J. Mochon (1972) used lexico-reconstruction to determine whether Siouan-speakers or Muskhogeans were the more important as bearers of the major cultural tradition called Mississippian. The Mississippian was a comparatively advanced way of life that spread in late prehistoric times from Mexico to the Mississippi Valley and the Southeast. Its characteristic features included advanced agriculture, a complex social organization, the construction of temple mounds, elaborate iconography, and a variety of ceramic types quite different from earlier ones. Mochon discovered that concepts relating to the characteristics and complexities of this tradition could be expressed more readily and clearly in Muskhogean (Creek and Choctaw) than in Siouan tongues (Osage, Ofo, Biloxi) of the Mississippi Valley. In other words, the lexical content of the languages bolstered the view that the Muskhogeans are to be identified closely with the Mississippian tradition.

In devoting so much space to the topic of language, I do not imply that linguistics is necessarily a more important adjunct to archeology than is, say, physical anthropology or ethnology. But some interactions of archeology with the last two, or even with history, are well known, and other such interactions could be envisioned readily. The literature of archeology has had considerable overlap with that of physical anthropology, ethnology, and history, but not much with that of linguistics. The study of language has its own special aims, methods, and outlets for publication; and in pedagogy, linguistic studies of any kind have traditionally been carried on in a school of languages rather than of social disciplines. But as mentioned in chapter 1, language is a part of culture. It is a highly distinctive part, of course; and there is ample warrant for a study of it through a series of specialized approaches. But this does not militate against archeological consideration of it as an aspect of past culture as well. Only a minority of extinct languages are recoverable by any method; and it is reasonable to ask how linguistics, with its concentration upon historic tongues, could be employed to illuminate prehistoric events. In the present chapter I have tried to show some ways in which this might be done.

CHAPTER THREE

Archeology and Toponymy

Perhaps surprisingly, archeology also has the possibility of usefully extracting data from toponymy, the study of place-names. This possibility is better known, and has been more often acted upon, in the Old World than in the New.

Toponymy, in the sense of the present work, is the study of place-names, their meanings, and the circumstances of their original applications. Obviously, the study is of maximum archeological usefulness in areas where a good many such names have persisted from an early time. Parts of Europe are noted for toponyms whose original bestowers have long since vanished. For example, the Celtic subfamily of languages is now confined to limited portions of France and the British Isles. However, geographic names of Celtic origin straggle eastward across Europe into Asia Minor. They are relics of Gaulish or continental Celtic expansion at quite an early date; a bit of Gaulish was written down in the North Etruscan alphabet around the second century B.C. Other bits were written down in the Greek or the Imperial Roman alphabets. In the fifth century A.D., when the continental branch of Celtic was dying out, the insular branch was introduced from the British Isles into France. Today, French areas of Celtic speech (Breton) are restricted to parts of the Armorica Peninsula, but place-names in France reveal a much wider distribution of this speech in former times.

Just as toponyms indicate the former existence of Celtic-speakers far to the east of their present holdings, so do they demonstrate that

Baltoslavic-speakers once held sway farther west than they now do. Germany's most famous state bears a name—*Preussen* or Prussia— that is from Lettish, a Baltic tongue. Geographic names suggest the Elbe River as a former western boundary of Baltoslavic speech. And as a final comment on the persistence of place-names in Europe, top- onyms of Danish origin can be mapped to show how the Danes spread into England in the ninth century A.D.

Contrary to what might be expected, toponymy holds considerable promise for archeologists in the United States, and not just in con- nection with "historic site archeology." Once again I shall draw an illustration from Florida.

The Florida aborigines, such as the Calusa and the Timucua, soon vanished under white onslaught; the close-knit weave of their culture came all unraveled in the face of strange new diseases, military ag- gressions, missionization, and a flood of trade goods. By the early 1700s, the original inhabitants of Florida were extinct or nearly so, and the Muskhogeans of Georgia began pushing southward into the rich country that had been left almost unoccupied. The first Muskhogean immigrants were Hitchiti-speakers who had been restive under Creek domination; but after the American Revolution, some of the Creek Indians also found it expedient to join the exodus to Florida. The new Floridian peoples, both Hitchiti and Creek, came to be known as the Seminole. Having an agricultural and pastoral economy, the Seminole occupied those areas of the state that were most suitable for the rais- ing of corn, other vegetables, fruit, cattle, hogs, and horses. From such areas they were eventually extirpated by the Americans; but for roughly a century they held much of northeastern and peninsular Florida, where numerous place-names attest to their former pres- ence.

History and toponymy were in agreement that the Seminole had been widely distributed in Florida, but where were their village sites? How could these sites be identified, and what would they yield? The answers to these questions proved elusive.

As late as 1948, a Seminole Period in Florida was known from his- toric sources only; not one site had been identified as Seminole. John M. Goggin (1949b) reported on the excavation of Spaulding's Lower Store, a trading post site dating approximately from the period 1763 to 1784. Among other things, it yielded potsherds with a brushed surface. These did not fit into the pre-Seminole ceramic sequence, but had close counterparts in material from historic Creek sites in Georgia. They were therefore identified as being of Seminole origin.

Also in 1949, Goggin and others described an Indian burial from the Zetrouer site near Gainesville. With the bones were a glass mirror, an iron trade tomahawk, iron knives, musket balls, gunflints, a gun lock, a silver brooch, a brass kettle, brass buckets, iron tools and nails, and several other items of non-Indian manufacture. The burial was regarded as that of a Seminole.

In 1950, Ripley P. Bullen (1950a) described brushed sherds from sites in the Chattahoochee River valley of northern Florida. These specimens were assigned, tentatively, to Lower Creek Indians who were on the verge of becoming Seminole. And in that same year of 1950, John W. Griffin reported plain and brushed sherds from the Negro Fort, which lay a little to the south of Bullen's localities. The fort had been occupied first by British troops and some Creek Indians, later by numerous runaway slaves and a few Indians of Choctaw and Seminole origin. Thus, at the opening of the 1950s, the presence of brushed pottery seemed the most likely clue to the existence of a Seminole site. Such pottery was, however, remarkably hard to find. For example, Alachua County (the Gainesville region of Florida) had been a focus of Seminole settlement, according to historical sources; yet after 260 Indian sites of the county had been investigated, only one brushed sherd had been found (Goggin 1964:181). A few other scraps of presumably Seminole pottery came to light in other counties of the state, and several brushed vessels were located in museum collections.

In 1952, Julian Granberry found a large Seminole village site (Mizell) near Winter Park, and in 1953 I found a small one (Halfmile Creek) near Silver Springs. During 1953 and 1954 I investigated the Fort King site near Ocala. This fort had played a major role during the Second Seminole War, and its sutlery had supplied both the garrison and the Indians. Although artifactual material was abundant on the site, very little of it suggested Seminole presence: only a few faceted glass beads of a kind favored by these Indians, and two plain sherds that differed from the local pre-Seminole types. Later, Goggin and I walked over the site with his archeology students, one of whom picked up a single brushed sherd.

Until 1955, Seminole pottery seemed to be accumulating scrap by scrap—this in a state where archeologists were accustomed to collecting hundreds if not thousands of sherds from a single village site. At this point I turned to the toponymic literature, at first not for clues to Seminole site locations but for information bearing on a different project, the interpretation of Indian place-names in Florida.

Popular writings were found to include quite a bit of misguided speculation about the circumstances under which Indian names were first applied to various natural and political features in Florida (and elsewhere). I say misguided because, in most cases, records had been kept of these circumstances; speculation was needless. For decades, the U.S. Department of the Interior had maintained a special bureau, staffed by linguists and historians who studied American place-names, their origins, and their meanings. The investigators' findings are of some archeological interest, but their sources of information are more so. Certain of these sources may be summarized briefly, with reference to Florida.

Very soon after the Seminole were extirpated from northeastern and central Florida, their former lands (and other lands) were platted. That is to say, they were surveyed, and officially subdivided according to a grid system of section, township, and range. The government surveyors made field notes and maps, both of which were often detailed. When a surveyor learned the Seminole name of a lake, river, abandoned village, or other landmark, he wrote it down; and in this fashion, many a locality first acquired its official name. Often, a surveyor put down the location not only of Seminole villages but even of the Indians' cornfields, gardens, and isolated huts, as well as the trails that connected one village with the next. Localities were recorded at least in terms of quarter-section, if not in terms of chain lengths from a section line or corner. (A surveyor's chain was 66 feet long.) Since the original section-township-range grid is still in use, I found it possible to identify most of the spots that had been noted or mapped as Seminole villages in the field reports that were examined. These reports related mostly to Marion County and vicinity, the region I was studying at that time.

In many cases, lands wrested from the Seminole were platted and then promptly transferred by the U.S. government to private citizens. At the time of such transferral, some of the Indians' village sites and fields were still conspicuous, and so were mentioned in applications for land. These applications therefore were a useful supplement to surveyors' reports. So were county deed record books, which permitted the tracing of property ownership from the end of the Seminole Period down to modern times. Surveyors' notes and maps, supplemented at times by land grant applications and deed record books, enabled me to locate Osceola's Village site, near Ocala (Neill 1955b). It had been occupied by the famous Seminole leader at the start of his resistance to removal. Also located were Tsalo Emathla's Town, Jumper's Town, Coe Hadjo's Town, Abraham's Old Town, and Abraham's New Town. It was particularly gratifying to discover Wacahoota, Bowlegs' village at the edge of a Spanish land grant, for it had been one of the largest Indian settlements of its day. Surveyors' reports also permitted the discovery of Seminole villages whose existence was not mentioned in any other historical source, and even identified a few spots where battles were staged or treaties signed.

Once the sites had been found and explored, it became evident that the earlier Seminole, although well provided with the white man's trade goods, also made pottery in abundance and in a variety of distinctive types. However, by the opening of the Second Seminole War in 1835, these Indians were using chinaware, glassware, and ironware almost to the exclusion of their own ceramics. Nevertheless, each site would yield at least a few sherds of the Seminole's own brushed and fire-clouded plain pottery. As far south as Osceola's Village and Spaulding's Lower Store, sand-tempered sherds might have a micaceous paste, as though some vessels had been brought from the Apalachicola River region where the clays have micaceous inclusions.

As it turned out, half-a-dozen artifactual criteria collectively permitted the identification of a site as Seminole, although such identification was most readily made through the pottery. Also, village locations had certain ecological features in common, features reflecting the Indians' agricultural and pastoral economy. But the initial discovery of Seminole sites was made possible less by archeological reconnaissance than by an excursion into the toponymic literature.

In the preceding example of archeology-toponymy interaction, language played little part; for once the surveyors' reports had been studied, it became possible to locate the Seminole sites no matter how they had been named. But as it turned out, a good bit of cultural data were recoverable when attention was turned to the meaning of place-names from the Seminole. I shall briefly review both the pitfalls and the possibilities of toponym translation, with special reference to these Indians.

Would-be users of such translations should proceed circumspectly, for misinterpretations abound, particularly although not exclusively in the popular literature.

Several processes have confused the issue of toponym translation. Thus, an imaginary translation, usually of a romantic nature, and often coined to fill a promotional need of the moment, comes to be widely accepted in later years. Or perhaps an original spelling becomes so changed with time that the late version of a name may baffle even the linguist if he does not see the earlier versions. A change of spelling may have been brought about intentionally by well-meaning cartographers or historians whose aim was to make sense out of earlier and well-nigh incomprehensible orthography. Also troublesome are transpositions or other miscopyings, especially when they result in an accidentally meaningful combination of letters. Finally, the difficulties of toponym translation have several times been compounded by loss of pronunciation while the orthography stayed intact. That is to say, some place-names were originally transliterated about as well as possible, but remained for a while thereafter in a sort of limbo, to be revived decades later. Once the original pronunciation was forgotten, it was not easily recovered from the written word that remained; for English phonetics are capricious, with several sounds often being assigned to a single letter.

In preparing a list of toponyms for analysis, it is also important to weed out those that were imported, coined, or applied only by the white man at a comparatively late date. Such Indian names as Catawba, Cayuga, Erie, Kalamazoo, Manhattan, Mohawk, Petaluma, Shasta, Umatilla, and others are quickly dismissed as importations into Florida, however significant they might be in other states. Wabasso and Wimauma look as though they could be Seminole, but the first is Ossabaw (a Georgia locality) spelled backward; the second is an acronym constructed from the names of three sisters called Willie, Maude, and Mary. Sumica acronymizes the title of a mining company. Aripeka, a town in the study area, bears the name of a Mikasuki resistance leader; but the name was first adopted by a logging company and later attached to a locality where logging was done. The present town of Aripeka was not the home of the Seminole who bore that name.

More troublesome are the numerous Seminole names that were given to twentieth-century communities by their founders. In southern Florida, the local Seminole were occasionally asked to supply an appropriate designation for some city in planning; but farther north in the state, developers often turned to the literature for euphonious toponyms. During Florida's "land boom," especially, when every little crossroad and whistlestop was hopefully being laid out as the site of a future metropolis, there was quite a demand for colorful Seminole names. Usually, the demand was filled through reference to the popular writings of Minnie Moore-Willson, who between 1896 and 1935 turned out numerous semi-factual articles about the Florida Seminole. It is generally easy to recognize a place-name from Mrs. Moore-Willson's Seminole vocabulary, for her orthography was *sui generis* to say the least. Also, the developers selected Seminole words that the Indians would not have used as toponyms; and so various Florida localities were given names meaning "day," "twins," "lantern," "knife," "what is it?", and other improbable designations.

A detailed map of Florida will reveal a large number of Seminole names in the eastern part of the peninsula from Seminole County to Okeechobee County: Osceola, Kolokee, Chuluota, Bithlo, Pocataw, Wewahotee, Salofka, Tohopkee, Holopaw, Illahaw, Nittaw, Apoxsee, Lokosee, Yeehaw, Osowaw, Hilolo, and Opal. The recent origin of these names becomes evident when it is noticed that the localities are aligned. They were stations or sidings on a former railroad line, and it is obvious that the names for them were selected mostly from Mrs. Moore-Willson's writings. One cannot mistake her spellings, such as Yeehaw for *yaha* ("wolf"), Osowaw for *fuswa* ("bird"), Illahaw for *yalaha* ("orange"), Opal for *oba* ("owl"), Lokosee for *nokosi* ("bear"), and others.

In recovering past culture through the translation of place-names, the first step is not reference to a dictionary; it is the tracing of the toponyms backward in time to their original application and orthography. The possibility of such tracing does not seem to be widely known. In Florida, and no doubt elsewhere, it involves use of government surveyors' notes and maps, as described above; but the use, also, of other maps which were published separately, or in atlases, or in books. The number and variety of published maps is astonishing, even excluding those of the last half-century. Surveyors' reports and early cartography, along with historical documents, constitute the primary sources of information pertaining to toponyms. Also useful are secondary sources compiled by seriously motivated authors, who of course examined much of the primary material and who often were in a position to examine old maps and writings that are now hard to come by.

To someone who has struggled with the linguistic portion of the toponymic literature, the primary sources often prove admirably incisive. As an illustration, the Seminole name for scrub vegetation was transliterated as Etonia or Eton-ai-ah. A Seminole town called "Etanie" once existed near Etonia Creek, a little north of central Florida's Big Scrub country; and Swanton (1922:412), who did not know the Seminole term for scrub, tried improperly to see some connection with the Timucua name Utina. The Ettini Ponds, also a little north of the

Big Scrub, received their name from Seminole Indians whose villages were located among them. Accordingly, a toponymist suggested that Eton Creek and Lake Eton, both in the Big Scrub, bear the Seminole name for an expanse of scrub vegetation. The suggestion was reasonable, but let us turn to the primary literature. The government surveyor R. B. Ker, in his field notes for 1835, said of the lake, "a fine sheet of water. . . . I have named it after the present governor of Florida, Eaton. The Indians have no name for it—excepting their general appellation—wewa—which is the Seminolese for water. . . . The creek and said lake had no name—the Indians say so. I have named them after our present governor." While Etonia, Eton-ai-ah, and Ettini are of Seminole origin, Eton Creek and Lake Eton bear no more than the misspelled patronymic of John Henry Eaton, who was U.S. Secretary of War before he became governor of Florida.

The aforesaid primary and secondary sources not only help clear up problems of original application and orthography; they likewise augment the list of true Seminole toponyms by adding to it a good many that have vanished from recent maps. Also, a few toponyms have persisted but only in translation, the Indian name having been too difficult to write and pronounce. Thus, the Seminole called a certain stream of southern Florida by a Creek name that means "fish eating-place river." The Indian expression was impossible to transliterate, since the Creek word for "fish" includes—in two places—a sound that does not exist in English and that cannot be written in English characters. (This sound is approached, although not closely, by the "thl" of "athlete"; it is the voiceless "l," best known for its occurrence in Welsh.) The early cartographers came up with such transliterations as Flathlopopkahatchee, Thlothlopopkahatchee, and Thlath-to-popka-hatchee; but later ones settled for a rough translation, Fish-eating Creek, and the stream is so called today.

About 45 miles west of Fish-eating Creek was another stream, which the Seminole called "peas river," in allusion to pea vines. The Seminole term for "peas" had the literal meaning of "long beans," with reference to the trailing vines; and so the stream's name was, literally, "long beans river." Early cartographers tried their hand at this toponym, penning such terms as Tolopchopko Hatchee or Talahk-chopko Hatchee; but later ones preferred rough translations such as Peas River or Pease Creek. ("Pease" was an old collective plural of "pea.") Today, the stream is called Peace River. The alteration of "Pease" to "Peace" reflected an effort to identify the stream with the Rio de la Paz or Flumen Pacis, a "river of peace" named by the Spaniards two centuries before the emergence of the Seminole. The Rio de la Paz was somewhere on the Florida west coast, but its location is otherwise unknown. Without reference to the primary literature, such names as Peace River, Fish-eating Creek, Spring Creek, Old Town, Billy's Branch, and a few others could not be identified as assuredly Seminole.

Few previous workers, if any, have attempted to recover information about American Indian culture through analysis of all the toponyms left by some tribe or other grouping; and so I have written at some length about the obstacles that might lie, unexpectedly, in the way of such analysis. What with my discussion of spurious names, perplexing orthographies, and frequent mistranslations, it might be supposed that there is a dearth of place-names that are old, Indian, and amenable to translation. But this is not the case. Thus, the translatable Indian toponyms of Florida, dating back to or well before the Second Seminole War, are numerous; and collectively they constitute a previously untapped source of cultural data, in addition to the possibilities they hold out for the locating of Seminole archeological sites.

Of culture periods recognized by Florida archeologists, the Seminole Period was the last to be identified, and it is still inadequately known, even though it began and ended in historic times. For history in the usual sense does not throw much light on culture history of the kind that would interest archeologists; and most ethnographic studies on the Seminole were made after these Indians had been decimated, despoiled of their herds and crops, dispossessed, and forced back into a swampland environment that was strange to them. Toponym translation can combine with archeology to reveal details of Seminole life that are not recoverable from history in the strict sense, or from ethnography. Of course, the Seminole Period can be seen most clearly when all pertinent data—archeological, linguistic, toponymic, historical, ethnographic, physicoanthropological, environmental—are integrated; but here I shall do no more than present a few conclusions to which I was led by an investigation of place-names, their meanings, and their applications.

Physical features of the Florida environment, regarded by the early Seminole as nameworthy, included little more than bodies of water, sharply bounded stands of certain vegetation types, and a few expanses of distinctive soils. But of course, such features are about the only ones offered by Florida, which is rather monotonous of topography. Named bodies of water included what we would call rivers, creeks, spring-runs, lakes, ponds, swamps, and marshes. The Seminole did not distinguish between river and creek, or between lake and pond. (A meaningful distinction could not actually be drawn, since bodies of water form a gradient in size.) However, a word meaning "large" might appear in the name of a sizeable river or lake. When a word meaning "little" was used, the intention generally was to contrast a certain body of water with a similar but larger one nearby. The Seminole distinguished toponymically between the flowing waters and the still ones; also between the ordinary streams and those that welled up, spring-like, from the ground. Intermittently flowing springs were also noted as such.

Toponymy suggests that the Seminole were categorizing the Florida fresh waters in an ecologically sound fashion. Let us pursue the topic of ecological subdivision a bit further, with reference to the land rather than the waters.

In Florida as elsewhere, plants are not distributed randomly over the landscape; rather, each species can grow only where its climatic and edaphic (soil-related) needs are met with. Species with fairly similar needs are rather consistently found growing together; they form what are called plant associations, some of which are so distinctive as to have received vernacular names. Each association has its characteristic animal species, also; and it is often convenient to describe the whereabouts of an animal species in terms of the plant associations to which it is confined. Archeologists have lately become interested in plant and animal habitats—so interested that an archeological expedition may also gather much ecological information (e.g. Coe and Flannery 1967); and it is worthwhile to see what toponymy tells about Seminole knowledge of plant associations in Florida.

Conspicuous in northern and central Florida is an association known to local residents as high hammock, and to ecologists as mesic hammock. It is the Florida variant of the eastern hardwood forest, familiar to archeologists as the Eastern Woodland. The Seminole did not make use of an expression that would distinguish mesic hammock from other kinds of forest, perhaps because the association is complex, and their attention was centered less upon the totality of plant species than upon a few important ones. However, the Seminole often gave name to a stand of this forest, in other words to an individual hammock. The name might be based on some nearby cultural feature rather than on any peculiarity of the stand itself. In addition, these Indians several times used a toponym meaning a stand of hickories, and once used another meaning a stand of basswoods. Such usages provide further evidence that the Seminole were interested in the mesic hammock, to which association the Florida hickories and basswoods are largely confined.

Also conspicuous in Florida is an association called scrub by the locals, or sandpine and rosemary scrub by ecologists. Except for a patch or two on the Alabama coast, scrub is confined to Florida, where it occupies coastal dunes and certain interior expanses of relict dunes. When the Seminole came to Florida, they saw scrub for the first time, and coined for it a designation roughly meaning, "go elsewhere." The name, applied by the Indians to several large areas of scrub, was appropriate; for this vegetation offers little but deep sand, dwarf pines, and coarse underbrush.

A third major plant association of Florida is called high pine by the locals, turkey oak and longleaf pine by ecologists. It was no novelty to the Seminole, for it extends well into Georgia. A special name for the high pine association was applied by these Indians to several large expanses of it. In addition, the Seminole made occasional use of a toponym meaning a stand of pines. The high pine association had its own name, and the pine stands that warranted separate reference were those of the flatwoods. In the vegetation mosaic of northern and central Florida, pine flatwoods form a matrix in which various other associations are set.

Another toponym signifies a grove of oak trees. The reference here was to stands of the association called liveoak hammock. This exists as scattered but numerous patches, each dominated by towering liveoaks, and with but little underbrush. Similarly, a toponym translatable as "cedar grove" designated spots where southern red cedars formed stands. This tree exists in mesic hammock but is scattered there; actual groves of cedars develop around limestone outcrops and on prehistoric shell middens where the soil is unusually limey. One island, in the Cedar Keys group, bears a Seminole name meaning "cedar island." Here the cedars grow upon middens that date from Weedon Island and earlier periods. (Not that the trees themselves are so old; the midden debris altered the soil in a fashion that encouraged the growth of cedars after the prehistoric Indians had left.)

Swampy tracts simply called "cypress" had an abundance of cypress trees. In Florida there are two varieties of cypress, ecologically separated; the pond or dwarf cypress occupies shallow basins of still water, while the much larger bald cypress follows the rivers and the shores of the riverine lakes. The Seminole did not insist upon distinguishing, toponymically, the stands of pond cypress from those of bald cypress. However, it is occasionally possible, from a place-name alone, to determine the kind of cypress that was locally conspicuous; for example, "cypress river" would refer to the large, riparian variety. The so-called Big Cypress Swamp, where a sizeable percentage of the Seminole still live, bears an English name that is a bit equivocal; does "big" allude to the size of the trees or of the swamp? If the former, the trees would have to be the bald cypress; if the latter, they would probably be the pond cypress, which occupies large, swampy basins. The English toponym was derived by rough translation from an old Seminole one that was less equivocal, and that meant a broad, level expanse with cypress trees. Big Cypress Swamp is Florida's largest unbroken expanse of pond cypress.

Widespread in Florida are patches of freshwater marsh, of a kind known locally as "prairie." The Florida "prairie" is essentially a shallow basin overgrown with sedges, grasses, or other herbaceous vegetation, and flooded during at least part of the year. The Seminole made toponymic use of an expression that designates this kind of vegetation in general, and also gave individual names to various "prairies." The name might be descriptive, or might be based on some nearby cultural feature. The old Mikasuki—or at least Hitchiti—designation for the Everglades meant, roughly, "water grassland"; and modern writers have referred to this great marsh as a "river of grass."

Turning now to the brackish-water associations, I find no toponym alluding to saltmarsh; but on one occasion, the Seminole name for the red mangrove tree was given to a locality with the plant association called mangrove swamp.

In short, place-names reveal the Seminole to have recognized almost every major plant association in northeastern and central Florida, the only conspicuous omission from the toponymic list being the low or hydric hammock. In this part of Florida, a low hammock usually exists as a very narrow strip between a high hammock and a body of water. As the land drops off toward the water, the tree species of the high hammock are gradually replaced by those of the low; and the two associations are not so much separated as united by an irregular, vaguely defined zone of transition. Along some rivers, the distinctiveness of the low hammock is further blurred because the association passes irregularly into bald cypress swamp as the water's edge is neared. It is therefore not surprising that the Seminole found no particular need to name a spot on the basis of some bit of low hammock.

Let us turn now from plant associations to soils. As might be expected, the early Seminole employed no place-name that mentioned the local presence of the ordinary, more or less grayish, sandy soils that extend so widely through northeastern and central Florida. (Toponyms are, of course, based on features that are locally distinctive, not those that are well-nigh ubiquitous.) But interestingly, these Indians made at least one toponymic reference to almost every other kind of soil within their area. These other kinds stand out locally by virtue of unusual coloration, texture, or both. Soils recognizable in Seminole toponymy include red clay, which is conspicuous especially toward the base of the Florida Panhandle; relict dunes of white sand, existing in the interior of the peninsula; expanses of black, peaty dirt in basins that have gone dry; the muck that widely borders some streams; and exposures of clay suitable for pottery-making.

Our knowledge of Seminole ethnoecology might be enhanced, of course, by an investigation of these Indians' present attitudes and terminology relating to ecological subdivision of Florida waters, plant associations, and soils. However, the modern Seminole concepts, pertaining to environments that exist today in southern Florida, cannot convincingly be used to disclose the ecological thinking of the early Seminole farther north in the state. Such disclosure can come only from toponymy, for the ethnographic literature does not provide the needed information.

Although the Seminole were keen observers of Florida's ecological diversity, and reflected their observation in toponyms, they did not share the white man's urge to name every distinguishable feature of the landscape. In general, they did not name a body of water, stand of vegetation, or expanse of soil unless it often commanded their attention. If a locality bears an old Seminole toponym, then these Indians knew the spot well. Many of their place-names, although mentioning some natural feature, actually served to identify a village. This point is important especially to archeologists who want to find Seminole sites.

Seminole place-names were not flowery, poetic, or mystical; they were down-to-earth, and often descriptive in a simple but appropriate fashion. Take, for example, toponyms referring to rivers, lakes, or other bodies of water. (For present purposes, it does not matter whether a body of water was considered nameworthy per se, or whether its appellation was also that of a nearby village.) These toponyms—and they are exceptionally numerous—yield such translations as big lake, round lake, long lake, black water, yellow water, clear water, slimy water. As for the streams, they were called big river, cypress river, cedar river, snake river, black river, clay river, alligator river, horse river. Others were called wolf creek, fallen tree creek, long and winding, bullfrogs, boggy, spring, small spring, high footlog, earthen bridge (i.e., natural bridge), deep valley. Some of the water names suggest human activity in the vicinity: bloody creek, walk in the water, white people, somebody drowned, shriveled corpse.

A good many toponyms, often but not necessarily connected with bodies of water, referred to the local occurrence of some particular food. Thus we have such translations as bass eating-place, turtle eating-place, and potato eating-place. The bass was the large-mouthed black bass, and the turtles were species of the genus *Pseudemys*. Contrary to the claims of some authors, the potato was unequivocally the sweet potato, not the yam, the Irish potato, or the wild bogpotato. Toponymy identifies one locality in peninsular Florida as an acorn eating-place, and suggests that the acorns were those of the liveoak. It is not surprising that the Seminole utilized acorns as food, for the Creek Indians were reported to do so around the time the Hitchiti began the exodus to Florida. In some years, the liveoaks drop an enormous number of acorns, a rich and easily gathered source of food. In some species of oaks, the nut is large and palatable; in others it is small, bitter and astringent, edible only after special preparation to remove a toxic principle. The liveoak's acorn is not as tasty as that of some white oaks, but it can be eaten when raw. Several methods of detoxifying bitter acorns were known in the Southeast, although the ethnographic literature does not ascribe any of them specifically to the Seminole.

Other Seminole toponyms, alluding to locally available foods, include one already noted, "fish eating-place river," and Chassahowitzka, "hanging pumpkins." Alafia, variously rendered as Alafia's, Alfiers, or Elfers, is customarily translated as "hunting-ground." The translation is tolerable, but the full significance of the name has not previously been remarked on. It did not refer to just any kind of hunting-ground, but to one that lay at a considerable distance from a village. The Seminole had (and still have) the custom of establishing a hunting camp at some promising spot miles from home. One man, or at the most two or three, would occupy a hunting camp, where they would erect only enough shelter to cover their firearms or other pos-sessions that might be damaged by rain. From this base they would make forays in search of game, especially deer. "Far-off hunting there" would be a literal translation of the Alafia toponym. In Hills-borough, Manatee, and Pasco counties, the toponymically recognized hunting-grounds were small rivers with an exceptional diversity of plant associations in the vicinity.

Wild animals, mentioned in old Seminole toponyms, include pan-ther, black bear, wolf, white-tailed deer, manatee, turkey, turtle (of the genus *Pseudemys*), alligator, snake, bullfrog, fish, and large-mouthed black bass. Wild plants include cedar, pine, cypress, dog-wood, red mangrove, red bay, sweetgum, basswood, Spanish moss, cabbage-palm, and grass. Domestic animals and plants include cow, horse, hog, chicken, corn, sweet potato, the Seminole pumpkin, pep-per (probably chili), tobacco, pea, bean, orange, and peach. Of the domesticated species, only corn, squash, and tobacco were assuredly native; perhaps the peas and beans were also, but toponyms do not distinguish between the native and the introduced varieties. The cow, horse, hog, orange, and peach were assuredly introduced into the Southeast by the Spaniards.

Spanish words appear in a scattering of Seminole place-names, and toponymy can throw a little light on Spanish-Seminole culture con-tact; but the subject must be approached cautiously; the likelihood that Spanish words entered Creek and Hitchiti at an early time, prior to the emergence of the Seminole, must be kept in mind. A few Spanish loan-words exist in both Creek and Mikasuki, a few more in Mikasuki or Creek alone. Most of these words relate to items of Spanish material culture—rice, wheat, orange, tomato, coffee, sugar, certain alcoholic beverages, cow, goat, horse, housecat, a kind of paint, flask, jug, coat, nail, flag, a kind of fence—that probably or surely arrived in the Southeast before the Seminole began their exodus to Florida. Seminole terms for soldier and captain are also of Spanish origin, and probably date from an early time. Two other Spanish loan-words—names for Christ and the Devil—doubtless were early borrowings also, for Spanish missionization was terminated by English soldiers and Creek mercenaries before the Seminole Period began. Earliest of all borrowings was a name for the Spaniards them-selves; this appears in several versions, but all of them are based on España.

Hence, no special significance can be attached to the few Seminole place-names that incorporate a Spanish-derived name for the orange;

or to the considerable number that are based on a Spanish-derived name for the cow. These latter toponyms yield such translations as "cow ferry," "Cowkeeper's Town," "cow home" (i.e., pasture), "there are cows," and "encircling cows" (i.e., cattle enclosure); at least they reveal the importance of cattle in the Seminole economy.

A different class of toponyms includes those coined by the Spaniards and adopted by the Seminole. With one or two exceptions, these names originally designated missions, but they were eventually extended to nearby rivers or lakes. Sampala, an old designation of a North Florida lake, was the Seminole version of San Pablo; the Franciscan mission of San Pedro y San Pablo de Potoriba once stood nearby. Interestingly, early cartographers reported the lake to have been called both Sampala and Sampelee; these would be Creek and Hitchiti variants respectively. Santaffy, a river name, was the Seminole attempt at Santa Fe; the Franciscan mission of Santa Fe de Toloca had been located near the stream. Santa Fe Talofa was a Seminole settlement; "talofa" means "town," and is only accidentally similar, phonetically, to Toloca. Seguana is the Seminole rendering of San Juan, another river name. (After Spanish influence waned in Florida, the Rio de San Juan Bautista was Anglicized to St. Johns.) The Spaniards in northern Florida looked on the Suwannee River as a sort of lesser St. Johns; hence early reference to the Suwannee as the "little Seguana." The name Suwannee itself is from the Seminole, but was derived originally from the Spanish toponym San Juanito. Sanfelasco, traditionally a locality of Spanish and Seminole occupation, bears a name intended for San Francisco.

The aforesaid toponyms, adopted by the Seminole from their Spanish predecessors, and perpetuating mission names in most cases, are confined to northeastern Florida. Thus, toponymy accords with history and archeology: the Spaniards had a chain of missions and ranchos extending across northeastern Florida, no farther south than Alachua County.

One Seminole and pre-Seminole toponym was involved with the Spaniards in a curious fashion that warrants separate mention. This place-name, which has come down to us in English translation as Fowl Town, was puzzling to the ethnologist Swanton (1922: 178, 409), and so to toponymists who followed him. There were several Fowl Towns scattered over Creek, Hitchiti, and Seminole country; and Swanton could only suggest that in these settlements the people raised chickens. Initially, however, the reference was to the turkey, which in English was long known as the Turkey fowl. In Creek, and inferentially in some other languages, the name for the Spaniards sounded like the word that meant turkeys collectively. The Southeastern tribes were all divided into clans, and the Turkey Clan bore a name phonetically similar to an expression that meant "Spanish people." Even in fairly literate societies, much less in preliterate ones, an unfamiliar word is commonly pronounced in a fashion that conforms with local speech, and may be twisted into some more familiar word without loss of semantic content. The early, pre-Seminole "Fowl" Towns were really "Spanish" Towns, which was merely to say that they were occupied by Christianized Indians. The ramifications of the misunderstanding will not be pursued here; suffice it to say that, contrary to some authors, a Fowl Town in Florida need not have been an offshoot of an earlier Fowl Town farther north.

In the old mission area, the Seminole also perpetuated some Timucua and Apalachee names, most if not all of which originally identified villages of missionized Indians. Thus, the English raids of the early 1700s destroyed a Timucua village called Lachua, but by 1750 the locality was occupied by an important Seminole town called Alachua Talofa. Again, the mission of Santa Maria de los Angeles de la Arapaha once stood near the Suwannee River. "Arapaha" was the name of the Timucua tribe or village that was missionized; but after the destruction of the mission, a Seminole settlement called Alapaha Talofa ("Arapaha Town") existed in the vicinity. The Aucilla River bears a Timucua name that dates well back into pre-Seminole times, but a Seminole town called Oscillee later occupied the river's bank.

A bit farther north in the state, the Apalachee mission of San Juan de Ospalaga was succeeded by a Seminole town called Aspalaga. On the St. Marks River, a missionized Apalachee village bore the name of Vasisa; later, the Seminole town of Wacissa Talofa was located in the area. The Apalachee name for Lake Jackson, Ocalquibe, reappeared as a Seminole appellation, Okaheepee.

Some hypothesis should be advanced to account for the frequency with which the Seminole took over Timucua and Apalachee village names. The report of Diego Peña (Boyd 1949) guides the direction of such hypothesizing. Peña led a few Spaniards and Creek Indians through the mission area about a decade after it had been devastated. The land was empty of people, but the old village locations were still evident, along with cleared fields, groves of fruit trees, and stray cattle. Someone in the party, presumably the Indians, knew the Timucua or Apalachee names of the abandoned villages and of conspicuous natural features; and Peña faithfully recorded them. When the

Seminole arrived about 40 years later, they must have found ready-made village locations, and well-situated fields that needed but minimal clearing. In other words, the reoccupation of older sites by the Seminole does not imply their connection with earlier occupants; rather, the Timucua and Apalachee, both of them agricultural (and pastoral too, around the missions), had chosen to live in places that the Seminole also found attractive.

This hypothesis could be tested by turning to the situation in central Florida, south of the missionized area. There, in both the Gulf and the St. Johns drainages, the cultural debris of Seminole occupation almost invariably lies atop that of some late prehistoric or early historic people. I use the word "atop" loosely, for at the sites under discussion, not much windblown sand or plant debris has accumulated over the pre-Seminole materials. It might be better to say that the brushed pottery, chinaware and glass scraps, faceted glass beads, gunflints, trade pipe fragments, cow teeth, and other remains of Seminole occupation are more or less commingled with the pottery and flint work of a somewhat earlier time. Evidently, when the Seminole first began moving down into northeastern and central Florida, they were much inclined to settle upon preexisting village locations, whether or not the former inhabitants had been missionized.

This circumstance explains the comparatively frequent occurrence of Seminole toponyms translatable as "old town," "old house," "burnt village," and "abandoned fields." It is not surprising that the Seminole did not adopt Timucua place-names in central Florida as they did a bit farther north. Northeastern Florida, the missionized area, was the territory with which the Creek Indians, the Spanish, and the English were vitally concerned, at a time when the interior of central Florida was virtually *terra incognita*. Spanish and English exploring parties, Creek raiders, bands of slave-catchers—these kept alive the Apalachee and Timucua toponyms of northeastern Florida during the 40 years that elapsed between the destruction of the Spanish missions and the arrival of the Seminole.

The primary toponymic literature has also revealed a hitherto unsuspected Seminole-Spanish relationship in the interior of Florida, developing in the period after the passage of the state into American hands (an event of 1821). After this passage, certain Florida tracts were not divided into section, township, and range, for by special agreement they had been set aside as Spanish land grants. When I began to examine surveyors' field notes, I was impressed by the way

Seminole sites were concentrated in or just peripheral to these granted lands. Thus, in Marion County alone, five sites (three Seminole and two Seminole Negro) lie in or not far outside the Catalina de Jesus Hijuelos Grant. Two more are located in the F. P. Sanchez Grant, and another not far outside the Antonio Alvarez Grant. The largest known Seminole site lies near the border of the Domingo Acosta Grant. In addition, there are records of Seminole settlement in the F. M. Arredondo, the Domingo Fernandez, and the J. Hernandez grants, although I have not found the sites. It is toponymy, more than history in the strict sense, that draws the archeologists's attention to a Spanish-Seminole association in the interior of central Florida, after the transferral of that area to the United States.

In devoting so much space to toponymy, I do not mean to overemphasize its importance as an adjunct to archeology. But it is readily imaginable, or discoverable from the literature, that archeology profits from involvement with such disciplines as ethnology, physical anthropology, or history; whereas toponymy has generally been neglected, at least in the United States, as a source of information about bygone cultures. Yet, some place-names of this country have survived through five culture periods, all of archeological interest. Thus, some Florida names originated with the pagan Timucua or Apalachee, and then were carried over into the mission era, when the state seemed destined to become another Latin-American country. They persisted through the English period, although the land was laid waste; were given new life in the Seminole period; and were passed on to the Early American period (if not indeed to the present). A study of Florida geographic names has permitted location of otherwise elusive Seminole archeological sites, and has thrown light on several aspects of these Indians' culture: their ecological concepts, their attitude toward the naming of localities, their subsistence activities, their domestic animals and plants, their contacts with the Spanish, their limited heritage from Timucua and Apalachee predecessors.

I should think that an investigation into place-names, carried on in the approximate fashion that was rewarding in Florida, should prove equally productive in other parts of the United States, and in other countries where cultures have proven more fleeting than their own toponyms.

CHAPTER FOUR

Some Interactions of Archeology with Physical Anthropology

One relationship of physical anthropology to archeology is evident: if physical anthropologists are to study any but modern man, they must make use of human remains excavated archeologically. Customarily, archeologists uncover human burials with great care, and a site report may include an appendix in which a physical anthropologist describes the skulls and other skeletal parts that were found. Less evident, perhaps, are the ways in which an analysis of human remains could be of use to the archeologist whose principal interest is culture. These ways are numerous, however, and it is worthwhile to discuss them.

Under exceptional conditions, the softer parts of the human body, such as the skin, hair, muscles, and viscera, may be preserved along with the bones. The requisite conditions may be environmental, cultural, or (most often) a combination of the two. In the southwestern United States, bodies have persisted in fair shape from Basketmaker II times (about 100 B.C.–400 A.D.) partly because they were placed in caves or rock shelters which protected them from weathering, but also because the very dry air desiccated them. In Egypt, mummies have withstood decay partly because they were artificially prepared, but also because the Egyptian climate is arid. Artificial mummification in the Egyptian fashion would be futile in a damper climate; and conversely, predynastic Egyptian bodies were remarkably well preserved by natural desiccation although they were not deliberately treated to ensure mummification. In the Andes of South America, Inca remains have lasted partly because of the way they were prepared and interred, but also because the region is cold and dry. In caves of Tennessee and Kentucky, decay of Indian bodies and their wrappings was slowed by natural salts such as nitre, copperas, and alum. In Europe, well-preserved bodies have been recovered from bogs, where they had been "tanned" by the acid medium in which they reposed. Copper salts can also act as a preservative; and in at least one instance, the ears of a prehistoric American Indian remained recognizable because they had been in contact with copper ear-ornaments. Human hairs have more frequently persisted as a result of contact with copper artifacts in Indian burials. In a very old Indian skull, discovered in a deep spring of peninsular Florida, the brain had been preserved.

But in most cases, human remains recovered by archeologists consist only of bones and teeth. If such remains are not too fragmentary, they permit determination (to within a few years) of the deceased person's age at death; for there is a fairly predictable rate at which the milk teeth are replaced by adult dentition, and at which certain changes take place in the skeleton. The latter changes are various, but many of them involve continued ossification; some cartilage is replaced by bone, various separate skeletal elements become fused, and a tighter junction may be formed between already fused elements. In the human embryo, the number of bones (or more accurately, independent centers of ossification) is about four times greater than in the middle-aged adult; and it is possible to construct a fairly reliable timetable for the reduction of skeletal parts through fusion.

The sex of the individual can also be determined from the skeleton. The pelvic girdle is especially useful in this connection, for it is sexually dimorphic even in children; other skeletal elements develop such dimorphism only after puberty, if at all. A roughened groove, the preauricular sulcus, lies on the ilium above and in front of the auricular area of the female pelvis. This groove, which is lacking from the male pelvis, is a notably constant, qualitative indicator of female sex. The male pelvis also differs from the female in shape, massiveness, and about eight details of structure; these are quantitative differences with some degree of overlap, and need not be reviewed here.

Sexual dimorphism in the human skull becomes evident only after puberty. Within any particular population, the females have thinner, lighter skulls, and a cranial capacity about 10 per cent less than that of the males. A human skull, or for that matter almost any bone, exhibits facets, grooves, or prominences whose function is likely to baffle the nonspecialist. Some of this modeling accommodates muscular attachments; and in general, the coarser modeling of the human male skull, as compared with the female, reflects the heavier musculature of the male jaw and neck. Sexual differences in skull characteristics are average, with some degree of overlap at least in large samples; and the same is true of certain sexual differences in stature, ribs, sternum, and thorax structure. Although males and females show some overlap in most sexually dimorphic skeletal features, a great majority of skeletons can be sexed convincingly.

Since features of the pelvic girdle, and especially the presence or absence of a preauricular sulcus, provide virtually unassailable indication of sex, it might be asked why attention should be given to other bones when sex determination is the aim. The answer is that skeletal remains often are not intact. For example, in Florida a prehistoric pelvis is rarely encountered. In that state, the great majority of Indian burials date from the Weedon Island Period or its temporal equivalent. During that time, most dead bodies were not buried speedily, but were disjointed and cleaned of flesh; the bones were then left in a charnel house, perhaps for years. When the time came for interment in a mound, often only the skull and a few limb bones were selected for burial. These were made into a small bundle; hence archeological reference to the practice of "bundle burial" in Florida and elsewhere. Primary interment (burial of the entire body) was known in Weedon Island times, and so was cremation; but the rule was secondary interment of selected bones. Excavating a burial mound, and confronted only with secondarily interred bundles, the archeologist is grateful for any data that can be extracted from skulls, femora, and other limb bones.

I mention femora because they hold special possibilities. Femur length bears a fairly predictable relationship to standing height in life; and so the former can be used to compute the latter, by means of carefully devised formulae (Cornwall 1956). The relation of femur length to standing height varies a bit from one race of mankind to another, and from male to female within any single race. Hence, the anthropometrist must select formulae appropriate to the skeletal material he analyzes.

Although anthropometric attention has centered upon the femur as an index to stature, the tibia, humerus, and radius are also useful in this connection; for tibia, humerus, and radius lengths also bear calculable relationships to stature. If a femur, tibia, humerus, and radius are all available from a single individual (as is commonly the case, even with bundle burials), and if all four bones are used independently to compute standing height by means of appropriate formulae, the arithmetic mean of the four computations will provide the most nearly accurate result. An individual's standing height in life cannot be determined with absolute accuracy, for it may be almost an inch greater upon arising than upon retiring, and may decrease in old age as a result of changes in the vertebral column without concomitant change in limb bone length. But certain other variables—such as racial diversity, sexual dimorphism, and postmortem changes—are taken into account by the aforesaid formulae, which permit determination of stature to within about an inch.

The practice of secondary interment is by no means the only factor responsible for the incompleteness of skeletal remains in some burials. The preservation of bones depends on the physical, chemical, and biotic characteristics of the medium in which they repose. Thus, in Florida, the dampness of the soil may soften buried bones, which are soon invaded and fragmented by plant rootlets. Even in the case of a primary interment, excavation of an intact skeleton may accordingly be impossible. In addition, anywhere in the world, remains may be disarranged by forces of nature, or (more often) by human activities such as amateur digging.

The major physical types of mankind—"races" in popular speech—are generally identifiable from skulls alone. For example, in the United States it is easy to distinguish the skull of an American Indian from that of a Negro or a white person. While identification is customarily made on the basis of a series of proportionate measurements, the experienced anthropometrist can identify a good many skulls at a glance. Efforts have been made to categorize a series of varieties within each physical type. Thus, Georg K. Neumann (1952) examined over 10,000 American Indian skulls from various prehistoric and historic horizons at localities north of Mexico, and sorted this material into eight varieties. There had been mixing of the varieties through the millennia, but these eight apparently represented genetically distinctive groups, each of which had considerable continuity in time and space.

Sex, age at death, stature, and physical variety—these are common concerns of the physical anthropologist who examines human remains from archeological sites. In keeping with my emphasis on the usefulness of an interdisciplinary approach, I should note that they have also been the concerns of practitioners of forensic medicine; and the literature of that subject holds much that should interest both the physical anthropologist and the archeologist.

The archeological possibilities of physical anthropology are revealed with particular clarity when attention is turned to some report that presents a detailed analysis of abundant human remains from a single site. In this connection, an especially interesting report is that of Charles E. Snow (1962), who studied burials excavated by William H. Sears in 1960 from Mound B of the Bayshore Homes site in St. Petersburg, Pinellas County, Florida.

Near the end of Weedon Island times, about 500 individuals had been interred in this mound, most if not all of them as bundles. Bones were often fragmentary, and those of one burial were sometimes intermingled with those of another; so analysis of skeletal remains was limited to 115 individuals. Of these, the ones that could not be sexed were mostly under 12 years of age, an expected situation. Sexed individuals were about equally divided between males and females, suggesting that the sample was a random one. Age distribution ranged from fetus to middle-aged adult. There was a high mortality rate (nearly 80 per cent) before the age of 35. This approximate rate characterized prehistoric populations in many parts of the world, and is met with today in most underdeveloped nations which know little of modern scientific medicine. In fact, it is noteworthy that about 20 per cent of these Weedon Island Indians did live beyond the age of 35; the figure was only 5 per cent in the Indian Knoll culture of Kentucky (5,000 B.C.–2,000 B.C.) and among prehistoric Hawaiians of Oahu. Subadult mortality was 26 per cent at Bayshore Homes, as contrasted with about 50 per cent at Cockroach Key, a site in Hillsborough County, Florida.

The males of the Bayshore Homes series averaged about 5 feet 6½ inches tall, the females 5 feet 4½ inches. This stature is typical of prehistoric Indians from the Southeast. The people of the Bayshore Homes site tended to be robust, with broad shoulders. They had well-formed, muscular feet with widely spreading toes.

The skulls were assignable to Neumann's (1952) "Walcolid" variety, which, under the name "Gulf," was fairly well defined long ago by Aleš Hrdlička. In historic times, Walcolids were widely scattered, from the Southeast to the Pacific Northwest and southward through Mexico and Central America into South America. Walcolid remains are widespread in archeological sites of the Southeast, but not from early time levels. Neumann thought this variety might have entered North America from Asia at a fairly late date. In the Bayshore Homes series, the vault of the cranium was high, rather short but quite broad, its bones thick. The face, orbits, and nose were of moderate dimensions, the teeth very large. The skulls were noteworthy for marked relief, of the kind that accommodates muscular attachments.

Bones of the body and limbs were also muscle-marked to an exceptional degree, an indication that these people were quite muscular. In most of the females, but in only a few of the males, there was a slight backward slope of the tibial plateau; this condition characterizes individuals who walk with the knees slightly bent. So-called squatting facets, at the ankle joint of tibia and talus, were particularly characteristic of the males. These facets, and certain others, form in individuals who habitually rest in a squatting position, with the buttocks on the heels and the feet flat on the ground. Most individuals walked on the outside borders of the feet.

Snow reported that in some of the skulls, the cranium was artificially deformed. To judge from his photographs, deformation was limited to a kind that is generally ascribed to the use of a cradle-board. A baby's skull is flexible because certain of its component bones have not yet fused tightly, and so an infant's sleeping habits can affect the eventual shape of its skull. If a baby is frequently cradled and carried about on a cradle-board during the first year or so of its life, the back of its skull will become somewhat flattened, even if a pad is kept between the board and the infant's head. This occipital flattening often is asymmetric because a baby generally develops the habit of sleeping with the head turned to one side. In an unstated percentage of the deformed crania from Bayshore Homes, the forehead also appeared to have been somewhat flattened. This circumstance suggests that the infant's head was held firmly in place by some kind of tight band across the forehead.

Cradle-board deformation of the cranium was common and widespread in much of the United States; but not so in Florida, where it is infrequently encountered and was mostly limited to the Weedon Island culture.

A particularly interesting section of Snow's paper related to pathological conditions in the Bayshore Homes series. Healed fractures, such as those of the arm, leg, clavicle (collarbone), and ribs, were more common in males than in females. With but one exception, the fractures had healed in good alignment. Among the males, congenital or developmental abnormalities included one case of gaps in the auditory floor, and one of uneven annular rings in the dentition (a condition indicative of an arrested growth period early in life). Two females exhibited tilting of the head, and one had "boomerang shins," a bowing of the tibiae. Some minor physical irregularities need not be recounted. Dental abnormalities (both sexes pooled) included one case of broken teeth, six of apical abcesses in which the teeth were worn through the dentine, and two in which necrosis and bone recession suggested pyorrhea. Osteoarthritis was a common affliction, its crippling effects variously noted in the sacroiliac joint, the vertebrae of the lower back, the foot, wrist, elbow, shoulder, hip, knee, and jaw.

Some bones exhibited lesions, porosity, or swelling. These specimens were brought to the attention of pathologists, with the idea of discovering whether the abnormalities were of syphilitic origin. Most of them proved attributable to pyogenic inflammations, traumas, and skin infections. However, one individual exhibited multiple abnormalities consistent with a diagnosis of syphilis. A search was made by an archeologist for comparable pathological conditions in the numerous fragmentary remains that had not been brought to Snow's attention. The search revealed seven more individuals with abnormalities that were grossly similar, at least in the eyes of the non-specialist, to those that had been identified by specialists as probably syphilitic in origin. Thus, the Bayshore Homes series added to the scant but growing body of archeological evidence that syphilis was a disease of New World origin.

So much for Snow's paper. It introduced the subject of paleopathology, which might therefore be pursued at this point.

Man's ailments are numerous. Many of them are produced by pathogenic or parasitic organisms, dietary deficiencies, genetic abnormalities, or the degeneration of various tissues and organs from one cause or another. Accordingly, a detailed explication of paleopathology would necessitate an excursion into the literature of microbiology, parasitology, human biology, endocrinology, genetics, and various branches of medicine. However, only a small minority of these ailments manifest themselves identifiably in the decayed remains that are recovered through archeological excavation. In practice, it is usually the physical anthropologist who evaluates the abnormalities of these remains, perhaps consulting a pathologist if some special problem arises.

Needless to say, mummified bodies yield evidence of some diseases whose existence cannot be determined from mere skeletal remains. At one time, the ancient Egyptians removed the viscera from a body that was to be embalmed, cleaned them, placed them in four jars, and saved them separately from the body. At another time, however, the Egyptians cleaned the viscera, wrapped them, and restored them to the body cavity from which they had come, packing them with sawdust or other material. In consequence, radiography of mummies can reveal details not only of bones and muscles but also of the internal organs in some specimens whose dissection might be regarded as inadvisable. The Egyptians were beset by arteriosclerosis, pneumonia, osteoarthritis, cirrhosis of the liver, anthracosis, appendicitis, gallstones, several kidney diseases, pleurisy, traumatic childbirth, and broken bones, among other ailments. Occasionally, radiography may reveal the probable cause of an individual's death. Thus, the famed Egyptian king Tutankhamen was found to have an open wound on the side of the head, and cerebral hemorrhaging farther back. He probably died from blows to the head.

Of course, radiography is not the only approach to the study of mummified material; I mention it separately because it is a new technique, and one that has yielded fresh data. Naturally, the older paleopathologists seldom were free to autopsy such rarities as mummies; but even so, in the ancient Egyptians they detected Potts' vertebral caries, skin eruptions (perhaps smallpox), skin lesions (perhaps leprosy), inguinal ulcer (possibly from bubonic plague), multiple abscesses, parasitization by the urinary blood fluke, enlarged spleen (probably from malaria), vesicovaginal fistula, prolapsus of the rectum and of the female genitalia, and several other maladies.

In the southwestern United States, Basketmaker mummies have yielded evidence of silicosis, anthracosis, pneumonia, and kidney stones, as well as sinusitis, mastoiditis, and other conditions that would have been detectable even without mummification. Peruvian mummies have revealed arteriosclerosis.

Both nits (eggs) and adults of the head louse were found in the hair of American Indian mummies from Peru and the southwestern United States. This insect is believed to have evolved into a number of slightly different varieties, each infesting a different race or genetically isolated population of mankind. But the varieties can interbreed, and they have done so, especially in modern times when some peoples have moved widely across the face of the globe. Thus, much interest attached to an investigation of lice from New World mummies. The Peruvian insects turned out to differ from the prehistoric North American ones, but both lots were most closely similar to Aleutian and Chinese specimens. They were not particularly similar to specimens from living Indians of the United States; for this country has been the melting pot of lice, the European and the African varieties having interbred here with the indigenous one. Nits have also been observed in the hair of Egyptian mummies.

An unusual find was the frozen remains of an Inca child who had been buried in a stone building at an elevation of 17,658 feet in the Andes near Santiago, Chile. The burial was late prehistoric, dating from about 30 years before the arrival of Francisco Pizarro in Inca country. A parasitic roundworm, *Trichuris trichiura,* was abundantly represented in feces from the rectum of the well-preserved body (Pizzi and Schenone 1954). Previously, it had been supposed that Europeans brought this parasite to the New World, but evidently the supposition was in error. It is also interesting to note that the child had not been infected with the roundworm known scientifically as *Ascaris lumbricoides.* When cultural and environmental conditions are suitable for parasitization by the *Trichuris,* they are suitable for parasitization by the *Ascaris* as well; so presumably the latter species, now a common and widespread parasite of man and the domestic hog, had not reached Inca country by late prehistoric times.

Surprisingly, even in areas where bodies were not well preserved by cultural or environmental processes, it would often be possible to examine feces for evidence of parasites. With remarkable frequency, the fossilized droppings of animals have persisted from very remote times in paleontological sites, and so one might expect human feces to have persisted from less remote times in archeological sites. In the United States, human coprolites have come most frequently from the arid Southwest. Specimens from Mesa Verde, Colorado, revealed that about 1,000 years ago, the local Indians were parasitized by the human pinworm, *Enterobius vermicularis.* This species was also found by Gary F. Fry and John G. Moore (1969) in human fecal material from Hogup and Danger caves, Utah; one coprolite from Danger Cave, containing this parasite, was radiocarbon-dated at 7837 B.C. ± 630 years. *Enterobius vermicularis* invades man only, so coprolites containing it were unquestionably of human origin. With this point ascertained, it became possible to erect criteria that would distinguish the droppings of humans from those of all other mammals that might have entered the caves. The human coprolites were unique in containing a mixture of diverse plant material, bone, and charcoal. A similar situation is to be looked for in other parts of the world.

The Indians who occupied the Utah caves were also infested with some kind of acanthocephalan, or thorn-headed worm. Unlike pinworms, thorn-heads can bring on severe symptoms, including pain, diarrhea, exhaustion, and lassitude. Thorn-heads bore into the intestinal wall, producing sores which might become infected; sometimes they even perforate the intestine. Thorn-head life histories are various, but in general there is a young stage that is encysted in the tissues of some small animal such as a grubworm, roach, crab, or fish; the adult stage is spent in the intestine of a predaceous vertebrate that has eaten the parasitized small animal. At least some acanthocephalans can spend their adult stage in any one of several vertebrate predators, including man.

Coprolites are sometimes encountered in the freshwater shell middens of the southeastern United States. I have identified certain Florida specimens as dog droppings, but the matter would bear further investigation. In any event, knowledge of human paleopathology would doubtless be augmented by a study of canine coprolites. Even now in civilized countries, fastidiousness and the principles of sanitation are suspended by a remarkably large percentage of people in matters relating to close contact with dogs and the waste products therefrom; and accordingly, the canine population serves as a reservoir for a considerable number of parasites that also infect man. Among these are at least two kinds of hookworms, a gnathostome roundworm, various dog ascarids, certain heartworms, an intestinal threadworm, the trichina worm, the eye worm, the Guinea worm, the giant kidney worm, the double-pored tapeworm, a hydatid tapeworm, a many-headed tapeworm, the broad tapeworm, the dog tapeworm, several echinostome flukes, the large intestinal fluke, a blood fluke, a lung fluke, and a tongue worm, along with a diversity of pathogenic bacteria and protozoa—to say nothing of external parasites such as fleas, mites, and ticks, which themselves may transmit pathogenic organisms. Uncivilized peoples of the past no doubt were as unsanitary as the civilized ones of the present in their association with dogs, and a goodly segment of prehistoric man's parasite fauna should be detectable in dog droppings from archeological sites.

Since the general public, even the reading public of civilized nations, seem ignorant of the extent to which dogs can transmit parasites and pathogens to man, it may be well to note that under the proper cultural and environmental conditions, such transmission can undermine the health not just of scattered individuals but of an entire community. For example, a serious medical problem in several parts of South America has been the transmission of a hydatid tapeworm from dogs to people; in Iceland, where 70,000 people lived with 20,000 dogs, hydatid disease became so common that control and treatment of the canine population proved imperative; and in China, the high incidence of kala-azar in Kansu Province was found to result principally from the close association of children with dogs. Hence, it is likely that the destiny of some prehistoric communities was influenced, unbeknownst to the inhabitants thereof, by the debilitation that can result from unsanitary coexistence with dogs.

It is also worth noting that while many parasites are soft and delicate in the adult stage, they are likely to have a younger stage (usually the egg) that is tougher and more apt to be preserved; for this younger stage is passed out with the feces of the host, and so must withstand environmental rigors from which the adult parasite is shielded. The egg, encapsulated embryo, or other young stage often has characteristic details permitting identification. Quite a bit of work has been done on the diagnostic features of parasite eggs recoverable from modern fecal smears, and this work is applicable to coprolite analysis also.

Another approach to paleopathology is provided by the realistic portrayal of diseased individuals in ancient painting, sculpture, or ceramics. The approach is fairly limited, for only a minority of maladies produce unmistakable external signs.

Nevertheless, a few abnormalities can be identified from figurines or other portrayals. Some prehistoric Peruvians turned out a remarkable variety of ceramic vessels, modeled or painted to show numerous aspects of their own life and culture; this was particularly true of the Moche (also called Mochica) in the first few centuries A.D. These vessels provide evidence of *veruga,* which is restricted to the Peruvian region and is carried by sand flies; of *uta,* a disfiguring leishmaniasis; of hunchback, resulting from tuberculosis that attacked the spine; and of plantar lesions in consequence of sand-flea bites. These maladies could not have been identified so readily without knowledge of modern Peruvian pathology; the earlier paleopathologists were unfamiliar with *veruga* and *uta,* and diagnosed portrayals of these conditions as syphilis or leprosy. Moche figurines also reveal pathological conditions tentatively diagnosed as idiocy, harelip, goiter, clubfoot, edematosis of the face and feet, facial paralysis, myxedema, sarcoma, blindness, and two kinds of "Siamese" twinning.

Egyptian sculptures show hunchback, and a foot or leg malformation probably attributable to poliomyelitis.

Occasionally, figurines or other portrayals also reveal cultural practices that altered the individual's physical structure. Thus, various prehistoric American Indian ceramic vessels show extreme distention of the earlobe; perforation of the earlobe, nasal septum, or lower lip for the reception of a bauble; intentional deformation of the cranium; and partial depilation of the head. The bearers of the Moche culture consistently portrayed themselves and their captives as having been circumcised, and we may suppose that circumcision was standard practice in the Moche country.

In the field of paleomedicine, which of course is closely related to paleopathology, Moche figurines show amputation of the foot, leg, hand, arm, lips, nose, and male genitalia; also simple orthopedic devices to aid those who had lost hands or feet. Scattered American Indian cultures turned out ceramics modeled to show a parturient woman (or goddess). In present-day Mexico, some Indian women get down on their hands and knees to give birth, and some of the Mexican ceramic specimens show parturition in this posture. In late prehistoric specimens from the Mississippi Valley, however, the woman is on her back.

Archeological interest extends into the historic period. Several early bodies of medical lore—the Greco-Roman, the Arab-Turkish, the Indian, the Korean, the Japanese, and the Chinese—collectively refer to a host of diseases, their symptoms and signs, and their treatment. But in the early medical writings (and in some fairly modern ones, for that matter), a number of different maladies might be lumped under one name; for example, it is likely that several kinds of infections or eruptions were mistaken for leprosy at one time or another. In any event, a firm medical diagnosis often is hard to make on the basis of written descriptions alone, and early writings may be more suggestive than explicit in their approach to the past incidence and distribution of diseases.

Of exceptional interest would be studies that combine data from archeology, history, pathology, and sometimes linguistics. Such a combination has not often been attempted, but would be feasible in quite a few cases. Consider, for example, what is known of syphilis, a disease whose spread has had considerable effect on man's history.

Syphilis is often regarded as having been native to the New World, although an African origin has also been suggested. The problem of its origin is complicated by the existence of several diseases related to it. One of these, yaws, is transmitted (mostly in children) by direct contact or by certain flies. The individual, external lesions of yaws are larger and more persistent than those of syphilis; since they may involve the bones, they can be detected, at times, in archeological material. Serological tests for syphilis give a positive result in the case of yaws, and both diseases are responsive to penicillin. But unlike syphilis, yaws is confined to the tropics. It may have originated in Africa, although it now occurs in scattered parts of both the Old World tropics and the New.

Less publicized, yaws-like maladies are pinta (most characteristic of the Central and South American tropics although reported in the Old World also), and bejel, which affects some semi-nomadic peoples of the Middle East. Then there are certain yaws-like syndromes that are geographically localized and that have received vernacular names, although they have not as yet been recognized as clinical entities. Examples are njovera in Rhodesia and dichuchwa in Botswanaland.

Three species of the spirochete genus *Treponema* have been named and credited with the production of syphilis, yaws, and pinta respectively; but in the study of microorganisms, species are erected on grounds that would be unfamiliar to taxonomists who work with other groups of living things. Faced with such complexities, some workers have avoided commitment by using the name "treponematosis" to cover all the syphilis-like or yaws-like diseases produced in man by spirochetes of the genus *Treponema*. Some of these organisms will infect other mammals, at least experimentally; subhuman primates of central Africa harbor a spirochete similar to the one that produces yaws in man; and venereal spirochetosis of rabbits is a treponematosis in all but name.

With so many complications hampering syphilology, the thing to do now is to concentrate on available facts. Although osteomyelitic conditions can be produced by several clinical entities, including some that are not related to treponematosis, it now seems possible to identify certain of these conditions as being rather surely of syphilitic origin. The best evidence of prehistoric syphilis comes from Florida, Alabama, Kentucky, Oklahoma, and Texas.

Turning to written records, the European, Arabic-Persian, Indian, and Chinese bodies of medical literature all announce the dramatic arrival of a new disease, syphilis, just a decade or two after European discovery of the New World. While these medical writings are less precise than one might wish, it seems fairly clear that syphilis had reached England by 1496, Poland by 1499, Russia and Scandinavia by 1500. The army of Charles VIII, King of France, contracted the disease in Naples in 1495. Syphilis reached India in 1498, simultaneously with the arrival in Calicut of Vasco da Gama's fleet from the New World. The malady appeared in China in 1505.

Turning to languages, it is probably true that some European names for syphilis reflected a desire to blame the disease on a foreign country; but most of these names also seem to indicate the directions in which the malady spread. In Spain, syphilis was called the royal disease. (One recalls that men who led expeditions to the New World had access to the royal court, even if they were not noblemen.) In France, syphilis was called the Spanish illness. Charles VIII's soldiers, mercenaries from several countries, spread the name "Neapolitan sickness" to scattered localities in France and elsewhere. To the Germans, syphilis was the French disease; to the English it was the French pox. In far-northern Europe it was the Polish disease; in China it was the Canton sickness. Syphilis did not reach Japan until 1569; there, it was dubbed the Chinese illness. Gonzalo Fernández de Oviedo y Valdéz, who had been a page at the Spanish court when Columbus returned from the West Indies, wrote in 1526 that in spite of geographic appellations, syphilis ought to be called the West Indian disease. Oviedo was official historiographer of the Indies, where he spent much of his adult life, and where he saw what he took to be syphilis among the tribespeople. It is probably not coincidence that the early treatment of the malady in Europe was with guaiac, a resin obtained from certain West Indian and South American trees.

One school of thought explains the origin of syphilis as follows: Yaws was introduced into Europe by the slave trade from Africa, nearly 50 years before Columbus started out for the New World. In the European environment, the yaws organism somehow changed, producing syphilis; this was then taken to the New World by early Spanish and Portuguese explorers, and by Negro slaves who were shipped to the West Indies in large numbers during the period 1500–1503. However, the evidence favors an alternative view: that syphilis was indigenous to the New World, and was taken back to Europe by the explorers. As suggested by vernacular names and the dates of arrival, it spread from Spain to France, thence to Germany and England, from Germany to Poland, and so northward to Russia and Scandinavia. It also moved eastward from Spain, probably by way of seaport towns, reaching Naples among others; from there, it was introduced to scattered parts of Europe when Charles VIII's mercenaries were disbanded. In India, it probably spread from the port of Calicut, and in China from the port of Canton.

In any event, it will be seen that a solution to the problem of the origin of syphilis will most likely come from paleopathological studies. If certain bone abnormalities have been correctly identified as syphilitic in prehistoric American material, the New World origin of the disease could scarcely be questioned. It is probably significant that comparable abnormalities are not known from European material older than 1500. Quite likely, Europeans carried syphilis to some parts of the New World where it did not originally exist. Before people began to move en masse from one continent to another, the various treponematoses may well have been mutually exclusive in distribution.

Now to other aspects of paleopathology. In spite of possibilities offered by the occasional preservation of soft parts of the body, and by the occasional existence of useful data from history and languages, most paleopathological work involves examination of teeth and bones that have persisted from some earlier time. Teeth are exceptionally persistent through the millennia; for the enamel of the vertebrate tooth is the hardest tissue produced by any living organism, and extreme hardness makes for preservation. In many parts of Florida, where almost every week another Indian mound or village site is bulldozed out of existence, quite a few localities are littered with human teeth although the associated bones have been reduced to crumbs. Many of these teeth, becoming buried beneath modern subdivisions, will probably fossilize, perhaps to be excavated by archeologists of the far future. And if they are so excavated, no doubt they will be recognized as those of American Indians; for the teeth of prehistoric Indians are noteworthy in that the crowns are worn down to an unusual degree, and in that the incisors are shovel-shaped.

The Indian incisor is naturally shovel-shaped; that is to say, its posterior face has a thickened rim around the lateral and lower borders. This characteristic, presumably of genetic origin, allies the American Indian with some Asian Mongoloids, and was also noted in an Asian specimen of the near-human *Homo erectus*. The occlusal wear of the teeth, however, is ascribed to a coarse diet. In some cases, at least, it could be regarded as pathological, small abscesses having developed in the tooth after so much of the enamel and dentine had been worn away. The term "caries" is sometimes extended to cover the cavities that may develop on the occlusal surface of a tooth that has been worn down to the pulp; but it is important to distinguish this condition—call it occlusal caries—from the kind of tooth decay that is so common in civilized man today. Occlusal caries is not peculiar to man, but has also been noted in the sea otter, a mammal that may wear its teeth down in feeding upon shellfish, crabs, and sea urchins.

Another type of dental caries, the one so common in modern man, is independent of occlusal wear, and its attack need not be upon the tooth's crown. According to current views, this type of caries is produced by microorganisms; their proliferation is encouraged by acids formed through the fermentation of certain carbohydrates that encrust the teeth. It has also been suggested that a chronic emotional or systemic upset, of a kind that renders the saliva more acid, could also foster the growth of these microorganisms. The ratio of tooth size to jaw size also may have something to do with susceptibility to dental caries, for the crevices between crowded teeth are likely spots in which carbohydrates and microorganisms may accumulate. In women, the teeth could be softened, perhaps rendered more susceptible to caries, by a calcium-deficient diet during pregnancy; for calcium is abstracted from the mother's system to build the embryo's bones. "For every child, a tooth," as the pioneer women used to say. In adults of either sex, the teeth and bones can be decalcified by several conditions, especially a shortage of Vitamin D. Evidently, then, the paleopathologist may have to take a number of factors into account if he is going to suggest why certain skulls have carious teeth.

It is interesting to note that with but a single exception, carious teeth have not been found in any of the extinct races of man, or in any of man's near-human ancestors and allies. The exception is Broken Hill man, whose remains were found in what is now Zambia. Apparently, Broken Hill man was a late survivor of *Homo erectus*, persisting in Africa after other populations of the species had vanished. At any rate, his teeth were carious to a noteworthy degree.

In prehistoric man of our own species, dental caries of modern type was rare or nonexistent in pre-Neolithic populations. Its first European appearance was in the Neolithic of Scandinavia. In the class-stratified society of ancient Egypt, it beset the wealthy. A study of New World caries was made by Adelaide K. Bullen (1964), who reported on skeletal remains from an early historic site (Savanne Suazey) of Grenada, in the West Indies. She suggested that caries of modern type appeared there concomitantly with the Europeans, and that carious teeth might be a time marker for the historic period, in the West Indies and perhaps elsewhere. While her series was too small to prove this point, her suggestion would be worth following up. Having been advised by a dentist who believed that caries was linked with concentrated sugar in the diet, she wondered if the introduction of sugarcane into the West Indies could have been responsible for the carious condition of the teeth in the Savanne Suazey material.

Mrs. Bullen also remarked that in the historic series of skulls from Grenada, occlusal wear was not as pronounced as in the Weedon Island Period series from the Bayshore Homes site of Florida. To this I might add that occlusal wear is comparatively minor in the few known historic Seminole skulls from Florida. I have seen little evidence of dental caries, except of the occlusal sort, in Florida Indian skulls from any time period, but think that reduction of occlusal wear might well mark the historic period in that state and in several other parts of North America.

Other dental abnormalities—including root-canal abscess, impacted molars, rotated teeth, and malocclusion—have been reported now and then. Pyorrhea first appeared with Neanderthal man. In man of modern type, it is fairly common in series of prehistoric skulls from North America, South America, Europe, Egypt, Hawaii, and elsewhere. Syphilis can cause some of the teeth to become peg-shaped, but as far as I know, this condition has not been seen in prehistoric material; it might be looked for. Certain deficiency diseases can manifest themselves in the teeth, but might better be discussed in connection with the bones, which they also affect.

In prehistoric skulls, certain dental peculiarities are of cultural origin. These might be discussed at this point, even though they are not pathological in the usual sense. Ablation—the deliberate knocking out of one or more teeth—was practiced at many scattered localities of both the Old World and the New. According to the ethnographic literature, tetanus (lockjaw) was so prevalent in some parts of Africa that the tribespeople habitually knocked out two front teeth, thus making a gap through which a patient could be fed when the disease struck, as it almost inevitably would. The tetanus bacillus lives in the intestine of herbivores, and contaminates the soil where the animals' droppings fall. One might therefore expect tetanus to have been most common among cattle-raising people. However, ablation was carried on far outside the pastoral regions—Hrdlicka (1940) traced it from Siberia through North America to southern South America—and in many cases may have been ritual, not practical. Negro slaves reintroduced the custom into the New World in historic times.

The front teeth, the ones that were visible, were the ones that were modified ritually or ornamentally. Prehistoric skulls, including some from burial mounds of the Tennessee River drainage, occasionally reveal the removal of a rear tooth. Such removal is probably to be regarded as dental surgery, undertaken to rid the jaw of a tooth that was giving trouble.

Negro slaves also brought to the New World the custom of chipping the teeth into some abnormal shape. Although the prehistoric Americans may not have chipped the teeth, they filed or ground them occasionally, especially in the Maya area and the Andes. Among the Maya, one side of the tooth's occlusal border might be ground away; or both sides of the border might be ground partly away, leaving a prominence in the middle. Sometimes the front teeth were not only filed but also inlaid with jade or iron pyrite. Among the Andean peoples, a V-shaped or W-shaped notch might be ground into the occlusal border, and inlaying was done with gold.

In both the Old World and the New, some historic peoples ate meat by biting down on a large piece of it, then using a knife to cut off a bite-sized chunk of it. Lately, it has been found that certain prehistoric peoples, eating in this same fashion with flint knives, left recognizable knife-scratches in the enamel of the front teeth. When more skulls have been examined for these scratches, it will be possible to trace the spread of a distinctive method of eating. In the southwestern United States, one or two historic Indian tribes knew how to make an arrowhead by biting flakes from the edge of a scrap of flint, and this practice should also have scarred the teeth recognizably. It might therefore prove worthwhile to examine prehistoric skulls for evidence that the jaws were used vise-like on flint.

Although teeth can provide useful data, bones are the main focus of paleopathological study. The pathological conditions they display might be grouped under seven headings.

The first of these is osteomyelitis, produced by syphilis, yaws, tuberculosis, pyogenic inflammation, fungus infection, or other agency. As suggested by the review of Snow's work on the Bayshore Homes specimens, problems may arise when an effort is made to determine the cause of osteomyelitic abnormalities in dry-bone material. The problems are not insoluble; they simply have not attracted many investigators. Bacterial invasion can result in inflammation, followed by the destruction of old bone tissue and the formation of new. Examples of such inflammation include periostitis ossificans, from the Neolithic of Europe; sinusitis, from prehistoric North America, Peru, and France; and mastoiditis, from prehistoric North America, Peru, and Egypt. In prehistoric human bones from Europe, the Middle East, China, and Japan, certain inflammations were once ascribed to syphilis; but at least some of the specimens are now regarded as evidencing Paget's disease of the bone, a malady that also beset prehistoric American Indians. Tuberculous affection of the bone is readily identifiable when it manifests itself as Potts' vertebral caries, a disease resulting in angulation of the spine. Tuberculosis was prehistoric in both hemispheres, although very little evidence of it has come to light from Europe. Old World tubercular specimens are most numerous from Egypt; New World ones have come from both North and South America.

A second type of pathological condition is the tumor, which may be benign or malign (cancerous). Among benign tumors, osteomata are known from prehistoric Peru and the Neolithic of Europe. In Peru, osteomata were most often manifested in the auditory duct. Multiple myeloma has been diagnosed in specimens from Peru and the Neolithic of France. Among malign tumors, osteosarcomata have been reported in crania from Egypt and Peru. Both of these areas have yielded crania with lesions perhaps residual to sarcomatous meningiomata. From Peru and parts of Europe have come both crania and sacra with defects perhaps attributable to cancer in nearby soft parts.

A third type of pathological condition is degenerative disease. In prehistoric material, osteoarthritis is the commonest and most widespread malady of this category. The term "arthritis" popularly covers a variety of joint disorders whose postulated causes range from syphilis to chronic emotional disturbance; but osteoarthritis usually develops at or after middle age, and shows its effects most noticeably on the weight-bearing joints of the body although other joints are sometimes involved as well. This disease appeared with Neanderthal man, and has characterized many later populations in both hemispheres. It was common among prehistoric Indians of North and South America. Spondylitis, which is osteoarthritis of the spine, existed in the days of Neanderthal man and has continued to the present. In prehistoric populations, as in modern uncivilized ones, it usually involved the lumbar but not the dorsal or the cervical vertebrae; the ancient Egyptians, with considerable dorsal involvement, were an exception. Cervical involvement, common in modern civilized peoples, is rarely seen in prehistoric remains.

Temporo-maxillary osteoarthritis was noted in Neanderthal man but not in other prehistoric Europeans. It was rather common among prehistoric Indians of both North th and South America; and in modern times it has been reported among certain West African and Melanesian tribespeople. It seems to have developed in individuals who used and strained their jaws a great deal, presumably in masticating a coarse diet daily. Indeed, osteoarthritis in general seems to develop in joints that receive much physical stress and strain as the years go by.

Rheumatoid arthritis may have quite a different origin. Its prehistoric occurrence is hard to evaluate from the literature, for only in very recent times has it been set apart from other arthritic maladies. Whereas stress-related osteoarthritis was widespread in time and space, rheumatoid arthritis was localized.

A fourth type of paleopathological anomaly is metabolic disease. Osteoporosis symmetrica, a childhood malady, has been discovered at archeological sites of Peru, the Maya country, the southwestern United States, and Egypt. Today it is rare except in some Africans and Asians. Perhaps an avitaminosis akin to scurvy, it is characterized by symmetrically placed areas of porosity; thus, in skulls, it may involve both orbits or both parietals. Its lesions were once mistakenly regarded as of syphilitic origin. Osteomalacia reflects a deficiency of Vitamin D in adults, whose bones begin to decalcify; it is known from prehistoric Peru. Rickets is the result of Vitamin D shortage in infants or very small children. It is very rare in prehistoric material, although it has been reported in the Neolithic of Europe and Indochina. On the human skin, a sterol is converted by solar ultraviolet to Vitamin D_3, which is then absorbed; and rickets is primarily a disease of industrialized areas, where some babies are kept indoors or swaddled most of the time, and where the atmosphere is smoky.

A fifth type of pathological condition, detectable in skeletal remains, might be called gross congenital abnormality. I say "gross" in order to exclude some minor anomalies that seemingly do not discommode the bearers thereof, and so are not pathological in the usual sense. By "congenital" I mean present from birth, whether or not the abnormality is genetically produced.

Exemplifying the fifth category is achondroplasia. Also called achondroplastic dwarfing, this abnormality is of genetic origin, produced in man by simple Mendelian dominance. Remains of a dwarf, probably of the achondroplastic type, were discovered in one of the Huntoon Island burial mounds, Lake County, Florida. The molars had nearly all been lost in life, and the sockets reabsorbed; so presumably the individual was fully adult. The stature in life was estimated to have been about 3 feet 6 inches. The cultural context of the find was not reported, but to judge from other work done on the island, it may well have been St. Johns II, roughly contemporary with the latter part of the Weedon Island Period. The Belle Glade burial mound, Palm

Beach County, Florida, also yielded the bones of one or more dwarfs. These have not been described, but a physical anthropologist has referred to them as probably achondroplastic. Once again, the cultural context went unrecorded; but the mound was in intermittent use from fairly late prehistoric to early historic times.

From one of the Adena burial mounds, near Waverly, Pike County, Ohio, came the bones of a stocky, undersized individual who may have been an achondroplastic dwarf. The heavy sculpturing of bones suggested muscularity, and the teeth exhibited less occlusal wear than is usual in prehistoric Indian skulls. In Ohio, the Adena culture existed between 800 and 200 B.C.

Of exceptional interest was the discovery of two adult achondroplastic dwarfs, a male and a female, who had been buried near (not in) Mound G of the Moundville site, Tuscaloosa and Hale counties, Alabama (Snow 1943). The cranium of the male exhibited posterior flattening of the kind I attribute to use of a cradleboard; that of the female was too fragmentary to permit comment on deformation. Both burials were without grave goods. Post holes revealed that the male, at least, had been buried beneath the earthen floor of a hut. Perhaps it was his home, for some of the historic Muskhogeans practiced subfloor interment, and Moundville was one of the great sites marking Muskhogean irruption into the Southeast. Both dwarfs had been buried face down. Prone burial was not otherwise noted at Moundville, and in fact was rare throughout the world.

To judge from a goodly number of ethnographic references, many historic Indians of the Southeast believed that careful orientation of a burial was necessary if the spirit of the deceased was to find the proper trail to the hereafter. Among the Muskhogeans, or some of them, a corpse was buried in a sitting position with the face to the east, or else was stretched out supine with the head to the west. East-west orientation of burials is a practice that can be traced, archeologically, back into late prehistoric times. Perhaps, then, the bodies of the Moundville dwarfs were interred face down with the hope of pointing their spirits away from whatever hereafter was imagined for ordinary people. Nevertheless, the dwarfs may have been pampered when they were alive. Even in modern times, most achondroplastic dwarfs die during their first year, and only 20 per cent survive to adulthood; yet, even among prehistoric Indians, for whom 35 years must have been a ripe old age, these stunted people reached maturity. Also, the minor occlusal wear of the Adena specimen suggests a more refined diet than usual. It may be significant that one of the

Adena mounds yielded a tobacco pipe, probably of ceremonial import, and realistically modeled to portray a costumed man with the proportions of an achondroplastic dwarf.

This type of dwarfing was not peculiar to any one race of mankind, although archeological reports of it are few.

Other congenital abnormalities include cretinistic dwarfing, known from Egyptian skeletons and figurines; anencephaly (absence of the brain), observed in one Egyptian mummy; hydrocephaly, reported from prehistoric Peru, Roman Egypt, Turkey during the Copper Age, and ninth-century Germany; and congenital luxation (dislocation) of the femora, seen in Peruvian, North American, and European material. As noted, "Siamese" twinning was shown in Peruvian Moche ceramics. Paintings or other portrayals, especially but not exclusively from the Classical civilizations, show individuals with certain rare congenital deformities such as two-headedness; but it is possible that the artists were inspired by myths rather than models.

A sixth category is virtually limited to poliomyelitis, a disease of viral origin. In acute anterior poliomyelitis, the central nervous system is affected; motor neurons are destroyed in the spinal cord, with resultant flaccid paralysis. Until very recent times, polio was mostly a disease of children, and a victim of it might be permanently paralyzed in one or more of the limbs, which would therefore atrophy. Egypt has yielded one mummy and a good many portrayals of individuals with stunted limbs, probably the aftereffect of polio. This disease has also been diagnosed in a skeleton from the Neolithic of Europe.

A seventh type of skeletal abnormality reported in archeological material is the trauma or wound. Often, inferences about culture can be drawn from traumas. For example, in the Bayshore Homes series, almost all broken bones had set in good alignment, and from this circumstance one might infer that the local Indians knew how to treat fractures. True, some workers have held that breaks will usually set themselves in satisfactory alignment, without any treatment. I believe this contention was based on a study of the gibbons, long-armed apes of tropical Asia; their numerous fractures healed admirably in most cases. Nevertheless, there are series of American Indian skeletons—I have in mind especially some from the Tennessee Valley shell middens—in which many breaks healed irregularly and in poor alignment. In ethnographic times, Indians of the Southeast had ways of treating fractures. The historic Creek Indians treated a broken arm or leg by splinting it with the inner bark of the cottonwood tree, and by pouring over it an infusion of this bark. The historic Cherokee fitted the parts of a broken limb together as neatly as possible, splinted it with sticks as a first-aid measure, later replaced the sticks with a board casing, and blew a decoction of tulip-tree bark over it. Bark extracts probably had no healing effect, but splinting surely made it easier for the broken parts to knit in good alignment. Perhaps some earlier Indians, such as those who left the shell middens of the Tennessee Valley, did not know the technique of splinting.

Or perhaps they stoically refused to pamper an injured limb. In one remarkable specimen, both femora had been dislocated; the individual had walked, and the head of each femur had ground a new socket into the pelvis. Burial mounds of the Tennessee Valley also included the remains of several individuals in which one or both elbows had been dislocated, and it is tempting to speculate that some cultural practice was responsible for this pathological condition, which in other areas was rare. At any rate, the dislocations had not been set. Of course, anomalies of this kind—luxations, in medical parlance— are sometimes hard to evaluate, because they might have been congenital rather than traumatic. One anomaly, noted in Tennessee Valley material, and medically unique as far as I know, was surely traumatic: a broken arm had been used so determinedly that a pseudo-joint had formed at the broken ends.

Not surprisingly, broken bones have been observed in prehistoric remains from many parts of the world. One healed fracture was noted in Neanderthal man, many in early Egyptians, Neolithic Europeans, and prehistoric American Indians. Such injuries occasionally give a clue to cultural practices beyond the paleomedical. For example, broken bones at Bayshore Homes were more numerous in males than in females, and from this one might infer that the more strenuous activities were left principally to the men. The inference is bolstered by the observation that among historic Indians, hunting and warfare were assigned mostly to the men, along with the more violent sports.

Head injuries have been reported in *Homo erectus* and Neanderthal man, as well as in Cro-Magnon man and later Europeans. Such injuries are widespread in the New World, especially in Peru where their locally high frequency probably reflected use of the mace as a favorite weapon. Trephining, the surgical removal of a bit of skull, may sometimes have been performed in Peru and Neolithic Europe with the hope of remedying a cranial injury, although it may also have been performed as some sort of magical rite. Crania were opened in one of three fashions, depending on time and place: drilling, scraping, or sawing. The last was most common, and was done by means of a flint or obsidian knife. In prehistoric Peru, cranial surgery was sometimes followed by prosthesis; a plate of metal or shell was used to cover the trephined hole. At least in the New World, trephined skulls usually are those of males.

In the United States, as in Neolithic Europe, a fairly common bone injury resulted from the deep penetration of a flint arrowhead or spear point, which remained in place when the body was interred. This circumstance backs up the supposition, from ethnographic analogy, that warfare was carried on by prehistoric Indians and Europeans who had attained the tribal level of social organization. Sometimes the point was embedded in the viscera, and so was left lying free among the bones after the softer tissues had decayed; but other times, the point penetrated deeply into a hard bone, and one may be sure that the projectile was hurled (or shot, in the case of an arrow) with great force.

When a certain type of flint point is found embedded in a bone, that type might reasonably be identified as having tipped a projectile, not a knife, drill, or other tool. Some large points from the Perry and Mulberry Creek sites, in the Pickwick Basin of northern Alabama, could easily have been misidentified as knives, had not they been found piercing a vertebra, sacrum, or other bone. Again, a small, triangular point is known to amateurs as a "bird point," and is popularly supposed to have been reserved for the hunting of birds. Thus, it is interesting to note one of these points in the sacrum of a human burial from Mound No. 2 of the Ausmus Farm site in the Norris Basin of Tennessee. (Actually, the small triangle, which appears late in the archeological record of the Southeast, is merely a true arrowhead, in contrast with larger, heavier specimens, which tipped lances or spears.) In Arkansas, a long, slender, cruciform type of flint point was thought to have tipped a drill, until specimens were discovered embedded in bones. In Denmark, a slender bone point, easily mistaken for a tool, was found piercing the skull of a Neolithic man.

At the Woodward site in Micanopy, Alachua County, Florida, the skull of a child was pierced by a scrap of chert (a flinty material) (R. Bullen 1950). The scrap had not been worked and was not even pointed, yet it had completely penetrated the skull; thus, it may have tipped an arrow, perhaps a child's arrow whose lethal possibilities had not been foreseen. If this bit of chert had been found loose in the sand of the site, probably it would have received scant attention; for chunks and thin flakes of flinty material occur in abundance at most localities where prehistoric Indians lived, and are generally dismissed as knapping debris. The chert scrap from the Woodward Site draws attention to the desirability of examining flakes closely. In Florida, much flinty debris was used for cutting or scraping, and low magnification often will reveal characteristic use-spalling along the margins of an otherwise unmodified flake. Most scraps of dark green bottle glass, recovered from Seminole sites in central Florida, also exhibit use-spalling; probably they were scrapers.

Remarkable skeletal specimens, suggestive of prehistoric Indian warfare, are crania showing evidence of scalping. American Indians are popularly supposed to have carried on scalping rather generally, but actually, in early historic times the practice was limited mainly to the Southeast and scattered parts of the Northeast; it was best developed among Muskhogeans, Iroquoians, and adjoining tribes whom they had influenced. It was spread in later times by the white man, who paid bounties for Indian scalps. An older and more widespread aboriginal custom was head-hunting. In the Southeast, burial mounds occasionally yield headless bodies, perhaps the remains of people who were beheaded by enemy raiders. Sometimes they yield an intact body that had been buried with an extra skull, possibly a battle trophy. Even in the historic period, some villages of the Southeast were decorated with enemy skulls. It is suspected that around late prehistoric times, the custom of taking heads was supplanted by that of taking scalps. From Moundville came a skull exhibiting a pathological groove completely encircling the cranium (Snow 1941). The skull was that of a woman who had been scalped alive; the incision left by the scalping tool had become infected throughout its entire length. A central Illinois site, roughly the same age (late prehistoric) as Moundville, yielded a cranium that was girdled by an incision. A similar specimen came from a site of the Fort Ancient culture in Illinois. The bearers of this culture were not the builders of the Fort Ancient earthworks, but lived from late prehistoric into historic times.

In some widely separated parts of the world, a distinctive trauma was produced by the custom of lopping off a finger joint at the death of a relative. This custom is best known from historic New Guinea, where it continues today. Usually, the donor of the joint is a young girl or an old woman; and in a grandmother who has known many bereavements, most of the fingers may be reduced to stumps. However, men may also make the sacrifice, although they try to keep intact enough of their digits to handle the bow and arrow. Curiously, some historic plains Indians of the United States also sacrificed a finger joint at the death of a relative; and even as late as the nineteenth century, many a digit was so mutilated after the defeat of a tribe in battle. Edwin T. Denig (1953), a principal observer of the Plains Indians during the period 1833–1858, wrote of the Crow, "When anyone dies, the immediate relatives each cut off a joint of a finger. This is done by placing an axe or butcher knife on the joint, and striking the same with a good-sized stick. . . . The blow [sometimes] misses the joint, and the finger is divided between joints. . . . . . . Both men and women mutilate their hands in this manner, so that at the present day there is scarcely an entire hand among them. The men, however, reserve entire the thumb and forefinger of the left hand, and thumb and two fingers of the right . . . But even these fingers often want a joint or so when all the others are cut off to the stump."

Obviously, it would be desirable to trace the spread of this curious practice, which would be readily identifiable in prehistoric remains. Unfortunately, both the New Guineans and the Plains Indians often built aerial sepulchers, leaving a dead body above ground on some kind of scaffold or support; and under such conditions, bones are not preserved for long. Nevertheless, archeologists have been interested in the custom of sacrificing a finger joint, for the walls of some European caves bear very old, stenciled portrayals of human hands with mutilated digits.

In man, the local incidence of a disease often reflects cultural factors; and such factors can even affect the manifestations or prognosis of some more nearly ubiquitous malady. Accordingly, paleopathological studies may provide clues to problems in the fields of modern medicine and public health; conversely, details of past culture can be revealed when paleopathological conditions are identified and interpreted in the light of modern medical knowledge.

To conclude the discussion of human remains from archeological sites: the bones sometimes exhibit peculiarities that are noteworthy even though they are not pathological in the usual sense. One such peculiarity, of cultural origin, is fronto-occipital deformation of the cranium. To my way of thinking, this is a very different matter from cradleboard deformation as described in connection with the Bayshore Homes series. The board was primarily a cradle and carrier; its use deformed the cranium inconspicuously, and perhaps only incidentally. In contrast, fronto-occipital deformation was practiced only by people who were determined to mash an infant's head into a shockingly grotesque shape. To accomplish this end, some historic tribes used a cradle with a moveable flap that could be lashed down in such a way as to flatten the baby's forehead; others applied a sand-bag, or clay and two boards, to the head of the cradled infant; still others fitted the head into a wooden frame, which could be worn in the cradle or out. Such extreme reshaping of the cranium was a drastic procedure. A witness of it among the Natchez remarked, "The infant cries, turns completely black, and the strain it is made to suffer is such that a white, slimy fluid is seen to come out of its nose and ears when the mother presses on its forehead." In the Pacific Northwest, an observer commented that an Indian baby, with its little black eyes popping out from the pressure of the deforming device, reminded him of a mouse caught in a trap. Fronto-occipital deformation is not a practice that might be independently developed at many different localities, and much interest would attach to an analysis of its distribution on prehistoric and historic time levels.

In the New World, this kind of cranial deformation occurred in widely scattered areas from Argentina northward through the Maya country to Vancouver Island, British Columbia; also through the West Indies to the Gulf coast and lower Mississippi Valley of the United States, with an outlier in the Carolinas. Occurrences are consistent with the view that the practice spread from south to north, and was carried mostly by coastal voyagers who bypassed large stretches of land.

Obviously, an investigation of fronto-occipital deformation might prove rewarding to those who are concerned with the diffusion of culture traits, even though the description of the misshapen crania has generally been left to physical anthropologists, whose specialty is not culture. To judge from the ethnographic literature, or at least the portion of it that relates to the New World, this type of deformation was a privilege of the elite; people who flaunted it were haughty, aristocratic. No great surprise if, at several localities, its initial appearance coincided with the introduction of important new culture traits, in other words with the beginning of a new culture period. Extreme deformation of the cranium was practiced among the Inca, Maya, and Aztec, advanced peoples who influenced less advanced ones. Perhaps cradleboard deformation, where intentional, reflected earlier emphasis on more extreme reshaping of the cranium.

The fronto-occipital was not the only type of extreme cranial deformation; there was also the annular, which was produced by binding or bandaging the infant's head tightly. In southern South America, the annular type may be older than the fronto-occipital. In North America, annular deformation was restricted to northern Vancouver

Island. In the Old World, one or another kind of cranial reshaping has been reported from such diverse peoples as the French, the Wends of Germany, the Avar of Siberia, the Turkomans, the Malays, and a few African tribes.

Before leaving the subject of paleoanthropology and culturally induced abnormalities, it might be well to mention obesity. Paleolithic Europe, especially, has yielded small sculptures of a stout woman with huge buttocks, fatly bulging thighs, and heavy breasts. It is not clear whether the sculptors were expressing their culturally determined standard of feminine pulchritude or desirability; but, at least in some cases, they had assuredly seen obese women, whose conformation they portrayed with near-clinical accuracy.

Some work of the physical anthropologists is of concern to archeologists even though it is directed primarily toward the study of present-day man. Of particular interest in this connection are studies on racial characteristics, for they provide a clue to past migrations. Such studies are responsible for the conclusion that the American Indians are of Mongoloid affinity. Their relationship is, however, not so much with the late or classic Mongoloid, but with an earlier or proto-Mongoloid stock that has persisted in out-of-the-way places of Asia. The Eskimo more closely approximates the Asian norm, but physical distinctions between Indian and Eskimo have probably been overemphasized in the earlier literature. The Eskimo type has been altered, here and there, by admixture with the Nadené and other Indians, and with the Chukchi of Siberia. Admixture with Norsemen probably accounts for the so-called "blond Eskimo" of Canada.

For a time, there was speculation about the physical type of the earliest inhabitants of the New World. American archeologists, following the lead of Hrdlička, once found some reason to reject every find that pointed to the existence of man in North America before the end of the Pleistocene; but they had to abandon this stand with the discovery of the Folsom site in New Mexico. There, a herd of bison, belonging to an extinct species, had been killed and butchered by Paleolithic-level hunters, who had left some of their characteristic flint points embedded in the giant carcasses. With archeologists looking for, not automatically rejecting, evidence of Pleistocene man in the Americas, a good many early sites were located. The Clovis artifact complex, widespread in the United States east of the Rockies and south of the old glacial border, was the handiwork of elephant-hunters who preceded the Folsom bison-hunters (Cotter 1937, 1938; Wormington 1958). The Suwannee artifact complex of Florida was closely similar to the Clovis, and was similarly associated with a late Pleistocene (Rancholabrean) fauna (Neill 1958, 1964, 1971; Mason 1962). The Sandia Cave complex, older than the Folsom if not older than the Clovis, included single-shouldered points like those of the Soultrean culture of France and Spain (Hibben 1941).

And there were other finds of cultural debris attributable to early Americans. It became clear that man was widespread in North America by about 10,000 B.C., before the last glaciation had begun its retreat; he was a contemporary of mammoth elephants, mastodons, ground sloths, sabertooths, and other great beasts. But his remains proved harder to come by than his work in flint, bone, and elephant ivory. It was suggested that the makers of these artifacts be referred to as Paleo-Americans rather than Paleo-Indians; for in the absence of skulls, one could not be sure that the early hunters were physically Indian.

Today, however, sufficient material has accumulated to permit identification of these hunters as basically Indian. The earliest known Americans were small and gracile. The cranium was long and narrow, the cheek bones not especially prominent, the face of moderate size, the brow ridge heavy, the temples depressed, the nasal aperture high and rather narrow. In most parts of the country, this physical variety (the Otamid, in Neumann's classification) was swamped out by that of later comers; but it persisted here and there in out-of-the-way places, mostly in marginal habitats. The historic Karankawa of the Texas coast exemplify the Otamid variety, from which the historic Pima, Papago, and Mojave were not far removed.

Two other varieties of American Indian, second only to the Otamid in age, were almost as long-headed and narrow-nosed. There was also a late migration of long-heads into North America, but the significant point is the absence of short-headed varieties in earlier times. In South America, the earliest known short-headed people were Japanese who carried their Middle Jomon culture from Kyushu to Ecuador around 5,000 years ago (Meggers et al. 1965). James A. Ford (1969) suggested that when advanced culture trait-complexes diffused northward from Ecuador to Central America and North America, they were carried for the most part by short-headed peoples who were moving in long strides through an older stratum of long-heads. Genes for comparative short-headedness were also introduced into the New World across Bering Strait; the Deneid variety, which characterized the Nadené speakers, was noteworthy for a broad, round head.

If the Otamid physical variety is to be associated with the Paleo-

Indian hunters of Pleistocene big game, then it should date back almost 12,000 years, as does the Clovis artifact complex. But evidence is gradually accumulating to show that the New World was reached between 30,000 and 40,000 years ago, by people who had not yet learned how to make bifacially flaked projectile points. In the absence of skulls, one could not even guess at the physical appearance of such extremely early Americans. Their postulated time of arrival corresponded with the replacement of Neanderthal man (an extinct species) by Cro-Magnon man (a Caucasoid) in Europe, and with the first European production of bifacially flaked points.

A physical variety represents the norm of a population. But also of potential archeological interest are certain genetically induced characteristics that are abnormal, present only in a minority of a population. I did not discuss these in connection with paleopathology, for they are not pathological in the sense that they are harmful to the individuals who display them; they simply are departures from the genetic norm. They can reasonably be treated at this point, since our knowledge of their genetic basis comes mostly from a study of modern man.

As an example of a minor genetic anomaly, the Huff site in Morton County, North Dakota, yielded the remains of three adult females. One of the women had 25 presacral vertebrae (24 are normal) and 13 left ribs (12 are normal); two of the neural arches were separate, articulating respectively with the fifth lumbar and the first sacral vertebra. Another of the women had 13 thoracic vertebrae (12 are normal); the fifth lumbar vertebra had fused with the sacrum, while the sixth and seventh thoracic vertebrae had fused with each other. Such anomalies of the ribs and vertebrae are occasional in all races of mankind, but it is remarkable to find them so concentrated at one site. Furthermore, all three women were long-heads—this at a time when and place where a fairly short, broad head was usual.

The Huff site was occupied at some time during the period 1400–1600 A.D. by people who became known to history as the Mandan. Ethnographic accounts indicate these people to have had a longer head, straighter and narrower nose, and less prominent cheekbones than nearby Plains tribes such as the Sioux. Gray eyes, reddish hair, and albinism were also reported to have occurred more frequently among the Mandan than among their neighbors. Physical anthropology and ethnography combine to suggest that the Mandan were inbred, genetically isolated to some degree, a remnant of a physical variety that had vanished from most other parts of the Plains;

for inbreeding, which can perpetuate an early variety, also increases the local frequency of genetic anomalies.

A widespread physical anomaly is the presence of a Wormian bone. This is a supernumerary bone of the cranium, produced when the sutures take an irregular course. One type of Wormian bone forms between the parietals, and so is an interparietal. This type is often called an Inca bone, having been unusually common among the Inca. Its presence has been noted among other Indians, for example among the Weedon Island Period Indians of Florida.

Minor dental anomalies also exist, noted more often in the adult dentition than in the juvenile. A supernumerary tooth is of surprisingly frequent occurrence among adult American Indians. It is a small, cone-shaped structure, enamel-covered, usually inserted near or between the upper median incisors. Another dental anomaly, notably common among Indians, is the presence of an extra cusp on one or both of the upper lateral incisors; but in prehistoric skulls, this characteristic might often have been obliterated by occlusal wear.

Taurodontism is a remarkable condition of a molar tooth: a deep pulp cavity extends to the roots, which are fused into a sort of stump. Taurodontism was once thought to have been peculiar to Neanderthal man, but it was eventually discovered as a rare, minor anomaly in Neolithic or later peoples of Europe, the Middle East, and South America.

Genetically induced characteristics, studied primarily in modern man but of some archeological concern, are not limited to those of the bones and teeth; they extend also to blood group systems. Archeologists have hoped that serological studies on existing populations might provide clues to past migrations, especially those of Old World stocks into the Americas (Boyd 1953, 1958). Of blood group systems, the ABO has been known for the longest time, and has been most frequently investigated. The only populations lacking both A and B are certain American Indian tribes. However, some other American Indian tribes are noteworthy for a moderate to high frequency of A. The only other peoples with a high frequency of A are the Australian aborigines. Elsewhere in the world, variation is chiefly in the frequency of B, which ranges from about 4 or 5 per cent in western Europe and the Caucasus up to about 30 per cent in parts of Asia. The Basques are characterized by a virtual absence of B. The blood antigen A is itself divisible into A_1 and A_2. The latter is found only in peoples of Europe, the Middle East, and Africa. The proportion of A_2 to A_1 is higher in Africa than in Europe, with the Middle East a transition zone. Where A exists among American Indians, Australian aborigines, Pacific islanders, and peoples of eastern Asia, it is always A_1.

It is tempting to draw some conclusions from geographic variation in blood type frequencies, but several factors complicate the issue. In the New World and elsewhere, many an area must have been populated by the numerous descendants of a small, ancestral, immigrant group; and a small group may not typify the genetic norm of the larger population from which it broke away. As an imaginary example, a large population might be low in O, yet include some families (perhaps related among themselves) that are high in this antigen. If these families moved away, isolating themselves in a new locality, they could found a new population that was mostly O—or even entirely O, for mere chance could result in the disappearance of genes responsible for other antigens. In fact, granting that natural selection is not at work, purely random processes could account for almost any gene frequency in a small population, although some frequencies are statistically much more likely to develop than others.

More significantly, however, there is growing evidence that blood types are not selectively neutral, in the biological sense of selection; rather, they are involved with resistance or susceptibility to various diseases. Thus, the frequency of A was found to be high—that is, significantly higher than in a control group—among sufferers from stomach cancer and from pernicious anemia. Or to phrase the matter differently, the other antigens were apparently associated with more resistance to these maladies than was A, at least under the cultural and environmental conditions that obtained where the studies were made. The frequency of O was high in sufferers from gastric ulcer and duodenal ulcer. There is somewhat more equivocal evidence that A is associated with susceptibility to bronchopneumonia, diabetes mellitus, salivary gland tumor, cancer of the cervix, ovarian tumor, and cancer of the pancreas; O with susceptibility to pituitary adenoma. Efforts have been made to link blood type with rheumatic fever and paralytic poliomyelitis, also. Hemolytic disease of the newborn results from serological incompatibility involving the ABO and Rh systems, and such incompatibility may limit the fertility of certain matings.

As mentioned previously, many ailments have been concentrated at certain times and places. Cultural and environmental factors commonly are involved with such concentration, but there may be a genetic factor at work also. It has repeatedly been observed that when a group of people arrive in a new land, they are likely to introduce diseases to which they are innately more resistant than are the aboriginal inhabitants. Of course, the newcomers should be comparably susceptible to the indigenous maladies; but the established inhabitants are likely to have a geographically extensive network of trade or social connections, along which the newly introduced diseases can move rapidly. These inhabitants may die of diseases that are regarded as minor by the newcomers who brought them; witness the mortality of European whooping-cough and measles among the Hawaiian islanders. And as for maladies that were serious even among the newcomers—they might become pandemic, sweeping across the land, wiping out one community after another. Thus, about 15 years after European discovery of the New World, the Spaniards introduced smallpox into Mexico; and in a short time, an estimated 3.5 million Indians died of it. Whole tribes vanished. In both Mexico and Peru, the indigenous peoples were so reduced in numbers that other Europeans, arriving just a few years later, could scarcely believe the earlier accounts which had portrayed those lands as populous. In the 1800s, the artist-explorer George Catlin, who had seen smallpox rage through the tribes of the western United States, estimated that 6 million American Indians had died of that disease. Although perhaps an overestimate, the figure gives an idea of the virulence of smallpox in the Americas.

Less dramatic than the arrival of an introduced malady, but still impressive, is the abrupt spread of an indigenous disease as a result of some cultural or environmental change. Although direct evidence is lacking, it is at least possible that most survivors of a pandemic had above-average resistance to the scourge, perhaps because of or correlated with their blood type in some cases.

The ABO system was not discovered until 1900, and it was well into the twentieth century before studies were made on the blood types of American Indian groups, Pacific islanders, and other distinctive populations. In many cases, these populations must have descended from the comparatively few survivors of pandemics, and so may well have exhibited average differences from their prehistoric ancestors in certain characteristics, including blood type frequencies.

Studies on the ABO system, originally carried on with the aim of making blood transfusions possible, were soon extended to apes and monkeys. When 108 chimpanzees were typed, 96 turned out to be A, while 12 were O. Of 24 orang-utans, 9 were A, 10 were B, and 5 were AB. Of 11 gibbons, 2 were A, 7 were B, and 2 were AB. Two mountain gorillas were A, 13 lowland gorillas all B. Of 24 Javanese macaques, 12 were O, 9 were A, 1 was B, and 2 were AB. There is no need to summarize the numerous later studies; suffice it to say that man's ABO system is a part of his primate heritage, and one supposes that each component of this very ancient system must have had considerable selective value at certain times and places.

In addition to the ABO, there are other systems, such as MN with its associated Ss. Geographic variation in this system is not as great as in the ABO. However, the incidence of N is notably low in American Indians, notably high in Pacific islanders, especially the New Guineans. The antigen S is absent from Australia but present in New Guinea, thus confirming the evidence from other sources that Australoids are racially different from New Guineans.

The exceptionally complex Rh system also holds possibilities. One of its genes, r, is of high frequency among the Basques, of moderate frequency in African Negroes, but lacking from Asians, American Indians, and Pacific islanders. Another of its genes, R^0, is high in black Africans, low in other races, absent from American Indians. And there are about ten other blood group systems, such as the Lewis, the Duffy, the Kell, the Lutheran, the Kidd, and the Diego, whose geographic variation may eventually demonstrate former connections among peoples who today are widely dispersed. Furthermore, techniques have been devised to test the blood type of mummified and skeletal material. What with continued advances in serology and an upsurge of interest in human genetics, it may soon become possible to comment more meaningfully on the blood antigens of prehistoric populations.

CHAPTER FIVE

Paleoanthropology

Other interactions of physical anthropology with archeology include those in the field that has generally been called human evolution. The physical anthropologists, with their orientation toward biology, have generally been called upon to tell the story of this evolution. But perhaps more than any other story within the purview of the social disciplines, this one necessitates constant attention to the interweaving of biological and cultural factors. For cultural activities far antedate *Homo sapiens,* and the process of hominization—evolution leading toward man—was accompanied by an elaboration of these activities. Thus, it is gratifying to note the emergence of a new paleoanthropology, which utilizes data not only from physical anthropology and evolutionary theory but also from archeology, psychology, animal behavior, functional morphology, systematic zoology, paleontology, and paleoecology. Focusing upon man's prehuman ancestors and extinct near-human relatives, paleoanthropology is in effect a new discipline; for although more than 80 years have elapsed since Eugène Dubois found bones of the Pithecanthropus— now called *Homo erectus*—in a fossil bed beside the Solo River in Java, not until after World War II had enough field work been done, enough primate remains unearthed, to provide raw material for detailed studies.

These studies have yielded many surprises, and knowledge of primate evolution has been considerably refined in the last few years, by paleontologists, paleoanthropologists, and archeologists.

The early or paleontological part of the primate story has a bearing on the later parts, and is worth recounting here. (In so doing, I draw

111

heavily on Kurtén 1972.) It has become evident that the placental mammal order Primates appeared in the latter part of the Cretaceous Period, when dinosaurs still walked the earth. The earliest primates were not monkey-like in build; superficially, they must have looked more like shrews or mice. About 65 million years ago, the Cretaceous came to an end, as did the long reign of the dinosaurs; but the primates survived into the next period, whose first epoch is called the Paleocene. One genus of primates, Purgatorius, is known from both the late Cretaceous and the early Paleocene of Montana. By middle Paleocene times, some of the primates had evolved a rodent-like dentition: chisel-like incisors at the front of each jaw, well separated from the cheek teeth by a toothless gap. In general conformation, also, these animals were reminiscent of squirrels, rats, or other rodents. Remarkable as it may sound, it is likely that the true rodents, the order Rodentia, evolved from Paleocene primates, perhaps from some member of the family Plesiadapidae, which was distributed over Europe and North America.

At any rate, by the late Paleocene a true rodent, Paramys, had appeared in North America. The emergence of the order Rodentia has a bearing on our story. A rodent-like way of life evidently had much to recommend it, for at least five groups of early mammals independently evolved into pseudo-rodents, complete with chisel-like incisors. The true rodents soon displaced most of these others, including the rodent-like early primates. As the rodents took over the terrestrial niches, the primates became more restricted to the arboreal ones. In time, a minority of the rodents would take up a more or less arboreal existence; but the principal rodent domain would be the surface of the ground, or the upper soil in which to burrow. And in time, a small minority of the primates would become terrestrial to a greater or lesser extent; but the principal domain of the primates would be the branches and vines high above the ground.

Man is a dominant species, and he is a primate; therefore it is natural to think of primates in general as having been adaptively superior to other animals. But the rodents evidently had some kind of superiority—perhaps anatomical, or physiological, or behavioral—over the earliest primates. For the rodent-like way of life was in great demand, so to speak; and it was the Rodentia that managed to usurp it, leaving the primates to the trees. Furthermore, while arboreal existence may not be back-to-the-wall, it is possible only where there are sizeable expanses of forest, and this vegetation can develop only under certain climatic and edaphic conditions. Thoroughgoing adaptation to the trees can prove an evolutionary cul-de-sac, if climatic change replaces forest with some more open vegetation type. And to judge from fossil plant remains, not only did the primates become committed to forest existence at an early time; they were limited to tropical or subtropical forest. One might say that the primates evolved to fill the arboreal niches of the wet tropics or near-tropics, where the temperatures were uniformly warm and the rainfall was heavy enough to support forest vegetation. As a result of this original evolutionary commitment, few primates would ever be able to spread into temperate lands.

The early restriction of the primates to the wet tropics might at first seem inconsistent with the presence of Purgatorius in Montana, or of the plesiadapids in both Europe and North America. However, the world of the early primates was quite different from the one we know today. The present continents and some large islands were originally combined in a single land mass, Pangaea. At an early time, this was split by a seaway into northern and southern components, which might be called supercontinents. The more northerly of these supercontinents, dubbed Laurasia, was destined to break up into North America and Eurasia (minus the Indian peninsula); the more southerly, Gondwanaland, into Antarctica, Australia, Africa, the Indian peninsula, and South America (Tarling and Tarling 1971). It was around the late Cretaceous and Paleocene, especially, that the supercontinents began breaking up, the fragments drifting apart. Some lands now far outside the tropics had a tropical climate in the Cretaceous and Paleocene, principally because at that time they lay much closer to the Equator.

Certain evolutionary trends, established in the early primates and continued in their descendants, can be identified as adaptations for arboreal existence. Most wild mammals rely heavily on their sense of smell to locate and identify food, mates, rivals, enemy predators, and territories; but this sense is of limited value in the trees, where there is no unbroken substratum on which scent trails may be laid down. On the other hand, vision could be extremely useful to an animal that spends its life on a series of high vantage points. Agility is desirable in the trees, and is fostered by an ability to grasp twigs and branches. Thus, the trends within the primates were toward improved vision and more dextrous paws. With time, visual improvement culminated in binocular vision, while improved manual dexterity culminated in the opposable thumb. Arboreal existence does not necessarily lead to bipedality, but in manually dextrous mammals it can lead to the frequent adoption of a bipedal stance while the hands are busy at some task.

Certain other primate trends could also have been involved with fitness for arboreal existence. Living primates have color vision, and in this they are unique among mammals, as far as is known. Perhaps they evolved the ability to see color, or perhaps they inherited and improved upon this ability; but in any event, color vision is another aspect of the primates' visual acuity. The members of this order are also noteworthy for an elaboration of social behavior; most of them cope with the world not as individuals but as groups, usually composed of several to many families. It might be an overstatement to say that in the primates, there was also a general trend toward a larger "vocabulary"; but social animals must communicate with one another, and sound is an ideal medium of communication among tree-dwellers. A good many living primates have a repertory of meaningful sounds, and a few have special anatomical structures that amplify the voice.

Evolutionary improvement in vision, dexterity, agility, and social behavior would not have been possible without an increasing complexity of the nervous system, including the brain; but of course, this system is rarely amenable to direct study in fossil material.

Not that primate trends were carried very far in the Paleocene. When that period ended, about 55 million years ago, the order Primates must still have been a drab lot of little animals. The next epoch, the Eocene, saw the extinction of the rodent-like members of the order; saw, also, the rise of lemur-like and tarsier-like primates, highly adapted for arboreal life. During the Eocene, there was still a broad connection of eastern North America with Europe, and perhaps an intermittent connection of western North America with eastern Asia. At least for the most part, this great land mass still lay within a zone of tropical forest, and the arboreal primates came to range widely across it. Indeed, it was in the Eocene that the so-called prosimians—the primates below the level of monkeys, apes, and men—reached their peak of diversity.

The Eocene passed into the Oligocene around 36 million years ago. At that time, South America had not yet become connected with North America, although there may have been islands in the water gap between them. In any event, one of the North American prosimian species somehow managed to cross the gap, probably carried on drifting vegetation. (During floods, rainforest trees are often uprooted and washed out to sea, where they may drift for months along with some of their inhabitants.) When the North American prosimian stock reached South America, it began to evolve there into the New World monkeys. It is unfortunate that the name "monkey" is popularly used for certain primates of both the Old World and the New. In many ways, the monkeys of the New World are very different from those of the Old; and the two groups had different origins. Certain of their similarities reflect parallel evolution. Of primate parallelism, more later.

It is not known just which North American prosimian drifted to South America and began the evolution of the New World monkeys. It may have been a member of the family Omomyidae; it is easy to visualize a colony of these small, tarsier-like primates, drifting in the ocean on some great tree that had been their home, and finding enough to eat among the branches and vines. However, some workers have suggested derivation of New World monkeys from some North American member of the lemur-like family Adapidae.

Nor is it known exactly when a prosimian first reached South America; but by the late Oligocene, the monkeys of that continent had already diverged into two families, both of which exist today. One of these, the Callithricidae, embraces the marmosets; the other, Cebidae, includes all the other New World monkeys.

In the Oligocene, Africa was more widely separated from Eurasia than it later became, but it was moving close enough to permit a little faunal exchange. The Oligocene mammals of Africa included many with a long history on that continent, and a few that were recent arrivals from Eurasia. In Africa, just as in South America, some prosimian stock arrived from the north and gave rise to advanced primates. Parapithecus, from Oligocene deposits near El Faiyûm, Egypt, was more or less intermediate between a prosimian and an Old World monkey. Concomitantly with the emergence of advanced primates in both South America and Africa, the prosimians began to die out. A scattering of them have survived to the present, however. Three families of lemur-like primates exist on the great island of Madagascar. For all their present diversity, these three may well have evolved from a single prosimian stock that arrived on floating vegetation. In other words, the living Madagascan prosimians exemplify adaptive radiation into a variety of ecological niches that were open for the taking. Probably they would have been displaced from all of these niches, or most of them, if monkeys or apes had reached the island; but these higher primates never arrived. Perhaps Madagascar, a fragment of Gondwanaland, had drifted well out into the Indian Ocean by the time the higher primates evolved in Africa.

In the Asian and African tropics, a few prosimians have survived into modern times, probably by virtue of nocturnality. These few are given to foraging by night and hiding by day; thus they occupy ecological niches that are avoided by Old World monkeys, gibbons, and great apes, which are strongly committed to diurnality.

The aforesaid Egyptian deposits, which span most or all of the Oligocene, yielded not just Parapithecus but an assortment of advanced primates. Among them was Apidium, whose probable descendant will play an extraordinary role later in the story. Also present was a possible gibbon ancestor. From the lower and therefore older Oligocene levels of El Faiyûm came Oligopithecus, which may have initiated a line that would lead to the great apes. Aegyptopithecus, from upper levels, was rather surely on this line. Propliopithecus, from middle levels, was probably ancestral to man.

In describing certain primate genera of El Faiyûm as forerunning various later groups, I do not mean that these genera already were highly differentiated. They were in fact a rather compact lot. If they were alive today, no doubt they would all be called "monkeys" by the layman. The largest of them, Aegyptopithecus, was no bigger than a modern gibbon; it had a monkey-like head, a rather long snout, and a tail. Propliopithecus, from whom we may be descended, was no bigger than a cat. The Egyptian Oligocene primates provide another instance of adaptive radiation; in the El Faiyûm material we see this radiation before it has progressed very far.

From an evolutionary standpoint, the most significant thing about Propliopithecus might have been adaptation to a vegetation type more open than forest. The Oligocene deposits of El Faiyûm were laid down in the delta of the primeval Nile, a delta that kept moving northward as the river endlessly dropped its great burden of silt. Often it carried enormous trees as well. Most of the mammal fossils have come from two levels, an upper and a lower, in which huge logs and other plant remains were abundant. Between these two, and dating from middle Oligocene times, is a level without trees, and rather poor in mammal fossils. All specimens of Propliopithecus have come from this middle zone, whose characteristics probably reflect a mid-Oligocene shift toward a drier climate. Under this new climatic regimen, the local forest was temporarily replaced by some comparatively treeless vegetation; and the proto-ape line was temporarily replaced, locally, by Propliopithecus.

Some workers have suggested that during the middle Oligocene, the forest around El Faiyûm gave way to savanna, a tropical grassland in which trees form widely scattered clumps. This type of vegetation is now widespread in Africa, but its existence there in the Oligocene is doubtful. Not until after that period is there fossil evidence of floras with adaptations for existence under climatic conditions too dry for forest. Also, the origin of savanna has been a controversial topic. Climate, soil, fires, human activities, and other factors have all been invoked, at one time or another, to explain the existence of this vegetation. It would be highly desirable to know the habitat of Propliopithecus. Such knowledge will probably come from the further discovery of fossils, both plant and animal, in the middle Oligocene levels of El Faiyûm. Many organisms are good indicators of past climates: various plants, reptiles, amphibians, certain fishes, mollusks, some insects, and others. Among mammals, a diet of grasses is reflected in dental adaptations, and so fossil teeth alone can sometimes indicate the former existence of grassland.

Around 25 million years ago, the Oligocene passed into the Miocene. New seaways formed, separating North America from both Europe and eastern Asia. These seaways were narrow; of themselves, they would not have been significant barriers to faunal exchange between North America and Eurasia. But the two continents were still drifting northward, and their northern parts were outside the tropics. As a result, exchange was limited to species that could stand the cooler conditions of the latitudes where the narrow seaways existed. The primates, adapted for tropical and subtropical life, would no longer be able to pass between the Old World and the New. (At least, not until a hominid had developed the cultural attainments—use of fire, snug shelters, warm clothing, and boats—that would counteract his biological limitations. Of course, such development came long after the Miocene.)

In North America, one tarsier-like prosimian, Ekgmowechashala, survived into the early Miocene but then became extinct. It was the last New World prosimian, as far as is known—a remnant of the family Omomyidae, which in earlier times had given rise to the New World monkeys in South America. During the Miocene, South America was still not in contact with North America, and faunal exchange between these two continents was limited to species that could cross sizeable water gaps. In the Old World, however, Africa had drifted close to Eurasia, and a good many mammals passed between the two great land masses. Hedgehogs, shrews, aardvarks, rhinoceroses, swine, giraffe-like animals, members of the cat family and of the dog family—these entered Africa for the first time, coming from Eurasia.

African Miocene primates were varied. Among others, they included a prosimian closely related to the modern bush baby, a monkey ancestral to the langur group, and the gibbon-like Pliopithecus. Although forerunning the gibbons, Pliopithecus still had a short tail, and its arms were not greatly elongated. The long arms of the modern gibbons—long in proportion to the legs—were a post-Miocene adaptation for progress through the trees by brachiation (swinging hand over hand). Another important Miocene genus was Dryopithecus. It was represented in Africa by two species, probably ancestral to the chimpanzee and the gorilla respectively. Dryopithecus was not especially long-armed; like the gibbons, the apes would later take up brachiation, and would evolve disproportionately long forelimbs. Apparently there were no brachiators on the line that led to man.

At one time, Dryopithecus was regarded as a possible ancestor of man. It was clear that man was closely related to the great apes, the family Pongidae; clear, too, that the hominid line became more simian the further back it was traced in time. Accordingly, such tracing would eventually reach a common ancestor of pongids and hominids. Dryopithecus, a rather unspecialized genus of apes, looked as though it might be that ancestor. By this interpretation, the hominids would be an offshoot of the pongids, albeit an offshoot sufficiently specialized to warrant recognition as a separate family. But as previously suggested, the hominid line may have been distinct long before the pongid genus Dryopithecus had evolved; for the line probably stems from the Oligocene Propliopithecus.

In the Miocene, some African animals pushed into southern Europe, which was still sufficiently tropical for them. Both Pliopithecus and Dryopithecus entered Europe, and the Apidium line may have produced Oreopithecus of Italy. This last primate was a remarkable one. Its fragmentary remains were discovered over a century ago, but not until the 1940s were its superficially man-like characteristics emphasized in the literature. Further interest in Oreopithecus was stimulated in 1958 by the discovery of a complete skeleton in a Tuscan coal mine. In newspaper accounts of the find, this primate was described as some kind of ancestral human (or, whimsically, as the Abominable Coalman), but it was no such thing. It suggested man in having somewhat reduced canine teeth and a two-cusped lower premolar. Its face was short, the profile not especially prognathous. The hipbone was sufficiently man-like to suggest an upright posture. The cranium was rather rounded, and the attachment for the neck musculature was far down on it, as though the head had been balanced on a vertical neck. The arms were scarcely longer than the legs. Oreopithecus may have been superficially the most man-like primate of its day, but it represented an independent evolution leading toward a humanoid type. Just as the Old World monkeys and the New World monkeys represent parallel evolution from prosimians, so do Oreopithecus and the family Hominidae represent parallel evolution from an advanced primate stock.

If the hominid line had suffered a mishap, or had not moved out of Africa, perhaps Oreopithecus would have evolved further, to become the dominant primate of the world. The reduced canines of Oreopithecus have led some workers to suggest that it relied on artificial weapons for offense and defense. Perhaps so; even the chimpanzee will occasionally make and use tools, or hurl branches. But paleontologists have held, and rather convincingly demonstrated, that dentition reflects diet; and there seems no justification for abandoning this dictum in the case of a few primates. In the gibbons and great apes, the canines of the upper jaw interlock with those of the lower jaw when the mouth is closed. Hence, these primates cannot work the jaws with any sort of lateral movement; they cannot grind food, man-fashion. Oreopithecus had strange-looking incisors and molars, prima facie evidence of dietary specialization; and the reduction of its canines is probably to be regarded as additional evidence of this specialization, whatever it may have been.

Apidium of the African Oligocene may have been ancestral to Oreopithecus of the Italian Miocene. But what of the line that was generated by the little African Oligocene primate Propliopithecus? The Miocene genus Ramapithecus was probably its descendant, and is clearly a member of the Hominidae, whose culmination we are. Ramapithecus remains have been unearthed at a number of scattered localities, but usually they have been in very fragmentary condition, and comments on them must be circumspect. The canine teeth were reduced, but from this circumstance one cannot infer reliance on artificial weapons. The African Miocene yielded mammal bones that had been smashed as though to extract the marrow, and animal skulls that had been opened as though to get at the brains; but the association of Ramapithecus with such debris has not been demonstrated. The pelvis of this primate has not been found, and so we do not know whether it walked erect.

One thing is clear: Ramapithecus was a very successful genus. Although confined to Africa in the Miocene, it became widespread in Eurasia during the next period, the Pliocene; in time, it reached Germany, India, and southwestern China. In other words, the genus had wide geographic extent and considerable duration in time. It is reasonable to ask whether this circumstance implies some unusual mental abilities, foreshadowing the ones that later enabled man to cover the globe. No such inference can be drawn, for some other animal genera spread out of Africa more dramatically than did Ramapithecus. For example, the order Proboscidea, which culminated in the elephants, originated in Africa. One of its genera, Mastodon, was present in both Africa and Europe in the early Miocene, and by the middle Miocene had spread all the way across Asia to enter North America. From distribution alone, one cannot visualize Ramapithecus as anything more than a genus of animals, whose persistence and geographic spread resulted from innate responses to environmental stimuli.

The Miocene ended around 12 million years ago, passing into the Pliocene. North America became joined to South America by a land bridge roughly corresponding to, but a little wider than, the modern Central America. Faunal exchange between the two continents was therefore facilitated, although not until the next epoch, the Pleistocene, would it become a highly significant factor in the evolutionary history of the New World mammals. Also in the Pliocene, northwestern North America was again connected with northeastern Asia; so in effect there was a continuity of land from Africa through Eurasia and North America to South America. But obviously, an intercontinental land bridge does not offer a continental range of environmental conditions; such bridges are filters, permitting passage only of species that can survive on them. As a result of continued northward drift, the Alaska–Siberia bridge had become too cold to permit movement of primates across it.

As far as is known, there were no North American Pliocene primates to move into South America with the emergence of the Central America bridge. Thus, between the start of the Pliocene and the arrival of man in the late Pleistocene, the only noteworthy zoogeographic development of the primates in the New World would be the movement of South American monkeys northward into the forested tropics of Central America and southern Mexico, plus a little island-hopping northward through the West Indies.

Some of the South American monkeys evolved prehensility of the tail. Such a development never took place among Old World monkeys, numerous stories and illustrations to the contrary. One group of South American prehensile-tailed monkeys became so highly adapted for brachiation that the thumb degenerated, leaving the hand with only four digits. The circumstance bolsters the view that an opposable thumb was primarily an adaptation for grasping branches during locomotion. With the evolution of a different type of locomotion, one in which branches were grasped only by the four hooked fingers (and sometimes the tail), the thumb was useless and was lost.

Among Old World primates, there were Miocene happenings aplenty. It will be recalled that the Indian peninsula, although now a part of Eurasia, was originally a fragment of the southern supercontinent, Gondwanaland. By Miocene times it had rammed into Eurasia, wrinkling the Earth's crust to form the Himalayas, the Arakan range of Burma, and the two great island arcs of Indonesia. By the Pliocene, India had formed a homeland for primates in variety, some of them ancestral to surviving groups. Spain, too, has yielded a goodly lot of Pliocene primates; evidently it was still in tropical latitudes during at least a part of that epoch.

The ape genus Dryopithecus, which we met in the Miocene of Africa, was widespread across southern Eurasia in the Pliocene. In the latter continent it was represented by two general types. One of these, medium-sized, was chimpanzee-like, while the other was bulkier and more gorilla-like. So far, Eurasian fossil beds have yielded few clues to the early history of the orang-utan. Today, it is restricted to the islands of Borneo and Sumatra, although in the Pleistocene it lived also on the Asian mainland. Probably, the orang genus (Pongo) evolved from Dryopithecus, as did the chimpanzee genus (Pan) and the gorilla genus (Gorilla).

A remarkable Asian primate was Gigantopithecus. Most specimens of it are from the early and middle Pleistocene of China, but a member of it has been found in the Pliocene of India, and so the genus warrants mention at this point. For a while, Gigantopithecus was known only from its enormous molar teeth. In shape, these molars were very like those of man, and they even showed the human type of occlusal wear. Such wear is possible only when the canines are so reduced that the jaws are capable of lateral or rotary grinding movements. Many mammal stocks produced giant species in the Pleistocene, and it was tempting to guess that Gigantopithecus represented Pleistocene gigantism in the hominid line. But with the accumulation of more and better specimens, it became evident that this huge primate was an ape. Like the chimpanzee and the gorilla, Gigantopithecus was descended from Dryopithecus. Nor was Gigantopithecus as large as had been supposed from the size of its molars;

it had reduced front teeth but exceptionally large rear teeth. Still, it was as bulky as any gorilla.

What of Ramapithecus? As mentioned previously, this hominid genus was confined to Africa in the Miocene, but spread in the Pliocene to lands as far away as Germany, India, and southwestern China. Even though Pliocene specimens of Ramapithecus are fragmentary, they yield some new information about this important genus. The Pliocene saw the origin and spread of scrubland, grassland, and other vegetation types not dominated by trees; and in that period, just as today, each type had its characteristic animal life. Thus, some Pliocene fossil beds can be identified as having been laid down in wooded country, others in grassland. Often, this grassland is referred to as savanna, but I should not care to be so specific. In any event, Eurasian Ramapithecus was not part of any grassland assemblage; it left its remains in wooded regions. One may doubt whether these regions were covered with forest, however; more likely they supported woodland, a vegetation type in which the fairly numerous trees are scattered and do not form a closed canopy.

Unfortunately, Ramapithecus remains have not come to light from the Pliocene of Africa. In the late Pliocene of that continent, the hominid line was represented by the genus Australopithecus, probably a lineal descendant of Ramapithecus. Australopithecus survived into the Pleistocene, and I should like to review some of the early Pleistocene finds, than trace the story back into the Pliocene.

As early Pleistocene fossils began to accumulate, it appeared that eastern Africa was inhabited by a hominid species, *Australopithecus africanus,* about the size of a modern pygmy and rather slender of build. Although upright of posture, this being was not as thoroughly adapted for bipedality as is modern man. The middle toe was the largest, bearing the greatest share of the weight; the buttock musculature, so important in striding, was less well developed than in man; the gait may have been a bit waddling. The thumb was proportionately smaller and probably less manipulable than ours. As in Gigantopithecus, the front teeth were small, the rear teeth large. The cranial capacity was about a third that of modern man, roughly equal to that of a gorilla.

For a time, it seemed that *Australopithecus africanus* was the direct ancestor of man, but as more specimens were found, the situation grew complicated: there were two lines of Australopithecus descent in the Pleistocene of Africa. The second of these was represented by *Australopithecus boisei* in the early Pleistocene, and by *Australopith-*

ecus robustus in the middle Pleistocene. For convenience we may refer to the *boisei-robustus* group as the robust line, in contrast with the gracile *africanus* line.

As suggested by the name, the robust line was comparatively stocky. The cranium bore a longitudinal crest for the attachment of powerful jaw muscles. (A crest of this kind is present in the gorilla and orang-utan, but not in the chimpanzee or in any hominid except a robust Australopithecus.) The jaws were wide; the front teeth were very small, but the rear ones were enormous grinders. Evidently, the two lines of descent were ecologically separated, the robust one being adapted for consumption of plant foods that required hard grinding. The teeth of the robust species were not only worn but also scratched, as though by sand grains; and it may be that roots and tubers formed a large part of the diet. The gracile line, on the other hand, was probably omnivorous like ourselves, and certainly had a human fondness for meat, as shown by food remains.

To further complicate the matter of hominids in the early Pleistocene of Africa, there was the problem of Australopithecus culture. In caves of southern Africa, early Pleistocene levels were sometimes rich with horns, teeth, and smashed bones of game animals. The suggestion was advanced that this debris represented an "osteodontokeratic" culture—in other words, a tool-making industry based on bones, teeth, and horns rather than on flint. A countersuggestion attributed the fragmentation of the animal remains to the powerful jaws of hyenas that supposedly laired in the caves. But some of the sites contained the skulls of baboons that had been knocked in the head by a powerful blow from a club-like implement that had left a double fracture. The sites also yielded remains of a large antelope whose humerus (upper arm bone) had double ridges in the lower end. These ridges neatly fit the double fractures in the baboons' skulls. Especially at Makapansgat in the Transvaal, some primate species of the early Pleistocene was preying heavily on baboons, bludgeoning them to death. About 95 per cent of the blows had been struck righthanded, 5 per cent lefthanded. (In modern man, the proportion of righthandedness to lefthandedness is also 95 to 5.) Some of the baboons had been struck from the rear, as though they had been fleeing, but most had been struck from the front; presumably they had confronted their attackers. Baboons are dangerous animals, even singly; and customarily they live in troops, which are formidable indeed. To have killed these beasts, the hunters themselves must also have operated in troops.

At Olduvai, Tanzania, the evidence for early Pleistocene cultural activities was unequivocal. In that region, there were a series of deposits spanning much of the Pleistocene. At several levels in the stratigraphic sequence, volcanic material had been laid down. Such material is ideal for dating by the potassium-argon radiometric technique, and so it was possible to establish absolute dates for various levels in the sequence. Dating was also facilitated by faunal changes through time. It was clear that some being at Olduvai was chipping flint in the early Pleistocene. This being lived by the shore of a lake that has long since vanished, and to his lakeside home he brought flint pebbles gathered miles away. Some of these pebbles could have been used as missiles, but others were chipped into a variety of rude tools: choppers, hammer stones, anvil stones, scrapers, and ovate knives, along with flakes and cores that remained as the debris of knapping and that were themselves utilized. The deepest Pleistocene level of Olduvai yielded a large ring of piled stones, set in place perhaps to form or hold down the base of a thatched shelter.

Enough artifactual material was eventually uncovered, not just at Olduvai but at other sites as well, to permit recognition of an early Pleistocene culture, dubbed the Oldowan. (Oldoway is an alternative spelling of Olduvai.) Traces of this culture were nearly limited to the simple but distinctive flint work described above, although the ring of stones was also Oldowan. To put the matter in another way, the Oldowan culture is represented mostly by a series of flint industries. Flint tools were turned out according to patterns that were handed down from generation to generation for thousands of years. During that time, the patterns were gradually modified and improved upon. The tangible relics of the Oldowan industries are to be viewed as evidence of cultural activities. Their existence accounts for my statement that if archeology deals with past culture, then it must cover a time span that began at least 2 million years ago; for such is the age of the lowest artifact-bearing level of Olduvai.

But who were the bearers of the Oldowan culture? Candidates for the position were the gracile *Australopithecus africanus* and the husky, big-toothed *Australopithecus boisei*. It was generally supposed that the gracile species, being more nearly human, was the toolmaker. But then excavations were made into what had been an ancient ground surface, a "living floor" of an early Pleistocene hominid; and there, reposing atop the substratum on which Oldowan flint work had been dropped, was the skull of a robust Australopithecus. This specialized primate—specialized in a direction that did not seem to forerun man—appeared to be the culture-bearer. Opponents of this view held that the gracile species had left behind its own flint work and the head of a robust congener.

In science it is always desirable to fit the available facts together in the most meaningful fashion, always with a tacit understanding that new facts may necessitate a recombination of the old ones. This necessity arose after further excavations at Olduvai—excavations that revealed the hitherto unsuspected presence of a third hominid species in the early Pleistocene. In brain size and dental characteristics, this one was a bit more man-like than the most advanced Australopithecus, a bit less man-like than *Homo erectus* of the middle Pleistocene. The newly discovered species was given the name of *Homo habilis*. The oldest specimens came from the lowest Pleistocene levels of Olduvai. Later specimens—later by about three-quarters of a million years—were more like *Homo erectus*.

As it turned out, *Homo habilis* was consistently associated with flint implements. Wherever such implements accompanied Australopithecus remains, *Homo habilis* was present also, and was the more likely fabricator. The South African sites, with Australopithecus but not *Homo habilis*, yielded no flint work but only horns, teeth, and smashed bones. In short, *Homo habilis* was the bearer of the Oldowan culture. The similarity of the Oldowan flint industries to those of *Homo erectus* is now understandable: as *habilis* evolved into *erectus*, the Oldowan flint work of the former was slightly improved upon to become the Abbevillian flint work of the latter.

Thus, early in the Pleistocene of Africa, there were three lines of hominid descent in Africa, three closely related species representing adaptive radiation into as many different ecological niches. And they were closely related, even though one is assigned to Homo, the other two to Australopithecus. Since there was a morphological and presumably an evolutionary continuum from one of these genera to the other, the paleoanthropologist must be a bit arbitrary in deciding the point at which one of them passed into the other. The tool-making ability of *habilis* was a factor influencing the choice of a separate generic position for it.

For simplicity we may say that *habilis*, *africanus*, and *boisei* were three early Pleistocene developments from an Australopithecus stock. *Habilis* evolved into *erectus*. *Africanus* persisted to the beginning of the middle Pleistocene, at which time it became extinct, probably from inability to compete with the *habilis* line, which was just becoming *erectus*. The fate of *boisei* is uncertain. It was specialized in a direction quite different from that of *africanus* or *habilis;* but the middle Pleistocene representative of that line, *robustus,* seems less specialized along that direction. One possibility is that the robust line evolved in a fashion paralleling the *habilis-erectus* line. In other words, *robustus* might be a lineal descendant of *boisei.* Alternatively, *robustus* might represent a part of the robust line that evolved outside eastern Africa, and that moved into that area around the beginning of the middle Pleistocene. In any event, the robust line held on longer than did the gracile line, probably because an ecological specialization kept it out of much competition with *habilis.* But soon after the latter became *erectus, robustus* vanished.

Obviously, with three closely related hominid lines in the early Pleistocene of Africa, the thing to do is to go back into the earliest Pleistocene and the Pliocene of that continent to search for their common ancestor. This is being done, although with some difficulty, for not many earliest Pleistocene or Pliocene fossil beds have been found in Africa, and the known Pliocene ones are concentrated toward the northern part of the continent. Nevertheless, remains of Australiopithecus have come to light from the earliest Pleistocene and late Pliocene of Africa, with specimens dating from 3 to 5 million years ago. While some of these specimens have not been reported on in detail, they suggest that in the late Pliocene, Australopithecus began the adaptive radiation that produced *africanus, boisei,* and *habilis* of the early Pleistocene. A recently discovered specimen, not yet adequately described, may be the oldest *habilis,* and may date from near the Pliocene-Pleistocene boundary. No flint work has been found with Pliocene Australopithecus.

Nor have skeletal remains been found that would stand intermediate, morphologically and temporally, between Ramapithecus and Australopithecus. It is of course possible that the first of these genera passed into the second somewhere outside the African regions that are now being searched intensively for hominid fossils.

Much interest attaches to the ecology of the Australopithecus line that gave rise to Homo. At Olduvai, remains of *Homo habilis* were concentrated in the lowest levels. As noted, these were of early Pleistocene age. However, they did not date back to the very beginning of the Pleistocene. They were deposited at a time when the region was at its driest, with a maximum of grassland and a minimum of wooded expanses. It is unlikely that this hominid was rigidly bound to one vegetation type. Troops of *Homo habilis* probably went wherever there were supplies of wild game and edible plants. *Australopithecus boisei* probably was more strongly committed to existence in wooded areas, and to a plant diet. *Australopithecus africanus* hunted in the grassland, and brought back an abundance of game. Animal bones, horns, and teeth, the debris of hominid feasts, have been found in numbers at sites of eastern and southern Africa, but it is not always possible to decide which hominid accumulated them. Before the discovery of *habilis* it was customary to regard *africanus* as a meat-eater who hunted and perhaps scavenged, especially in the grassland. This still seems likely, although *habilis* left some of the food remains formerly credited to *africanus*. These two species may have differed more in hunting techniques than in dietary preferences.

When attention was drawn to the evolutionary importance of the African finds, a search was made through fragmentary hominid material in the hope of discovering comparable specimens from other areas. A broken, weathered, and distorted cranium from Chad, in north-central Africa, was once thought to be an Australopithecus, but it now appears to be either *Homo habilis* or *Homo erectus*. Teeth and scraps of cranium from Israel, while suggestive of Australopithecus, are more likely Homo, species unidentifiable. Teeth from China, once referred to as Hemianthropus, might be Australopithecus or *Homo habilis*, but more material is necessary before identification can be made. Bits of broken jawbones from Java, dubbed Meganthropus, are assignable to a hominid slightly more advanced than Australopithecus, possibly *Homo habilis*. Whatever Meganthropus may be, it is not as old as *Homo habilis*, but comes from the early part of the middle Pleistocene. Thus, we have no more than tantalizing hints that during the first half of the Pleistocene, hominid evolution was going on in Asia as well as Africa.

In discussing the hominids of the early to middle Pleistocene, I have said nothing about the glaciations that characterized that period; for the glaciers grew in the high latitudes, while Australopithecus and *Homo habilis* lived in the tropics. But beyond the *habilis* level, the hominid line would eventually confront glacial ice, and so we need to consider certain climatic episodes of the Pleistocene.

Climatic oscillation—a cooler, rainer regimen alternating with a warmer, drier one—probably began in the Miocene, becoming more pronounced and rhythmic as time passed. In the late Pliocene, there may have been a waxing and then a waning of ice in the Arctic and Antarctic; and in the early Pleistocene, also, there probably was temporary glaciation in the high latitudes. Subsequently, there were four more glaciations; the remnants of the last one still cover Greenland,

Antarctica, and some smaller areas. These four are the ones to which reference is usually made in standard works on the Pleistocene. The first of the four began shortly after the start of the middle Pleistocene.

Ecological effects of glaciation were numerous and far-reaching. Enormous expanses of country were covered by ice sheets up to 10,000 feet thick. The third of the classic glaciations was the most extreme, at least in terms of ice extent: one of its ice sheets covered more than 2 million square miles of Europe, another covered about 6 million square miles of North America, and several others occupied large areas of Asia. There was growth of ice in Tasmania, New Zealand, and southern South America, also. Outside the main glaciated regions, minor glaciers capped a great many mountains. In North America and Eurasia, another ecological effect of a glacial episode was the telescoping of the life-zones in a southward direction. Today, the far-northern parts of these continents are occupied by treeless tundra, while south of the tundra is a belt of cold-temperate coniferous forest. Still farther south are hardwood forest, grassland, or desert, depending on rainfall. But at a peak of glaciation, tundra was pushed far down into Europe and the United States. South of the tundra, the cold-temperate coniferous forest extended to the Gulf states in the United States, and was pushed out of Europe except for some small areas near the Mediterranean. In past times, as today, each great vegetation belt had its characteristic animal species, and the geographic ranges of these were shifted far to the south at times when glacial ice occupied so much of the north.

Toward the low latitudes, there was progressive attentuation of the chilling that accompanied glacial episodes. Nevertheless, even in the tropics, such episodes were marked by a slight cooling, an increase in rainfall, and the growth of ice caps on various high mountains.

Even at peaks of glaciation, small parts of northern North America and large parts of northern Eurasia were not covered with ice sheets; for glacial ice is frozen rainwater and snow, and glaciers did not develop where precipitation was scanty. This circumstance draws attention to another major ecological effect of glaciation. Moisture evaporates from the sea, is carried inland by the wind, falls as rain, and eventually runs down to the sea—an endless cycle. But as a glacial episode got under way, more and more precipitation was bound up in the ice, and so did not return to the sea. Thus, sea level began to fall. Its maximum drop was during the third glaciation, when it fell to more than 500 feet below its present stand. Such a drop turned many a strait into dry land, for example connecting Alaska with Siberia, merging Australia with Tasmania and New Guinea, and uniting south-eastern Asia with Borneo, Sumatra, and Java.

The four glaciations were separated by episodes of deglaciation. During these, the ice began to melt, returning more and more water to the sea. The first of the three classic deglaciations was the most extreme in this regard; most of its ice melted, and sea level rose to about 200 feet above its present stand. The life-zones shifted to the north as the climate grew warmer. Rainfall decreased over vast expanses.

Thus, since the beginning of the middle Pleistocene, several principal factors of the environment have fluctuated markedly. As a matter of fact, there were more such fluctuations than might be suggested by this brief account; for neither a glaciation nor a deglaciation proceeded smoothly. Instead, each progressed by fits and starts, sometimes with temporary reversals of the trends.

By about one million years ago, at the beginning of the middle Pleistocene, *Homo habilis* had evolved into *Homo erectus*, known in the older literature as the Pithecanthropus. A bit larger and in some ways more man-like than its predecessor, *erectus* used fire for warmth and cooking, as well as to set blazes that would stampede wild game. The flint work of *erectus* included a hand-axe, a large chopper or cleaver, a smaller chopping or cutting tool, knife-like flakes, and what might have been a gouge. In Africa, sites with this flint inventory also yield rounded, fist-sized stones in groups of three. These probably indicate use of the bolas, a weapon consisting of three stones bound together by long sinews. The device is whirled around and then cast at an animal, which it strikes with great force.

Not that all populations of this species were culturally identical. *Homo erectus* existed for about three-quarters of a million years, perhaps longer in some areas. The later populations were more *sapiens*-like than the earlier ones, especially in cranial capacity, and had made some additions to or improvements in their cultural inventory. Hearths, evidence for the use of fire, have not been found at the earlier sites. The early variety of hand-axe, shaped by blows from a hammerstone, was not as neatly made as the later variety, which was shaped by blows from a baton of antler, bone, or hard wood. Evidence of huts comes from only one site, a very late one in the *erectus* time span. Nowhere is there indication of intentional burial of the dead, but at two of the fairly late sites, one near Peking and the other in Java, *erectus* had taken the skulls of its dead, cleaned them of the brains, and left them in a cave. Neanderthal man, a descendant of *erectus,* often removed the brains from bodies that were to be carefully buried; and it is tempting to interpret such removal, by both *erectus* and the Neanderthalers, as ritual cannibalism. Even in historic times, some uncivilized peoples ate the brains of the dead, with the belief that the eater would thereby acquire the qualities of the deceased; and of course, the general outline of the old superstition is still detectable in the transsubstantiation ritual of the Christian mythology. Certain historic tribes of the southwestern Pacific, mistakenly believing the liver to be the seat of self-awareness, ate the liver of a fallen enemy. Among historic American Indian tribes, ritual cannibalism was widespread, and was virtually limited to eating of the brains, heart, blood, marrow, or muscles of a brave enemy. Perhaps it was at the level of late *Homo erectus* that the hominid line began to take its fancies seriously, fancies that would in time be elaborated into a wide variety of religious mythologies.

It is sometimes asserted that *Homo erectus* produced no art. Such a state of affairs would be altogether remarkable, for even the chimpanzee has a rudimentary artistic sense. Perhaps we should forget the famous "painting" that was daubed by a chimpanzee, entered by a prankster in an art show, and awarded a prize; the episode probably tells more about human nature than subhuman. But seriously motivated experimenters found that a chimpanzee had a sense of composition. It would center its rude designs on the canvas. It had an impulse toward symmetry; presented with a semi-circle already drawn, it roughly sketched in the rest of the circle. The hand-axes of late *erectus* also demonstrate an impulse toward symmetry. A hand-axe probably was an all-purpose tool, used for chopping, slicing, scraping, and digging. Whatever the function of the implement, its usefulness was not impaired by rudeness of manufacture. Yet, late *erectus* turned out thousands of hand-axes, ranging in outline from trianguloid through oval to lanceolate, that were neatly symmetric. In other words, late *erectus* manifested an artistic sense, at least in crafting a symmetrical hand-axe where a rude one would have sufficed for practial purposes.

The remains of an early variety of *Homo erectus* have come to light from southern, eastern, and northern Africa, as well as from Java and China. Presumably, much of this distribution was accomplished during the first glaciation, when sea level was far below its present stand. Thus, the presence of *erectus* on Java does not lead to the inference that this species could cross sizeable water gaps, for Java was united with the Asian mainland during glacial episodes. Both Java and Africa have produced *erectus* specimens close to one million years old. Not long after the first deglaciation, this species entered Europe. The few and fragmentary European remains from that approximate time exhibit comparatively advanced physical characteristics. It is hard to put a specific name to these remains; for in the evolutionary continuum, they represent a point at which *erectus* was beginning to give rise to Neanderthal man in one direction, and to man of modern type in another direction.

In South Africa, China, and Java, later populations of *erectus* were more *sapiens*-like than the earlier ones. But in the African and Asian tropics, *erectus* would hang on, here and there, long after Neanderthal and modern man had evolved elsewhere. "Broken Hill man," from a relict population of African *erectus,* was remarkable not only for severe dental caries but also for a small, circular hole that had been cut neatly into his skull, above the left ear. It was cut while he was alive, for the bone showed signs of healing. The operation might have been the first known trephining.

The advanced variety of *Homo erectus,* who existed during the latter part of the middle Pleistocene, gave rise to both the modern and the Neanderthal types of man. Neanderthal man was first discovered and studied intensively in Europe. There, he looked very different from ourselves. He was stocky and bull-necked, barrel-chested and bandy-legged, with wide forearms. The length of his cranium and the heaviness of his brow ridge gave him a "low-browed" look, although in actual measurement his cranium was as high as ours. Neanderthal man of Europe should be considered specialized rather than primitive. In other words, the hominid line was producing a species adapted for life in chilly Europe during a time of glaciation. In that region, Neanderthal man had an average cranial capacity exceeding our own. In arm and leg proportions, he was less simian than we are.

Neanderthal man used fire, and this is not surprising since *Homo erectus* had done so at an earlier time. However, it is at the Neanderthal level that we find the first evidence of an ability to make fire, not just to use it. Like *erectus,* Neanderthal man often knocked pieces of flint together while roughing out tools. Surprisingly, sparks are not all of the same temperature, and when they are produced by striking flint on flint, they will not kindle a blaze. However, if a Neanderthal knapper used a lump of pyrite to batter flint, he would produce fat sparks that could set tinder alight; and a pyrite lump has been found in a French cave, in a stratum with the flint implements of Neanderthal man. In several sites of early European *Homo sapiens,* a lump of pyrite has been found beside one of flint, the two constituting a primitive "lighter."

The Neanderthal flint industry, called the Mousterian, was based largely on flakes struck from a core. It was the flake, rather than the core, that would be shaped into the desired tool or weapon point. At some times and places, Neanderthal man trimmed the core in such a fashion that the flake would need no further shaping after it was struck off. Mousterian flint work includes a hand-axe made from a core in the style of late *erectus,* and a disc-shaped core that was used as a tool after blades had been struck from it; but the inventory consisted principally of flake-based implements for cutting, perforating, and scraping. Flint balls probably were bolas weights. Neanderthal man may have made clothing of skins, as suggested by the abundance of his perforators and scrapers, and by his residence in glacial Europe. Using flint tools, he fashioned wooden ones, including spears; nor did he neglect bone as a raw material for implements. Occasionally, he did a little scratching on bone—simple, apparently nonfunctional scratching that might represent artistic efforts. Both red and black pigments have been found in sites of Neanderthal man; evidently he painted something, perhaps his own face or body.

Holding meat in his jaws, Neanderthal man would use a flint knife to cut off a bite-sized chunk. The knife left scratches on the enamel of his teeth, and the direction of these scratches reveals the knife to have been wielded with the right hand.

Contrary to popular belief, Neanderthal man did not always make his home in caves; he left many of his characteristic implements at campsites far outside the cavern regions. He erected artificial shelters, as shown by postholes and hut floors at a few sites. But of course, traces of occupation are more likely to be preserved in caves than in the open. When Neanderthal man did frequent a cavern, his living area was around its mouth; the depths were reserved for disposal of the dead, and for certain rituals.

At Savona, an Italian city on the Mediterranean, Alberto C. Blanc found evidence of a Neanderthal ritual in a cave—evidence that had been preserved because a landslide had blocked the cavern mouth not long after its occupants had gone. In the clay of the cave floor were the characteristic footprints left by the short, broad feet of Neanderthal man, feet unlike those of any European *Homo sapiens.* Also in the clay were holes with the charred remains of the torches that had lighted the scene. A group of Neanderthal adults had stood at one side of the cave and thrown mud balls toward the opposite side, where an irregularity of the cavern wall suggested an animal shape. But the shape was not the target. Blunt Neanderthal fingers had scraped away the mud that had hit it. Beside the irregularity, a Neanderthal youth had stood. Evidently he had stood there for a long while, for his footprints were deeply impressed into the clay. He had been the target. The procedure strongly suggests the rites whereby a boy was initiated into manhood; roughly comparable rites have been carried on in historic times by many peoples, both civilized and uncivilized.

If *Homo erectus* had not already invented the fiction of an afterlife, Neanderthal man did. Evidently he regarded death as a kind of sleep, for he consistently arranged a dead body in a sleeping position, often with one arm under the head as a pillow. He began the custom of placing red ochre in a burial. Perhaps he associated the powdered red mineral with blood and the blush of life. At any rate, he began a practice that was carried on by man of modern type—carried on up into the seventeenth century in some areas. In the burials he put flint objects and haunches of meat, thus beginning another practice that was destined to persist; it continues to the present in a few societies.

Just recently, Shanidar Cave in Iraq yielded the skeleton of a Neanderthal man. He was quite old for a Neanderthal, in his early forties. Throughout life, one of his arms had been useless, probably as the result of both a birth defect and an injury. He must have been cared for to have reached so great an age. With the bones was a circular area of dark, carbonized plant material. This was examined for pollen grains that might be identified. Amazingly, the plant material turned out to have been a wreath, made up of a dozen kinds of brightly colored wildflowers. Today, of course, floral tributes to the dead are made in almost all societies.

Neanderthal burial usually was in the soft dirt of a cave floor. Sometimes a rock was placed over the filled grave. In one Italian cave, a Neanderthal skull, minus the lower jaw, had been placed on the floor and surrounded by a ring of stones. The individual had been killed by a blow to the temple.

In Europe, a Neanderthal man's principal animal enemy and competitor may have been the cave bear. This beast was abundant, well adapted to a glacial climate, and given to lairing or denning in caves that were ideal for hominid occupancy. Certain activities of Neanderthal man may have reflected an effort to manipulate the shaggy beast through magic; for at one locality he dug a pit, lined it with stones, and filled it with a stack of cave bear skulls. At a second locality, he inserted the limb bones of one cave bear into the skull of another, and placed the assemblage atop an arrangement of still more cave-bear bones. It is the irrationality of Neanderthal man, as much as his technological accomplishments, that allies him to us.

As already mentioned, not long after the beginning of the first deglaciation Europe was occupied by a hominid probably ancestral to both Neanderthal and modern man. As the millennia went by, the two descendant types became so different that they might well be regarded as two separate species, *Homo neanderthalensis* and *Homo sapiens;* for when man of modern type began to push into Europe during the last glaciation, he did not interbreed with the Neander-thalers who were already established there. Surely, extensive in-terbreeding would have taken place if it had been biologically pos-sible, and reproductive isolation is an important criterion when one must decide whether two congeners are conspecific. In other words, once again there had been parallel evolution in the hominids. Of course, man of modern type had the potentiality of evolving into sev-eral species, for he developed several geographic races, all of which could have become reproductively isolated if their geographic isola-tion had persisted long enough. But these races began to move about, their peregrinations facilitated by cultural attainments. In their movements, they interbred frequently, thus lessening whatever de-gree of genetic divergence they might once have evolved.

It was quite late in the fourth glaciation, around thirty to forty thou-sand years ago, that man of modern type began to migrate through-out much of the habitable world. By this time, he had already di-verged into some of the geographic races that have persisted, with more or less admixture, to the present. Negritos spread through In-donesia and eastern New Guinea to Australia and Tasmania, followed on this route by Australoids. Mongoloids probably entered the New World soon after spreading in eastern Asia. An African race, similar to the Bushman but a bit taller, took over large parts of Africa, but were later displaced from most of their territory by Negroids. Early remains of the latter race have not come to light, probably because its charac-teristics were developed in the African rainforest, where environ-mental conditions militate against fossilization. Caucasoids—the so-called Cro-Magnon man—entered Europe and eventually replaced Neanderthal man there.

Previous accounts of human evolution occasionally went astray be-cause of difficulty in deciding whether an ancient hominid was di-rectly on the line that led to man, or whether it was on a parallel line that died out. This kind of difficulty still exists, although it has been minimized by the accumulation of more specimens and the refinement of dating techniques. But in any event, a Pleistocene hominid morphological sequence leads from gracile Australopithecus through earlier and later *Homo habilis,* thence through earlier and later *Homo erectus,* and so to a common ancestor of modern and Neanderthal man. Here the sequence forks, leading in one direction to modern man, in the other through a less specialized variety of Neanderthal man to a more specialized.

What with the current interest in paleoanthropology, many significant finds will probably be made in the near future, and some present ideas about hominid evolution may have to be revised. The late Louis S. B. Leakey, who did so much excavation at Olduvai and other African sites, was never quite convinced that *Homo erectus* was an ancestor of modern man. He visualized *sapiens* as a direct descendant of *habilis,* with *erectus* as a side branch that had evolved from some undiscovered Australopithecus. The weight of accumulated evidence militates against this view, but it is worth bearing in mind.

Newspaper articles have lately described some finds that will be spectacular if they live up to their advance billing. Remains of *Homo neanderthalensis,* older than any previously known, have been reported from Russia; and remains of *Homo sapiens,* likewise older than any previously known, have been reported from Africa. A supposedly *erectus*-like cranium has been unearthed in Australia, and a *neanderthalensis*-like one in South America. The presence of Neanderthal-like man in South America is not highly improbable. The earliest known American Indian skulls exhibit some primitive features: a long, narrow cranium, a deep depression at the temple, a heavy brow ridge, and a prognathous jaw. Such skulls characterized the big-game hunters who might have driven still earlier peoples southward. It might not be coincidence that more pre-projectile point sites have been found in South America than elsewhere in the New World. An apparent concentration of taurodontism in South America might be a legacy from a very early occupation.

Paleoanthropologists study the flint industries of early hominids. However, I shall omit a discussion of these industries, for they are described in detail in various purely archeological works (e.g. Bordes 1968).

It should be obvious that paleoanthropology abstracts a great deal of its data from environmental sciences, notably animal behavior, functional morphology, systematic zoology, paleontology, paleoecology, geology, and geophysics. Paleoanthropology has a sort of philosophical import, too. But on that subject, more in Epilogue.

CHAPTER SIX

Interactions of Archeology

with Economics, Geography, History,
Sociology, Psychology, and
Other Disciplines

The four preceding chapters have been especially concerned with ways in which archeology interacts with other branches of anthropology, but it can interact as readily and as meaningfully with non-anthropological disciplines as well.

Consider economics, for example. True, an economic text discusses many topics that seem to have little bearing on archeology: profits, price systems, national income, inflation, banking systems, monetary policy, wage-price controls, and dozens more. But in broad view, modern economics has two principal concerns, economic policy and the economic analysis of production and distribution. In even the simplest Paleolithic-level society, there was some production of goods (e.g., tools and weapons), perhaps to be distributed only within the society; and production had an economic foundation consisting of raw materials and foods gathered from the wild. In societies at a full-fledged Neolithic level, there was food production through the domestication of plants and sometimes animals; there was exploitation of natural resources in considerable variety. In many or most Neolithic-level societies there was a surplus of some edible or otherwise useful product, which could be traded away to some other society. Power accrued to a society that controlled the distribution of

136

some necessary or highly desired article of commerce. Money, i.e., a medium of exchange with an arbitrarily fixed value, was used by at least a scattering of Neolithic-level societies, although such use might have been stimulated by contact with some contemporaneous but more advanced society.

In the time of the early civilizations, economics became complex. Intensive study of Classical affairs has made possible the writing of a good many large books on the economy of the Greek world, Asia Minor, Syria-Palestine, Egypt, Mesopotamia, Iran, and the Roman Empire. The general history of these civilizations is subdivisible into four periods, and the economic history into four phases.

The first phase began around 3,000 B.C. Agriculture dominated the economic system, but animal husbandry was also important, both to pastoral nomads and settled farmers. Crops were of three general types. Most important was grain, first barley and later wheat; second was fruit, especially of the grape vine but also of various trees from Asia; third was a selection of oleaginous plants, especially the olive but also sesame, castor bean, croton, and others. Some oils were edible but others were used for lighting or as cosmetics. Livestock included cattle, sheep, goats, and asses; later, horses were raised. The horse's utility was limited by lack of a yoke that would take maximum advantage of the animal's strength; the stirrup was unknown, also.

Industries included the construction of buildings, dikes, bridges, and ships; the manufacture of clothes and carpets; the production of ceramics; and metallurgy. Raw materials were mostly of local origin, but in some areas it was found necessary to import timber. Copper, silver, and gold were worked. Alloying began, with resultant emphasis on bronze, an alloy of copper and tin. Later in the first economic phase, iron was extracted, but for a long while it remained scarce and expensive. While clothes often were made at home, most construction, ceramics, and metallurgy was carried on by professional artisans. Many of the mines were state enterprise and were operated by slave labor. International trade involved luxury goods, with high value and low weight; slaves; and certain minerals that were of wide utility but of limited geographic distribution. Long-distance transportation was by overland, river, and maritime routes. Along with legitimate trade, piracy and military conquest were important in providing slaves and goods.

Egypt and Mesopotamia were the first two great economic powers. Egypt's felicitous combination of climate, soils, and midsummer flooding had great possibilities for agricultural exploitation, given the proper crops and sufficient human cooperation. The necessity for such cooperation resulted in state control, which was extended to matters far outside the scope of agriculture. Writing and mathematics were encouraged; they facilitated the accumulation of governmental red tape. Mesopotamia was on some major trade routes, and developed a class of middlemen, nonproducers who took a profit from handling goods produced by others. Standards were set up for weights and measures; forms were developed for business contracts involving sales, hiring, and partnerships. In time, Babylon's name became synonymous with the crassest sort of commercialism, in which profit-taking was placed above most other considerations.

During the first phase, the Phoenicians and then the Greeks began long-distance maritime exploration and colonial expansion. The Phoenicians emphasized a carrying trade, and took their profit mostly fom the sale of goods produced by others; but the Greeks generally carried their own productions, and regulated much of their industry to fill export demands. The Phoenicians rarely attempted navigation out of sight of land or by night, and so established closely spaced way stations along the routes that they followed. Placing such economic reliance on the product of others, the Phoenicians displayed little inventiveness. In the field of material culture, their principal contributions were a purple dye extracted from a mollusk, and a clear or colored glass superior to the opaque Egyptian product. The Greeks, cautious mariners at first, became bolder as time went by. Not content to establish mere way stations, they began to colonize along their trade routes. Eventually, they transported heavy goods such as wine, oil, dried or salted fish, wheat, hides, wool, and timber.

Money appeared at quite an early date in Egypt, but as an accounting device rather than for payments. A gold ring weighing about 7.5 grams was a standard, in terms of which the value of some other item could be expressed; but the rings themselves did not change hands when goods were bartered. At various places and times during the first economic phase, values were expressed in terms of grain, oxen, or metals. Coined money appeared around 700 b.c. in western Asia Minor; and in time, a barter economy gave way to a monetary economy. As Greece forged ahead, Athenians became familiar with production loans, simple and compound interest, banks, letters of credit, stock exchanges, and bottomry loans at a high interest rate that amounted to an insurance premium. Capital was mobile; there was speculation, and constant new investment. Industry profited from this mobility, but agriculture suffered in the long run.

The first economic phase has been called the Hellenic, for during it Greece came to take the lead. It was terminated by the conquests of Alexander, and was over by about 330 B.C. The second phase, the Hellenistic, was one in which an essentially Greek civilization was spread by the victories of Alexander. The third phase was that of the Early Roman Empire; the fourth, that of the Late Roman Empire. After the fall of Rome, economic systems of the Classical lands collapsed almost to the level they had occupied at the beginning of the first phase; and for centuries thereafter, they did not recover.

Obviously, Classical economics could be discussed at much greater length, but the foregoing brief summary suffices to reveal just how stimulating the subject can be to the archeologist. In many cases, the economic practices of the first phase had pre-Classic roots, and some clearly seen Classical trends might be projected backward, so to speak, into fully prehistoric times. For example, much archeological effort has been expended in order to discover the circumstances under which plants and animals were first domesticated, and to trace the spread of agriculture and animal husbandry. Noting that grain and livestock were raised together early in the first phase, one might ask whether agriculture encouraged animal husbandry and vice versa. (For grain yields fodder; domestic animals produce manure for fertilizing crops, and perhaps supply motive power for plowing and other agricultural practices.) It is conceivable that some types of agriculture were highly productive but only in conjunction with animal husbandry; and if so, these types would spread only to areas where the appropriate domestic animals were available. It is also conceivable that the notably early emphasis on domestication of plants in the Fertile Crescent to some extent reflected the presence there of animals that were exceptionally amenable to domestication.

Early in the first phase, if not at a much later date also, most trade was over routes that had been established in remote prehistoric times. It is interesting to learn that luxury goods accounted for such a large part of early Classical trade. Long before the rise of the first civilizations, there had been a trade in beautiful mollusk shells; also in obsidian or volcanic glass, a material from which it is possible to knap some exceptionally fine implements. In the New World, just as in the Old, early trade involved mollusk shells, obsidian, copper nuggets, crystals, and other luxury items.

Noting that several Classical and early Asian civilizations developed along river valleys and deltas, one might ask whether flood-plain agriculture was an ineluctable first step in man's rise above a Neolithic level of culture. If so, outside stimulus rather than local invention should be invoked to account for the rise of civilizations that were not "hydraulic," not oriented toward control and utilization of the flood-plain environment. The New World civilizations come to mind in this connection. Seeing how much is known about Classical economics, and recalling that so many elaborate culture trait-complexes of the Near East (Sorenson, no date) reappeared in the early civilizations of Middle America, one might also ask whether any sizeable group of Middle American economic practices hearkens back to some specific Classical civilization. It would also be useful to study Classical shipping, with particular reference to ship's cargo and crew capacity, techniques of navigation, and attitudes toward maritime exploration.

Students of Classical economics have also had to ponder the downfall of Rome, for this was sometimed ascribed to economic factors. One hypothesis blamed this downfall on too much state planning, which strangled individual initiative. A second hypothesis blamed it on too much taxation, a third on the drain of precious metals to the East. In another book (Neill 1969) I have emphasized deterioration of the natural environment in the Mediterranean world, as a result of agriculture, timbering, and other activities of man. But in fairness, economists have also had to consider hypotheses that laid Roman decline to essentially noneconomic factors: too much reliance on slavery, too much intermixture with non-Romans, a decrease in population, debilitating diseases such as malaria, or infiltration by vigorous, aggressive barbarians. Edward Gibbon, in his famous (and often proscribed) *Decline and Fall of the Roman Empire,* blamed much of that decline on the rise of Christianity. Gibbon and his followers pointed out that early Christianity substituted mythology for rationality as a basis for action; emphasized passivity and acceptance, even though in the face of well-nigh intolerable social conditions; and discouraged sociocultural improvement in favor of preparation for existence in an imaginary hereafter.

Many questions are called to mind by investigations into Roman downfall. In early Classical times, the Aryans poured into India, where they found an advanced but rather static civilization in the valley of the Indus River. They brought with them a vigor, an aggressiveness, and a pantheon of nature gods who (like the Greek Olympians) were regarded as manipulable by man. But in time, the Aryan élan bogged down in the passivity and mysticism of Buddhism, the passivity and irrationality of Hinduism. To some extent, India was revitalized by the coming of the Moslems, and then of the British; but

among nations it never attained a stature commensurate with its resources. It became noteworthy for emphasis on religion, and for an
extraordinary amount of human misery and degradation. Can a society become too god-ridden for its own good? Did the remarkably advanced Hopewell culture of the United States decline and vanish because so many man-hours were conscripted into the construction of
burial mounds, the importation of rare materials for the manufacture
of religious paraphernalia, and the constant burying of the most la-
boriously crafted items as grave goods?

Clearly, it would be desirable to search history and archeology for
correlations between sociocultural decline and a rise of religiosity.
Probably, such correlations would prove numerous. If so, the next
question would relate to cause and effect: Did preoccupation with
mythological irrationality bring about sociocultural decline, or did the
members of a declining society turn to mythology for psychological
soothing? It is conceivable that the two processes operated simultaneously, each accelerating the other.

Pursuing a slightly different line of speculation, China's Han Dy-
nasty paralleled the Roman Empire in a good many ways. Subequal in
geographic extent and cultural level, the two declined and fell at
about the same time. Shortly after the last Classical period of Western
civilization had ended, the Middle American civilizations began to fall
one by one; the so-called Classic stage of Middle American culture
came to end. Was it just coincidence that so many early civilizations
declined in sequence, or were there inevitable cultural processes at
work? Or could there have been a worldwide climatic shift, gradual
but nonetheless sufficient to erode the economic foundation of agricultural societies? Such matters warrant investigation, especially in a
discipline that searches for causality and regularities.

Without pursuing the subject at greater length, it will be seen that
the writings of the economists might help the archeologist to frame
some important questions and answers. There is, however, another
reason why the archeologist might wish to become well grounded in
the basic principles of economics: some theorists have held that
there is a vital relation between production and most other aspects of
culture.

By this view, the structure of a society is determined in the long run
by the food quest and the technology involved with it. A society will
develop a set of social relations that are appropriate to its degree of
success in exploiting food resources through its technology, and it
will also invent or come to accept a set of ideologies that justify and

help to maintain the social relations. As a corollary to this view, it is held that a change in technology leads to a change in the economy, with resultant modification of social relations and their supporting ideologies. But some of these relations and tenets may be more resistant to change than others, with the result that a society's culture will have aspects that conflict with or contradict one another. Effort to resolve these contradictions provides the motive power, so to speak, behind culture change.

Some archeologists and other students of culture may regard the aforesaid theory of economic determinism as an oversimplification. Indeed, they may reverse the position of the economic determinists, and hold that the food quest and the related technology are determined socioculturally. Still, in uncivilized societies, there are certain fairly predictable correlations of economy with social structure and ideologies; and the writings of economists, including the great economic theorists, hold much that is of importance to anyone who investigates sociocultural problems. European archeologists, more often than their American colleagues, have turned to this body of literature for aid in the interpretation of raw data recovered through field work.

The field of economics is widely overlapped by that of human geography, with its emphasis on natural resources and the routes along which societies have extended their territories. It is instructive to review some general principles relating to the effect of geography on the human story.

The extreme environments, such as the arctic or the desert, permit a society little choice of action, as compared with the milder environments. In large part, material culture is adjusted to the possibilities and limitations of the environment; and ideologies are so adjusted, at least to some extent. Mineral, water, animal, and plant resources are environmental factors offering the aforesaid possibilities and limitations; so are climate, topography, and soils. The size, shape, and location of a society's territory may affect its historical trends. Even when such trends are controlled by nonenvironmental factors, they are likely to bring about a movement of the society into new territory, or into new habitats of the old. Large-scale migrations may be triggered culturally or environmentally, but the routes they follow are governed principally by the geography of the land and the waters.

Certain environments—desert, grassland, mountain range, sea— can be barriers to the spread of a society; but when that society becomes culturally able to cope with that environment, the former barrier becomes a highway. When a society has successfully populated a given expanse of its favored environment, it may attempt to invade nearby expanses of different environment. If a society's territory is provided with a heavily indented coastline and an abundance of navigable rivers, the members of that society will be encouraged into exploitation of marine resources, and into maritime ventures. Within its sphere of contacts, a society may rise to dominance or sink into oblivion; to a considerable degree, the position it occupies will depend on whether or not it is geographically fit to take advantage of the technological changes that are going on in that sphere.

The foregoing geographic principles were modified from the writings of Derwent Whittlesey (1941), who was concerned principally with the historic period; but reading them, one feels the urge to test their pertinence to prehistoric times. On the one hand, they would be refined by such testing; on the other hand, certain prehistoric episodes would be clearer in the light of them.

Archeology can interact with history, also. The older archeological writings are history-like in being limited to simple narration, and one or two modern archeologists have held out in favor of the old approach to their subject. Even though archeology is becoming scientific, there will probably remain a need for history-like narration of past events, for example in the summarizing chapter of a regional study, or in a work that is intended for a general readership. History differs from most archeology in that its authors can investigate the influence of personality on events. This difference may not be as trenchant as it seems. Some thinkers have guessed that the times call forth the man; that even the great personages of history were caught up in a tide of events, which they might have slowed or speeded, but which they never could have turned completely aside.

At any rate, there are at least four ways in which archeology can interact with history. First, as already noted, Classical archeology combines historical and archeological data with elements from the humanities. The approach of this discipline has been used outside the Classical lands, for example in Indonesia, where many ruined or restored buildings, statues, and other artifacts date from ancient yet literate times. Second, protohistoric archeology combines historical with archeological data, investigates past cultures, and focuses upon times and places in which preliterate peoples coexisted with literate ones. In the United States, protohistoric times may be regarded as those in which American Indian tribes were still engaged in their aboriginal pursuits, but were under ocasional observation by Spaniards or other early European explorers. Third, several new archeological approaches, such as industrial archeology and historic site archeology, deal with time periods for which written records are abundant yet are not highly revealing in some regards.

Fourth, much so-called ethnography is from a body of literature more widely considered as historical. For example, in the eastern United States, most of the Indian tribes were exterminated or dispossessed before they were visited by anyone whose primary concern was their ethnography; and knowledge of tibal customs must be gleaned from old writings by traders, travellers, priests, administrators, and other people who spent some time on the frontier of white settlement. Such gleanings are appropriately known as ethnohistory. In many parts of the world, an archeological-ethnographic comparison is likely to involve ethnohistorical data abstracted from historical works.

Early historic American Indian cultures have been studied mostly by ethnologists using ethnographic data from a body of literature generally catalogued as historical, while the late prehistoric antecedents of those cultures have been studied by archeologists. As noted in a previous chapter, not much effort has been made in the United States to trace the culture of a society from late prehistoric into historic times. The archeological approach has differed from the ethnological, especially in shying away from human concerns. Of course, some difference between the two approaches is justifiable, considering the nature of the materials with which the respective specialists have to work; but obviously there should be a search for cultural continuities from late prehistoric into historic times. Indeed, since the contact period was a crucial one for American Indian societies, and since the topic of culture contact is of enormous importance today, every effort should be made to correlate the archeological findings with the ethnohistorical and historical.

Some work has been done along this line. Thus, for the Indian River area of Florida, Irving Rouse (1951) erected a series of local periods, extending from early prehistoric times into the nineteenth century, and he made considerable use of historical documents in the interpretation of archeological material from early historic sites.

More recently, William M. Gardner (1969) studied regional variants of the Fort Walton culture, which succeeded the Weedon Island culture in the Florida Panhandle and some nearby areas. The Fort Walton Period extended from late prehistoric times into early historic. According to written records, the Fort Walton culture area was occupied in early historic times by several Muskhogean tribes or chiefdoms. The westernmost of these spoke Choctaw. Linguistic kinship to Choctaw decreased progressively toward the east. At the extreme eastern end of the area, Muskhogeans were replaced by the Tocobaga Timucua, bearers of the Safety Harbor culture rather than the Fort Walton, and speakers of an Arawakan tongue. Gardner found that in the area of the Fort Walton archeological culture, shell-tempered pottery decreased progressively eastward from the Choctaw-speaking region, being replaced by grit or sand tempering. Incised and punctated decoration, as opposed to incised decoration alone, increased toward the east. The Pensacola series of pottery types characterized the Pensacola, Mobile, and Sawokli, whose language was Choctaw. Farther east, the Fort Walton series characterized the Chatot, whose language was Choctaw-related. Still farther east, the Lake Jackson series typified the Apalachee, whose language was not particularly related to Choctaw except in being Muskhogean. The Pinellas series typified the Tocobaga Timucua.

Although it deals with regional problems, Gardner's paper has wide implications. It would appear that, contrary to previous supposition, it may be possible to identify ethnic groupings within an archeological culture area. Gardner thought it would be possible to trace such groupings back into Weedon Island times.

Strangely enough, there are ways in which archeology could profitably interact with sociology, even though the latter discipline is rather generally committed to the study of modern civilizations. Much of sociology is concerned with social institutions. These, by definition, extend through large numbers of societies, have existed through long periods of time, and are characterized by an elaboration of both material and nonmaterial culture around fundamental human functions. Material culture trait-complexes, associated with these institutions, range from the utilitarian to the symbolic. It would be desirable to follow the social institutions (family, religion, government, business) from archeological times through ethnological to sociological.

It has sometimes been held that the institutions of past societies cannot be reconstructed through archeological techniques. Perhaps they cannot be reconstructed in their entirety, but selected aspects of them can be clarified. As an illustration, postholes often reveal a village to have included a number of huts, each with a hearth; and it is reasonable to suppose that a hut sheltered a family. Patrilocal residence has been inferred for certain societies in which the women's manufactures are homogeneous in style, the men's heterogenous, over the same wide area; for a man usually remained throughout life in his own village, but a woman would move to another village if she married a man who resided there. Division of labor within the family might be indicated by grave goods; in a prehistoric cemetery on Gotland, sealing harpoons were buried with men, fishhooks with old women. Cave paintings of eastern Spain include hunting scenes, and the hunters are always men; but a woman is shown gathering wild honey. Healed fractures in skeletal remains may reveal the men of some particular society to have suffered more broken bones than the women, a circumstance correlated with assignment of more vigorous activities to the male.

Although religion supposedly deals with the immaterial, it has generally been manifested materially, and to a greater extent than some other institutions. It has left abundant archeological traces in burial practices, iconography, priestly trappings, domestic shrines, ceremonial centers, and temple furnishings. One gets the impression that religion had much to do with the development of a social organization above that of a tribe. A ceremonial center, serving a number of scattered villages, tended to unify them, and the high priest came to wield secular power. In both the Old World and the New, a good many of the most advanced cultures were theocracies. Badly needed is a general assessment of the role of religion in prehistoric societies. Archeological materials are probably adequate for such an assessment.

Early stages of government are not easily recognized archeologically. To judge from ethnography, the conduct of a tribal society was regulated in large part by intangible precepts. Some charismatic individuals might acquire a following; certain lineages were apt to be especially prominent in public affairs, and clans to have specific responsibilities. Clans might occasionally be recognizable archeologically, through their specific productions or their totemic representations; but in general, it would be unusual to excavate anything revelatory of tribal government, except perhaps the traces of a structure in which councils were held. At the level of a chiefdom, government leaves more evidence of its existence, but even there it may not be separable from religion: the ceremonial center may function as a council house, the councilmen may include priests, and the paramount figure may be a high priest. The separation of church from state was a slow process, and even some of the early civilizations did not bring it about. Indeed, the process is far from complete in some parts of the modern world. Unlike sociologists, archeologists might at times have to consider government and religion as two aspects of a single institution.

In contrast with government, the institution of business can be traced back probably to Upper Paleolithic times, when mollusk shells from the Mediterranean were traded far inland in Europe. Upper Paleolithic trade may have been little more than the fortuitous passage of small items from one band of hunters to another, along unpredictable routes. But soon after Paleolithic times, trade routes became definite and far-flung; along them passed a variety of goods, both finished products and raw materials. It is unfortunate that so little effort has been made, especially in the New World, to determine the approximate courses of the ancient routes; for along them passed not just material objects but ideas of every sort. Archeological needs include an assessment of trade routes as a factor in the diffusion of culture. Such assessment is feasible, for in many cases it would be possible to pinpoint the origin of trade goods found in a site.

In the archeological record, business may not be manifested materially to the same extent as religion, but an investigation into prehistoric business is not limited to matters of trade. For example, evidence of craft specialization has been excavated. From the Modoc site in Illinois, Melvin L. Fowler and Paul W. Parmelee (1959) reported a human burial that included a cache of about 160 bird bones, mostly goose radii but a few tarsometatarsals of the sandhill crane. A minority of these bones had been worked into awls. In the culture that yielded this cache, a special type of awl was made from the limb bones of large birds, and I would interpret the burial as that of a professional awl-maker who was interred with a sampling of his raw materials and finished products. There is a close parallel with a prehistoric burial uncovered during the Tennessee Valley excavations: a professional flint knapper had been buried with his bone and antler flaking tools, a supply of flint blanks, and some of his finished projectile points. His workmanship was so distinctive that points made by him were recognizable in distant sites to which they had been imported. In Mexico, certain prehistoric societies turned out an abundance of ceramic figurines that were made in a mold. Mold-made ceramics are good evidence of craft specialization, for with a mold, one ceramicist can supply the needs of an entire community.

At times, village specialization is also detectable from the archeological record. Near Port Richey, Pasco County, Florida, there existed a large midden of Weedon Island times. The site, which has lately been hauled off for fill, is known as Big Midden. It was unusual especially in the depth of the midden debris, the vast quantity of sherds, and the presence of limestone pebbles in great abundance. The pebbles could easily have been acquired a few miles to the west, along the coastline where the sea had exposed and cut into an eroded limestone formation; but their presence in the midden in such great numbers was puzzling until it was recalled that most of the sherds were tempered with pulverized limestone. The site was bordered to the north and east by a small, intermittent stream with clay deposits along its bed. Just east of the site, there were a series of large, irregular pits that had been dug into the stream bed. I interpreted these pits as evidence of aboriginal clay mining; the pebbles were to have been pulverized into tempering. Mollusk shells, and implements cut from the walls thereof, were numerous and could have been potters' tools. In other words, the Big Midden site was locally unique in the concentration of raw materials and tools necessary to the potter's art; and I inferred that its occupants specialized in ceramics, turning out Pasco Plain bowls in quantities that far exceeded village needs.

Warfare may not be listed as an institution, but it has been of sociological concern, and some aspects of it are evidenced archeologically. I have already commented on human bones pierced by projectile points, and skulls smashed by the blow of a mace.

Less direct evidence of warfare was provided by a Weedon Island Period site in New Port Richey, Florida. Called the Homecrest site, it was unique (for this area and period) in combining decorated pottery with village midden debris; for the local village sites of this period yield plain pottery, the decorated types having been reserved for mound burial. It is not surprising that one of these sites should have an abundance of decorated sherds in an otherwise ordinary midden context, for the Indians acquired or made a great many decorated vessels, and must have kept them somewhere while awaiting the next construction of a mound. It was not customary for a village to keep the decorated vessels that would be buried with its dead; if it had been, decorated sherds would turn up consistently on village sites. It is reasonable to suppose that a single village served as a repository for the fine vessels that were destined for eventual interment in a mound. The midden debris of the Homecrest site consisted of a thin layer of mollusk shells with abundant vertebrate remains, charcoal, a scattering of flint artifacts, and numerous sherds referable in large part to the decorated types of the Weedon Island Period. The outline of the midden formed a sharply defined, nearly perfect oval, and there was an abrupt change from culture-bearing deposit inside the

oval to sterile soil outside. I infer that the village had been surrounded by a palisade, inside of which the villagers had left their
debris.

Palisaded villages were common in Florida during early historic
times. I had thought of them as a post–Weedon Island development.
Only once in Florida has palisading been demonstrated through excavation; this was at a site of the Fort Walton Period, which succeeded Weedon Island in parts of the Gulf coast lying north of the
study area. Perhaps palisades, like temple mounds, spread in advance
of other ideas that remodeled Weedon Island culture into Safety Harbor. A single village that served as a regional depot for ceremonial
ceramics—this too is a cultural development that seems a bit precocious for Weedon Island times. At any rate, a palisaded village implies
that the villagers felt themselves to be in danger of attack. The Homecrest site is indicative of warfare at a time when the local variant of
Weedon Island culture was first being exposed to strong influences
from outside.

Turning from sociology, archeology can also interact with psychology. Thus, the archeologists John M. Goggin and Frank H. Sommer, III
(1949) made the following comment about the decoration of prehistoric pottery from Upper Matecumbe Key, Monroe County, Florida:
"Design is conceived in terms of small units and their regular repetition. In this way esthetic experience is organized in terms of unity
rather than disparity. To follow a design around the rim of a vessel
would be to experience the constant repetition of identity." The comment takes the reader into the field of psychology. So does a study of
Moche pottery for evidence regarding the extent to which the potters
were conformists. This study was an outgrowth of an earlier one on
"doodling," scribbling in an idle moment; it had been discovered
that the scribblers' feelings of social pressure had much to do with
the freedom or restriction of their designs. Moche modeled pottery
furnished psychological data of quite another sort. The Moche (= Mochica) culture, which flourished about 200 to 700 A.D. on the north
coast of Peru, turned out some exceptionally fine, naturalistically
modeled and painted ceramics, including portrait heads and figurines
showing numerous details of daily life. But Moche pottery is also
noteworthy for an extraordinary emphasis on the erotic. Many vessels
were modeled to portray coitus (sometimes in unusual positions),
multiple unions, fellatio, cunnilingus, *soixante-neuf*, sodomy, bestial-
ity, male masturbation, female masturbation with the aid of an artificial instrument, pederasty, male and female homosexuality, and

sadism. Other vessels were modeled in the shape of a man, skeleton, or monster with an enormous phallus, while still others portrayed grotesquely deformed, mutilated, or diseased individuals. While the role of these vessels in Moche life is not clear, they provide some insight into the sexual psychology of their makers.

It may be mentioned in passing that in the archeological literature, erotic art has been neglected. Examples of it have seldom been described, much less figured. But such art might be revelatory not only of sexual psychology and customs but also of culture contact. That is to say, among human societies there has been considerable variation in sexual behavior, the portrayal of it, and the social role of it; the patterning of such behavior is determined socioculturally, and can be transferred from one society to another. Unfortunately, in the past the archeological tendency has been to shy away from description of material that might throw light on such patterning. When Gordon F. Ekholm searched for Asian influences in prehistoric America, he concluded that erotic or sexual motifs were almost lacking from the Classic period art of Middle America. I wonder if this is true, or if specimens exist but have gone unreported. Certainly, many other New World areas have yielded specimens that were never described. For example, it is well known that sites in Panama have produced a variety of small figurines and ornaments in gold, but nowhere have I seen published reference to the fact that this gold work includes male and female figures performing sexual acts.

In the eastern United States, erotic portrayals have been found, especially in sites of the Southern Cult or of the Long-Nosed God. I do not refer simply to the "bilobed arrow" motif which some archeologists have regarded as a bit of phallic symbolism in Cult iconography. When Warren K. Moorehead dug into the spectacular Cult site of Etowah, Georgia, he found scrotum-shaped concretions, each of which had been placed in the pelvic region of a skeleton. He threw them away, and their existence would not be known if local residents had not salvaged them. Etowah also produced clay phalli.The Spiro site in Oklahoma and the Gahagan site in Louisiana both produced large effigy pipes in the shape of copulating frogs and human couples. Tobacco pipes in the shape of the male genitalia came from both the Lamar and the Mossy Oak sites near Macon, Georgia, and the Macon site itself yielded a clay phallus with a cross inscribed on the glans; I do not know the cultural context of these specimens, but they were from an area that was dominated in early historic times by the Muskhogeans, whose late prehistoric ancestors were responsible for some Southern Cult and Long-Nosed God representations. In the 1700s, the Creek Indians of Georgia would paint various figures on the clay-plastered walls of a ceremonial house; the pioneer naturalist-explorer William Bartram (1791) described some of these paintings as "obscene . . . the privates of men are sometimes represented."

Directly or indirectly, sexuality has played such a major role in human affairs that archeological evidence of it should be studied vigorously, not diffidently.

A further possible interaction of archeology with psychology relates to religion. It would be very desirable to trace religious belief from paleoanthropological into sociological times, with emphasis not on its social role but on its psychological foundations. It is often said that religion distinguishes man from the beasts, but this little homily, stemming from Descartes, has obscured the reality of the situation: religion consists of overt, socioculturally determined responses to innate genetic urges that man shares with lower organisms. The "awe-struck" behavior of a chimpanzee when confronted by an incomprehensible object—this is proto-religious behavior at its simplest. The incomprehensibility of so many manifestations of nature, especially to hominids at a low cultural level; the biological events of sleeping and waking, with which Neanderthal man perhaps equated death and an afterlife; dreaming, another biological event, one easily giving rise to belief that the personality can exist in a world other than the real one; the innate impulse toward survival, assuaged by the notion that death is not really the end; the widespread mammalian urge that is gratified by the discovery of paternal strength; the equally widespread mammalian urge that is gratified by maternal care; the impulse, ubiquitous among social species, to accept and follow a leader—these are the foundations of religion, along with temporary mental disorders (so-called religious experience) that result from hysterical states, diseased conditions, or toxic chemicals taken into the system.

Upon these foundations have been built an elaborate superstructure of fictions: animistic belief in sentient rocks, trees, grottos, volcanos, and other insensate objects; a long series of heavens, nirvanas, zions, and happy hunting grounds; an array of strong father-figure gods and of occasionally severe but usually warm mother-goddesses; various almighty leaders who, being imaginary, do not share the mortality and fallibility of flesh-and-blood ones. Where these imaginings are given concrete expression, as in burial practices or in iconography, they come within archeological purview.

It would also be gratifying to have psychological studies on the mentality of shamans and charlatans who claim to have special rapport with imaginary supernatural beings; but I suppose these studies would involve an interaction of psychology with sociology rather than with archeology. Still, the latter discipline probably could contribute to any investigation into the way societies have been manipulated, cynically or otherwise, by religious systems that take advantage of basic human drives.

It would be easy to cite other disciplines with which archeology might interact. It may not be possible to recover the cultural ecology of vanished societies; but cultural ecologists will reach the point in their studies where they can offer generalizations, and these will be of much archeological interest. Human ecology could and should be traced back into the Pleistocene. Political science offers stimulating ideas, especially about the processes whereby governmental power is acquired, exercised, and retained. But perhaps the point has been made that a scientific archeology, taking its place in a science of man, would have a great variety of directions in which it could expand.

CHAPTER SEVEN

Directions in Archeology

The preceding chapters have necessitated at least brief excursions into biogeography, ecology, systematics, botany and its applications, a selection of zoological sciences, geology, oceanography, parasitology and medicine, paleontology, evolution, and climatology. These are the fields with which a scientific archeology would most frequently and profitably interact in a science of man, the fields upon which archeologists would most frequently draw when trying to extract the maximum information from archeological sites. But almost any environmental science might, on occasion, aid in the interpretation of archeological findings. There is no predicting when some bit of specialized knowledge, seemingly remote from cultural studies, will throw a welcome light on a problem of wide archeological interest. One illustration of this point may be given.

In 1903, 1906, and 1917, Clarence B. Moore dug into the Crystal River site, Citrus County, Florida. The site lay about four miles east of the Gulf of Mexico, near a river. It offered two temple mounds, each with a ramp; two burial mounds; a long midden of shell; several mounds of heaped-up shell; and various other features. In one of the burial mounds, Moore found decorated pottery, much of it reminiscent of midwestern Hopewell types. There were incised, modeled, and negative-painted vessels, some with tetrapodal supports. Also in the mound were copper objects, including discs, ear ornaments, a conjoined tube, and an embossed plate. Likewise present were sheets of mica, pendants of rock crystal, pipes of soapstone, and celts of diorite—artifacts of imported materials if not workmanship. Moore also discovered numerous plummet-shaped pendants of stone and shell, as well as ornaments and dippers of shell. In later years, several other archeologists dug at the locality, or analyzed the material therefrom. In spite of these studies, in 1951 Ripley P. Bullen felt constrained to characterize the site as "enigmatic." By 1953, when Bullen correlated his own results with those of other excavators at Crystal River, at least two dozen published works had dealt with the site. It appeared to have been a ceremonial center that was used, perhaps not continuously, during three culture periods.

As usual, the archeological importance of the locality did not prevent its being menaced by the activities of modern man. Houses were built on the midden, and a start was made toward destruction of the larger temple mound for the sake of its shell content, which would be used as fill. Fortunately, in 1962 the site became a state park, and removal of its contents was halted. In the meanwhile, it was slowly becoming evident, at least to a few archeologists, that many comparatively advanced culture trait-complexes had reached North America from the south, not by gradual diffusion but by great leaps; and in 1964, Edward V. MacMichael was ready to see midwestern Hopewell as having been derived from Veracruz by way of Crystal River. MacMichael had his opponents, however.

When the Crystal River site was made into a park, it was cleared of heavy brush, and this clearing revealed significant features that had been overlooked previously. On each side of the larger burial mound was a stela, a large, standing boulder. The two boulders were equidistant from the mound. One of them had been rudely incised with a human head. The ramp of each temple mound pointed slightly to the east of a stela, and the maximum horizontal dimension of each boulder was at right angles to a line leading from the stela to its associated temple mound. The face of the incised stela was turned away from its temple mound. Bullen (1966) realized that the whole arrangement was typical of lowland Maya sites. There were ceremonial deposits—a cache of flint chips, a cobbled pathway, food remains, and charcoal—beneath or in front of the incised stela. The charcoal gave a radiocarbon date of about 440 A.D. Beneath the second stela was a cache of flint chips, along with food remains and two sherds of a common indigenous pottery type. After Bullen's paper had been written, a third stela was discovered. Smaller than the others, and rudely incised, it had been displaced probably by some activity of modern man.

Next, Clark Hardman, Jr. (1971) brought to the study of the Crystal River site his special knowledge of astronomy, a science that no one suspected would throw light on Florida archeology. He pointed out that the major features of the site had been aligned with the solstitial and equinoctial positions of the sun. The incised face of the first stela was turned toward the sunrise at summer solstice. If an observer stood cn the cobblestoned area and faced the stela, he would be looking over its right side into the sunset. If he stood on one of the larger rocks beside this boulder and then looked west, he could align the sun, the top of the boulder, and some aspect of one of the shell mounds. The displaced stela may originally have capped that shell mound. If the observer on the larger rock made a half-turn right at sunset on summer solstice, he would see the sun over the second stela. From the latter boulder, at winter solstice he would see the sun go down directly behind one of the shell mounds.

The second stela and the larger burial mound formed an equinoctial alignment: at the time of the equinox, an observer at the second stela would see the sun rise over the center of the burial mound.

Other astronomical observations were possible at the Crystal River site, which could be thought of as a primitive solar observatory or as a huge calendar. Hardman believed that priest-chiefs, presiding over this center, could determine the day of the year to within a week's accuracy. In its arrangement, to permit calendrical determination through observation of the sun, the site reveals impressive similarities to those of the lowland Maya. Hardman also showed that the Moundville site of Alabama and the Winterville site of Mississippi had been constructed to form solar observatories; and he listed several other United States sites with solstitial or equinoctial alignments if not both. No doubt archeologists, following Hardman's lead, will search for alignments comparable to those of Crystal River. For example, the Big Circle mound group of Palm Beach County, Florida, includes several alignments that apparently were chosen very carefully.

Thus, knowledge of astronomy has opened a whole new chapter in United States archeology.

The content of this chapter, and of the succeeding one, may seem sprawling, diffuse. This is inevitable; environmental archeology is so new, and so rapidly expanding, that it has not yet been brought into any sort of order, or arranged into any disciplinary framework. True, a few workers have tried to define the experimental procedures, terminology, logical schemes, and generalizations that they regard as characterizing environmental archeology. However, that discipline persists in escaping its boundaries.

Environmental archeology was called by that name and was fairly well organized in England at a time when it was just beginning in the United States. As an illustration of this point, in 1956, with H. James Gut and Pierce Brodkorb, I attempted to extract as much cultural, environmental, and zoological data as possible from certain vertebrate and invertebrate remains. These had been excavated at four roughly coeval sites in the same culture area and subarea of Florida. As far as I know this was the first fairly intensive effort in the southeastern United States to discover some environmental relations of a single culture through the application of zoological, anatomical, taxonomic, and ecological knowledge to a wide range of faunal remains. But simultaneously with the appearance of that paper, there appeared I. W. Cornwall's large book (1956) on the identification of mammal bones for the European archeologist—and in that work, Cornwall was described as a lecturer in a Department of Environmental Archeology at the London University Institute of Archaeology, where candidates for the Diploma in Prehistoric Archaeology had to take a course in human and animal osteology!

It is natural that environmental considerations have so frequently commanded the attention of Europeans. Dominant themes of European history include warfare over natural resources and the establishment of colonies for the exploitation of such resources. As already noted, some European theorists have emphasized economics as a determinant of culture, and of course economics is closely involved with aspects of the environment, especially natural resources and trade routes. Any list of "books that changed the world" will include several by Europeans who were concerned with environment, especially as related to the economics of societies. Among these books are Adam Smith's *An Inquiry into the Nature and Causes of the Wealth of Nations*, Thomas Malthus's *An Essay on the Principle of Population*, Karl Marx's *Das Kapital*, Halford J. Mackinder's *Democratic Ideals and Reality*, and Oswald Spengler's *The Decline of the West*. Another European book, equally seminal but in the natural sciences, was Charles Darwin's *The Origin of Species by Means of Natural Selection or the Preservation of Favored Races in the Struggle for Life*. This work drew attention to environment as a factor controlling evolution. Thus, the European intellectual atmosphere has long been conducive to investigation of past environments.

Furthermore, in Europe, and in the Classical lands where most of the archeology was carried on by Europeans, the time span of human occupancy was very long, so long as to have overlapped several profound changes in climate, flora, fauna, and the relationship of land to sea. Evidence of environmental change was not something that had to be searched for painstakingly; it fairly cried out for notice. Also, some of the world's most important cultural advances were first made in Europe or in some Classical lands peripheral thereto; and it was only natural to wonder what environment had to do with this cultural precocity.

Main currents in European environmental archeology have included the use of environmental materials for dating, environmental clues to the existence and extent of archeological sites, the effect of environmental conditions on the preservation of archeological remains, the economic basis of prehistoric societies, testing of the theory of economic determinism, the discovery of trade routes through location of sources for raw materials, identification of the (usually fragmentary) plant and animal remains from archeological sites, the spread of agriculture, and the spread of metallurgy. The principal accomplishments and aims of European environmental archeology have been described at considerable length in the writings of V. Gordon Childe, Grahame Clark, S. J. de Laet, Stuart Piggott, and others. In the next three chapters, which review some directions of environmental archeology, the European accomplishments are not neglected, but the American ones are considered in more detail because they are not as well known and have not previously been summarized.

Several of the earliest excursions into American environmental archeology were efforts to determine just what was to be found in shell middens. Some middens were so large that they were taken to be natural formations rather than cultural deposits, and much digging was necessary to prove that they included scattered artifacts from top to bottom, and had been heaped up by men. Thomas Jefferson determined to his own satisfaction that middens were man-made, but not until the latter 1800s had enough digging been done to warrant unreserved acceptance of Jefferson's view. In 1903, D. W. Prentiss discovered a previously unknown species of mink in coastal middens of Maine, thus arousing zoological interest in archeofaunal specimens. In 1916, E. W. Gifford produced one of the first detailed studies on the composition of New World midden; his work was done in California, where coastal shell heaps had attracted the attention of several early archeologists. But American environmental archeology did not begin to grow until about the 1930s and 1940s. Then, it was sparked by zoologists who believed that sites would yield faunal remains of much zoological importance. These workers believed, too, that cultural data could be extracted from such remains, and urged a rapport of archeologists and zoologists in preserving and analyzing excavated materials of a zoological nature.

In 1929, Hildegarde Howard studied bird bones from a California midden. The bones included those of young birds belonging to resident species, and those of adult birds belonging to migrant species. She inferred that the midden was occupied during the warm season when the residents nested, and during the cold season when the migrants passed through. In 1938, the ornithologist Lyndon L. Hargrave issued a plea for preservation of all biological materials from prehistoric sites. He pointed out that such materials must be identified by competent biologists working in the appropriate fields. He thought that sites might yield the remains of extinct birds. More importantly, there might be evidence of local changes in the bird fauna, changes correlated with fluctuations of climate or other environmental factors. Hargrave noted that excavated biological materials, although perhaps not immediately revealing, might prove exceedingly useful to future students who would have improved techniques of analysis.

The investigation of archeofaunal remains, with special emphasis on their zoological interest, has continued to the present. Prentiss's sea mink is the only extinct vertebrate to have come to light in North American shell middens, ignoring a few species (e.g., the passenger pigeon and the great auk) that were exterminated by civilized man. And as it happened, the sea mink existed up into historic times; a few skins of it were handled by fur traders. But numerous organisms have turned up archeologically at localities well outside their present respective ranges. In 1939, Hargrave reported on bird bones from 22 abandoned Indian dwellings of northeastern Arizona and southern Utah. Some of the sites were in the San Francisco Mountains, others in a plateau region. In age, the sites ranged from fairly late prehistoric to early historic. In their vicinity, the modern bird fauna was extensively sampled, in order to procure comparative material. Bones from the plateau sites included two species, the saw-whet owl and the turkey, not present in the area in modern times. Domestication of the turkey was inferred. Bones from the montane sites included seven species (scaled quail, Gambel's quail, sandhill crane, thick-billed parrot, short-eared owl, screech owl, American magpie) no longer present in the general area; four (snow goose, prairie falcon, long-eared owl, saw-whet owl) now rare there; and five (pied-billed grebe, Canada goose, green-winged teal, bald eagle, coot) now lacking from the vicinity of the sites. Hargrave inferred that the inhabitants of the montane sites had been living under environmental conditions quite different from the present ones.

In 1957, Paul W. Parmelee and Donald F. Hoffmeister reported remains of the prairie spotted skunk from the Modoc Rock Shelter, Randolph County, Illinois. These remains were scattered through levels dating from about 4500 B.C. to 2500 B.C. The species had not been reported from modern Illinois. The site also yielded remains of Shaw's pocket-gopher, a species that presently does not range quite as far south in Illinois as the Modoc vicinity. In 1958, from the Cahokia site of central Illinois, Parmelee reported bones of the fisher, another mammal no longer ranging so far south. Cahokia was occupied in late prehistoric times.

Also in 1958, Parmelee described the remains of rare, vanishing, or extinct birds from a number of Illinois sites. (By "rare" was meant rare in Illinois today, however abundant elsewhere.) The sites ranged in age from fairly early prehistoric to late prehistoric. Noteworthy species included the white pelican, brown pelican, trumpeter swan, whistling swan, swallow-tailed kite, Mississippi kite, greater prairie chicken, sandhill crane, marbled godwit, whimbrel, long-billed curlew, passenger pigeon, Carolina parakeet, ivory-billed woodpecker, and common raven. Parmelee noted the comparative abundance of deer and waterfowl remains in sites older than the late prehistoric. There was evidence of more selective hunting in the late prehistoric sites, and Parmelee attributed this to the arrival of the bow and arrow. He noted that tools were made from deer and turkey bones; beads were cut from eagle and swan wing bones; the ulna of a whooping crane had been made into a whistle or flute.

Ichthyologists began to take an interest in fish remains from archeological sites, especially in the Southwest. Ever since the fourth glaciation began to retreat, the general ecological trend of the Southwest had been progressive drying, with the concomitant disappearance or restriction of many waters. Accordingly, fish distribution had been restricted or fragmented, and the ichthyologists suspected, correctly, that some species had been more widely distributed in past times. In 1955, Robert R. Miller described fish remains from sites of the lower Colorado River basin, Arizona. In 1961, Frederick R. Gehlbach and Miller reviewed fishes from sites of northern New Mexico. They found the longnose gar in a site near the Colorado River, from which stream the species is now lacking; and they called attention to portrayals of garfish on pottery from sites of the upper Rio Grande, another area today without gars. The blue sucker also occurred in a site of the upper Rio Grande, outside its present range.

Mollusks also yielded proof of shifting geographic ranges, and of extirpations resulting from modern silting or polluting of streams. In 1956, Parmelee compared past with present populations of freshwater mussels in Illinois.

More than any other state, Florida provided evidence of shifting ranges in vertebrates, invertebrates, and plants. However, I defer discussion of Florida material, since it will be taken up later in a different connection.

While archeofaunal remains were being analyzed primarily for zoological data, some zoologists began to concern themselves more and more with cultural problems also. Often but not invariably, they coauthored with archeologists in this work. In 1958, Parmelee reported 21 species of marine shells from Illinois sites. These shells began to appear in preceramic times, and became more numerous as the millennia went by. Illinois Indians worked the imported shells into spoons, pendants, dippers, and beads. Parmelee did not attempt to identify the waters from which the shells came. Most of the species range widely along the southern coasts of the United States, in both Atlantic and Gulf waters. Thus, their origin cannot be pinpointed. The lightning conch is likely to have been taken in Florida waters, the yellow helmet and jasper dwarf olive along the Atlantic coast somewhere south of Cape Hatteras.

In 1959, the archeologist Melvin L. Fowler and the zoologist Parmelee discussed the interpretation of ecological data from the Modoc Rock Shelter. They concluded that the site had first been occupied not long after the Valders substage of the fourth glaciation had reached its peak. At most times, the Indians were gathering mollusks in variety and abundance. The mollusk fauna had changed little from the time of earliest occupancy to the present.

Ten species of fishes were identified from Modoc. Among these, there was a predominance of kinds that could be taken in the shallows or backwaters. Turtle remains were mostly of kinds that could be taken in such places, or on land. Fishes and turtles characteristic of the deep, fast water were poorly represented. Bird remains, with a predominance of waterfowl, suggested that much hunting was done along a river or in the marshes; but some of the birds, as well as the eastern cottontail and the prairie spotted skunk, were taken in prairie or brushland. Turkey bones were few. The white-tailed deer was the most important prey species, but smaller mammals were also taken.

Opossum remains were common in this site as compared with later ones. Tools were made of deer and turkey bones. A cache of 160 goose bones (Canada goose and either snow or blue goose) and 6 sandhill crane bones accompanied a human burial; some had been made into awls. (This is the burial that I regarded as providing evidence of craft specialization.)

A terrestrial snail, *Allongona profunda*, was found only in the lowest levels of the Modoc site. Today this mollusk ranges only into northern Illinois, where it inhabits cool, damp, wooded areas; and the circumstance bolsters the evidence that the rock shelter was first occupied during or soon after cool, moist Valders time. But there was not much indication of any post-Valders change in the local ecology.

During the earliest period of the site's occupancy, the Indians took a wide assortment of animal prey. During the middle part, they relied heavily on fishes, snails, and clams. During the latter part, they concentrated on deer and waterfowl, and may have used the shelter only as a hunting camp to be occupied in the fall. Hunting tools, notably projectile points, were most numerous in the period between 3000 and 2000 B.C. In terms of response to environment, habitation of the site was divided into three phases: initial occupation, local adaptation, and specialized adaptation.

Also in 1959, Parmelee described the use of mammal skulls and jaws by prehistoric Indians of Illinois. The study was of more than local interest, for the working of mammal jaws into ornaments had been rather characteristic of the midwestern Hopewell culture, an advanced culture for its time; and archeologists had wondered whether such ornaments, found in other areas, represented Hopewell influence. Summarizing the literature and reporting new material, Parmelee showed worked mammal jaws to have had a wide distribution in time and space. In Illinois, ornaments were cut from the jaws of the black bear, raccoon, wolverine, otter, badger, domestic dog, coyote, gray wolf, puma, bobcat, white-tailed deer, and man. While these objects were concentrated in Hopewell sites, they also occured on earlier and later horizons. The Hopewell specimens were the most neatly finished.

Quite a few other zoologists concerned themselves with cultural affairs as seen in the light of archeofaunal remains. Conversely, in 1948 the archeologist John M. Goggin began to concern himself with zoological and other environmental matters. His approach was pragmatic: he summarized the kinds of environmental data that archeologists might be expected to recover from excavation of Florida Indian sites. He drew attention to the way cooperation of archeologists with natural scientists had aided the interpretation of a cave site in Oregon, the Boylston Street fishweir in Massachusetts, and the Grassy Island site, also in Massachusetts. He pointed out that the approach of these studies had been developed in the Old World, where a sequence of cultures spanned numerous ecological changes; but he suggested that refined analysis would permit detection of such changes in the New World even though the cultural time span was shorter there.

According to Goggin, Florida sites revealed five kinds of ecological changes. First, there had been a rise of sea level, the sea having encroached upon some sites that were originally built on dry land. Second, there had been a rise of ground-water level, the water table having encroached upon some interior sites that had once been dry. This latter rise would have been concomitant with that of sea level, but could also have been affected by increased precipitation or (locally) by the natural partial damming of a stream. Third, there had been changes in local ecology. These were noted in coastal sites, where oysters had appeared at one time but disappeared at another, to be replaced by coquina clams, Donax. (A comparable situation exists at a few sites in Louisiana, where oysters are replaced by a clam, Rangia.) In several prehistoric culture periods of the Southeast, oysters were gathered in quantity by coastal peoples; and a few middens or levels thereof, containing marine shells but not oysters, were probably accumulated when local water conditions did not meet the oysters' rather rigid environmental requirements.

Fourth, Goggin noted changes in faunal composition. Thus, the West Indian top shell (Livona) is virtually ubiquitous in middens of the lower east coast of Florida, but the species does not inhabit the state today; the nearest modern occurrence is in the Cay Sal Banks, between Cuba and the Florida Keys. Fifth, there had been change in the size and proportions of certain freshwater mollusks. This had been noted by the pioneer Florida archeologists, Jeffries Wyman and Clarence B. Moore, while E. S. Morse had reported something similar in the shells of Maine middens. Freshwater middens of Florida are composed of the shells of a mussel (Unio), a small snail (Vivipara, also called Paludina), and a large snail (Pomacea, also called Ampullaria). The two snails were comparatively small in preceramic times, became larger in early ceramic times, and then became small again; they have continued small to the present. The Vivipara of early ceramic times differed from earlier and later ones in certain shell proportions.

Goggin's remarks on sea-level changes stimulated a good bit of work. In 1956, at a meeting of the Florida Anthropological Society, I discussed submerged sites along the Gulf coast of peninsular Florida. At one shallowly submerged flint quarry, just south of what I have called the study area, there was "horizontal stratigraphy": pottery of late types occurred on the fore-dune, earlier types were in the inter-tidal zone, and projectile points of preceramic varieties were abundant farther out in the water. Flint chipping of uncertain age was noted two miles offshore.

In 1957, I attempted to explain why the east coast of peninsular Florida, but not the west, offered middens of the Late Preceramic Period and of the succeeding Orange Period, which latter was characterized by the earliest Florida pottery. The west coast, heavily embayed and with a rich marine fauna, provided an ideal environment for littoral existence; and one would expect that coast to have been the more heavily populated during Late Preceramic and Orange times, when the Florida Indians were rather consistently living on the seacoast and the banks of the larger rivers, and were subsisting mostly on aquatic life, especially mollusks. The continued rise of sea level, as the fourth glaciation melted and returned its water to the sea, would drown the formerly littoral sites, but to an equal extent on all stable coasts. Accordingly, I postulated that the obvious westward depression of the Florida Plateau (the part of the continental shelf on which Florida rests) had continued into archeological times. Such depression resulted from the great weight of sediments deposited by the Mississippi River, and was greatest near the Mississippi delta.

In 1960, Rhodes W. Fairbridge, who had long been interested in worldwide changes of sea-level, pointed out that tide-gauges, located near large deltas or other regions of heavy sedimentation, consistently show local subsidence. Using data from all available sources, Fairbridge constructed a graph of sea-level changes over the past 18,000 years. In some areas, the geographic position of an archeological site, with respect to the present shore line, will depend not only on postglacial rise of sea level but also on local processes such as deltaic deposition, uplift, and several others.

In 1964, at a meeting of the Florida Anthropological Society, I described the One Fathom site in the Gulf of Mexico, off the coast of the study area. The site was about three miles off the present shore line, ignoring a fair-sized peninsula constructed in recent years by dredging and filling. It was submerged to a depth of about six feet at low tide, eight feet at high. It was a shell midden, roughly oval in outline, the long axis paralleling the modern shore line. The midden followed the course of a long, low rise of sand, similarly running parallel to the present shore. Along this part of the Gulf coast, the sea bottom is mucky for the most part, with scattered, small, rocky expanses; and the sand rises, even though low, are distinctive bottom features wherever they occur. No doubt they represent the drowned remnants of what were once dunes.

Years of residence on this coast had convinced me that absolutely no stratigraphy remains in a site that has been covered by a rising sea. When the highest tides (usually storm tides) first reach a midden, they begin to cut into its base; and as the deposit is progressively undercut, material from its upper strata continually falls down to mingle with that from its lower. Consequently, on the beach slope just in front of a vanishing midden, materials from all levels are intermingled. The height of the midden deposit is decreased by submergence, the horizontal spread of it increased. Accordingly, the possibility existed that the One Fathom site had been one of multiple occupation. However, all the artifactual evidence was consistent with the view that the site had been occupied only during a part of the Deptford Period (about 500 B.C. to 500 A.D.).

Although now well out in the Gulf, the midden was made up of shells of mollusks characteristic of shallow, brackish water. A very small percentage of the recovered potsherds represented the type Norwood Plain, a "semi-fiber-tempered" ware that immediately succeeded the earliest (fiber-tempered) pottery of Florida. The rest of the sherds were Deptford Simple Stamped, Deptford Linear Check Stamped, and Deptford Plain.

Two general kinds of projectile point were recovered, both in fair numbers. One of these was comparatively short and broad, roughly triangular, and stemmed. Stem shape varied. This kind was a carryover from an earlier type, Florida Archaic Stemmed, Marion and Alachua variants. The Deptford specimens were smaller and a bit more rudely made than the average of the earlier ones. The second type of point was comparatively long, slender, with weak shoulders and a straight stem. I have not seen this type from above-water sites of peninsular Florida, but it is fairly common and widespread in dredgings from the Gulf of Mexico between Tampa Bay and the mouth of the Withlacoochee. West of Florida, the type has close counterparts in cultures approximately coeval with Deptford.

Like some Deptford Period sites in Georgia, One Fathom yielded an abundance of blades struck from flint cores. The core-and-blade technique was exceptionally well developed for the Southeast, especially considering the refractory nature of the local siliceous material. Along the coast of the study area, both above and below the present sea-level, there are outcrops of nodules that could be taken for ordinary limestone rocks, but that contain a core of somewhat translucent flinty material. Some of this material is orange-brown, the rest bluish to blue-black. From a boat over the One Fathom site, one can see on the distant mainland a prehistoric flint quarry and knapping station, from which flint was widely exported in Weedon Island times; but the bluish to blue-black flint from this quarry did not appear in the One Fathom site, where the orange-brown material was used consistently. The aforesaid quarry is at and just below the present shore line, where it has been exposed by wave action; but in early Deptford times it would have been about three miles inland, and probably was not visible above the surface of the ground. Flint artifacts from the One Fathom site had developed a very heavy patina, a bit of which had to be flaked off if the underlying material was to be identified. Exhausted cores were of the so-called "horse's hoof" type, which has also been reported from dredgings along the coast of Pasco and Pinellas counties, Florida.

The One Fathom site yielded a selection of other flint artifacts, including broken quarrying tools. These heavy implements must have been hafted, possibly as hoe blades, for it would surely be impossible to snap so many of them across when digging with them by hand. I am dubious of identifying these artifacts as agricultural tools, for they have a wide distribution in both time and space at quarry sites of the Southeast, and evidently were used by the Indians to dig out flint nodules and boulders. Shallowly submerged outcrops of nodular flint, now overgrown with oysters, are locally numerous.

In the category of stone implements made by grinding rather than knapping, a significant find was the broken wing of a bannerstone. It was made of a conglomerate material that does not occur locally, and was shaped like a wing of the so-called "bow-tie" bannerstone. "Bow-ties" are widely distributed from Georgia to the Great Lakes; where dated, they are roughly coeval with Deptford. They are always of some conglomerate rock. One Fathom also produced bone artifacts and vertebrate remains. There were no shell hoes of the kind so common on Weedon Island Period sites.

I concluded, solely on the basis of the cultural debris, that the One Fathom site had been occupied quite early in the Deptford Period, say around 500 B.C. William C. Lazarus (1965) approached the date problem from another direction, that of postglacial sea-level rise and Gulf coast subsidence. He concluded that if the site had been a littoral one at the time it was occupied, then such occupancy would have been possible early in the Deptford Period. The sea-level dating technique was compatible with the ceramic materials.

I have discussed the One Fathom site in some detail, for it gives an idea of both the problems and the possibilities of a submerged site and its interpretation.

While Florida archeologists were trying to extract useful information from geologists' accounts of sea-level changes and Gulf coast subsidence, geophysicists demonstrated the reality of continental drift, and the existence of forces powerful enough to move continents about. This scientific breakthrough, made possible by worldwide scientific cooperation during the International Geophysical Year, led to the realization that continents do more than drift: they also rise, fall, rotate, and tilt. Coastal elevations may be altered because a great crustal plaque is thrust beneath the edge of a continent by sea-floor spreading. Other scientific advances have revealed additional factors that complicate the relationship of sea to land: gravity pulls down more strongly in some regions than in others, and winds can keep the waters "piled" in certain parts of the seas. Thus, sea level is far from level; it varies in elevation from place to place, by as much as 50 feet. To the archeologist, the new findings mean that problems involving sea-level changes will have to be considered in the light of purely regional conditions.

Nor have we reached the end of the list of factors that might locally alter the water relations of sites that were originally littoral. Along formerly glaciated coastlines, the continued melting of the ice takes a great weight from the land, which accordingly rises and so lifts the local sites to a higher elevation than they once occupied. Also, after severe earthquakes, stretches of coastline are sometimes reported to have been raised or lowered a distance of several yards.

Environmental conditions, affecting the water relations of formerly littoral sites, can vary markedly over a fairly short distance. For example, along the northern part of the peninsular Florida Gulf coast, southward through the Cedar Keys, village sites (middens) of the Deptford and Santa Rosa–Swift Creek periods are common on land. They are not far from the modern shoreline, and their great abundance of marine mollusk shells (food debris) shows that they were not far from the shore when they were occupied. But a little south of the Cedar Keys, Deptford and Santa Rosa–Swift Creek village sites disappear into the water. In a stretch from 50 to 80 miles south of the Cedar Keys, the only village sites with Deptford and Santa Rosa–Swift Creek sherds are middens that have been encroached upon by the sea, if indeed they have not been completely submerged. In some of these middens, the aforesaid sherds are mixed with those of Perico Island types, a local ceramic development. Several of the middens were occupied into Weedon Island times.

Although they lived on the coastline—a former coastline now well out in the Gulf—the Deptford peoples occasionally went inland (usually up a river) to erect a burial mound. For example, in Tarpon Springs, Pinellas County, Florida, the Safford mound yielded Deptford Period grave goods in abundance. A mile or so east of the Safford site, and similarly on high ground bordering the Anclote River, a burial mound was hauled off for fill; and on the spot it had occupied, I found Deptford ceramic materials. But nowhere in the surrounding area has anyone found a village midden of that period, except the submerged One Fathom site. No doubt other Deptford middens are now beneath the waters of the Gulf. From St. Petersburg, Pinellas County, came a sherd of Deptford Linear Check Stamped in dredgings that also produced a "horse's hoof" core.

Thus, between St. Petersburg and the Cedar Keys vicinity, there is a considerable difference in the relationship of Deptford Period sites to the present coastline. Of course, the difference may reflect both cultural and environmental factors. In the Cedar Keys vicinity, the middens had Deptford Bold Checked Stamped and the Santa Rosa–Swift Creek types; One Fathom lacked these and so should be older, especially since it had semi-fiber-tempered sherds.

Furthermore, it has lately been shown that the rate of coastal submergence may vary from place to place as a result of down-warping, produced by plate tectonics, the movement of the vast plates that make up the Earth's crust. This movement is submerging the Cedar Keys five times faster than the South Florida Keys (and parts of New Jersey are being submerged faster than either).

When drowned sites are mentioned, Florida comes immediately to mind. Six miles off the coast of Pasco County, the water is only about eight feet deep at mean low tide; and the figure gives an idea of the way the state slopes gradually into the Gulf of Mexico. In a coastal region with such a gentle gradient toward the sea, even a slight rise of sea level can inundate a broad horizontal expanse of land, and all the archeological sites thereon.

Coastal dredgings commonly contain sherds referable to types whose presence so far south was not previously suspected; they also contain projectile points of types that are rare on land, or even unknown from above-water sites of Florida. Thus, it is evident that important chapters of Florida archeology are hidden beneath the sea.

Submarine archeology will probably turn out to be important not just in Florida but also in other lands that similarly slope gently into the sea. Off the Gulf shore of peninsular Florida, the postglacially drowned expanse of sea bottom is a limestone plateau, probably karst at the time when it was above water. A similar formation exists on the opposite side of the Gulf, off the northern coast of the Yucatán Peninsula. This latter expanse should likewise have many drowned sites.

An unusual situation exists along the Louisiana coast. There, the water relations of many sites have been altered by postglacial rise of sea-level, deltaic deposition (which builds land but also dams streams), compaction of sediments, and extreme depression of the delta region from the weight of sediments. Geologists have also reported a "seesaw" effect, northern Louisiana having been elevated as the delta region was depressed. Elsewhere I have suggested that at the present state of knowledge, reference to geological studies probably would not date Louisiana archeological materials as accurately as would typological comparison with accurately dated materials from other areas.

Finland and Scandinavia form an area in which certain sites have been dated with fair accuracy through study of their position in relation to the present sea level. In this region, however, an environmental change has elevated the sites, not drowned them; for Finland and Scandinavia were once depressed by the great weight of glacial ice, and have been springing back up at a fairly constant rate now that the glacier has gone. Thus, the age of some rock carvings, shell middens, and other archeological manifestations can be approximated by their present elevations.

For a time, not much attention was given to archeological evidence of changes in ground-water level. Before Goggin wrote of such changes, it had already been observed that, in a few sites, the bottom of the cultural deposit was beneath the water table. The most one could say of these sites was that they had been occupied at a time when the local ground-water level had not risen to its present stand. The rise was hard to evaluate, partly because the water table is not level. It may stand higher beneath a hill than beneath a valley; it may rise markedly during a rainy season, or fall during a drought.

In the early 1950s, Florida was drought-stricken. Large lakes contracted, to leave fishing camps far from water. Small lakes vanished; and in the flatwoods, former pond bottoms burned over as the muck dried. Streams fell, and their waters became unusually clear in the absence of rainwater runoff. This drought was directly responsible for the sudden development of underwater archeology and underwater paleontology in Florida. The falling of the waters exposed great numbers of archeological sites or rendered them more accessible. Prehistoric dugouts, wooden pestles, and other artifacts came to light when local residents began to farm the newly exposed mucklands. Divers found it easy to see and reach the artifacts and fossils that littered the stream bottoms of Florida.

In 1952, as the drought was just getting under way, archeologists visited the Bluffton site on Lake Dexter, a part of the St. Johns River system in Volusia County, Florida. This was one of the state's largest and most important sites, having been occupied for thousands of years, from Late Preceramic into historic times. Midden debris covered about seven acres to a depth of 20 feet or more. The site was hauled off for fill. It was visited day after day by a stream of trucks, loading shell with a rich burden of artifacts, all to be dumped wherever fill or shell paving was desired. Archeologists could do no more than test the site hastily. Ripley P. Bullen (1955) reported the results of the testing, and I examined about 500 artifacts salvaged by local residents from Bluffton shell that had been dumped into low spots. This material included pendants in shell, baked clay, and sandstone; a red-painted disc of clay; a clay effigy of a bird; gorgets of shell and stone; a shell spoon; bannerstones and celts of imported stone; and numerous artifacts of more usual nature, including stemmed projectile points and shell tools. A published account of the test excavations was nearly limited to a discussion of a zone with fiber-tempered pottery, although the bulk of the midden lay below this zone.

At the time of my preliminary remarks on the site in 1954, I stated that its lower levels were at least four to five feet below the water table, even at times of low water. Later on, hard rains resulted in a temporary rise of the water table to a more usual stand; and in the meantime, a dragline had been digging deeper into the site. At a depth of about 12 feet below the water table, the machine was still digging shell, and had not reached the bottom of the midden.

The St. Johns has, or had, one of the world's greatest concentrations of shell middens. Nearly all of these had been dug into, at one time or another, for fill. Nowhere had I seen a midden that extended as far beneath the water table as did Bluffton. It was concluded that this site was the oldest observed midden of the region; it was begun quite early in the period now called Late Preceramic, when sea level and ground-water level were substantially lower than at present. A large, heavily patinated projectile point or knife came from deep in the Bluffton site, well below the water table; and I noted that typologically it appeared to be early. The type has since been named: the Stanfield point. A marker for the early part of the Late Preceramic Period, it may date back to about 5000 B.C. Thus, conclusions about the age of Bluffton, based on observation of the ground-water level, were eventually confirmed archeologically.

During the 1950s, I found the Snyder site, on high ground overlooking the St. Johns River valley east of Paisley, Lake County, Florida. It was a stratified site without midden debris. Its upper zone had stemmed projectile points, while the lower had Paleo-Indian material representative of what I have called the Suwannee artifact complex. This material included Suwannee projectile points; Suwannee knives, which are fluted more strongly than the points; a blunted-back blade; disc-shaped scrapers with steep retouch; and denticulate flakes. Returning to the site during a comparatively rainy part of the year, I found that the water table had risen above the Suwannee zone, even though the river, at a lower elevation, had just begun to flood its valley. A situation like this can exist in Florida (and some other parts of the Southeast) especially because so many localities have a hardpan, a buried stratum of limestone or clay, impervious to water. Where a hardpan exists, rainwater cannot sink deeply into the ground; it can only evaporate at the surface or flow off laterally, and neither process is rapid under usual conditions. Thus, attention was drawn to the possibility that Paleo-Indian habitation zones might be beneath the present water table, at least during the rainier part of the year.

In Florida, the Paleo-Indian tradition is typified by the Suwannee artifact complex. This includes lanceolate projectile points, flake-based gravers, other denticulate flakes, spurred flakes, steeply retouched scrapers, utilized cores, beveled foreshafts of bone and elephant ivory, bits of cut ivory and fossil shell, long bone points, and a subspherical stone object that has been regarded either as a clubhead or as a bolas weight. The Suwannee complex is very similar to the Clovis one, as manifested at sites in New Mexico and Arizona, and could scarcely be much younger. Like the Clovis, the Suwannee complex is associated with the Rancholabrean (late Pleistocene) fauna. This is in contrast with the Folsom complex of New Mexico and Colorado; Folsom slightly postdates the Rancholabrean. The mammoths, mastodons, giant ground sloths, camels, horses, and other large beasts of the late Pleistocene had vanished by Folsom times; only Figgins' bison lived on in the western plains, to be pursued by Folsom hunters. Hence, the Suwannee complex dates back roughly to Clovis times, during which the sea level was far below its present stand. There is probably some margin of error in graphs on which sea stand is plotted against time, but for present purposes we need only an approximate idea of where the stand was in Suwannee times. Around 13,000 years ago, the sea was about 240 feet below its present level, and by 11,000 years ago it had risen to about 140 feet below the present level. But then came the Valders advance of ice; it abstracted more water from the sea, which fell to an estimated 160 feet below its modern stand.

The foregoing figures may be too conservative, but they make it clear that in Florida, the environment of Suwannee times was very unlike the modern one. Characteristic features of present-day Florida include innumerable bodies of water and patches of vegetation whose existence reflects a water-table not far below the surface of the ground. Water-table fluctuations over the millennia need not have exactly paralleled the rise and fall of sea-level, but they did so approximately; and in Suwannee times, Florida was not the swampland it later became. (For example, the Everglades did not come into existence until about 6,000 years ago, to judge from calibrated radiocarbon dating of its most deeply buried peat.) Water sources were comparatively scarce in Florida when Suwannee hunters pursued the great beasts of the Pleistocene.

Now we can begin to see why the great majority of Suwannee points are associated either with the great springs, spring-runs, and rivers of Florida, or else with the slash-pine and wiregrass flatwoods. With the water table far below its present stand, the springs, runs, and rivers would have constituted one of the two main sources of water. The other source would have been certain flatwoods, where the hardpan kept rainwater from percolating into the ground, and allowed pools to stand during at least a part of the year.

In modern Florida, especially but not exclusively in the central part of the state, huge springs well up through vertical chimneys and horizontal caves in the underlying limestone. In Suwannee times, with a low water table, many of the caves would have been dry, and the chimneys would have been rocky shafts into which the Suwannee hunters could have driven their prey. Where a spring did flow, wild beasts congregated at it and along its run, perhaps to be driven into bogs by the hunters. Flatwoods ponds also served as waterholes, attractive to animals and men.

Most Suwannee sites fall into one of five categories. First, there are cave sites, now deeply submerged beneath the water table. They have Pleistocene mammal remains in variety (and sometimes human remains), along with a fairly wide range of artifacts belonging to the Suwannee complex. Second, there are stream-bed sites with mammal remains and numerous Suwannee points. They may also have a few clubheads or bolas weights and some rude scrapers, but they lack most items of the Suwannee complex because they were not habitation sites. Ben I. Waller in 1970 and I (Neill 1964a) have interpreted these stream-bed occurrences as kill-sites where game was bagged and butchered. They do not have Suwannee habitation sites on the adjoining high ground. Third, Suwannee points and long bone points are scattered over the bottoms of the large springs. Fourth, Suwannee habitation sites, with a wide range of Suwannee complex artifacts, are located on high ground bordering a large spring-run or river. Fifth, Suwannee habitation sites occur in the slash-pine and wiregrass flatwoods. They have a wide range of Suwannee complex artifacts, which rest on the hardpan and are usually beneath the water table during a part of the year.

Elsewhere, I have reviewed occurrences of Suwannee material, and will note only a few finds indicative of water-table rise since Florida Paleo-Indian times. In 1958, Stanley J. Olsen described exploration of an underwater cave in Wakulla Springs, Wakulla County, Florida. The mouth of the cave was submerged to a depth of about 200 feet, and the floor sloped downward to about 220 feet. Even an experienced Scuba diver has difficulty in working at this depth, and the explorers determined only that the site was littered with elephant, deer, and giant ground sloth remains, along with charred wood and hundreds of long bone points. At the time the discovery was made, the relatively great age of the Suwannee artifact complex was just becoming evident, and Fairbridge had not yet published his graph of sea-level changes. Thus, it was hard to realize that the water table could have risen more than 200 feet since Indians first occupied Florida. It had to be supposed that the bones, artifacts, and charred wood reached the cave through a sinkhole that had somehow vanished without leaving a trace behind.

In 1960, William Royal and Eugenie Clark described their investigation of an underwater cave in Warm Mineral Springs, Sarasota

County, Florida. Submergence was to a depth of about 80 feet. The cave ceiling had stalactites, which form in air and not under water. On the floor were a burnt log and the bones of seven human beings. The log gave a radiocarbon date of about 10,000 years before the present. (But radiocarbon dates for such old materials are consistently too young, as noted later on in the present chapter.) Artifacts from this cave were reported to include a "bone needle," no doubt what I have called a long bone point.

About a mile from Warm Mineral Springs is Little Salt Springs. The latter had a horizontal cave submerged to a depth of about 70 feet, and containing human bones and artifacts. Human bones were also found on the spring floor at a depth of 200 feet. At the present writing, Warm Mineral and Little Salt springs are being reinvestigated by archeologists. I have not seen the skulls that have been recovered from these underwater sites, but one specimen has been figured in the newspapers. It had a long, narrow cranium and a high, narrow nasal aperture; thus it agreed with the earliest (Otamid and Iswanid) skulls from the Southeast.

In 1964, I described material from the Cavern Site, submerged to a depth of about 35 feet beneath the waters of Silver Springs, Marion County, Florida (1964a). It had the bones of extinct Pleistocene animals, human remains, charcoal, and artifacts. There were no sinkholes leading into the cavern, no fissures that would have permitted passage of elephant limb bones and enormous tusks, no downwardly directed currents of water, and no nearby Pleistocene fossil beds. The animal remains were taken into the cave through its mouth—taken selectively, for entire skeletons were lacking. For the most part, haunches and tusks had been brought in. Florida mastodon and Columbian mammoth were identified, although some tusks were so large that I suspected the presence of the imperial mammoth also.

The aforesaid remains were at the top of an earthy deposit that extended from the back of the cavern to a ledge at its mouth. In this deposit were a broken Suwannee knife, variously worked or utilized spalls of flint, unused spalls, a scrap of mastodon tooth, a worked bit of horn-like material, the molar of a large Pleistocene horse, a piece of elephant ivory with two apparently worked edges, a fluted projectile point, and a fragment of human skull. The projectile point was described as a "distinctive variety" of the Suwannee point, more Clovislike than the usual Suwannee; it has since been named the Simpson point. The human skull may well have been broken when efforts were made to remove the bulky elephant remains.

In 1971, I reported a second exploration of the Cavern Site. This produced three noteworthy specimens from the earthy deposit well back in the cavern: a Clovis point, a Suwannee clubhead or bolas weight, and the claw-like terminal phalanx of a giant ground sloth. The phalanx had been nibbled on by small rodents. Today, certain small rodents or their nests are commonly encountered in Florida caves, and it is well established that wild rats and mice will gnaw avidly on fresh bones and antlers. The gnawed phalanx was additional evidence that the Cavern Site had once been above water.

Thus, a knowledge of water-table vagaries proved necessary for an interpretation of Florida Paleo-Indian sites. Goggin did well when, in 1948, he commented on archeological evidence of a postglacial rise in sea level and water table. I defer further discussion of Goggin's other propositions, and pass on to additional directions in environmental archeology.

One such direction was taken by workers who wished to determine the age of sites. These investigators were from both the Old World and the New. Two general kinds of dating are possible: relative and absolute. Relative dating is possible because younger cultural debris normally accumulates atop older; this stratigraphic relationship is maintained thereafter, unless the site is badly disturbed by natural forces or the activities of man. With due care in excavation, either kind of disturbance is identifiable. Various natural deposits build up in the same fashion as man's cultural debris, the strata becoming younger toward the top. At a great many localities, a vertical cut into the ground will reveal several natural strata, each deposited under different environmental conditions. The general nature of these conditions may be determinable, and their sequence at one locality may be repeated at others. Widespread repetition of a sequence can usually be laid to climatic fluctuations that were felt over a wide area. These fluctuations were more or less concomitant with waxing or waning of the glacial ice, but were manifested far beyond the glacial border. Accordingly, in some regions it has been possible to determine a sequence of climatic phases, and to date a site in relation to natural deposits or to the phases they represent.

Much work along this line was done by Ernst Antevs (1945, 1948, 1953a, 1953b, 1955) and his associates. They concentrated upon the Great Basin and other parts of the arid Southwest, where vagaries of climate were most sharply reflected in soil stratigraphy. However, a sequence of climatic phases has also been erected for the Southeast, and another for Alaska. American students, unlike their European counterparts, have had little reason to consider phases antedating the last part of the fourth glaciation. Geologic-climatic dating, applied so effectively by Antevs to sites of the Southwest, was refined but not replaced by radiocarbon dating.

Geologic-climatic dating was not the only chronographic system that proved especially applicable to Southwestern sites; there was also dendrochronology. The latter, which provides absolute dates, was developed by A. E. Douglass (1936) and his associates.

Douglass was an astronomer, and he first investigated the annual growth-rings of western pines in the hope of finding some correlation between tree growth and sunspot cycles. From an archeological standpoint, the importance of his work was the discovery that in certain common trees of the Southwest, the width of a growth-ring was determined by the amount of rain the tree received during its growing season. In the past, rainfall had varied, often from one year to the next as well as over longer periods of time; and so the rings of any particular tree were not uniform in width. Each very dry year was marked by an exceptionally narrow ring, each wet year by a wide one; five narrow rings in sequence would reflect a five-year drought, and so on. Over a good part of the Southwest, the ring-width pattern of one tree would be duplicated in many other trees, which had been exposed to about the same fluctuations of rainfall. It was therefore possible to prepare a master chart, tracing the patterns as far back in time as was permitted by the age of the oldest trees. A series of timbers, some from old churches or missions and others from still older Indian sites, permitted extension of the chart still further back in time. Proceeding in this fashion, dendrochronologists worked out ring-width patterns back to 11 A.D. For a time, it seemed as though they would never "break the B.C. barrier," but then a beam of Douglas fir was recovered from Mummy Cave on the Navajo reservation. It had been cut in 304 A.D., but its ring record went back to 59 B.C.

The master chart therefore revealed rainfall fluctuations from 59 B.C. to the present in the arid Southwest; but more importantly in the present connection, it provided a method of dating logs, timbers, and other wooden objects from many sites of that region. The ring-width pattern of the archeological specimen could be checked against the chart, into which it would fit somewhere; and of course, each ring of the chart was of known date.

It might be asked why dendrochronologists did not begin their work with the sequoia or the redwood, trees reputed to reach great age. But a chart based on these trees, which grow in high-rainfall areas of California, would be of dubious applicability to wood from sites of the arid Southwest, and the latter region was the one in which so much wood had been preserved. Dendrochronologists did indeed investigate the growth-rings of giant trees, not just the sequoia and redwood but several others as well. They found, among other things, that the largest species did not set records for longevity. The bristle-cone pine, which grows at high elevations in the Rockies, reaches no great size but lives much longer than any of the giants. Students of the bristle-cone pine made a discovery of great value to archeology. But of that discovery, more later; it is necessary first to introduce the topic of radiocarbon dating.

The technique of radiocarbon dating was invented by Willard F. Libby and his associates. The theory behind it was as follows: In the upper atmosphere, cosmic ray bombardment converts nitrogen into a radioactive isotope of carbon. In carbon dioxide of the atmosphere, a constant percentage of the carbon atoms are of this isotope. Green plants take in carbon dioxide from the atmosphere, and animals feed directly or indirectly upon plants; so each living organism has in its tissues the same percentage of radioactive carbon as does the atmosphere. But when the organism dies, it ceases to take in carbon. In its tissues, the radioactive isotope breaks down at a predictable rate: any amount of radioactive carbon will be halved in 5,568 years, plus or minus 30 years. Thus, if the percentage of radioactive carbon in the tissues of a dead organism is half of that in a live one, then the organism died about 5,568 years ago. If the percentage is just a quarter of that in a live one, the organism died about 11,136 years ago. In its early stage of development, the technique of radiocarbon dating was not accurate for remains older than 20,000 years, but recent refinements permit dating back to 70,000 years. Of course, dates are obtainable only from bone, shell, wood, charcoal, or other organic materials.

The advent of radiocarbon dating caused quite a stir in archeology. Dates in some cases bolstered, in other cases refuted, the informed guesses that archeologists had made about the age of various cultures. A small minority of the dates were wholly incredible. Most of these could be blamed on faulty collecting or processing of a sample, or contamination of it by younger material such as plant rootlets. In Florida, some mollusks could not be used for dating, because they built their shells in part from dissolved limestone in which the carbon was radioactively "dead." In several lands, special environmental conditions had resulted in very heavy mineralization of bones, whose comparatively weak radioactivity was attributable not to great age but to nearly complete absence of any organic material. In some cases, a date was accurate enough, but the dated specimen was not of the same age as cultural debris found near it. Of course, as radiocarbon dates accumulated, the anomalous ones could be discounted if not explained away. Culture chronologies, based on radiocarbon determinations, were worked out for many parts of the world. In the arid Southwest, dates from such determinations were not in much conflict with those from dendrochronology.

Then, dendrochronologists began to take an interest in the bristlecone pine. It was possible to count growth-rings without cutting down an ancient tree; a special implement could be used to take a core that extended from the bark of a tree to the center, leaving only a small perforation that would heal. Borings revealed some of the living pines to be more than 4,000 years old. From living pines, Charles Wesley Ferguson and his associates built up a growth-ring chronology that extended back to about 2630 B.C.; a series of dead pines carried it back further, to about 6230 B.C. It was discovered that radiocarbon dating was in approximate agreement with dendrochronology back to 1500 B.C., but before that the two systems diverged more and more; the radiocarbon dates were too young. This was no surprise to Egyptologists. In Egypt, historical sources guided chronology back to about 3000 B.C.; and in the southern Aegean region, sites were dated by Egyptian trade goods. Workers in that part of the world had used the historical chronology, in terms of which the local radiocarbon dates were much too young.

Hans E. Suess calibrated radiocarbon dates, bringing them into line with dendrochronological findings. A radiocarbon date of 2500 B.C. is in fact about 700 years too young; one of 5000 B.C. nearly 1,000 years too young. It has become evident that the percentage of radioactive carbon in the atmosphere has undergone numerous minor fluctuations as well as a long-term change. The latter may have resulted from changes in the strength of the Earth's magnetic field, which deflects some cosmic radiation; the minor fluctuations could have been correlated with solar activity. Also, the percentage of radioactive carbon in the deep sea is not identical with that in the atmosphere, and in times of lowered sea level, the deep waters are more readily mixed with surface waters; thus, carbon from the depths becomes more readily available to the atmosphere.

The revision of so many radiocarbon dates had archeological repercussions, especially in the great region extending from Europe through Egypt and the Near East. In the eastern part of that region, absolute chronology was based on history; in the western part, on radiocarbon determinations. It had generally been supposed that most of the major advances that led toward civilization had first been made in Egypt or the Near East, and then had diffused into Europe. The unrevised radiocarbon dates had not negated the supposition; but when the dates were calibrated, it appeared that Europeans had sometimes been donors, not mere recipients, of advanced trait-complexes. For example, Spanish megalithic shrines and Balkan metallurgy both were older than their supposed prototypes in the Near East.

Wherever they are based on unrevised radiocarbon dates, absolute chronologies will have to be corrected for cultures older than 1500 B.C. For example, Florida workers have generally accepted 2000 B.C. as marking the local arrival of pottery, but the proper figure may be close to 2500 B.C. The earliest Florida shell middens may date from 6000 B.C., not 5000 B.C. as previously supposed. It is not known how much correction will be needed for radiocarbon dates older than 6000 B.C. The Suwannee artifact complex, often regarded as dating between 9500 B.C. and 9000 B.C., may in fact date from 12,000 B.C. or earlier.

Absolute dating through radiometry is not limited to radiocarbon determination. Also useful to archeologists is determination of the potassium–argon ratio in certain deposits; for potassium has a radioactive isotope that decays into argon at a predictable rate. (Calcium is also produced but is not used in dating.) This technique was invaluable at Olduvai and other localities of East Africa, where volcanic tuffs were especially amenable to its application. In general, potassium–argon dating is not useful in testing deposits less than 100,000 years old. Proactinium–ionium dating to some extent fills the gap between the radiocarbon and the potassium–argon techniques.

So-called fluorine dating does not supply actual dates, at least not directly. Minute quantities of fluorine, in the form of fluorides, are present in the soils and ground-waters of sedimentary formations. Fluorine will combine with hydroxyapatite, a constituent of bones, antlers, and teeth. The enamel of a tooth is somewhat resistant to the passage of fluorine, and not many animals have antlers; so in practice, this technique of dating is generally applied to bones. The combination of fluorine with hydroxyapatite produces fluorapatite, which is stable and not readily dissolved; a chemical environment that

1. (Left) *The oldest and simplest type of artifact: a pebble chipped to an edge. In a later (but still very old) type, flaking extended across both faces of the pebble (right).*
[T. Wilson, Report U.S. National Museum 1896]

2. *A modern civilization is characterized by a considerable degree of cultural diversity. Here, Florida Seminole Indians join their white neighbors at a barbecue, but in many aspects of life the two peoples will go separate ways.*
[W. T. Neill]

3. Early diggers uncovered some extraordinary specimens. In 1894, a cache of 46 ceremonial flint implements was discovered on a farm near the Duck River, Tennessee. Two stone idols were also found. Many stone-lined graves were destroyed, the stones hauled off by the wagonload for building purposes.
[W. K. Moorehead, 1910, *The Stone Age in North America*]

4. From the Spiro Site of Oklahoma: a human effigy in shell, a double-effigy boatstone in rock crystal, two copper plaques embossed with human faces, and a stone pipe with mother-of-pearl inlay eyes.
[F. E. Clements, 1945, Contributions, Museum American Indian, Heye Foundation, Vol. 14]

5. An Auetö tribesman of the Upper Xingu River, Brazil, with cooking vessels and a grave. The picture was made by Karl von den Steinen who, in 1884, was the first European to ascend the Upper Xingu. Ethnographic studies, such as those of Steinen, aid in the interpretation of archeological remains.

6. *Projectiles from South America. The center one reveals how many stone points were mounted. The one at right is tipped with a bipointed sliver of bone. Similar bone points have a wide distribution in time and space.*
[E. Nordenskiöld, 1923, *Indianer und Weisser in Nordostbolivien*]

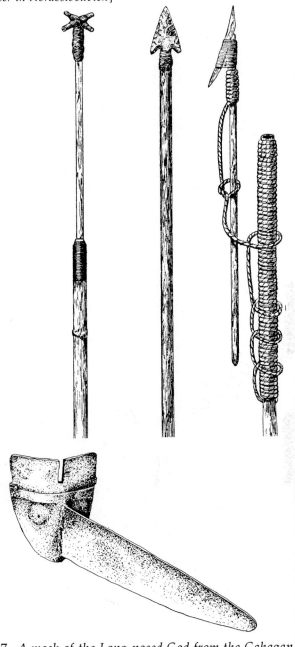

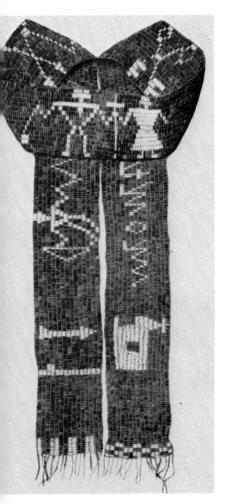

7. *A mask of the Long-nosed God from the Gahagan Mound, Louisiana.*
[S. Williams and J. M. Goggin, 1956, *Missouri Archeologis* Vol. 18, No. 3]

8. *Although wampum beads were used singly and in strings, they were als woven into bracelets and sashes. This sash, more than 6 feet long, was collected probably in the latter 1600s from one of the Northeastern tribes, perhaps the Huron.*
[D. I. Bushnell, 1920, Bureau of American Ethnology Bulletin 71]

9. *The four potsherds on the left are from Jomon Phase sites of Japan, the four on the right from Valdivia Phase sites of Ecuador. A great variety of Jomon pottery types were closely approached by Valdivia types.*
[B. J. Meggers, C. Evans, and E. Estrada, 1965, *Smithsonian Contributions to Anthropology*, Vol. 1]

10. (Upper) *The sand pine and rosemary scrub of central Florida. The Seminole name for it meant, roughly, "go elsewhere." (Lower) The mesic hammock of central Florida.*
[W. T. Neill]

11. *A scene in Annutteliga, Pasco County, Florida. The Seminole name means "brushy place." The plant association is turkey oak and longleaf pine.*
[W. T. Neill]

12. *What Floridians call a "prairie." Much of the year it is flooded.*
[W. T. Neill]

13. *A Seminole hacks a dugout from a fallen bald cypress in river swamp.*
[W. T. Neill, 1953, *The Florida Anthropologist,* Vol. 6, No. 3]

14. *A late prehistoric vessel from the central coast of Peru portrays a strabismic individual.*
[André Emmerich, Inc.]

15. *Culturally prescribed mutilations of the body are revealed by effigy vessels. The Peruvian Moche and their nearby enemies practiced circumcision, as shown by many vessels of baked clay.*
[Arts of the Four Quarters, Ltd.]

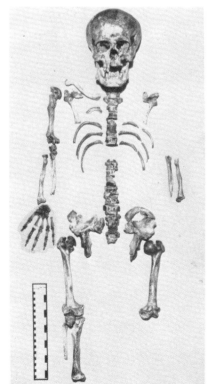

16. *A Moche copper mask reveals mutilation of the earlobes and nasal septum for the insertion of ornaments.*
[André Emmerich, Inc.]

17. *The male dwarf skeleton from Moundville, Alabama, found buried face down, as reassembled in the laboratory.*
[C. E. Snow, 1943, Alabama Museum of Natural History, Museum Paper 21]

18. *Peruvian mace heads of stone. Local preference for the mace as a weapon of war probably accounts for the high frequency of cranial injuries in Peruvian skeletal material.*
[Arts of the Four Quarters, Ltd., and André Emmerich, Inc.]

19. *An artificially deformed skull, that of the Chinook chief Comcomly. Similarly deformed skulls are known from scattered parts of North and South America, as well as the Old World.*
[T. D. Stewart, 1959, Annual Report Smithsonian Institution]

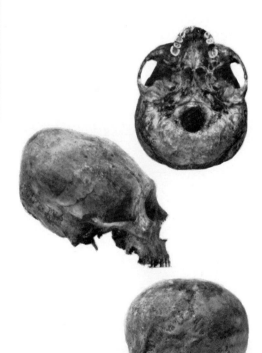

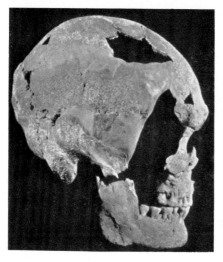

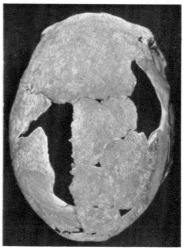

20. (Upper) Minnesota's
"Browns Valley Man," an
early skull of the Otamid
physical variety. The lateral
view reveals a heavy brow
ridge, the dorsal view a long,
narrow cranium and a depression at the temples. (Lower)
Projectile points of the Plano
series, found with Browns Valley Man.
[A. E. Jenks, 1937, Memoirs
American Anthropological Association, No. 49]

21. A Florida Seminole of Walcolid
physical variety. This variety appeared fairly late, and may represent a separate, late migration from
eastern Asia.
[Frances Densmore]

22. *A Florida Seminole of the Uinicid physical variety. Although this variety is concentrated in the Maya area, it also appears among the Creek and the Creek-speaking Seminole, and to a lesser extent among other Muskhogeans. (The vessels are modern creations, not in the old Seminole style.)*
[W. T. Neill, 1956, *The Story of Florida's Seminole Indians.* Silver Springs, Fla.]

23. *A Canadian Assiniboin of the Lakotid physical variety. This variety probably originated in North America, unlike other varieties whose characteristics were developed in Asia.*
[Canadian Govt. Travel Bureau]

24. *In the New Guinea uplands, tribesmen receive marine shells over long trade routes from the coast. A shell disc is worn around the neck, and held in the mouth while dancing. In several parts of the world, some of the earliest trade involved marine shells.*
[W. T. Neill]

26. *Peruvian Moche ceramics were remarkable for the number and variety of erotic portrayals. This specimen dates from Moche IV times, about 300–500 A.D.*
[André Emmerich, Inc.]

25. *Although religions commonly extol spirituality, as a rule they are manifested materially, often to a degree unsurpassed by other social institutions. A Buddha figure, adorning a gigantic temple built more than 1,100 years ago in Java, gazes toward other temples.*
[Indonesian Tourist Board]

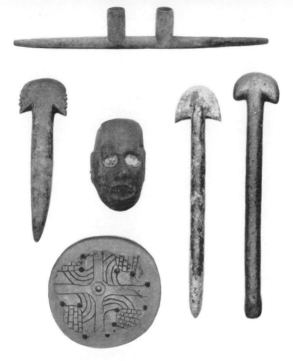

27. *Iconography of the Southeastern Ceremonial Complex or "Southern Cult": a double-bowled pipe, three ceremonial celts ("spuds"), a wooden mask with shell inlay eyes, and an incised shell disc. Scale varies.* [F. E. Clements, 1945, Contributions, Museum American Indian, Heye Foundation, Vol. 14]

28. *The Big Circle Mounds, Palm Beach County, Florida. The double ridge, leading off to a tree-covered mound at the upper left of the picture, is about 500 feet long, and is oriented north–south.* [Ross Allen]

29. *Artifacts and faunal remains from Florida middens of the Weedon Island Period: projectile points, sherds, columella pendant, deer ulna awl, deer mandibular ramus and phalanx, alligator jaw fragment and scute, fish vertebra and pharyngeal teeth, and others.*
[W. T. Neill]

30. *A specimen famous in the annals of tree-ring dating. A Douglas fir beam from Mummy Cave, Navajo Reservation, it "broke the B.C. barrier," dating back to 59 B.C.*
[P. B. Sears, 1957, Condon Lectures, Oregon State System of Higher Education]

31. *A cuneiform tablet from King Sargon II's palace at Khorsabad. It revealed the succession of 95 Assyrian kings from 2400* B.C. *to 746* B.C. *Workers in the Near East and Egypt preferred to base their dating on such written records, while workers farther west relied on radiocarbon determinations. The two systems were in disagreement for times earlier than 1500* B.C.
[Arabian American Oil Co.]

32. *An Inca drinking vessel clearly portrays a cornstalk with ears of corn.*
[André Emmerich, Inc.]

33. *A search has rarely been made for plants that prehistoric peoples might have domesticated solely for the blossoms; yet in ethnographic times, quite a few Neolithic-level peoples prized gaudy blossoms for personal adornment. Shown here is a Bororo Indian of the Mato Grosso, crowned with flowers.*
[R. H. Lowie, 1946, Bureau of American Ethnology Bulletin 143]

35. *Two specimens at left: supposed artifacts from a Maya site. At right, scute of a Pleistocene armadillo from Florida.*
[A. V. Kidder, 1947, Carnegie Institution of Washington, Pub. 576; E. H. Sellards, 1916, 8th Annual Report Florida State Geological Survey]

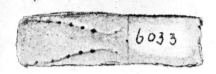

36. *Freshwater marsh, open and sunny, supports a comparatively great amount of small, edible game, but the supply of this game is easily exhausted unless the marsh is very extensive.*
[Florida State News Bureau]

← 34. *From left to right: a Clovis point, bifacially and strongly fluted; a broken Suwannee point, unifacially and strongly fluted; a Suwannee point base, unfluted; a Suwannee point, unifacially and weakly fluted. The three specimens on the right were from the Suwannee level of the Silver Springs site in Florida.*
[W. T. Neill]

37. *River swamp, thickly forested and deeply shaded, supports a comparatively small amount of small, edible game at any one time, but the supply of this game is continually being replaced as animals move in along the swamp and its borders.*
[W. T. Neill]

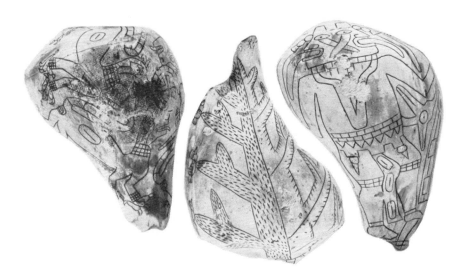

38. *Engraved shells from the Spiro Site, Oklahoma. They portray (left to right) four animals with bird-like feet; a tree, light on one side and dark on the other, with birds on the dark branches; a Janus-headed man-like being.*
[F. E. Clements, 1945, Contributions Museum American Indian, Heye Foundation, Vol. 14]

39. *A common Florida artifact is a Busycon shell, notched at the lip and perforated near the opposite shoulder. The beak has also been ground off.*
[C. B. Moore, 1900, *Journal of the Academy of Natural Sciences of Philadelphia*, Vol. 11]

40. *The specimens that provided a clue to the origin of certain curvilinear complicated stamped designs on pottery: a columella stylus, a cut Melongena shell, and a sherd of Tampa Complicated Stamped pottery, found together at the Hickory Hammock site, Levy County, Florida. The sherd had been stamped with the actual shell that had accompanied it.*
[W. T. Neill]

41. *The cut Melongena shell, impressed into plasticine, duplicated the design of the Tampa Complicated Stamped sherd.*
[W. T. Neill]

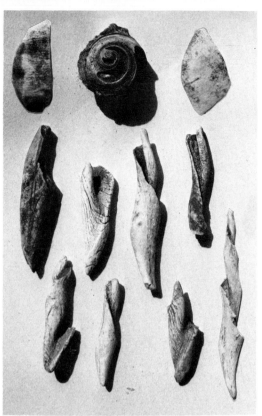

42. *Top row, another cut Melongena shell pottery stamp, flanked by pottery scrapers or smoothers made of shell. Beneath, eight columella styluses. All specimens are from the Hickory Hammock site.*
[W. T. Neill]

43. *This bromeliad is a larger relative of the Spanish-moss, and its Seminole names indicate that fact.*
[W. T. Neill, 1969, *The Geography of Life.* New York: Columbia Universit Press]

44. *The Seminole gave to the red mangrove a name that drew attention t its aerial roots.*
[Ross Allen]

45. *The Seminole gave the papaya (upper) a descriptive name, but gave the coontie (lower) a name transferred from the Smilax.*
[W. T. Neill]

46. *The American crocodile received Seminole names appropriately meaning "alligator with a long, sharp snout."*
[W. T. Neill, 1971, *The Last of the Ruling Reptiles.* New York: Columbia University Press]

47. *(Upper) An Afro-American gecko,* Hemidactylus brooki. *(Lower) In the tropics, large and small vessels may have a thatched cabin. The thatching often is inhabited by geckos and other organisms. This small vessel, with a thatched cabin, was photographed on the Amazon at Leticia, Colombia.*
[A. G. Kluge, 1969, Miscellaneous Publications, Museum of Zoology, University of Michigan, No. 138; Bruce Mozert]

48. *A scene in northern Belize, showing the quasi-rainforest that covers parts of that country and the nearby Petén of Guatemala. The railroad, which hauls mahogany, has cut through a Maya site.*
[British Crown Photograph]

49. *The savanna of northern Belize. Mostly open and dominated by grasses, with scattered palms, pines, and oaks, it is in sharp contrast with nearby forest vegetation.*
[W. T. Neill]

50. *A present-day Maya house in the savanna of Belize. In the distance, savanna is abruptly replaced by forest.*
[W. T. Neill]

51. *Looking toward El Petén, Guatemala, from atop of the Maya ruin of Xunantunich near Benque Viejo, Belize. A freshly cleared* milpa *is in the middle distance.*
[W. T. Neill and R. Allen, 1959, Publications of the Research Division, Ross Allen Reptile Institute, Vol. 2, N 1]

52. *The Maya turned out superlative work in several mediums. Shown are a monolithic axe in obsidian and a vessel in tuff-tempered red ware. Both are from San Jose, Belize. Elaborate ceramics and stone work are another manifestation of the Maya's flourishing economy, which permitted the expenditure of much time and effort on nonutilitarian items and embellishments.*
[J. E. Thompson, 1939, Carnegie Institution of Washington Publication N 506]

would break it down would probably destroy bones as well. The longer a bone remains in a fluoride-bearing deposit, the more fluorine it takes up and binds as fluorapatite. The amount of fluorine in a bone is not per se a direct indication of its age, because some soils and ground-waters may be richer than others in this chemical. But if a group of bones, taken from a single deposit, all contain about the same percentage of the chemical, then they are all of about the same age.

To give an idea of the way this method of dating has been used, a question once arose regarding the age of a fragmentary human pelvis, found with the bones of extinct mammals in a clay bed near Natchez, Mississippi. The mammals formed an assemblage typical of the late Pleistocene: a mastodon, various ground sloths, a horse, and a giant bison. But a sedimentary deposit can contain materials of differing ages, and the pelvis might easily have been younger than the animal remains. It turned out to have a higher percentage of fluorine than did a bone from one of the ground sloths, a Mylodon. Thus, human beings lived in the Natchez vicinity before that beast became extinct there. In the Old World, far more often than in the New, a fluorine test has been helpful in deciding whether human remains were intrusive into the deposit that contained them.

If human bones turn out to have been coeval with a faunal assemblage, interest naturally attaches to the age of that assemblage. Accordingly, we are led into the topic of what has been called stratifaunal dating. At any given time, a given region is inhabited by an assortment of animal species—the region's fauna. The composition of such a fauna changes with time; it is modified by evolution, extinctions, and shifts of geographic range in response to changing environmental conditions. Hence, the fossil record will permit chronological seriation of faunas if it is sufficiently studied. Paleontologists have concentrated on the seriation of mammal faunas. In Africa and Eurasia, hominid evolution spans a long sequence of these faunas; and in a good many cases, hominid remains were datable in terms of an associated fauna.

In North America, only two mammal faunas are of archeological concern. One of these, of late Pleistocene age, included ancestors of species that exist today, along with many other beasts that have since vanished. This rich fauna is called the Rancholabrean, after a California locality, Rancho La Brea, where many of its species had left their remains in asphalt pools. The Rancholabrean fauna was distributed completely across the United States, from California to Florida, but this does not mean that every species in it had a transcontinental range. The asphalt pools yielded a short-faced bear, a dwarf prong-horn, and the Shasta ground sloth, none of them known from Florida. On the other hand, the latter state has produced remains of species unknown from California: a spectacled bear (Tremarctos), a capybara, a giant armadillo, an armadillo-like chlamythere, a glyptodont or tortoise-armadillo, an enormous ground sloth (Eremotherium), a tapir, and a long-nosed peccary, among others. The stag-moose, shrub ox, and woodland musk-ox left their bones in deposits north of both California and Florida. The dire-wolf, a massive sabertooth (Smilodon), a gigantic cat (*Felis atrox*), a large horse, a flat-headed peccary, two kinds of ground sloths, a camel, a giant bison, a mastodon, and at least two species of mammoths were among the transcontinental components of the Rancholabrean fauna. In other words, this fauna exhibited some geographic diversity, both from east to west and from north to south.

The apparently exceptional richness of the Florida Rancholabrean fauna may be illusory, the result of exceptional opportunities for fossilization in that state. At any rate, Florida gives a better-than-average picture of mammalian diversity in late Pleistocene times. It has often been said that Pleistocene Florida must have resembled the present game fields of Africa, with herds of grazers and browsers, a variety of carnivores, and some scavengers to pick the bones of the carnivores' prey. This comparison could be misleading. Africa's spectacular wild-life assemblage is concentrated in savanna. Florida is now too cold and rainy to support this type of vegetation, and in the late Pleistocene, before the last glaciation began its retreat, it was colder and rainier than at present. While savanna may be able to support an unusually diverse mammal fauna, it is likely that most or all vegetation types could support a greater diversity of mammals in man's absence than in his presence. It was the spread of Paleolithic-level man that so dramatically depauperated the faunas of six continents.

A fairly abrupt shift of climate, with glaciation passing into deglaciation, might well have altered ecological relationships that had existed for millennia; but the Rancholabrean mammals, or their ancestors, had survived preceding episodes of glaciation and deglaciation. Shortly before the fourth glaciation began its retreat, a new ecological factor appeared in the land: man, equipped with the Paleolithic techniques of big-game hunting. Not just in North America but throughout the world, the depauperation of a late Pleistocene fauna followed hard upon the arrival of man, with his fire-drives, his stampeding of game into bogs and over cliffs, his determination and teamwork.

Australopithecus, *Homo habilis, Homo erectus,* Neanderthal man— all littered their habitation sites with mammal remains. Upper Paleolithic man (including the Paleo-Indian) pursued the biggest of big game. So successful was he in this pursuit that the great predators of the Pleistocene could not compete with him; and they died out. The ecological repercussions of man's presence profoundly altered the composition of the fauna. In North America, the Rancholabrean fauna was altered, by subtraction, to the modern one.

Two aspects of this alteration have not previously been mentioned, as far as I know. It could be said that Paleolithic man was a new and mighty force in the world, an ecological force, a selective force in the evolutionary sense of selection. But what made man so mighty was his intelligence. From Australopithecus to *Homo sapiens,* the significant feature of hominid evolution was an increase in brain size and complexity. Thus, the aforesaid new ecological and selective force really was intelligence. This was what the Pleistocene beasts really had to cope with. The beasts that vanished were, in my opinion, notably dull-witted. Not much work has been done on the brains of extinct mammals; and with rare exceptions, such work is of necessity limited to investigation of cranial capacity and sculpturing. We are told that the Rancholabrean sabertooth, although bigger than a lion, had a brain no larger than that of a kitten. If so, it must have had far less intelligence than a lion, and must have taken singularly unintelligent prey. The giant ground sloths also appear to have had a proportionately diminutive brain. Regardless of cranial capacity, the mammoths and mastodons that so often fell prey to Paleolithic hunters need not have been as sagacious as a modern elephant. The game animals of today probably average keener of perceptions and quicker in reactions than did the vanished Pleistocene beasts.

The second overlooked aspect of Pleistocene extinction is less speculative. As a general rule of biology, extinction is accompanied or soon followed by replacement. As a highly successful predator, Paleolithic-level man replaced a number of other and less successful predators. But what replaced the Pleistocene herbivores that vanished as a result of man's impact on the ecology? In North America, deer bones are uncommon in pure Pleistocene deposits. They are uncommon in Paleo-Indian sites. Unfortunately, food remains have seldom been found in Indian sites dating from the first few millennia after Paleo-

Indian times. But soon thereafter, deer bones appear in enormous numbers. In Florida, the white-tailed deer was a staple food at least from the beginning of the Late Preceramic Period (say around 5000 B.C.) up into historic times. Early historical accounts also emphasized the great abundance of this species. I take it that in Europe also, the disappearance of the Pleistocene herbivores was followed by a population explosion among some members of the deer family; for European paleontologists speak of a "deer zone," lying stratigraphically just above a late Pleistocene zone in which deer are comparatively scarce. It would seem that in some parts of the world, a deer replaced a number of Pleistocene herbivores when man replaced a selection of Pleistocene carnivores.

If the Pleistocene is defined geologically, it may be regarded as continuing today; the present episode of deglaciation might well be followed by a new glaciation at some time in the future. But commonly, a deposit is assigned to a period and epoch on the basis of the contained fauna; and from a biological standpoint, the Pleistocene was over at the end of the fourth glaciation, by which time the world's ecology had been drastically revised by man. In North America, the conversion of the Rancholabrean fauna into the modern fauna marked the passage of the Pleistocene Epoch into the Recent Epoch.

In broader view, the dispersal of Upper Paleolithic man in fact marked the passage of the Cenzoic Era, the Age of Mammals, into the Psychozoic Era, during which the destiny of most living things would depend upon the whims of sapient man.

CHAPTER EIGHT

Further Directions in Archeology

Sometimes, it may be possible to date hominid remains and artifacts through reference not to the totality of an associated mammal fauna, but to just one species thereof. As already mentioned, efforts are currently being made to discover additional hominid remains from Africa. The importance of a specimen would be enhanced if it were possible to provide a relative or an absolute date for the deposit in which it was found. Like hominids, the proboscideans originated in Africa. Appearing first in Eocene, they underwent adaptive radiation, and in time they diverged into a remarkable assortment of beasts, most of them large. The heavy bones, huge teeth, and great tusks of these mammals had a better-than-average chance of being fossilized, and paleontologists will probably acquire the fossils in such numbers as to permit detailed tracing of proboscidean evolutionary sequences in Africa. Thus, upon identification to species, the remains of a gomphothere, rhynchothere, true mastodont, deinothere, elephant, or other proboscidean might serve to date a deposit that also contained hominid remains or cultural debris.

In the New World, there has been little need for archeologists to consider evolutionary sequences of vertebrates, but such consideration might prove useful at times. In 1956, with H. James Gut and Pierce Brodkorb, I noted that remains of American coot and eastern diamondback rattlesnake both confirmed a post-Pleistocene dating for preceramic levels of certain shell middens in Florida. Probably, no archeologist seriously suspected that these levels would date from the Pleistocene, but their age was not definitely known at the time we wrote. The coot and the rattler were each represented in Pleistocene times by a subspecies differing osteologically from the Recent one, and it was worth remarking that in each case, the Recent subspecies was the one present in the middens.

More recently, I investigated a site near the coast of Pasco County, Florida. It yielded a bifacially fluted projectile point that differed from the Clovis norm only in that the projections at the base of the artifact were carefully shaped, somewhat spur-like. In association with the point were, among other things, some denticulate flakes, scrapers, a hammerstone, pieces of long bone points, bits of cut or worked bone, and a variety of faunal remains in fragmentary condition. Although most of the remains were mammalian, there were also a good many pieces of turtle shell. Some of these were referable to the species most commonly called *Pseudemys scripta*. The late Pleistocene subspecies of this turtle, *Pseudemys scripta petrolei,* had a thicker and more coarsely sculptured shell than any of the several Recent subspecies. The specimens from the site were intermediate in these characteristics. William G. Weaver, Jr. (1967), who had just finished a taxonomic review of this group of turtles, suggested that, in Florida, the late Pleistocene subspecies passed into the Recent one about 12,000 years ago. The figure accords well with the age of Clovis points.

I do not wish here to emphasize the archeological importance of this site, for it has not yet been described in the technical literature; but it draws attention to the likelihood that some natural and cultural deposits might be dated through reference to the evolutionary stage of *Pseudemys scripta* remains found therein. The subspecies *petrolei* ranged at least from southern Texas to central Florida. A slight approach to the Recent subspecies is seen in material as much as 17,000 years old, but the transition from late Pleistocene to Recent subspecies was completed around the end of Rancholabrean times. It may be noted in passing that in the Recent Epoch, the species fell back to the north, at least in some parts of its range. In Florida, *petrolei* ranged southward at least to the latitude of Tampa, while the modern subspecies does not occur naturally south of the Gainesville vicinity.

Some use has been made of bison remains in dating American sites. The genus *Bison* arrived in the New World around the end of the middle Pleistocene, and its arrival marks the beginning of the Rancholabrean provincial age. The genus underwent rapid evolution in North America, producing both long-horned and short-horned giants. One Rancholabrean bison, found in Florida and elsewhere, dwarfed the modern species, and had a six-foot spread of horns. On the western prairie, two or more species of Pleistocene bison (not long-horned) hung on after the demise of mammoths, mastodons, and other Rancholabrean faunal elements. I take this to mean that the Paleo-Indian hunters were comparatively late to invade the prairie. At any rate, the association of Folsom points with extinct bison first demonstrated the existence of early man in the New World. The Folsom was followed by a variety of other projectile point types, collectively known as the Plano assortment. Of this assortment, some types have been reported with extinct bison only, others with both extinct and modern bison, still others with the modern species only. Evidently, Plano points were in favor during that time when the number of North American bison species was rather abruptly being reduced to one. The more paleontologists learn about the evolution of the genus *Bison,* the more will remains of these animals prove useful in dating sites that are not readily datable in any other fashion.

Also, while Plano points are concentrated toward the western prairie, specimens much like them occur sparingly in other parts of the country. Thus, Eden-like points have been reported from Alaska to the Savannah River region of Georgia and South Carolina. It was principally but not exclusively on the basis of typology that I considered the Georgia–South Carolina material to antedate the local Late Preceramic shell middens. It is now clear that in the West, Eden points were used to kill not only bison of the modern species but also the extinct *Bison occidentalis.* Accordingly, Eden-like points should be quite old wherever they are found.

Oddly, even certain microscopic marine organisms, the foraminiferans, might command archeological or at least paleoanthropological attention. Foraminiferans are vastly abundant in the sea, where their minute shells build thick deposits on the bottom. Certain characteristics of these organisms, or of the assemblages they form, tell a great deal about the marine environment in which they lived. When a submarine core is drilled and examined, its foraminiferan sequences reveal fluctuations in the depth, oxygen content, salinity, pH, turbidity, and temperature of the water, as well as distance from shore and nature of the substratum. Fluctuations of water temperature are especially interesting in the present connection, for vagaries of temperature in the water presumably were paralleled on land. Investigation of these temperatures, through examination of foraminiferans in cores, has possibilities as a dating technique, also, for certain levels in a core might be datable radiometrically.

Recently, methods of dating the past have proliferated. The age of obsidian artifacts has been determined through a study of fission tracks and of surface hydration. Thermoluminescence has been used to date potsherds, and to test the genuineness of certain museum specimens whose purported antiquity was suspect. Not just biology but also physics and chemistry have facilitated efforts to reveal the age of archeological materials.

Physics and chemistry also interact with archeology in a new field called archaeological chemistry. The European spelling "archaeological" is customary here, for the subdiscipline crystallized and was named in the Old World. A part of archaeological chemistry is devoted to preservation and restoration of excavated specimens. Another part, more important here, is involved with chemical analysis of such specimens. Trace elements may reveal the source of raw materials used by prehistoric peoples, and such revelation may lead to additional conclusions. For example, obsidian implements were found in Greek caves, in levels dated by radiocarbon at about 7000 B.C. The obsidian was identified as having come from the island of Melos, and the identification provided evidence that goods were transported by sea at a very early date. Other European studies show a trade in obsidian to have begun in very early times, and permit a tracing of approximate routes along which this mineral passed. In the midwestern United States, the Hopewell culture was characterized by ceremonial spear points and other artifacts of obsidian. The Hopewell source turned out to be the vicinity of Yellowstone National Park, most likely the Obsidian Cliff quarry.

Chemical archaeology has shown the bluestones of Stonehenge, in southern England, to have been quarried in South Wales. Evidently, then, the builders of Stonehenge were able not just to cut and erect huge stones, but also to transport them dozens of miles. Certain stone axes of southern England were of material from North Wales and Westmoreland. In the southern United States, trace element analysis revealed some copper to have been imported from the Georgia uplands, and some from the Great Lakes region.

Another interesting project in archaeological chemistry involved the identification of a white cosmetic powder, found in graves of Greek women of the fourth and third centuries B.C. The powder turned out to be artificial basic lead carbonate. Evidently, then, the ancient Greeks were able to manufacture this substance. It was distributed widely, to the detriment of its users. (It is poisonous.) The new subdiscipline has helped distinguish copper from bronze, bronze from brass, lime mortar from gypsum plaster, and solid bitumens from resins.

One technique of chemical archaeology, called chemical microscopy, has thrown light on metallurgical techniques. For example, the Old Copper culture is one of the most extraordinary archeological manifestations in North America. In the vicinity of the Great Lakes, some early peoples began using "float" copper for the manufacture of socketed adzes and spears, long-tanged knives, and other implements. The Old Copper culture dates back at least to 5000 B.C., and may be older; the early metal-workers may even have been contemporary with an extinct bison. The characteristic flint projectile point of this culture was an elongate, side-notched type, in a style rather characteristic of Early Preceramic times. In most parts of the world, much effort would be expended to discover just who was working metal at such a remote time; but the Old Copper culture has been rather neglected. At any rate, chemical microscopy shows the early American metal-workers to have practiced cold-hammering and annealing of copper, although they did not smelt or melt the substance.

A recent discovery of archaeological chemistry is a method to distinguish human coprolites from those of animals. When a human specimen is dissolved in water, and sodium triphosphate is added, the solution turns brownish. Animal coprolites yield no such reaction.

An uncommon approach to environmental archeology was exemplified by the work of S. F. Cook (1946) and his associates on shell middens of California. These middens were considered with respect to nutrition and population, and investigated with reference to their physical and chemical characteristics. This work necessitated the examination of midden material in enormous quantities. Today, with middens and other Indian sites being destroyed so rapidly by the activities of man, an archeologist could scarcely take the time to investigate the entirety of a large shell heap; more likely, he would be content to test it stratigraphically for evidence of culture change from bottom to top. If he did remove any substantial portion of it, he would be in search of artifacts rather than compositional, physical, or chemical data. The work of Cook and his associates is especially important in showing what constitutes adequate sampling of a midden, and of some other kinds of sites, if the aim is to extract certain cultural and ecological data. It is to be hoped that Cook's methods of investigation will be applied to middens outside California.

Another fairly unusual approach to environmental archeology is exemplified by an aforementioned paper in which Gut, Brodkorb, and I studied faunal remains from Late Preceramic middens in the St. Johns area of Florida. Gut had specialized in the paleontology and osteology of mammals, Brodkorb in the paleontology, osteology, and taxonomy of birds, I in the biology of reptiles and amphibians, the ecology of Florida, and the natural history of Southeastern wildlife. In addition, both Gut and I were interested in Florida archeological problems as such. It was hoped that our combined efforts might extract considerable information, both cultural and biological, from the faunal remains in these sites. Our principal conclusions were as follows:

At least 47 species of vertebrates were identified, all of them present in the vicinity of the sites today. In Late Preceramic times, the environment of the sites was much as it is now (ignoring the havoc wrought by modern man). Near the sites there had been river swamp, but also some dry, sandy areas covered either with sand pine and rosemary scrub or else with turkey oak and longleaf pine. Pine flatwoods and mesic hammock may also have been present. The age of the sites was post-Pleistocene. The Indians hunted mostly along the river and its tributaries, less frequently in the dry areas. Most of the hunting was probably carried on by day. Fire-drives were not staged. No special hunting technique was employed, beyond prowling the river swamp and collecting any fair-sized edible game. All four of the sites were occupied in the winter, and at least two of them in the summer also. The Indians preyed most heavily on the white-tailed deer, raccoon, opossum, wild turkey, soft-shelled turtle, and two turtles of the genus *Pseudemys*; less heavily upon the otter, bobcat, rabbits, double-crested cormorant, alligator, gopher tortoise, and eastern diamondback rattlesnake. Other mammals, birds (mostly waterfowl), and a bullfrog were hunted sparingly.

The Indians at these four sites did not often collect small animals, odoriferous ones, or young individuals of the larger species; they devoted their attention mostly to flavorsome, meaty game, and presumably did not suffer from any shortage of food. They did not often prey on large carnivores such as the puma and black bear, but they did procure large alligators.

Deer carcasses were brought to the sites entire. *Pseudemys* and softshelled turtles were beheaded when caught. These reptiles were dressed, and alligators were at least cleaned. Most turtle shells were broken by pounding on the under side, but box turtles were opened by a special technique that took advantage of their peculiar shell construction. The Indians kept two varieties of dog, one large and one small; both were eaten. Considerable use was made of bone and antler. Most worked bone probably was that of the deer, but one artifact of turkey bone was found. The deer cannon-bone, especially, was used in the manufacture of implements. A pathological deer bone, consisting of a fused radius and ulna, had been incised as though to correct the abnormal fusion. A few marine shells had been obtained by the Indians, and a few fossils. The latter were easily distinguished from food remains by their color and mineralization. In the St. Johns drainage, fossils can be found by people grubbing for shellfish, and their occasional presence in a local midden is not significant. Three freshwater species of shellfish—a mussel, a small snail, and a large snail—made up most of the midden debris. Having temporarily exhausted the supply of one mollusk, the Indians would then turn to another. There were no important intersite differences in faunal composition.

Here, I shall not review the lines of reasoning that led us to the above conclusions. It might be worth mentioning that we also turned up some information of purely biological interest. It is well for archeologists to realize that biological discoveries can be made through investigation of archeofaunal remains. These workers usually will have to rely on biological specialists for identification and interpretation of such remains, and the specialists may be more willing to examine a mass of fragmentary bones and eroded shells if they can expect data pertinent to their own fields.

A very important direction of environmental archeology has involved the analysis of plant remains. The greater part of this analysis has been done in Europe and the Near East. G. W. Dimbleby (1967) has recently reviewed archeobotanical research in the Old World.

Some of this research has necessitated the identification of pollens. Surprisingly, in the proper environment, pollen grains will persist in excellent condition for many thousands of years; indeed, they can fossilize. Often, the size, shape, and sculpturing of a grain permits identification of it, if not to the taxonomic level of species then to that of genus. Accordingly, there has developed a science of palynology. Grains are searched for by microscope in the appropriate material, and usually they occur in enormous numbers; for many plants, especially the wind-pollinated ones, liberate myriad grains into the air. Some grains might be carried a long distance by winds, but most soon fall to earth. In any event, the palynologist concerns himself with the kinds of pollen that are to be found abundantly in the studied sample; their abundance is prima facie evidence that they were liberated from plants that grew near the spot from which the sample was taken.

This circumstance could be of archeological concern, as I have pointed out elsewhere (Neill 1957b). Palynological analysis of a boring from Marion County, Florida, revealed pollen of fir and spruce in a Pleistocene stratum. Pollens of cold-weather plants, such as fir, Canadian spruce, larch, and arborvitae, have been recovered from a number of Pleistocene localities between western Florida and eastern Texas, in some cases with cold-water mollusks. A pollen profile from Lake Singletary, in the coastal plain of North Carolina, included a stratum with fir, spruce, and pine, but almost no broad-leaved trees; and this stratum could be correlated with the Mankato advance of the fourth glaciation. Some workers, reluctant to grant chilling as far south as the Gulf states and the Carolina coastal plain, argued that in glacial times the pollen of northern cone-bearers blew down from localities hundreds of miles to the north. But these trees produce small amounts of pollen as compared with many common broad-leaved species; and if a deposit of the southern lowlands has abundant pollen of cone-bearers that are now northern and montane, then those trees once formed stands nearby. Thus, evidence accumulates that episodes of glaciation in the north were accompanied by chilling in the south. The makers of Clovis and Suwannee points lived under a climatic regimen quite different from the present one.

Obviously, the pollen of cultivated plants implies local agriculture. But in Europe, the spread of agriculture has been traced palynologically even in the absence of such pollen. Many plants, popularly lumped together as "weeds," are very rare in undisturbed situations, yet they proliferate where man has cleared away the natural vegetation. Some are indicators not just of clearing but of actual cultivation of the land. A pollen profile, say from a former bog, can reveal the local arrival of agriculture through the sudden appearance of weed pollens in quantity. A pollen-bearing deposit can sometimes be dated by geologic-climatic, radiocarbon, or some other technique, and so palynological analysis can make it possible to date cultural events.

Often, in Europe, an area was cleared to the bare ground prior to the erection thereon of a stone tomb or other structure. Pollen grains showered upon the cleared area from nearby plants. Through flotation, such grains are recoverable from the earth on which they fell; and upon identification, they reveal the nature of the local flora at the time the structure was erected. They may indicate agriculture, and tell something about climate. Comparable investigations could be made in the United States. For example, in the Southeast, some if not all Weedon Island Period burial mounds were built on a spot that had been cleared to the bare ground. Many mounds were located well away from any settlement, but others were built at the edge of a village area, and might have had cultivated fields nearby. Most Florida soils are acid, as they must be if pollen is to be preserved.

Deposits with pollen also contain minute organisms of various kinds, and in practice a palynologist may analyze more than pollen grains. If a deposit was originally laid down on the bottom of a pond or lake, it may contain the remains of aquatic organisms in great abundance and variety. The study of these remains is subsumed under paleolimnology rather than palynology. John DeCosta and Claude N. Warren (1967), who summarized the archeological possibilities of paleolimnology, held that aquatic organisms are even more sensitive indicators of environmental conditions than are pollen grains.

Needless to say, plants do not have to be identified solely by their pollen; leaves, fruit, or seeds sometimes chance to be preserved in a site, and identification of them may yield useful archeological information.

Thus, I described wooden rattles recovered from a large spring of central Florida (Neill 1952). Where water emerges from limestone to form such springs, it is low in oxygen and bacteria, fairly high in some dissolved minerals; and so wooden items might have persisted from prehistoric times on the bottom of a deep spring. One of the rattles was complete; it contained several kinds of hard seeds, which had originally produced a rattling sound when the implement was shaken. Among the seeds were castor beans. Castor is native to Africa and Asia. Castor oil has been used as a medicine, a lubricant, a flypaper glue, and a soap ingredient, while the castor oil pomace has been valued as a richly nitrogenous fertilizer. In earlier times, the oil was used to treat cotton cloth that was to be dyed a certain shade of red, and the plants were grown about dooryards in the belief that they would repel mosquitos and moles. Accordingly, castor has been introduced into many parts of the world outside its natural range. Its initial introduction into the United States probably took place in early historic times, from Europe where the plant had long been known. The castor beans indicate that the rattles are historic; they are generically similar to other American Indian specimens, but they definitely are not Seminole. Perhaps, then, they were the work of the Acuera, a Timucua-speaking tribe who lived near the spring in early historic times.

Whatever their origin, these rattles draw attention to the fact that floral remains from archeological sites need not be those of food plants. As noted in chapter 1, man has turned to plants for medicines, paints, gums, thatching, and many other items. Accordingly, the paleoethnobotanist would do well to bear in mind the historic ethnobotany of the area in which he works. Dimbleby's aforementioned book, on plants and archeology, devoted considerable space to ethnobotany. With regard to New World studies, I have cautioned (1968c) that the early European settlers and Negro slaves were themselves in possession of a vast body of plant lore, some of it practical and some of it superstitious. There was much swapping of this lore, and some uses of plants may not have originated with the Indians although ethnographically recorded among them.

Of course, in sites that date from after the spread of agriculture, domesticated food plants will usually predominate among the floral remains. In 1958, C. W. Meighan et al. provided an annotated checklist of cultivated plants that had been recorded ethnographically or archeologically, if not both. Under the heading of seed grains (which included not just the cereals but also the grain amaranths, the sunflower, and others), they listed 30 species. One of these, maize, was represented by six varieties. There were also 81 species of fruits, 12 of legumes, 22 of root crops, 11 of narcotics or stimulants, 16 of spices, 10 of fiber plants, 8 of nuts, 22 of vegetables (including Crescentia and Lagenaria gourds, used for containers), and 23 miscellaneous. The last category included some important dyes, rubber producers, oleaginous plants, and others.

Archeologically known plants of the Andean region were ragweed, sunflower, quinoa, one variety of maize, avocado, guama, jackbean, lablab bean, jicama, scarlet runner, kidney bean, sweet potato, sweet manioc, potato, Columbian potato, cinchona, coca, three species of cotton, peanut, squash, crookneck squash, summer squash, bottle gourd, pepino amarillo, indigo, and cacao. Tropical America, exclusive of the Maya area and Mexico, had yielded no archeofloral specimens, although numerous species of plants were cultivated there according to ethnographers. There was no archeofloral material from the Maya area, and Mexico had produced only one variety of maize and one species of cotton.

From sites of the southwestern United States had come three varieties of maize (ordinary maize, popcorn, and dent corn), jack bean, kidney bean, one species of cotton, crookneck squash, summer squash, and bottle gourd. Sites of the eastern United States had yielded ragweed and dent corn. Europe had produced oats, a species of pigweed, six-row barley, quadrangular barley, millet, rye, dwarf wheat, einkorn, spelt, bread wheat, apple, grape, lentil, pea, Celtic bean, flax, cameline, olive, a species of buckwheat, poppy, and saffron. From the Near East had come barley, six-row barley, quadrangular barley, emmer, bread wheat, some kind of melon, a species of cotton, flax, olive, and saffron. No domesticated plant species had been reported archeologically from southeastern Asia; other parts of Asia had yielded millet and emmer.

Harold C. Conklin (1959) added to the list of Meighan et al. a good many more cultivated plants, including those peculiar to Africa and Oceania. Reviewing the tabulations of botanists, Conklin concluded that more than 1,000 plant species had been taken into cultivation by 1500 A.D. The figure would have been much higher if subspecies or varieties had been counted separately. Needless to say, the number of archeologically reported species has been augmented since Meighan et al. and Conklin presented their lists. Nevertheless, five conclusions can safely be drawn from those lists.

First, in the tropics of both the Old World and the New, the cultivation of many plants was reported by ethnographers, often at quite an early date; yet these regions have yielded very little archeofloral material. This situation exists partly because tropical environments often are not conducive to the preservation of plant remains, but also because many tropical regions have received comparatively little archeological attention.

In these regions (and in some other parts of the world) there is indirect evidence of cultivated plants other than those that happened to be preserved in sites. For example, ceramic representations of maize are widespread in the New World; the lima bean was clearly portrayed on a ceramic vessel from Peru; pomegranate flowers and fruits were reproduced in gold by the Chaldeans. Occasionally, a pottery vessel retained the accidental imprint of an identifiable seed. The Classic civilizations, being literate, left references to cultivated plants, some of which are lacking from sites. Thus, a great Roman orator and writer, born 106 B.C., was called Cicero, "chick-pea," in allusion to a pea-like growth on his face; but the chick-pea, *Cicer arietinum*, was not listed by Meighan et al. This legume, widely grown in the Mediterranean region, is best known by its Spanish name of garbanzo.

As a second conclusion derived from the list of Meighan et al., if the remains of domesticated plants are comparatively abundant in some region, one cannot infer that the inhabitants thereof were exceptionally interested in agriculture. More likely, the region offered environments particularly conducive to preservation of plant remains (as in the cold, dry Andes), or has been exceptionally well studied (Europe).

Third, certain kinds of plants were more likely to be preserved than others. The grain seeds were notably amenable to preservation, followed by the legumes.

Fourth, medicinal plants were rarely cultivated. Of course, the category of medicinal plant grades into that of food or beverage plant, and into that of the narcotics, stimulants, and hallucinogens; and some plant species yield an actual or a supposed medicine in addition to another product. Still, the ethnographic cultures have generally attributed medicinal properties to a variety of plants, which were gathered from the wild and not grown close at hand.

By way of illustration, the Florida Seminole have used a Sagittaria and an Iris to treat shock brought on by alligator bite, and a Pilostaxis in cases of snake bite. They have treated colds and pulmonary ailments with a Xyris, nosebleed with a Cracca, sunstroke with a Viorna, toothache with an Atamosco, burns and skin irritations with a Commelina, kidney disorders with a Pityothamnus, stomach upsets with a Rubus, sore throat with a Crotalaria, and nausea with a Chamaechrista. They know a tranquilizing drug, but its identity is secret. Two species of Salix, an Eryngium, a Hypericum, a Persea, a Vaccinium, a Cissus, two or three species of Vitis, a Magnolia, a Pterocaulon, a Saururus, a Juniperus, and a Phoradendron have been mentioned as part of the Seminole pharmacopoeia or as ingredients of the "Black Drink" that is taken ceremonially. None of these plants is cultivated by the Florida Seminole; rather, each is gathered as needed. Ginseng, a highly respected medicine among the Seminole, is imported from Oklahoma.

There is a certain feeling among the Florida Seminole that medicinal plants acquire their power in the wild; but more importantly, medical lore is esoteric to a considerable degree among them. A plant, one that is to be used curatively or ceremonially, is not simply gathered; it must be gathered at the right time and place, by a person who knows the proper procedures for doing so. This person is likely to be a medicine man, or at least a member of a clan that is traditionally associated with medicine. Ethnographers have seldom descried local attitudes toward mysticomedicinal herbs, and from the literature I could not say whether the Seminole attitude is typical; but from a little experience in the Philippines, Indonesia, New Guinea, and Central America, I suspect that it is. If so, it is easier to understand why many prehistoric peoples readily cultivated food, seasoning, beverage, stimulant, narcotic, fiber, fodder, dye, oleaginous, and other plants, yet never grew the aforesaid herbs about the village. Of such herbs, tobacco is one of the few that was cultivated.

As a fifth conclusion, the cultivation of ornamentals is a subject that has been neglected. Manuals list vast numbers of cultivated plants—more than 31,000 species and varieties in the United States alone—but a majority of these are grown for their flowers or decorative foliage. No doubt, great interest in ornamentals has been most characteristic of comparatively affluent modern societies; and plants of the modern lawn or flower garden have been selectively bred for gaudiness, or for some other nonutilitarian quality, in the last few centuries. Still, there are hints that, in some parts of the world, certain plants have been prized for beauty.

The ethnographic literature has little to say about the circumstances under which uncivilized tribespeople might have raised a few plants for their esthetic qualities. In Papua, North-East New Guinea, and Irian Barat, I have seen flowering shrubs in fairly remote villages, and received the impression that they were valued simply for their blossoms. In this connection, it may be significant that the men of these regions often adorn themselves with flowers, which are stuck into the hair or beneath a sennit armband. The use of flowers for personal adornment is in fact quite widespread from New Guinea through Melanesia into Polynesia. Among the pygmy peoples of the North-East New Guinea uplands, I have noticed flowering shrubs grown in cemeteries. (Of course, missionary influence might be suspected here, even among the pagan tribes.) On the island of Bali, in Indonesia, flowers are used not only for personal adornment but also as tribute to gods of the Hindu pantheon. In India and the mainland of southeastern Asia, flower garlands and bouquets figure in many ceremonies. In and near the Orient, many plants have long been raised simply because they are pleasurable to look upon: hollyhock, rose of Sharon, peony, violet, camellia, deutzia, pear, yellow rape, hawthorn, flowering cherry, morning glory, chrysanthemum, paulownia, plum, yellow rose, and dozens more.

In any event, the paleoethnobotanists have a whole new pathway to explore: the cultivation of ornamentals.

Meighan et al. pointed out that even though the farmer modifies his environment, he must contend with limiting factors of both geographic and cultural nature. Grassland was not cultivated until the invention of methods whereby the tough sod could be broken up. American Indians never cultivated the prairie by aboriginal methods; agricultural tribes of the prairie country grew their crops in the river bottomlands. More advanced farmers, knowing of canalization, terracing, and damming, could live farther from water than could the less advanced ones.

Meighan et al. also pointed out that sites of a certain agricultural period may be correlated with a certain soil type, not necessarily the type we would now consider best for farming. However, some peoples may have restricted themselves to one soil type for reasons that had nothing to do with agriculture; its natural vegetation may have attracted them. (To this I would add that advanced peoples can force less advanced ones into marginal situations, where they cope as best they can with comparatively unfavorable environmental conditions.) In some areas, the line between a cultivated plant and its wild ancestor may be thinly drawn; such an area is likely to have been one in which the plant was first taken into cultivation.

Advanced farmers left implements (e.g., plows) indicative of agriculture, but less advanced ones often left small tools of equivocal function. Polished stone celts may have been used most often to clear fields before planting crops, but they were also used by some nonagricultural peoples to hew out wooden canoes. Sickles were used to reap cultivated plants, and wild plants also. Grinding stones, dibble sticks, hoes, and even spindle whorls had occasional uses other than those involved with agriculture. Ditches, canals, terraces, irrigated plots, granaries, and storage pits often provide good evidence of agriculture. With occasional exceptions, certain comparatively advanced culture trait-complexes were characteristic of peoples with an agricultural economy. Among these complexes were decorated pottery, wheeled vehicles, shaft tombs, constructed ovens (not earthen pits), arches and vaults, molds for casting, cylinder seals, lapidary work in stones harder than quartz, and pottery fired at high temperature. But neither smelting nor the production of clay figurines was limited to agricultural societies. A site of more than 10 acres in extent is likely to have been occupied by farmers, not hunters and gatherers.

I should also add that in some areas, a transition from a molluscan to an agricultural economy can be correlated with a change in the ratio of shell to soil in the middens. Thus, in central Florida, a pre-agricultural midden is composed of clean shells, with scarcely any dirt. Sites of unadvanced agriculture contain a good deal of black dirt with the shells. In the late prehistoric to early historic sites, those with advanced agriculture, the shells are irregularly and rather thinly distributed in a matrix of dirt; and this dirt usually is not especially blackened by organic materials. In still later Indian sites, those of the Seminole, shells are lacking, and the soil is not blackened at all. I should not be surprised to find that within some fairly restricted geographic area, actual measurements of the shell–earth ratio would produce a chronology more refined than the one I have suggested here.

An important recent work was that of Jane M. Renfrew (1973), who reviewed the prehistoric food plants of the Near East and Europe. The geographic restriction of this work was warranted, for of plant remains recovered from archeological sites, the most common and important are those of food plants; and of sites yielding such remains, the most important are those of the Near East and Europe. For as early as the eighth century B.C. in the Near East, man had already passed from a mere hunter and gatherer of wild foods to a more settled farmer who had taken several plants into domestication. The passage opened the way to the Neolithic and then to civilization, and Europe did not lag far behind the Near East in these cultural advances. Renfrew described, species by species, the wheats, barleys, rye, broomcorn millet, oats, apple, pear, almond, pistachio, wine grape, olive, flax, lentil, chick-pea, and other plants that were cultivated at an early time in the Near East and Europe. She also provided remarks on two drug plants, the opium poppy and hemp, along with a catalogue of the most common seeds of wild plants from Near Eastern and European sites. A considerable variety of Near Eastern and European plants—for example, wild strawberry, blackberries, red haws, wild plums, crabapples, wild cherry, vetch, elder, blueberries, acorns (i.e., oaks), cornel, hackberry, and sandspur—have close relatives in the New World, where they should be looked for in archeological sites.

There has been much speculation about the circumstances under which the domestication of plants first began. According to the standard view, the first agriculturists lived in the Near East, in the hills bordering the Fertile Crescent. There, they were very familiar with the wild ancestors of wheat, barley, and other present-day cultivated food plants; familiar, too, with the wild ancestors of several presently domesticated animals. Perhaps as much as 10,000 years ago, they began cultivating the plants, which they soon took down into the better-watered lowlands. Intensive field work in the New World, carried on especially by Richard S. MacNeish, revealed agriculture to be almost as old in the Valley of Mexico as in the Near East. Thus, supposedly, agriculture had two independent centers of origin. Most Old World agriculture is reasonably regarded as having been derived, ultimately, from that of the Fertile Crescent, although China has occasionally been looked on as a third independent center. New World agriculture is reasonably regarded as having been derived from that of Mexico, although the Andean region has occasionally been postulated as another independent center.

Lately, however, William G. Solheim, III (1972) has been accumulating evidence of very early agriculture in Thailand. He holds that from 13,000 to 4000 B.C., the most advanced cultures of the world were in the northern reaches of Southeast Asia, not in the Near East or the Mediterranean region. From a Thailand cave, occupied between 10,000 B.C. and 5600 B.C., he recovered a wide assortment of Asian plants, including pepper, butternut, almond, candlenut, betel nut, cucumber, bottle gourd, Chinese water chestnut, some kind of bean, a pea, and perhaps soy bean. Several species of the assortment were present at all levels, principally in association with artifacts of the Hoabinhian culture. I suppose it would be possible to assert that the inhabitants of the cave had been confirmed vegetarians who gathered wild plants that were destined to be taken into cultivation several millennia later. But certainly, Solheim's work draws attention to the circumstance that large parts of the world have received comparatively little archeological attention; and that many cultural advances—not just agriculture and animal husbandry but also ceramics and metallurgy, among others—might appear to be especially early in or near the Fertile Crescent simply because that region has been investigated more intensively than most others.

It would premature to theorize now at any length about the origins of agriculture. Environmental archeology is a new field, and before theorizing, we need far more basic data about plant remains from sites of the first few postglacial millennia, and about the environmental conditions that prevailed when those sites were occupied.

There are, however, several aspects of prehistoric farming that can be discussed usefully at this time. In this connection, it appears to me that archeologists have occasionally gone astray in approaching this matter of agriculture. I am especially disturbed by a tendency among archeologists to suppose that crops will of necessity grow well on soils that now support a lush natural vegetation, and to ascribe an abundant harvest to soil fertility alone. The relationship of soils to plant growth is a topic meriting discussion from the standpoint of environmental studies. It is a topic with several ramifications. Once again I draw most illustrations from Florida, but believe the situation there to have counterparts elsewhere.

In many regions, and perhaps everywhere, certain characteristic groupings of wild plants often mark the location of archeological sites. Thus, in Richmond and Burke counties, Georgia, the Savannah River has a broad valley that supports hardwood forest. Standing on the high ground overlooking the valley, the archeologist can locate distant mounds because they are covered with pines. In winter, when the hardwoods are leafless, the pines are very conspicuous. From northern Florida to northern Georgia, many expanses of red clay soil have been denuded of vegetation by agricultural activities of modern man. From some high vantage point, the archeologist can identify distant sites because their charcoal and other organic debris have been plowed through the upper soil, darkening it slightly. Thus, even in the absence of vegetation, it is evident that the soil was altered locally by prehistoric occupation. In parts of the St. Johns River drainage of Florida, where river swamps are covered with bald cypress, red maple, and water ash, mounds and middens may stand out because they support dense stands of cabbage palm. In some otherwise treeless, marshy parts of the Florida Everglades, small stands of trees grow on middens.

In much of Florida, the southern red cedar often indicates the presence of a site. Although this tree will grow in the mesic hammock and other plant associations, it forms its densest stands where limestone crops out at the surface or where midden shell has rendered the soil somewhat limey. Along the west coast of peninsular Florida, roughly from the Cedar Keys vicinity southward to the northern part of the study area in Pasco County, a sizeable timber industry once developed, based on the cutting of cedar from the shell middens. Along both coasts of peninsular Florida, the middens have also permitted essentially tropical plants to extend their respective geographic ranges remarkably far to the north. Mastic, gumbo-limbo, lancewood, ironwood, coral bean, saffron plum, white stopper, marlberry, myrsine, spice tree, wild coffee, snowberry, torchwood, butter bough, Jamaica caper tree—these and many more are generally regarded as characteristic of extreme southern Florida, but in actuality they follow the coastal middens northward.

In Pasco County, the outlines of a few Safety Harbor Period sites are identifiable by their vegetation. The sites date from the last part of that period, for they yield a little Spanish majolica. They are surrounded by the turkey oak and longleaf pine association, but themselves support a shrubby, treeless vegetation. Their outlines are recognizable from aerial photographs. In the southern Appalachians, the so-called "grass balds" develop on Indian sites and on well-beaten trails associated with them. Most of these "balds" are on a comparatively warm southwardly facing slope with a gentle gradient, and are located near a spring.

There are other parts of the world, from the Arctic regions to the equatorial, where sites are identifiable by their vegetation. It has even been hinted that occupancy of a site almost invariably changes its soil in a fashion that will somehow be reflected in its vegetation. This suggestion perhaps overstates the case a bit. In the southeastern United States, and I suspect in many other areas, there are no vegetational clues to the presence of sites dating from Paleo-Indian or Early Preceramic times; for these sites were occupied only briefly, they received little debris, and they are deeply buried. In the Southeast, sites of specialized activities (e.g., agricultural fields, flint quarries, knapping stations) may not be recognizable from vegetational criteria alone. Although some mounds support a distinctive plant cover, many do not; much depends on where and how the mound was built. In Pasco County, and in fact rather generally across central Florida, a large percentage of the burial mounds were constructed in one of the deep-sand plant associations, either the turkey-oak and longleaf pine or the sand pine and rosemary scrub. Choice of mound location probably reflected the local availability of much loose sand, easily dug. At any rate, mounds built of this sand often came to be covered with the same vegetation as that of nearby natural hillocks.

But in the Southeast, vegetational peculiarities are usually evident in what might loosely be called village sites, places where the Indians actually resided for a time. Residence might have been permanent, seasonal, or intermittent; at any rate, it was prolonged or intensive as compared with the transitory occupation of a campsite by nomadic hunters and gatherers. A village site, thus defined, need not have been inhabited by agricultural peoples. Coastal and riparian shell middens, left by Indians to whom agriculture was unknown or unimportant, offer a maximum degree of vegetational distinctiveness.

In short, the kind of vegetation that now covers a village site is not likely to be the kind that covered it when it was first occupied; for occupancy alters the soil, and plants are sensitive indicators of soil conditions. This dictum has an application beyond the mere discovery of sites. Failure to apply it has led to some dubious conclusions in Florida, where sites of or contemporary with the Weedon Island Period often are covered with mesic hammock. The supposition has been that the Indians sought out the areas of this vegetation because the presence of large trees guaranteed a rich, fertile soil on which crops could be grown most productively. The supposition is dubious for two reasons, one of which should be evident from the preceding discussion: the presence of mesic hammock on the site today does not lead to the inference that it was present there when the site was first occupied. In this connection, it is instructive to consider the situation at the Big Midden site mentioned previously.

The general vicinity of this site was one of relict dunes, composed of a characteristic white sand and covered with sand pine and rosemary scrub. The dune area was truncated on the north by a small creek with a border of mesic hammock. Occupancy was begun in Weedon Island times by Indians who left small patches of oyster shells atop the white sand of the northernmost dune. Oyster and other shells eventually accumulated deeply over the dune top, along with charcoal and other organic materials that left the shells in a matrix of dark earth. As a result of Indian occupancy, the soil of the site became less acid (because mollusk shells are alkaline), more retentive of moisture (because charcoal and other organic materials hold water much better than pure sand), and a bit richer in some minerals. In short, the soil was converted from one that would support the scrub vegetation to one that would support mesic hammock; and after the Indians had left, the hammock of the creek margin spread over most of the site. In modern times, before it was hauled off for fill, Big Midden was covered with mesic hammock, but this does not mean that the local Indians selected that plant association to reside in; on the contrary, they selected scrub, and their cultural activities were responsible for the subsequent invasion of their village site by mesic hammock.

Big Midden is not unusual; through the central part of the Florida peninsula, I have seen many village sites that were originally in the turkey oak and longleaf pine or else in the sand pine and rosemary scrub. Both these associations would be easy to clear as compared with mesic hammock; and the sand pines, so readily felled and trimmed, would provide ideal timbers for simple construction. Obviously, it would not be posssible to generalize about the plant associations that were selected by prehistoric Indians for their habitation sites; past cultures were diverse, and so were their environmental relations. In most cases, the original environmental relations of a village site could be determined by an ecologist who had intensively studied the local plant associations and the conditions under which they develop. If many sites were so investigated, it would probably become evident that choice of habitation locale was a culture trait. In other words, the bearers of each culture had strong opinions about the kind of surroundings in which a village should be built. But the point is that we cannot discern those opinions simply by looking at the plant associations that grow today on the long-abandoned sites.

There is no reason to suppose that the bearers of a prehistoric culture hacked their village sites and their agricultural fields both from the same plant association. The reverse is more likely to have been the case. A spot that is ideal for crops may have considerable drawbacks as a dwelling place, and vice versa. But in contrast with village sites, croplands never received much cultural debris, and they have but rarely been identified in the course of archeological investigation. In many parts of both the Old World and the New, Neolithic-level farmers practiced what is called swidden agriculture. A small patch of forest was burned, and the soil was automatically enriched by the resultant ashes. The burned patch was farmed for a few years, but then production dropped off rapidly, and so a new patch was cleared and planted. The old one would revert to forest, and eventually it could be burned and planted again. A few writings make it clear that in early historic times, some tribes of the eastern United States were practicing swidden agriculture; but unfortunately, these writings do not indicate the kind of forest that was being burned. I doubt that the mesic hammock, or any other variant of the eastern deciduous forest, was often selected by prehistoric Indians for conversion to cropland; for the trees of this forest were gigantic, the soil contained a network of cable-strong roots, and the association was never dry enough to support much of a blaze. Search should be made for evidence that the Indians of the eastern United States farmed the turkey oak and long leaf pine, the scrub, the clay hills with shortleaf and loblolly pines, and other associations that were drier and more open than deciduous forest. I know from personal experience that the turkey oak and longleaf pine association will grow excellent corn, beans, peas, squash, and pumpkins, even though its soil is deficient as compared with most others. Some of the deficiencies are easily counteracted by a simple farming practice, that of working organic material (leaf mould, manure, kitchen refuse) into the ground around the growing plants.

I stated that there were two reasons for questioning the supposition that Weedon Island Period Indians settled in mesic hammock because the great size of the trees provided assurance of soil fertility. One reason has been adduced: many of their villages were not originally in mesic hammock, and the whereabouts of their agricultural fields is unknown. The second reason relates to the nature of soil fertility, a subject that has been misunderstood in some of the archeological literature.

A soil that is rich and fertile for one species of plant may be intolerable for another. An excellent illustration of this is provided by the Homecrest site in New Port Richey. It is now occupied by suburban residences whose owners raise a variety of ornamentals. The locality originally supported mesic hammock, as shown by numerous large hickories, magnolias, and other trees that were left standing when settlement began. Charcoal, shell, and other organic materials were added to the soil by Indians in Weedon Island times, and modern residents have added several tons of commercial fertilizers. One could scarcely imagine a "richer" soil. It is slightly acid, an ideal condition for a majority of Florida ornamentals; but it will not grow certain species of morning glories that require an alkaline soil. If the soil were sweetened to the point where it would grow these morning glories, it would no longer grow azaleas satisfactorily; for the latter require a highly acid soil and can be poisoned by excess alkalinity.

If it be objected that ornamentals are atypically demanding, one has only to consult any basic agriculture text to learn that plant species differ among themselves in soil requirements. For example, in 1935 R. V. Tamhane et al. described an area in which the crops included pearl millet, lucerne, and rice. The pearl millet would grow on soil that was low in nutrients and water, while lucerne required a soil that was high in nutrients and constantly moist. Although lucerne and rice both needed much water, the lucerne had to have air mixed with it, while the rice did best when actually flooded.

The presence of a magnificent forest does not necessarily mean that the soil it grows in would be ideal for crops. Harold J. Lutz and Robert F. Chandler (1946) in their book on forest soils, summarized the situation admirably: ". . . agricultural crops differ from forest[s] in many respects. . . . Many investigators regard the physical properties of forest soils as of outstanding importance, whereas in agricultural soils the chemical properties may be most important. . . . In general, the requirements of forest trees for soil nutrients are much less than those of most agricultural crops. . . . In agricultural production the plants grown may not belong naturally to the soil, so that artificial conditions must be created to insure their development. Furthermore, in agriculture there frequently exists a desire to stimulate extraordinary growth in localized organs of the crop plants; such stimulation usually requires abnormal soil conditions, particularly from the standpoint of nutrients. . . ."

Crop plants are harvested annually or more frequently, and the continual removal of them depletes the soil if it is not deliberately fertilized. In contrast, a forest constantly returns its nutrients to the ground, as leaves fall and dead trees topple. The debris has an important effect on the physical, chemical, and biological characteristics of the soil. In a forest, but not in an agricultural field hacked therefrom, vagaries of weather are minimized by the plant cover. Beneath forest vegetation, the soil stays comparatively cool. In temperate lands, conversion of forest to cropland can alter the "soil climate" as though the denuded spot had been shifted southward by as much as two degrees of latitude.

In some parts of the world, special environmental conditions may affect the soil when forest is converted to cropland. In another book, I have discussed this circumstance in connection with the tropical rainforest of Indonesia. In that plant association, gigantic trees grow in abundance and variety on a lateritic soil that has little surplus of nutrients. The available nutrients are constantly cycled, and removal of the trees brings the cycle to an end. The more soluble minerals are soon leached out, and the soil of the denuded patch may be converted to brick-like laterite.

In summary, the archeologist should not assume that crops would grow excellently in soil that supports forest. Much depends on the kind of crops to be grown, on the local environmental conditions, and on the agricultural practices of the farmers. While a sizeable body of literature relates to the farming methods of historic Indians, not much is known about the methods of prehistoric ones. In general, archeological excavation can only reveal hillocks, ridges and furrows, terraces, irrigation channels—disturbances of the ground by farmers in the course of their work. However, I suspect that someone really familiar with farming could draw many inferences from the limited archeological traces of prehistoric agriculture.

For example, in the Florida Panhandle, two or three sites were excavated to reveal small garden plots, their rows carefully oriented in a north–south direction. Archeologists speculated about the reason behind this orientation: was it a matter of superstition, or did it carry out an alignment of something in the nearby village? But in all parts of the world, small-scale farmers know that row crops are to be aligned north–south, because the sun moves east–west. If the rows were oriented east–west, each plant would shade its neighbor. The north–south orientation of rows permits each plant to receive a maximum of sunlight. In the case of peas and beans, especially, the harvest is substantially reduced if the leafy plants are allowed to shade one another. Of course, it would be possible to set out plants so far apart that they would not shade one another regardless of orientation; but this procedure would necessitate clearing and tending a comparatively large patch of ground.

The archeological literature has gone a bit astray, at times, in invoking soil fertility alone as an explanation of an abundant harvest. We are told, for example, that at Ocos, Guatemala, the soil was so fertile that the Indians could raise three crops of maize a year; but surely sunlight, a long growing season, rainfall, and farming practices had something to do with the matter. Although a plant takes a small amount of minerals from the soil, most of its increase in bulk results from photosynthesis, a chemical process whereby water and carbon dioxide, in the presence of sunlight and chlorophyll, combine to form carbohydrates (sugars, cellulose, starches). Soils vary in their air and water content, as they do in their mineral content; but in general, it is an interaction of edaphic, climatic, and cultural factors that determines the productivity of a garden or farm.

The ecological relations of plants are complex, and human uses for plants are multifarious. Consequently, there exist quite a few more directions of study taken by environmental archeologists in their consideration of floral remains from sites. Dimbleby, in his aforesaid book on plants and archeology, drew attention to charcoal, which is present in most sites. One lump of charcoal looks about like another, but Dimbleby pointed out that this material often can be prepared and examined microscopically, in such a fashion as to permit identification of the wood that was burned. He also drew attention to wood that had been merely browned. In reexamining a supposed association of man and extinct animals at the Bon Terra Farm Site in northern Florida, I noted (1953) a slightly browned log, and attributed its condition to slow oxidation. Other archeologists have also invoked slow oxidation to account for some bits of wood that had been browned but not blackened. However, Dimbleby (1967) concluded that such browning results only from exposure to fire.

The topic of browning and charring has been of special interest in the Old World, where grains, especially wheat, often were seared. Dimbleby believed that grains were so treated in order to kill them and prevent them from sprouting while in storage. To this I might add that in the New World, the searing of maize renders it resistant to weevils, which otherwise would ruin a great deal of the stored grain. The early historic tribes of northern Florida sometimes constructed elevated granaries, under which fires could be built in order to sear the stored maize. Searing of grain might have led to the discovery of pop wheat in the Old World and popcorn in the New.

The topic of food storage merits more attention than it has generally received. To judge from the ethnographic literature, methods of preserving foods were not entirely unknown to nomadic hunters and gatherers; but storage was of particular importance to more sedentary peoples. Wild foods are likely to be seasonal in their availability, and of course crops are harvested only at intervals. If the domestication of plants is to provide a society with a firm economic foundation, techniques of farming must be accompanied by those of storing the harvest. The foundation of an early civilization was a storable food, usually of a starchy nature. Storage can be demonstrated archeologically through the excavation of granaries, storehouses, or jars of specially treated foods. In the Maya country of the Yucatán Peninsula, certain pits in the limestone turned out to be storage chambers for breadnut seeds. Of course, literate cultures may provide detailed accounts of their storage practices.

It often happens that two species of edible plants, cultivated or otherwise, are ripe for harvesting at different times of year. If the two are found in close association, say in the same jar or the same fecal specimen, then at least one of them was stored. It should also be noted that fermentation is a form of storage. Surplus fruits or grains, of kinds not readily dried or otherwise preserved, can be converted into beer; thus, their food value is not lost. Some archeologists believe that in the Old World, grains were brewed into beer long before they were baked into bread. Of course, in most parts of the world, fermentation has also been encouraged for reasons having nothing to do with storage.

An important direction in environmental archeology was stimulated by A. L. Kroeber's (1939) review of cultural and natural areas of North America. The subject may appropriately be introduced at this point, because natural areas are characterized in part by their vegetation, and because cultural adaptation to an area in part reflects the possibilities of the local flora, both wild and cultivated. Kroeber found a good degree of correspondence between cultural areas and natural ones. There was even a rough correlation between linguistic areas and natural ones. However, the presently distinctive natural areas, the ones that concerned Kroeber, have not been in existence throughout the full span of archeological times in North America. Accordingly, in 1954, George L. Quimby (1954) summarized knowledge of the earlier cultural and natural areas. He adopted a good bit of terminology from the geologic-climatic studies of Ernst Antevs.

Current views of the earlier natural areas are about as follows: The Mankato advance of the fourth glaciation came about 12,000 B.C., and was followed by the Two Creeks Interstadial during which the ice retreated. Then came the Valders advance of about 9,000 B.C. (All these dates are uncalibrated.) North America, north of Mexico, was a single natural area (in the broad sense of Kroeber) during Mankato to Valders times. The glacial ice and the Rocky Mountains were the only barriers to the movement of peoples. South of the ice was a narrow zone of tundra, and then a broad zone of taiga. South of the taiga were other forests, also grasslands; but there were no deserts and no tropical forests. Climate was cool and rainy; lakes were numerous in some areas from which they have since vanished.

By about 7000 B.C. the Valders ice was retreating, the climate becoming warmer and drier. The Anathermal climatic stage had begun, and would continue until about 5000 B.C. In eastern North America, pine forests pushed northward as the taiga fell back. In the rain-shadow of the Rockies and the more westerly ranges, dry-adapted vegetation kept spreading, although lakes remained numerous. But then the general climatic trend of the Anathermal was halted, and around 6000 B.C. there came the Cochrane advance of ice. This was but a brief episode, after which the trend was resumed and exaggerated.

By 5000 B.C., the Anathermal had passed into the Altithermal. The latter, a comparatively long period of warm, dry climate, was responsible for diversification of the natural areas. However, during the Altithermal, the climate became even warmer and drier than it is today. Some forests were replaced by grasslands, some grasslands by deserts. Tongues of prairie extended eastward into the eastern United States. Where rainfall was adequate, hardwood forest pushed north as more northerly types of forest continued to fall back.

Around 2500 B.C., the climatic pendulum began to swing back the other way; the Altithermal passed into the somewhat cooler and moister Medithermal. The natural areas took on essentially their present characteristics; they became the ones that were studied by Kroeber.

From Mankato times to the establishment of the present natural areas, North American cultural developments were complex. I shall not review them here, for they have lately been treated in detail by Gordon R. Willey (1966). He recognized ten cultural areas of North America, north of Mexico: Arctic, Subarctic (with eastern and western sectors), Northwest Coast, Interior Plateau, California, Great Basin, Southwest, Plains, Northeast Mexico-Texas, and Eastern Woodlands. His map of cultural areas is very similar to a map I prepared (1969) to show the vegetation provinces of North America. If the culture areas had been subdivided a bit further, the two maps would have been even more similar. This does not mean that cultures are adapted to vegetation; rather, vegetation reflects a variety of environmental conditions, to some or most of which culture is adapted. This statement needs to be "hedged" a bit further:

The general trend of the hominids, at least from the time of *Homo habilis,* has been one of progressive emancipation from the demands of the natural environment. Investigators have occasionally chosen to distinguish between a primary environment, which is of natural origin; and a secondary environment, which is produced culturally, and which may counteract some rigors of the primary environment. But in general, both the largesse and the demands of the natural environment were major concerns of most peoples during the time periods that interest the archeologist; and one might expect at least a fair degree of correspondence between natural areas and cultural ones. This statement does not constitute an endorsement of environmental determinism as any sort of general proposition. Certainly, environment can control some aspects of culture; its influence on technology is especially strong, and the archeologist deals primarily with the tangible traces of past technology. But if environmental control of culture were imperious, there would be no culture change within a natural area until the environmental characteristics of that area changed. In actuality, there were many instances in which culture was revolutionized independently of any change in the natural environment. And there were also instances in which a single natural area harbored two or more different cultures; e.g., both settled farmers and nomadic raiders.

The cultural and natural areas were conceived very broadly by Kroeber, his predecessors, and his successors. What is also needed, at least in archeology, is an investigation into the environmental relations of each past culture, considered separately; then, the investigations could be assembled and analyzed for patterns of environmental adaptation. By this approach, the combined efforts of many local workers would at least refine the broad schemes of the monographers, and might permit some new generalizations about the relationship of culture to environment. The needed kind of local work has not often been carried on, at least in the United States. Florida is one of the few states to have been formally divided into archeological areas—or perhaps I should call them subareas—that were more or less correlated with natural ones. Even in this case, the emphasis has been on cultural diversity as manifested by artifacts, not on environmental factors possibly correlated with such diversity; and little attention has been given to changes in the natural subareas between Paleo-Indian times and the present.

Now to another topic involving plants. Archeobotanical and other studies have combined to explore the likelihood that prehistoric man made transoceanic voyages between the Old World and the New. Man does not "independently invent" a plant, and if a plant species was cultivated in two widely separated areas, culture contact between those areas may be inferred. This apparently simple proposition has some hidden difficulties, however. Those who oppose it might argue that around the time of Columbus, the Spaniards and the Portuguese made some unrecorded voyages during which various crop plants were introduced into new lands. And if a plant demonstrably was present in both hemispheres before the official discovery of America, could not it have attained this distribution by natural dissemination? The transoceanic distribution of plants is in fact a complex subject, and one that has given rise to much controversy.

The bottle-gourd, *Lagenaria siceraria,* is one of the plants most often cited as perhaps having been carried across the ocean by prehistoric man. It was principally a domestic utensil, although it had other uses. In Mexico, the species has been radiocarbon-dated back to the period 7000–5000 b.c., so presumably it is of New World origin. There is no botanical reason why this should not be so. It existed in Africa and Asia, including the Mediterranean world, in pre-Columbian times. Its fruit forms a tough, long-lasting shell when hollowed and dried by man, but otherwise it rots so that the seeds may sprout. The species is not disseminated by water, and does not live on beaches. If it crossed an ocean with the aid of man, then some Old World voyagers came to the New World, acquired the seeds, and took them back home.

Archeologists have often balked even at the idea of storm-tossed castaways reaching the New World from the Old in prehistoric times, and no doubt would object even more strongly to the idea of a round-trip voyage. Still, there is some other evidence that such voyages were made. In ancient Pompeii, frescos portrayed two New World fruits, the pineapple and the soursop. These were shown on the walls of a building dubbed "The House of the Rich Man." Maize originated in the New World, where its ancestry has been traced archeobotanically back to an insignificant grass; but some Chinese scholars believe they have found references to maize in pre-Columbian literature of their country. Maize grown in Assam resembles archeological varieties, not modern varieties, from the New World; and the Assamese plant is the subject of myths resembling certain American ones. The night-blooming Cereus is a cultivated member of a New World genus, but it was first made known to science from a huge specimen grown horticulturally in China. In parts of Mexico, such a specimen may be grown in a village, where its flowering is the signal for a festival; but the species has not been found in the wild, except as an escape from some homestead.

The sweet potato has also received frequent mention in connection with transoceanic voyages. Its genus, *Ipomoea,* which includes the familiar morning glories, is most diverse in the New World but has some native species in the Old. Among the wild species, the nearest relative of the cultivated sweet potato is one from the New World tropics. The sweet potato was grown in a number of varieties from Mexico through Central America into South America, also in Polynesia and Melanesia. It was the proverbial staff of life for tribes in the remote uplands of New Guinea. The Maori of New Zealand grew some varieties that had become evolutionarily adapted to high latitudes and cool summers; and one hardly supposes that this evolution took place since Spaniards and Portuguese began crossing the Pacific. Although under unusual conditions the sweet potato may set seed, the plant is propagated through division of its sprouts or tuberous rootstock.

The coconut, *Cocos nucifera,* is another plant that was present in both hemispheres in pre-Columbian times. Transoceanic dissemination by man has been questioned because coconuts will float and will sprout in the supratidal zone. Experiments suggest, however, that the nuts could not survive a transoceanic drift voyage. The species may have originated in the New World, where it finds its closest relatives.

The banana and plantain also offer problems. Their genus, *Musa*, originated in the Old World tropics. The banana, prized by civilized man, may have been introduced into America in post-Columbian times. But in both the Old World and the New, the tribespeople and peasantry have been more interested in the plantain, also called cooking banana. If it was introduced into the New World in historic times, it spread with remarkable rapidity, and somehow acquired a diversity of indigenous names.

The case of cotton is singularly complex. Some species of the cotton genus, *Gossypium*, were native to the Old World, others to the New. Cultivation of cotton for the fiber may have begun in India, but was ancient in the Americas also. In prehistoric times, an Asian species was taken to Peru, where it hybridized with an American one. The resultant hybrid spread widely in the Americas, and was also taken back across the Pacific as far as the Galapagos, Hawaii, Polynesia, and Melanesia.

The peanut, *Arachis hypogaea*, is a New World species, and was widely grown in South America. There is no evidence that its presence in China and Southeast Asia resulted from historic introduction only; and the Oriental variety resembles the Peruvian archeological one. The jackbean, a species of *Canavalia* cultivated in prehistoric America, may be specifically identical with the swordbean that was occasionally grown in the Old World. The lima bean, *Phaseolus lunatus*, was domesticated in the prehistoric Americas; it was quite important to the Moche of Peru. A primitive variety of lima bean, virtually extinct in the Americas, is grown in Southeast Asia.

Tobacco is puzzling, also. Wild species of its genus, *Nicotiana*, are concentrated in warmer parts of the New World, but some are native to Australia and Oceania. Two South American species were taken into cultivation in prehistoric times, and one of these spread throughout much of South, Central, and North America. Oddly, tobacco apparently was first domesticated in the one part of the New World where smoking was not practiced. Perhaps, then, the plant was chewed in its original homeland, later to be replaced there by the chewing of coca, a stronger narcotic.

Among New Guinea tribesmen, tobacco is raised, and the smoking of it is integrated into ritual and ceremonial life. No doubt New Guinea had a native tobacco, and received an American one in historic times; but it is hard to believe that the Portuguese or other Europeans introduced a body of myth involved with the cultivation and utilization of *Nicotiana*. Elsewhere I have suggested that, in New

Guinea, smoking rituals antedated the historic introduction of New World tobacco. Whether these rituals were based on Old World to-bacco or some other plant, I do not know. But in any event, to get at the truth about the cultivation of tobacco and the smoking of it, we must consider separately such matters as narcotic indulgences, a body of myth surrounding the tobacco plant, and another body of myth surrounding the immolation of dried herbs.

The presence of pipes does not clarify the spread of tobacco, be-cause other plants might have been smoked in them. The origin of the pipe may have been in Asia, where a tube was used to blow or inhale the smoke of supposedly medicinal herbs. Such a tube, an-cient in Asia and Europe, may have been the prototype of the tubular (bamboo) pipe used in New Guinea. From the tube may also have been derived the first New World pipes, for they were oldest in North America and were tubular. In the New World, the tubular pipe dif-fused southward while the cultivation of tobacco diffused northward. A later development in North America was the platform pipe, which like the tubular was one-piece. The compound pipe—a cubical or elbow-shaped bowl with a detachable stem—may have originated in South America and spread northward. It arrived comparatively late in North America; but after its arrival there, both the platform and tubu-lar pipes continued in some use. The elbow pipe was in wide use at the beginning of historic times in eastern North America; it was soon duplicated by Europeans for the Indian trade. Mold-made specimens of fired clay, some of them glazed, occur as trade goods in early his-toric sites of the eastern United States. Soon, however, the Europeans introduced the one-piece, long-stemmed "church-warden" pipe of white ball-clay. This went through some stylistic changes before going out of fashion.

Thus, within some restricted area, pipes may serve as time markers, but it would be temeritous to say what was smoked in them. One might make out a case for the simultaneous spread of the compound pipe and the cultivation of tobacco.

Plants also figure indirectly in the postulated transfer of culture be-tween the hemispheres. Hindu-Buddhist iconography included a lotus staff, a lotus throne, and a panel in which the plant was treated in a stylized fashion. The lotus of the Old World has a close relative in the New; it figured in Maya iconography as a staff, a throne, and a similarly stylized portrayal on a panel. In and near Indonesia, a wide-spread custom was the chewing of betel nut. The pulverized nut was mixed with lime to liberate a narcotic, and there were special utensils for containing and dipping the mixture. Coca, a plant of South America, was unrelated to betel nut, but was similarly prepared and taken. Also in and near Indonesia, a kind of palm was felled and starch extracted from it by a special technique; the substance might then be baked into a sort of bread. In South America, starch was similarly extracted and prepared, from a different kind of palm. In northern and eastern Brazil, the starch was called by its usual Indonesian name, *sagu*, but this name may well have been transferred by the Portuguese.

Much less attention has been given to the possibility that animal species might also provide evidence of tranoceanic voyages. At least five animals may do so. First, the Mexican hairless dog has a counterpart in China. Second, the Chinese and Japanese custom of fishing with trained cormorants also existed in scattered coastal areas of South America. Third, a rumpless chicken that lays blue eggs was domesticated in Japan; but it was first discovered by Europeans in southern South America, and so became known as the Araucana hen.

Fourth, there are only two species of cochineal insects in the world. One of these, confined to the Mediterranean area, was "farmed"— placed on its food plant (the kermes oak) and protected from enemies. The second species, confined to Mexico and nearby parts of Central America, was similarly treated—placed on its food plant (the nopal cactus) and protected. Both species were gathered as the source of a red dye.

Some Mediterranean peoples, especially the Phoenicians, extracted a purple dye, the so-called Tyrian or royal purple, from a marine snail of the family Muricidae. When a clear juice, expressed from the mollusks, was boiled with salt, it gradually turned purple. The dye was used only to color the clothing of the elite. In Central America, Colombia, Ecuador, and Peru, another snail of the family Muricidae was treated in the same way, and its purple dye was similarly restricted in use. Incidentally, the production of this dye was not limited to the Mediterranean and the New World; it was also carried on in the British Isles, Morocco, the Madeira Islands, Java, China, and Japan.

Evidently, even though botanical and zoological studies may not actually prove transoceanic culture contact, they can help in evaluating the other evidence pertinent thereto.

A final direction of hypothesizing, inspired by archeobotanical remains: James B. Griffin (1960) attempted to explain why the Hopewell culture declined. This culture, which occupied the central Ohio River valley and the Illinois valley, was the culmination of a long developmental sequence. It was characterized by elaborate ceremonial earthworks and burial mounds, by quality craftsmanship in various materials, and by long trade routes extending from the Rockies to the Atlantic Ocean and the Gulf of Mexico. Its decline, after so auspicious a beginning, has been a puzzle.

Taking evidence from palynology, archeobotany, and geology, Griffin held the Hopewell culture to have reached its height between 200 B.C. and 200 A.D., during a relatively warm period; and to have declined during a cooler period, 200–700 A.D. As a result of this cooling, corn agriculture became unreliable in the Hopewell country, where the culture deteriorated for want of a reliable economic foundation.

It is well established that a less advanced culture can vanish when its country is invaded by a more advanced one; but nothing like this happened in the Hopewell country, where the Hopewellians were replaced by bearers of a much simpler way of life. The successors to the Hopewellians reverted to a mixed hunting, gathering, and agricultural economy. They let the trade routes break down, and built no more great earthworks. Sometimes, rather pathetically, they buried their own dead in the Hopewell mounds, with comparatively simple grave goods.

There are several instances in which natural occurrences have been invoked to explain cultural decay. It has been suggested, for example, that the Harappans of India were flooded out of their cities; that the Maya left northern Central America because their temples were brought down by earthquakes, or their agricultural soils were depleted by swidden agriculture; that the Romans succumbed to malaria, or to lead poisoning. But I am dubious of these simplicistic explanations for cultural decline.

The Hopewell culture apparently was spread by small groups of an elite, a priestly aristocracy who superimposed their ways upon those of other peoples. The Hopewellian degree of cultural complexity required not just a solid economic foundation but also a sizeable labor force. The vast majority of Hopewellians labored futilely at the behest of an elite. Trade routes were maintained solely to acquire exotic materials, for the manufacture of high-quality objects; and these were made solely for burial with the remains of certain dead. The earthworks were burial and ceremonial centers, even though some of them might also have served as fortifications. So-called Hopewell "culture" is little more than the material expression of funerary rites. Perhaps, after several centuries, the Hopewellian majority came to realize that they themselves took no profit from the arduous labors that made these rites possible. Climatic change, with its impact on local agriculture, may have been all that was needed to topple a culture that was already poised most precariously.

Perhaps a culture can decline because many of its bearers grow dissatisfied with it, coming to feel that its rewards are not commensurate with its demands.

In the preceding chapter I stated that environmental archeology was sprawling. If the reader had any lingering doubt about the matter, the present chapter should have removed it. Nevertheless, I have not wished to take up space with an attempted ordering of extant studies in environmental archeology. Such an attempt would rapidly be outdated, and I have preferred instead to show how environmental studies can provide new approaches to archeological problems large and small. Not that I claim to have solved the problems; I am merely trying to reveal new methodologies of investigation.

CHAPTER NINE

Some Environmental Studies and Their Application

In this chapter I review some additional work in environmental archeology, note a few more of the directions in which it has ramified. However, the greater part of the chapter is taken up with the application of environmental studies to archeological problems. It is hoped that some of the applications will prove interesting to the layman, useful or inspiring to the professional archeologist, and novel to both.

Sites of a culture may be restricted to a certain soil type, but it cannot automatically be assumed that the culture-bearers selected that type because of its agricultural possibilities. Instead, they may have been interested in some aspect of its plant associations, or in the animals that inhabited the associations. This circumstance, and discussion in previous chapters, emphasizes that the topic of soils is not readily discussed apart from that of vegetation. However, a few studies have focused upon soils. I. W. Cornwall (1958) wrote an account of soils for the archeologist, concentrating upon Britain and western continental Europe. From the standpoint of environmental archeology, a regional approach to soils is justified, for each archeological area has its own pedological complexity. The archeologist, hoping to extract useful information about the soil in and near a site, may not receive much help from pedologists or from other geologists who are familiar with soils; for in general, the geologists have concerned themselves with events of considerable geographic scope and time depth, not with the localized, short-term events of an archeological site. But the average archeologist, perhaps having studied a few publications on the geology of his area, might learn a great deal simply through observation of the local soils, minerals, and pedological processes. One illustration of this point will be given.

In Florida and southern Georgia, flatwoods soils are comparatively unsuitable for agriculture. They are very acid, soggy at one season and parched at another. Their plant associations are not particularly rich in edible or otherwise useful plant species, nor do these associations harbor any noteworthy abundance of edible wild game. It is not surprising that the flatwoods were largely avoided by the agricultural Indians, and by the Late Preceramic Indians who collected plants and animals from more productive situations. But as mentioned in an earlier chapter, Suwannee points date back to a time when the environment was quite different from the present one, and they do occur in flatwoods. As a matter of fact, a series of projectile point types characterize the flatwoods. In the slash pine and wiregrass flatwoods from central Florida into southern Georgia, a habitation site will generally yield Clovis, Suwannee, Arredondo, Bolen Beveled, Wacissa, Taylor, or Kirk Serrated points. These types collectively span the Paleo-Indian and Early Preceramic periods. Not that any one of them is restricted to flatwoods. Rather, in the case of each of them, a comparatively high percentage of specimens come from the flatwoods; whereas specimens of Late Preceramic types, although incomparably more abundant in the general region, hardly ever come from the flatwoods. The Late Preceramic types come mostly from riparian and littoral situations, usually shell middens.

In short, the transition from Early to Late Preceramic was marked by virtual abandonment of the flatwoods in favor of other situations. This cultural shift took place as the Anathermal passed into the Altithermal. There is local evidence of climatic change accompanying this shift; for in the early sites of the flatwoods, the occupation level is atop the hardpan and beneath the recent sands. Florida is plentifully supplied with relict dunes, not just coastally but also in the interior of the state. From these dunes, sand is blown by the trade winds, to a degree dependent on rainfall and plant cover. Evidently, not much sand blew from the dunes during the comparatively cool, moist Anathermal; it began to blow about during the warm, dry Altithermal.

Thus, the association of certain projectile point types with flatwoods soil leads to two conclusions: The climatic change, from An-athermal to Altithermal, was abrupt and was evidenced at least as far south as central Florida; and this change marked a cultural shift from Early Preceramic to Late Preceramic, as Indians moved into the ri-parian and littoral situations.

Also, in the absence of stratigraphic evidence, it is their restriction to flatwoods, as much as anything else, that leads us to assign Taylor, Wacissa, and Kirk Serrated points to the Early Preceramic. The assign-ment is bolstered by typologically early characters (basal grinding in Taylor, grinding and beveling in Wacissa, serration in Kirk Serrated), and by the absence of these types from Late Preceramic or later sites.

Interestingly, in Louisiana, Sherwood M. Gagliano (1967) used a dif-ferent ecological approach to show that the Kirk Serrated was Early Preceramic. In that state, these points were found to be associated with Early Recent stream terraces, in other words with a stream drain-age pattern that has long since vanished.

Turning now to other topics, there exist some papers describing how factors of the environment might lead the archeologist into mis-interpretation of his material. These papers are too few and diverse to be regarded as constituting a specific direction of environmental ar-cheology, but the topic is interesting, and it has ramifications to which attention has not been drawn.

Under special conditions, a wounded animal might carry a projec-tile point far outside the area where that type of point was made. This is most likely to happen in the far north, where some migratory ani-mals move southward at the onset of winter, then back northward in the spring. In latitudinal extent, the migration of the Barren Ground caribou is equivalent to an annual round trip between Philadelphia, Pennsylvania, and Charleston, South Carolina. Obviously, caribou could pass through the territories of several different peoples, all of them hunters. Along the Pacific Coast of northwestern North America, certain Indians harpooned whales, which ran for days be-fore dying and being cast ashore. Sometimes, a harpooned whale would be cast up in the territory of a far-off tribe.

The carrying of a projectile point by a large mammal must be of rare occurrence, although it has been reported. The carrying of nuts, seeds, and grains by small mammals is of common occurrence, how-ever, and has several times led to erroneous conclusions. In the newspapers, there have been numerous reports of viable nuts, seeds, or grains discovered in some ancient tomb or ruin. We are asked to believe that the plant propagules sprouted after a lapse of hundreds or even thousands of years. Actually, various mice and other small rodents will burrow deeply, and somewhere in the ground they will pile up a store of food gathered at the surface. These caches, so often left about tombs and buried ruins, are mistaken for the debris of prehistoric human occupancy. If the propagules germinate, their age is to be measured in years, not centuries.

Pack rats collect small objects, including modern artifacts of metal, stone, and glass. Sometimes they will drop one object in favor of another, a practice that has earned them the name of trade rats. One supposes that in caves and ruins of the southwestern United States, where these rodents may abound, small prehistoric artifacts are often moved about by them.

From an account (Kidder 1947) of excavations at the Maya site of Uaxactun, Guatemala, comes the following: "In two piles behind the head of the extended [human] skeleton . . . were 230 little bone objects, apparently of bird bone. . . . all were closely alike, exactly 2.3 cm. long, with four notches at the thinner end, an incised V in which were tiny drilled punctations, the thicker end plain or with a smaller V. As they have no suspension holes, they could not have been strung as a necklace; and their curving backs and thin ends render them unsuitable for inlays. Nothing similar has been recorded." Fortunately, two of these specimens were illustrated. They are merely scutes of the nine-banded armadillo. Their supposed incising and drilling are part of the scute's natural ornamentation. From published information, it cannot be determined whether an armadillo burrowed into the Maya burial and died there; or whether an armadillo (or just its scutes) was deliberately placed with the remains. But it is important to identify the objects as essentially non-artifactual, for similar ones have a wide natural distribution in the Pleistocene and Recent of the Americas.

The extent to which burrowing animals can disarrange a stratified site is astonishing. In central Florida, many streams have nearby sandhills covered with turkey oak and longleaf pine. Off and on during the millennia, these hills were campsites or village sites for Indians. Frequently, a test excavation will reveal several occupation levels, each neatly separated from the others by a foot or so of windblown sand. A situation of this kind would usually be ideal for further excavation; but unfortunately, some of the hills are infested with pocket gophers and gopher tortoises. Both of these burrowers rid their tunnels of hard objects. The pocket gophers, being small, seldom bring up anything but flint chips and charcoal; but the tortoises frequently bring up sherds and projectile points. Having brought up an artifact, the tortoise may give it a kick that sends it four or five feet away. Like postholes, pocket gopher and gopher tortoise burrows are distinguishable by the archeologist even after they have become filled in; but at some spots they have riddled the soil and ruined the stratigraphy. Even the deeply buried Suwannee points are brought to the surface.

The burrow of a large tortoise may be twelve inches wide, eight inches high, and 30 or even 40 feet long; at its deepest, it may be ten feet below the ground surface. On a tract of a few acres extent, the tortoises and pocket gophers can bring up tons of soil, and they will bring up quite a few artifacts if they chance to be burrowing through a site. In parts of central Florida, relic collectors find it profitable to return to a tortoise-infested locality every few months, because the reptiles continue to bring up cultural debris.

Chemical factors of the local environment also have the potentiality of leading the archeologist a bit astray. This circumstance was first brought to my attention at a time when I was occasionally called upon by certain police agencies to express an opinion about the age, sex, race, and time of death of unidentified corpses. It became evident that the surroundings of the body had much to do with its state of preservation. One body might decay more in two months than another in two years. Rotting was especially rapid in the low flatwoods of south-central Florida, especially slow atop the sandhills of north-central Florida. Admittedly, the chemical content of the soil was not solely responsible for the rate of decay; rapid desiccation makes for preservation. But evidently, some soils do not encourage preservation of bone (or shell).

From central Florida into southern Georgia, flatwoods sites of Paleo-Indian and Early Preceramic age yield only stone work. Yet, some long bone points are of Paleo-Indian age; and since the manufacture of these implements continued into Late Preceramic times, the Early Preceramic peoples should have possessed them also. And surely the Paleo-Indian and Early Preceramic Indians left food bones at their habitation sites. In the red clay hill country at the base of the Florida Panhandle, Early Preceramic sites yield stone work only. In the Savannah River drainage of the Georgia Piedmont, numerous red clay hills are capped with the quartz work of the Old Quartz culture, but there are no bone implements, no food bones or mollusk shells. The possibility should be considered that bone and shell do not last in flatwoods or red clay soils. They hold up excellently in middens, fairly well in deep-sand situations.

At the Silver Springs Site in Central Florida (Neill 1958b), an occupation level with rather Clovis-like Suwannee points lay atop a laminated formation of clay and sand, and beneath almost eight feet of windblown sand. The windblown sand contained lumps of claystone, which form in place as a result of chemicals trickling downward. The lumps were larger and more numerous toward the bottom of the windblown sand. Aside from stone artifacts and spalls, the Suwannee level yielded only a pentagonal bit of fossil shell, perhaps shaped by man, and what was possibly a fragment of an ivory foreshaft. But these two objects were so corroded, I suppose by soil acids, that I could not insist on their identification. Probably the Suwannee level, which was comparatively rich for Paleo-Indian times, once had bone and perhaps shell items that had decayed beyond recognition. From the level came two sandstone abraders, one of them with channels of the kind produced when long bone points are sharpened.

In sharp contrast with the site at Silver Springs was one in Pasco County, the one mentioned in chapter 8 as having yielded a Clovis point, denticulate flakes, and other items. This Paleo-Indian site had bone artifacts and food bones in good (mineralized) condition. The occupation level with this material was atop a limestone formation, and beneath less than a foot of sand. As a hypothesis, I suggest that limestone has much to do with the preservation of bone and shell. It will be recalled that these materials are also preserved in limestone caves and calcareous spring-runs of Florida. (And after Early Preceramic times, they are excellently preserved in shell middens, which are calcareous.) More importantly, bone and shell may vanish from Paleo-Indian and Early Preceramic sites in flatwoods, red clay, and perhaps some other soils of the eastern United States. I doubt that sites of these periods ever had more than a few shells, but they should have had bone artifacts and food bones at one time.

It is well known that organic materials can be preserved beneath the waters of the great springs of central Florida, but attention has not been called to the way in which these waters preserve the paint of certain red-painted pottery. In the vicinity of Silver Springs, sites on land produced a large quantity of St. Johns Plain pottery, and a much lesser quantity of Dunn's Creek Red. The latter is but St. Johns Plain with a red slip, and some workers do not regard the two as separate types; but I shall do so for convenience in discussion. Careful scrutiny revealed that quite a few sherds, catalogued as St. Johns Plain, actually bore a few tiny flecks of red. They had once been red-slipped, but the slip had almost vanished. Sometimes a sherd, perhaps because it had been half in the ground and half out, would show traces of red slip at one end only. It seemed possible that the original ratio of red-slipped to plain sherds was higher than present counts indicated. Then, special effort was made to recover sherds from the floor of the springs, and they were brought up in vast numbers. Red-slipped sherds from beneath the waters averaged much brighter than those from sites on land; but more importantly, in the submerged material the red-slipped sherds greatly outnumbered the plain ones.

The use of a red slip on pottery is a culture trait that apparently spread from Ecuador to the United States. In tracing this spread, it is important to realize that the popularity of red-slipping in some areas might have been much greater than is now indicated by ceramic inventories. For example, at the Colombian site of Puerto Hormiga, which figured significantly in the northward diffusion of culture, the use of red slip was regarded as doubtful; but some vessels had "small spots of red coloring," and I suspect they had been red-slipped at one time.

A misleading conception of a past culture may also result from failure to understand the deficiencies of the environment in which that culture existed. As an illustration, islanders might seem to have been in a pre-pottery stage, when in actuality they had given up the ceramic arts after movement to an island without clay deposits. The failure of metallurgy to reach some parts of South America may have resulted only from local absence of workable ores. In the Glades archeological subarea of Florida, the Indians' elaborate work in bone and shell constituted an effort to find a substitute for stone, which was scarce. The late spread of the bow and arrow, and its failure to reach some Florida tribes even by historic times, may reflect the absence from many areas of a suitable bow wood. Enthusiasm for the bow and arrow may have been limited until it became possible to obtain staves or finished bows of Osage orange, the only really good bow wood of the United States.

In past times, mineralization has occasionally misled archeologists. It was assumed that heavy mineralization of human remains or of bone artifacts was prima facie evidence of great age. As I have shown elsewhere (Neill 1957) this is not necessarily the case. Florida has produced a human skeleton in which the organic material had been completely replaced by limonite, and it has produced human skulls embedded in masses of breccia. But in that state, mineralization can be a mere matter of decades, at least under ideal conditions. I do not suppose modern archeologists will often go astray in the fashion of their predecessors; but as late as the 1950s, paleontologists were assigning a Pleistocene or earlier dating to any Florida bone that was heavily mineralized.

Patination of flint is another process that can be misleading. While a heavily patinated flint artifact is surely old, the degree of patination is not necessarily proportionate to the age. The most heavily patinated projectile points of Florida are Taylor, Wacissa, and Bolen Beveled specimens, mostly from sites in the red clay country of the Florida Panhandle; but these are by no means the oldest types of the state.

Before leaving the subject of environmental conditions that can give a mistaken conception of past cultures, I should note that modern settlement patterns can profoundly affect the knowledge of local archeology. This was recently made clear in western Pasco County, Florida. When I first began visiting the area, in 1956, its archeology was poorly known. From it, no more than four sites had been reported in the literature. These four merely revealed occupancy during the Weedon Island Period, and the receipt, during the latter part of that period, of some Englewood pottery from farther south. By the latter 1960s, however, I had located about 80 more sites, collectively demonstrating continuous occupancy of the area from Paleo-Indian times. This was not remarkable; one expects local archeological knowledge to be augmented when someone arrives with the specific aim of garnering it. Not only does he find new sites; his colleagues, working in nearby areas, show how to identify cultures whose presence had previously gone unnoticed.

But in the Pasco County area, the Safety Harbor Period proved remarkably elusive. It was present, but only at a few sites, usually atop a Weedon Island Period occupation. The situation was paradoxical. In the area, the Weedon Island Period was much better represented than any other. Weedon Island village middens were numerous along the coast and the lower reaches of the larger streams, and Weedon Island burial mounds occurred in expected numbers. During that period, the area had a comparatively dense population. It may be recalled that in late prehistoric times, the culture of the Southeast was revolutionized by advanced ideas that originated in Mexico, spread in the Mississippi Valley, and were carried eastward by the Muskhogeans. A major cultural tradition, called the Mississippian, had replaced the earlier Woodland tradition. This replacement was manifested in my area by the conversion of Weedon Island culture into Safety Harbor. But where, then, were the Safety Harbor Period sites?

In 1949, reviewing the archeology of the Florida Gulf coast, Gordon R. Willey had stated, "Safety Harbor village sites are middens, composed largely of shell, which are situated along the coast, bays, and rivers. The ecological picture is much the same as that observed for Weeden [*sic*] Island." The statement seemed to hold true for my area, where the few Safety Harbor Period sites usually had a thick Weedon Island level beneath a thin overlay of Safety Harbor materials. This was odd, for Mississippian supposedly was marked by a sharp ecological break, as the Woodland mixture of hunting, gathering, and simple agriculture gave way to agriculture of an advanced sort. After a decade's intensive search for sites, I could only conclude that the Pasco County area had somehow been depopulated, not advanced culturally, by the arrival of Mississippian ideas.

The mounds of the area did not negate this conclusion. In general, Mississippian culture was characterized by an emphasis on temple mounds and a declining interest in burial mounds. The area did have a goodly number of large mounds without burials; but the building of such structures began locally in Weedon Island times, and so their presence was not good evidence of Safety Harbor occupation. Both to the north and south of the study area, Safety Harbor peoples had continued to build some burial mounds even after adopting temple mounds. In the area, burial mounds with Safety Harbor pottery were very few, a circumstance in keeping with the idea of depopulation at the end of Weedon Island times.

But in the latter 1960s, the area underwent a "boom" and became one of the fastest-growing regions of the country. In a few years, its modern population increased from about 5,000 to about 100,000. The mystery of the Safety Harbor sites was resolved. Like the Weedon Island Indians, the white settlers had concentrated along the waterfront lands and in the nearby hammocks. But with the great influx of newcomers, the construction of subdivisions began moving inland, clearing away the sand-hills vegetation and the scrub. It soon became evident that the Indian population was greater in Safety Harbor than in Weedon Island times. With the arrival of the Mississippian tradition, most of the Indians had abandoned the waterfront localities, to which they had been bound by a dependence on the gathering of mollusks. They had moved a short distance inland to easily cleared situations where the only water was a pond or rivulet, adequate for drinking purposes.

Safety Harbor Period sites not only proved to be numerous; some of them were remarkably large, and rich in artifacts. Pinellas points, true arrowheads, were abundant. One site yielded a skull buried under an inverted bowl; such burial was a Mississippian practice not previously recorded so far south. Three sites were noteworthy for a cemetery rather than a burial mound. Only two Safety Harbor cemeteries had previously been reported, one to the north of the area and the other to the south. In the area, Safety Harbor burial mounds were a bit too few to accommodate the large population of the period, and I suspect that cemetery burial was more common than had been realized. Mounds are easily seen, and their whereabouts is generally known to local residents; but cemeteries go unnoticed until they are being bulldozed away. A few of the large Safety Harbor Period sites produced Spanish majolica, demonstrating occupancy into historic times.

In short, Safety Harbor is clearly a part of the Mississippian tradition, and not just in its ceramics. This conclusion would not have been reached, had not the study area received an influx of newcomers wanting houses and shopping centers. It was the new pattern of modern settlement that permitted a more accurate assessment of the Safety Harbor culture.

Perhaps in many regions, the knowledge of local archeology is limited, or augmented as the case may be, by the doings of modern man. Professional archeologists are few, and most sites are first located by other people. The activities of these people determine what they find. Sites are often revealed by the plowing of fields. The Leon-Jefferson Period of northern Florida had gone unsuspected until a farmer plowed up Spanish olive jars at a site of missionized Apalachee Indians. In England, hoards of Celtic coins and metalwork were turned up when tractor-drawn plows dug into the soil deeper than before. In that country, sites were discovered through the cutting of ditches, the mining of coprolites for fertilizer, the digging of chalk for marling, the building of stone walls using stones from cairns, the cutting of peat for winter fuel, the digging of gravel, the mining of diatomaceous earth, and the excavation of tracts to accommodate buildings and their utilities. Other archeological finds were made during the construction of airfields. The development of a chicken and egg industry led to the discovery of middens, because the midden shells could be ground and used in hen food.

In my Pasco County area, numerous large drainage and mosquito-control canals were dug through the coastal flats; with the flats drained, it became possible to walk freely over what had been mucky salt marsh, and the result was the discovery of many Perico Island Period sites. These had been occupied at a time when sea-level was somewhat below its present stand. Such extensive Perico Island occupancy along this stretch of coast would not have been suspected in the absence of canalization.

Near Augusta, Georgia, abandoned brickyards have yielded an abundance of prehistoric Indian ceramics; the earliest potters of the region, producers of the Stallings fiber-tempered types, had discovered the clay deposit almost 4,000 years before it was mined by the white man. Far more impressive were brickyards near Mexico City; they yielded prehistoric ceramics of much archeological importance.

In summary, it is clear that there are certain avenues leading to the discovery of archeological sites or specimens; but it might be well to investigate the likelihood that a conception of some past culture can be biased by the specialized direction of these avenues.

Having ventured a few admonitions, I offer one more. As a result of current interest in environmental archeology and human ecology, some archeological expeditions have included an ecologist or other biologist, who would collect biological specimens and study the environment of the sites. If the local residents were still living fairly close to nature, their ecological relations would be studied; the study might reveal clues to the way prehistoric peoples had utilized and coped with the environment in the same area. This approach is admirable, and no doubt will provide many insights into past culture. But I caution that an ecologist, or a zoologist with much field experience, may quickly grasp far more of the local ecology than the native peoples ever did.

Some peoples do not "think ecologically." The Papuan and Negrito tribes of inland New Guinea, whom I know well, live by hunting, gathering, and simple agriculture, but they are not good naturalists. They populate the forest with mythical beasts, which are just as real to them as flesh-and-blood ones; they ascribe wholly imaginary powers and propensities to ordinary animals and plants. They reject many natural resources as a result of irrational taboos, and avoid some potentially productive localities as a result of superstitious beliefs. Their limitations, as naturalists, are not entirely to be blamed on their absorption with the supernatural. In searching for some animal or plant species, they simply go to a locality where they have seen it before. They do not realize that each species has its characteristic habitat, and that the most productive way to search for a species is to investigate promising expanses of its habitat.

In parts of Indonesia, a different situation exists. There, some man in a village may be an excellent naturalist; but he will be in contrast with the majority of the villagers, who regard him as having some mystical rapport with wildlife. One might almost say that in these islands, skill as a naturalist is a specialized pursuit.

The finest naturalists I have ever seen are the Florida Seminole Indians of Big Cypress Swamp and the Everglades. While they have some superstitious beliefs, they know and can name a great number of plant and animal species. They recognize distinctive plant associations, soils, and aquatic situations, as might be anticipated from the chapter on toponymy. They know the habits of wildlife, and hardly ever ascribe imaginary properties to real animals. They note the subtle characteristics that distinguish two closely related species of plants or animals. They could teach something even to an experienced field biologist. And surely they did not acquire their knowledge from the local whites, who have but limited familiarity with the fauna and flora.

Oddly, language may have something to do with intercultural variation in ecological knowledge. The two Seminole languages, Creek and Mikasuki, are remarkable for a great number of specific names for plant and animal species. Two closely related species may be called by the same name, but with a different modifier for each; one is reminded of the biologists' binomial system of nomenclature, whereby two closely related species receive the same generic name but a different trivial name. Usually, the modifier is appropriately descriptive of some physical characteristic of the species. In contrast, the Papuan-speaking New Guineans will use one name to cover many species that are only superficially similar, and that are very different in habits and habitat. Seldom are these names descriptive; instead, they relate to some real or imagined usefulness or property of the animal or plant. Ethnoscience, including ethnoecology, may be hampered by the absence of an adequate and semantically sound vocabulary.

At any rate, it cannot be assumed that some prehistoric culture cleverly exploited the local fauna and flora, even if it had urgent need to.

To conclude this chapter, I shall review some aspects of environmental archeology, to which attention was called by Meighan et al. In two papers, those authors discussed ecological interpretations in archeology. One of the papers related to farming cultures, the other to hunting and gathering cultures. They thought it well to subdivide the work in this fashion, on the grounds that the hunters and gatherers were more intimately and directly affected by the environment. Their personal experience had been mostly in the western United States. In that region, ecological approaches had been used with exceptional frequency, because most sites were sparsely provided with cultural debris; excavators accordingly had an urge to extract as much data as possible from non-artifactual remains. To this I might add that ecological approaches have been used with exceptional frequency at Paleo-Indian sites, partly because these are sparse of cultural debris but also because they date back to a time when the environment was different from the one we know today. Lately, however, there has been a deliberate effort to determine the environmental factors that were associated with the beginnings of agriculture and the beginnings of civilization.

Meighan et al. noted that a good many studies had been made on the settlement patterns of prehistoric farmers, but not many on those of hunters and gatherers. Sites of a hunting and gathering culture might be correlated with some feature of the natural environment; Magdalenian sites were correlated with the distribution of reindeer, and the Sangoan culture was limited to areas of Africa now having over 40 inches rainfall anually.

With specific reference to hunting and gathering cultures: if a midden is deep but of limited area, forming a heap up to 10 meters deep but no more than 100 meters in diameter, the population was small; if it had been larger, the debris would have been more widely scattered. The social organization probably was of the band type, and included no more than 100 people; they subsisted by short-range foraging. If a midden is shallow but of considerable extent, say one meter deep and 300 meters or more in diameter, the population was relatively great, perhaps up to 1,000 people; they too subsisted by short-range foraging. When a very large area is occupied by many small patches of midden, each no more than 15 centimeters in depth and three meters in diameter, the locality was visited by long-range foragers who lived mostly in family groups.

The above conclusions, attempting to correlate midden configuration with population, were based in part on a study of debris left by historic tribes of coastal California. The rough applicability of the conclusions to many other areas is likely but has not been demonstrated. I suggest that a population of hunters and gatherers would have to be small if it subsisted by short-range foraging, because local food supplies would be exhausted by a larger population. A few years' assiduous collecting probably would suffice to exhaust many animal and plant resources within a radius of, say, a day's walk or canoe trip from a habitation site.

In the Southeast, and I think rather generally, freshwater marsh will produce more small game per unit area than any other situation. However, an expanse of freshwater marsh usually is small, and most of its resources can be used up in a few years' time. Reinvasion by marsh-dwelling animals, across dry land from other marshes, may be slow. But on a very large freshwater marsh, such as the Florida Everglades, a hunting and gathering society will not kill out the small game, because more animals keep invading the area to replace those that are removed. In effect, a society in this position is drawing upon the resources of a vast expanse of marshland outside the society's actual hunting territory.

River swamp will produce less small game per unit area than most other situations; less at any single point in time, that is. But a river swamp is a highway along which animals move; so is the river that borders it on one side, and the mesic forest that may border it on the other. Hunting in river swamp will rarely be richly productive of small game at any one time, but it will be continuously productive at a moderate level. Coastal waters resemble freshwater marsh in that the supply of small game is continuously being replaced from outside a society's foraging territory. Brackish situations have a very restricted flora and fauna, because not many species can stand the local fluctuations in salinity and (sometimes) temperature. The few species that can survive in brackish situations often are very abundant there.

When the reference is to hunting and gathering cultures of the southeastern United States, "midden" and "shell midden" are virtually synonymous. Food remains apparently have vanished from almost all Paleo-Indian and Early Preceramic habitation sites. Middens appear at the beginning of the Altithermal, when the first Late Preceramic Indians adopted a molluscan economy. Some Late Preceramic shell middens are of enormous size, and must have been occupied for thousands of years. Admittedly, occupancy might have been intermittent. But I believe that under ideal conditions, such as those that obtained along the middle and lower St. Johns River of Florida or along parts of the Florida Gulf Coast, a molluscan economy permitted the establishment of fairly permanent settlements, whose occupants were in a position to adopt agriculture when a knowledge of it arrived.

Two types of middens have received little attention in the literature.

In Florida, the arrival of agriculture reduced dependence on mollusks, but even cultures in the Mississippian tradition littered their villages with a scattering of shells. Where a Mississippian-level society existed near the sea, mollusks were gathered in fair numbers; most of the shells were not left underfoot in the village but were heaped up a short distance away, usually at the seashore. It is probable that the mollusks were opened at the seashore rather than at the village. In any event, the result was a small but high pile of shells, mostly oyster, virtually without food bones or artifacts. Such a midden could be misinterpreted if its association with a nearby village went unnoticed.

Another type of Southeastern coastal midden appears to me to represent the debris of shellfishing operations, carried on far from any village. Such middens range in size from small to enormous, and are made up mostly of oyster shells. They lack food bones, and much digging is necessary to find artifacts, such as a rude flint tool or the scraps of a broken pot. I believe the Indians would visit a rich oysterbed, shell the mollusks on some nearby islet or shore, and take the meat back to the village. Superficially, these middens might appear to be preceramic, but the few artifacts they yield suggest a later date for them.

Meighan et al. reviewed methods of estimating population at a site. An estimate could be made by counting contemporaneous house structures and multiplying by a factor for family size. There was a logarithmic relation between midden area and population, expressed by the formula log *population* = *constant* × log *area*. This was with particular reference to California middens. It seems to me that much would depend on whether the people were living directly atop their own debris, and whether they simply let this debris pile up wherever it fell. At scattered localities from Peru to Georgia, certain hunting and gathering cultures left middens in the shape of a doughnut.

Meighan et al. thought, logically, that cemetery size should be correlated with population. With reference to a hunting and gathering culture of California, the population of a site might have been six to ten times greater than the number of burials in its cemetery. The figure would hold true only for a cemetery that was in use over a short period of time.

The suggested relationship of cemetery size to population is hard to evaluate in the case of Southeastern hunting and gathering cultures. Paleo-Indian and Early Preceramic burials are rare, most of them coming from submerged caves of Florida. In that state and

Georgia, if not elsewhere in the Southeast, the Late Preceramic peoples did not often inter their dead in midden shell. In Florida, Late Preceramic skeletal remains are exceedingly rare. The peoples at that time may have practiced scaffold burial, or some other kind of aboveground interment that militated against preservation of the bones. Not until burial mound times do remains become abundant, and the builders of these mounds were carrying on at least some agriculture. Although a village site may have a burial mound in conjunction, many mounds are isolated and may have served several communities.

Meighan et al. did not touch upon one aspect of demography, the estimation of population not for a lone site but for an entire culture. How many Indians bore, say, the Weedon Island culture at any one time? How many bore it over its entire 900-year span? Perhaps it was well to avoid this aspect. Efforts have been made to estimate the population of a prehistoric Indian culture, but I am dubious of them after having watched events in the Pasco County area. There, many sites probably were built upon before they were seen by any archeologist. A few had been mentioned in the literature before my arrival. Many more, representing a 12,000-year sequence of cultures, were disclosed when new residents flocked in. The continued influx of such residents resulted in the expansion of settlement into the sandhills and scrub, with the concomitant disclosure of many Safety Harbor Period sites. Now the settlement is expanding into the flatwoods, the least favorable situation for housing and shops; no doubt many Paleo-Indian and Early Preceramic sites will be uncovered in the broad stretch of flatwoods that borders the study area on the east. But one archeologist cannot stay ahead of several hundred bulldozers, draglines, and other earth-moving machines, all working daily to obliterate sites. Quite a few sites must have been bulldozed away or built upon while I was busy in some other part of the area. The abundance and variety of artifacts in dredgings hint that unknown but fairly large numbers of sites are now beneath the waters of the Gulf.

I could not guess how many sites are in my area. The best I could do is to guess that the actual number of sites exceeds the number of presently known ones by a factor that varies from three to 20, depending on time period. At any period, the local population was far greater than anyone suspected a decade or so ago, even someone who admitted the existence of sites that had gone unreported. I doubt that this situation is peculiar to the aforesaid area. Probably, most regions had a heavier population of Indians than might be suspected from the number of known sites; and demographic estimates, intended to apply to a culture at a single time or throughout its entire span, have such a margin of error as to be of very limited usefulness.

Turning to another subject, Meighan et al. suggested that the archeologist himself might attempt identification of vertebrate remains from a site, although admitting that verification by a zoological specialist was desirable. This topic warrants discussion.

There exist a number of works that could guide the archeologist in the identification of vertebrate remains, indicate how such remains might be recovered and treated, or explain how a collection of comparative material might be assembled. No doubt the archeologist can learn to identify surely certain bones of certain species; but vertebrate remains usually are fragmentary, and the specialist can identify many scraps that would have to be discarded by the archeologist. Also, the remains might include those of some species whose presence was quite unexpected; it is the specialist who will more likely note that species, and its local presence might turn out to be of considerable ecological significance.

More importantly, what archeologists need is not just identification of remains but also interpretation of them. Here, the archeologist must turn to the specialist in animal habits, ecology, and distribution; for he cannot get the needed background information from handbooks, guides, or other readily available works. The author of such a work cannot have intimate knowledge of every species he writes about. Instead, in many cases he must rely on the published literature, which often is incomplete and occasionally is in error. The regional specialist will know many things that have not appeared in print.

As an illustration, take the matter of geographic distribution. Animal (and plant) distribution is very important in environmental archeology. If a species turns up in a site far outside its modern range, its presence might mean that some aspect of the climate had changed since the site was occupied. But the regional specialist may be able to point out where guides and handbooks go astray in the mapping or description of certain geographic ranges. A handbook or other work may assign too small a range to a species, either because biological collecting was incomplete, or because an inadequate search was made of published locality records and museum specimens. Conversely, the work may assign too large a range to a species, because hoaxes, mislabelings, misidentifications, and introductions were not weeded out. In general, it is the regional specialist who is in the best position to detect errors of omission and commission in mapping of geographic ranges. To him must be left, also, such matters as the habits and ecology of vertebrate species, for these have infrequently been described in the literature, at least in the kind of detail that is needed by archeologists.

While there are a good many specialists who are familiar with animal distribution, habits, and ecology, they may not be equally interested in osteology; they identify a species by the external characters, not by the bones. And of course, biological specialists of all kinds have their own researches, and perhaps would not care to invest time in tedious identifications which might contribute little to knowledge. The archeologist may therefore be hard put to find someone who will identify and interpret archeofaunal remains. Joint archeological-biological projects solve the problem, but their numbers are few, and not many archeologists can participate in them. In educational institutions, departments or sections of environmental archeology also are few, and may be equipped only to identify faunal remains, leaving interpretation to specialists elsewhere. I should like to offer a few suggestions for the average archeologist who wants to have archeofaunal remains examined by appropriate specialists.

First, remember that these specialists, having worked in some biological field, are accustomed to the scientific method. They are not impressed by the idea of excavating with the mere hope of finding something interesting. Their attention is more likely to be aroused if a problem is posed at the start: Do vertebrate remains suggest climatic change since the site was occupied? Did the arrival of the bow and arrow lead many peoples to hunt some kind of wild game they had previously let alone? Were the occupants of this site domesticating any animals? What animals, wild or domestic, might have supplied something other than food? Do vertebrate remains indicate that the site was occupied just seasonally?

Second, the biologist's attention might well be called to the circumstance that archeofaunal studies often yield new biological information. He may already know this. However, at least 20,000 journals publish biological research papers, and he may not have gotten around to reading the archeological journals in which archeofaunal finds often are announced.

Third, if the archeologist wins the agreement of a specialist to examine archeofaunal remains, he should make sure that the specialist receives the complete and unselected lot of material. Here I write from painful personal experience. On one occasion I visited a major archeological site, where the investigator persuaded me to identify and interpret the vertebrate remains that had been recovered. I agreed to do so principally because I had caught a glimpse of bear, panther, and wolf remains—carnivores whose bones are rare in most archeological sites, and are not well represented in most modern osteological collections. In the course of time, the remains were sent to me in a series of boxes. When I opened them, I found that the panther skull, the impressive wolf jaws, the bear canines, and other more striking specimens had not been sent. I would not have suspected their existence, had I not glimpsed them. An archeologist would not care to interpret a site on the basis of artifactual material from which all the more striking specimens had been removed before he had chance to examine them. The specialist who agrees to investigate archeofaunal remains should be assured that he is receiving the full complement of them.

Fourth, if remains are to be sent by mail or express, they should be carefully packed, not simply dumped into a flimsy cardboard box. Here again I write from experience. Archeofaunal remains are fragmentary enough to begin with, and they are fragile. Unless they are carefully packed, many of them will be smashed into unidentifiable bits while in transit.

Fifth (again from experience), when a zoologist devotes a good bit of time to any project, his aim is publication of his findings, for the advancement of knowledge. He will draw up for the archeologist a summary of his identifications and interpretations. He understands that journal space is limited, and will keep his remarks brief if brevity is desired. Unless some special arrangement has been made, he will not expect his summary to be published under his own name; usually, he will be satisfied with a mere indication that he is responsible for the identifications and interpretations. In fact, he could dispense even with that indication; but he expects some publication of his findings, even if they do not seem to be revolutionary. He may be exasperated if the published site report completely omits the archeofaunal summary he labored so hard to prepare.

Sixth, the zoologist or other biological specialist understands the principle of stratigraphy. He will be pleased to receive the archeofaunal material packaged by site level or zone. He will be interested in looking for local faunal change with time, whether this was brought about environmentally or culturally.

Seventh and last, a biologist will appreciate a few reprints (separates) of a site report if it has included his summary. Indeed, he may wish to order some in advance if such inclusion were assured. As compared with biologists, archeologists are remiss in the distribution of reprints. Of course, archeologists have had less need to exchange reprints with one another. The journals that publish archeological researches are comparatively few, and most archeological work has been strongly regionalized. Thus, the average archeologist can readily locate most of the published researches that are pertinent to his interests. In contrast, even a small subdivision of biology may have an extensive and widely scattered literature. For example, I once tabulated over 900 journals that had published something about the reptiles or amphibians of eastern North America alone. Most of these journals were published in the United States, but quite a few in Germany, Britain, France, and Canada, with the rest scattered over 52 countries of Europe, Africa, Asia, Oceania, and Latin America. Counting journal articles and non-serial publications, at least 75,000 titles have dealt with the herpetology of eastern North America.

As archeologists broaden their scope and adopt a scientific approach, they will take greater interest in the exchange of reprints. If someone sends copies of his own researches to, say, 1,200 colleagues, most of them will reciprocate with packets of their own studies; and there is no better away to keep abreast of the burgeoning literature.

Meighan et al. went on to say that the state of vertebrate remains is sometimes indicative of butchering practices. T. E. White (1955) had specialized in the study of such practices, especially as regards the way bison were cut up; and I had noted the aboriginal treatment of turtles and alligators in four preceramic sites of the St. Johns River drainage of Florida.

Inferences about butchering generally are drawn from the absence of certain skeletal elements; an animal was butchered where it was killed, and only certain parts were brought back to the habitation site. Such absences must be analyzed cautiously, with attention to all possible explanations for them. In middens of the St. Johns drainage, deer bones make up the bulk of vertebrate remains, but antlers are rather scarce. It could not be held that the Indians did not bring back deer heads, for jaws were abundant. Were they selecting does? The situation puzzled me until I had chance to study the deer herds of the Ocala National Forest, in the St. Johns drainage. Does outnumbered bucks by about 20 to 1. The ratio may be abnormal, since legal hunting is limited to bucks; but the species is polygynous, each buck having a harem of does. Also, bucks are much the shier; they stand quietly in the concealment of dense vegetation while the does show themselves boldly in the open spots. Thus, it is not surprising that the Indians killed far more does than bucks. In this species of deer, as in most but not all others, only the bucks have antlers. Remains from the St. Johns sites are consistent with the view that the Indians simply killed whatever deer they could.

Vertebrate remains have been used to demonstrate hunting trips from one region to some fairly distant one (especially from an inland locality to the seashore); and to show seasonal, or in other cases year-round, occupation of sites. If ethnographic-archeological parallels are allowed, still other inferences may be drawn.

Meighan et al. devoted a special section to mollusks. Since they wrote, these inveretbrates have received much more attention, and I should like to discuss them anew.

Mollusks have several qualities that commend them to man. Many of them are edible. The principal exceptions are some marine species that become poisonous through the absorption of toxins (such as the notorious "red tide") given off by microscopic organisms. Some land snails and slugs are protected by glutinous secretions that render them unappetizing; but in any event, they usually are too small and too widely scattered to form an important source of food. Some of the marine cone shells have a venomous sting, but they have been valued for their beautiful shells nonetheless. Many mollusks, especially but not exclusively of the sea, have a shell that is interestingly shaped, gratifying smooth to the touch, or extraordinarily colored and patterned. Whole mollusk shells have been strung as beads, and cut sections of shell have been used as jewelry, spangles, or inlays; but often, unmodified shells have themselves been prized for some esthetic quality.

The shells that are of especial archeological interest include the bivalves (such as the oysters and mussels) which have two half shells connected by a hinge; and the gastropods (such as the snails, whelks, and cones), which have a single shell that is spiraled in most cases. Externally, the spiral may form an interesting geometric figure. In many cases, when a section of gastropod shell is cut, ground, or sawed away, an amazingly whorled interior structure is exposed. Even blasé moderns purchase cut shells as curios, and there exists a world-wide trade in whole shells for collectors.

No doubt, many prehistoric peoples thought there was something supernatural in the exterior coloration and interior geometry of many shells. Large gastropods figured in the iconography of Southeast Asia, and in that of the New World's early civilizations. In South America, the iconographic uses of shells were notably diverse, involving not only actual shells but also portrayals of them in baked clay, gold, and other materials. Unusual South American specimens were trumpets made by hammering thin gold sheets over a large gastropod and then somehow extracting the shell; the result was a detailed replica of the shell in gold. In parts of North America, whelks and other large shells were placed in burial mounds with the bones of the elite. The Hopewell culture of the Midwest was noteworthy for the number and diversity of marine shells that were used as grave goods. Bearers of the Southeastern Ceremonial Complex incised a variety of mythological scenes on gastropod shells, and manufactured gorgets from cut sections of the shells. In early historic times, some Florida Indians quaffed the "black drink" from a gastropod. Large cups, made by modifying a whelk or other large gastropod shell, occur in Florida burial mounds, and some of them may have been used ceremonially.

Many other iconographic uses of shells could be listed, from both the Old World and the New. It has been asserted that the spiral design, which figured so widely in prehistoric art, was always intended to represent the whorls of a gastropod shell. The assertion is probably an overstatement, but no doubt many spiral motifs are to be so regarded.

A good many bivalves, of both freshwater and saltwater species, can form pearls; but many of them do so rarely. Only a few species produce pearls with sufficient frequency to provide a basis for a pearling industry, and then only in certain parts of their respective geographic ranges. In other words, pearls come from highly localized fisheries. Even at an unusually productive fishery, many thousand bivalves must be opened to disclose a single pearl. Thus, pearl-fishing beds can become exhausted. In some parts of the world, e.g., Indonesia, pearl fisheries may have been more numerous than present records indicate.

As a rule, pearls are badly corroded when recovered from archeological sites, and I do not know how to tell the saltwater specimens from the freshwater ones. In Levy County a coastal Florida burial mound yielded grotesquely flattened human skulls. The site also produced beads made from pearls that were small, hard, and rather drab. In contrast, pearl beads from Southeastern Ceremonial Complex sites are medium to small in size, light and fragile, bright pink in color. Perhaps they were from the queen helmet shell, *Cassis madagascarensis*, noted for the pink color of its pearls; the species is essentially Caribbean, but ranges northward to North Carolina. Pearls from an early historic Yuchi burial, excavated by me on an island in the Savannah River, Columbia County, Georgia, were large, heavy, but drab. I assumed that the pearls from this burial were of fresh-water origin, because, according to John R. Swanton (1946), an early historic pearl fishery supposedly existed on the river. However, I believe Swanton postulated a pearl fishery here simply because the Spanish explorer De Soto received many pearls at the Lower Creek town of Cofitachiqui, located on the Savannah about 25 miles down-stream of the island where I dug. The pearls of Cofitachiqui might well have been saltwater ones, imported by the residents of this prominent Lower Creek town.

Like many other rivers, the Savannah has long been silty, as a result of deforestation and agriculture in its drainage basin. Populations of pearl-bearing mussels—if it ever had any—have long since vanished. The same is true of various Mississippi Valley streams, supposedly inhabited by pearl-bearing mussels in early historic times. We may never learn the actual source of the pearls that were accumulated by prehistoric and early historic Indians of eastern North America.

At various localities from China through Southeast Asia to Oceania and Africa, the money cowrie, *Monetaria moneta,* was used as a me-dium of exchange. It is small and drab, without intrinsic interest; the value attached to it was artificial, a matter of cultural fiat. Archeologi-cal evidence suggests that the Chinese may have been the first to select this mollusk as a medium of exchange; but they may have gathered it for use in their East Indian trade, which began at an early date. This cowrie, an Old World species, has turned up in a historic site of Florida, and one supposes that the Spaniards were originally responsible for introducing the shells into America. At a later date, the Lewis and Clark expedition brought back an Indian dress, perhaps Cree, adorned with money cowries. Northern Indians may have ob-tained such shells from the Hudson's Bay Trading Company. But it is astonishing to learn that money cowries were found with prehistoric burials in the Roden mounds of Alabama, in the Tennessee River drainage; the supposed occurrence should be reinvestigated. Also puzzling is a money cowrie found near the Onotonabee Serpent Mound in Peterboro County, Ontario; perhaps the shell was not con-temporary with the mound.

In a previous chapter, I have discussed the way in which shell beads, the so-called wampum, were used as money in the eastern

United States. Tusk shells (*Dentalium*) were a medium of exchange on the Northwest Pacific coast.

Because shells were valued in so many ways, they figured prominently in prehistoric trade. The red helmet shell, a *Cypraecassis*, is native to the Indian and Pacific oceans, but a specimen of it was found with a Cro-Magnon burial in France. The tiger cowrie, a *Cypraea*, is likewise Indo-Pacific; it was found in a prehistoric pit-dwelling at St. Mary Bourne, Hants, England. The panther cowrie, also a *Cypreaea*, from the Red Sea and the east coast of Africa, turned up in Saxon women's graves at several localities in Kent, England. These finds hint at long-continued connections—not necessarily well-established trade routes—between Europe and the western shores of the Indian Ocean from a remarkably early time.

In the United States, *Dentalium* shells from the Northwest Pacific coast were traded eastward across the Rockies to the upper Missouri, and southward to southern California and northern Baja California. Away from the Northwest Pacific coast, the shells were used as ornaments, not money. The Pecos region of New Mexico was one where a shell trade from the Pacific met one from the Gulf of Mexico. Sites of the Pecos vicinity included such shells as *Haliotis* (abalone) and *Olivella* from the west, *Oliva* and *Cassis* from the east. *Glycimeris* clams were passed overland to New Mexico from the Pacific coast of Sonora. A trade in shells, extending from the Gulf and Atlantic coasts to the Great Lakes, began in preceramic times, and was concentrated in the Hopewell period.

During ethnographic times in New Guinea, marine shells were traded inland to the mountain tribes. Money cowries were used as a medium of exchange, while other shells, entire or somehow modified, were regarded as ornaments of great value. Among certain tribes, a large shell was used as a penis sheath. While culturally conditioned modesty was involved with such use, the shell was believed to divert evil spirits away from the genital organ. In some areas, dowels were incrusted with shells and inserted into the eye sockets of a skull, with the idea of neutralizing supernatural forces resident in such a trophy. While the archeology of New Guinea is not well known, it is clear that a trade in marine shells began well back in prehistoric times.

The meat of a mollusk does not keep very well. Even smoked or dried, it spoils more readily than some other products. In prehistoric times, peoples living far inland did not receive seafood; they received shells that had beauty, supposed supernatural qualities, or (in the case of the money cowrie) an arbitrarily assigned value. In contrast, coastal peoples relied heavily on marine mollusks for food, once they discovered this resource and how to exploit it. In Florida, the coastal villagers concentrated on *Ostraea* (oysters), but also gathered *Arca* (arc shell), *Pecten* (scallops), *Cardita* (heart shell), *Cardium* (cockle), *Venus* (hard-shell clam), *Donax* (coquina shell), *Strombus* (conch), *Cassis* (helmet shell), *Busycon* (whelk), *Fasciolaria* (horse conch), *Melongena* (crown conch), and others. *Busycon, Melongena,* and gastropods of similar shape were perforated near the shoulder so that the animal could be pushed out.

To inland peoples, marine shells were luxury items, but to coastal peoples they often were raw materials from which utensils could be manufactured. Uses of marine shells were more diverse in peninsular Florida than in most other parts of the world. Common in Florida sites are *Busycon* and *Melongena* shells that had been perforated near the shoulder and notched at the lip, so that a wooden handle could be inserted. There were in fact several different ways in which a gastropod shell was modified for the reception of a handle. Fortunately, specimens with the handle intact have been preserved in a few sites, and it is possible to say why so many large gastropods were variously perforated and notched. Even without such evidence, it could have been inferred that the shells were modified for use as tools. In some specimens, the beak was left unworked, and the hafted implement was used pick-like, with resultant wear on the tip. In other specimens, the beak was sawed or ground off, and the implement was used as a hammer, with resultant battering. A large *Busycon* shell, perforated and notched for the reception of a long, stout handle, was used as a hoe, and received wear along its blade.

Interestingly, the One Fathom Site (chapter 7), pure Deptford, yielded no such hoes, although the Deptford peoples are suspected of having introduced agriculture into Florida. *Busycon* hoes are common in Weedon Island and Safety Harbor sites, and should be indicators of fairly to highly advanced agriculture. It might prove worthwhile to trace the geographic and temporal distribution of hoes, picks, and hammers made by hafting a large gastropod shell. At a coastal Maya site of Belize, I saw implements closely resembling certain Florida ones, although made from the shells of *Strombus* and *Fasciolaria,* which were locally common large gastropods.

In the Pasco County area, Weedon Island Period village sites yield numerous *Busycon* and *Melongena* shells of very small size, modified in the same fashion as the larger tools. Whether the miniatures had some symbolic import, I could not say; perhaps they were children's toys.

Miscellaneous shell implements from Florida include cups or dippers made from *Busycon* shells, and chisels or gouges cut from the shell wall of some large gastropod. A rectangle of shell was used to scrape and smooth a pottery vessel before firing, and some vessels were patterned by impressing them, while still soft, with the sinuate edge of a *Pecten* or the sculptured back of some other bivalve.

The Glades archeological subarea of Florida has produced a distinctive lot of shell tools. The distinctiveness results in part from the presence there of essentially tropical mollusks that are absent or uncommon farther north, and in part from the usual Glades reliance on organic materials in the local scarcity of most useable stones. A *Macrocallista* shell was converted into a knife by chipping it along the edge as though it had been a flint blade. Very heavy *Noetia* and *Arca* shells were perforated and strung together in bundles to serve as boat anchors. Widespread (but not common) in Florida are celts cut from the very thick shell of a giant conch, *Strombus gigas;* presumably these were turned out in the Glades subarea, for the species does not range very far north in the state. *Strombus* celts were once thought to be copies, in shell, of the stone celts that were used farther north, but the situation is not that simple; tribes of central Florida had *Strombus* celts imported from the south, as well as celts of hard stone imported from the north.

As found in archeological sites of Florida, shell celts, gouges, chisels, and hoes seem rather soft, and easily dulled on the edge. However, they have been softened by soil chemicals. To understand the properties of mollusk shell, it is necessary to examine fresh specimens. A large, fresh gastropod shell is hard to cut even with a hacksaw. When shells are used in the manufacture of modern jewelry, they are worked with special saws, emery powder, grindstones, and buffing wheels. The prehistoric manufacture of *Strombus* celts, and of some shell pendants, might well be considered under the heading of lapidary work.

Although coastal peoples of Florida made workaday tools from marine shells, they also made ornaments such as beads, labrets, gorgets, and pendants. Some of these ornaments may have had ceremonial or mystical import, based upon the attribution of supernatural qualities to shells. For example, plummet-shaped pendants appeared in Deptford times and continued in use up into the early historic period. Some of them were made from imported stone, others from the columella (the interior supporting rod) of a large gastropod shell. In historic times, they were occasionally made from metal. In a Deptford context, the pendants occur in both village sites and burial mounds; usually if not invariably they are of stone. In Weedon Island, stone specimens are likely to be present in mounds, no more than one pendant to a burial; but shell pendants are common in village sites. Effigies and problematical objects of shell occur just occasionally in Florida middens, and may have had ceremonial significance.

William J. Webster, in 1970, found *Busycon* shells that had been used as cooking vessels by preceramic Indians of Florida. Presumably, the shell was suspended over a fire, and its long beak was used as a handle. In parts of Oceania, a large triton shell (*Charonia*) was used as a tea kettle. This shell has a long beak at one end and a long spire at the other. In life, the mollusk was provided with an operculum, a calcareous, door-like structure that would close the shell. When in use, the shell was suspended over a fire by a wooden hook, and the operculum served as a lid. The spire served as a handle, and the canal of the beak as a pouring spout.

Many parts of the world had localized uses of mollusks. Of especial interest is the extraction of a reddish-purple dye from certain marine snails. This I have discussed in chapter 8.

What with the multifarious uses of mollusks, shells obviously are to be expected in many archeological sites. As most species of mollusks are quite limited in their ecological tolerances, their presence in a site may provide an indication of certain environmental conditions that obtained when the site was occupied. Unfortunately, the ecological requirements of various mollusks are not easily ascertained from the literature; they are known to regional malacologists, and to those shell collectors who hunt for specimens as well as purchase them.

A site may contain shells of mollusks that arrived under their own power, for quite a few gastropods live on land. In Florida, site reports often list the cannibal snail, *Euglandina,* along with the shells of food species. But *Euglandina* is not edible. It is most abundant where limey materials occur at the surface of the ground. It is found around limestone quarries, on middens, in moist situations overlooking calcareous streams, near the coast where limestone is exposed at the inland border of saltmarsh, and in some suburban yards and gardens.

It feeds on other snails. Its presence in a site does not imply abandonment of that site; it will crawl into an occupied locality.

European archeologists have explored certain interesting possibilities of land snails, even though such mollusks may not have been gathered by prehistoric peoples. If some one of these peoples dug a deep ditch, it would gradually fill up with dirt. At all times, snails would be dying in the ditch. A stratigraphic change in the snail fauna, from the bottom of the ditch to the top, might reveal a sequence of environmental changes in the vicinity. Local deforestation, resulting from the arrival of agriculture, might be reflected in the snail fauna.

There are several ways in which a knowledge of molluscan habits and ecology could resolve archeological problems. For example, archeological materials often are dredged up in oyster shell from Tampa Bay and nearby waters of Florida. A good many Dalton projectile points have been recovered from the shell yards, and raise the question of whether the makers of these points were accumulating oyster shell middens. One supposes not; the Dalton point was in style near the beginning of the Early Preceramic, a good 2,500 years before Florida Indians adopted a molluscan economy. But it is scientifically sound to draw attention to the occurrence of the points in oyster shell.

The occurrence can be explained in the light of oyster biology. Although adult oysters are sedentary, the larvae drift in the water; they must settle out on something hard if they are to live and grow. Many of them settle out on preexisting oyster beds, but this does not explain how the beds were started in the first place. All along the coast of the Tampa Bay region, and of the Pasco County area a short distance farther north, there are shallowly submerged outcroppings of flint. Most of these outcroppings show evidence of prehistoric quarrying. Investigation of a local oyster bed will usually reveal that it began on boulders and nodules of flint, and on large spalls battered therefrom by prehistoric quarrymen. Projectile points occur around the quarry sites. In the canalized saltmarsh of the study area, Tallahassee points (a bit older than Dalton points) exist around flint outcrops; if the outcrops were flooded again, oysters would grow on them; if the oysters were then dredged up, Tallahassee points would appear with them.

Thus, the facts are consistent with the view that Dalton hunters left their projectile points at flint quarries on which oysters later grew after the sea had risen to the proper level. This hypothesis can be tested. The Dalton point was widespread across North America, from Florida and Texas to Canada and Alaska. Although the sea has encroached upon the Florida Gulf coast since Dalton times, there are many other coasts and numerous riverbanks that should still have Dalton middens if such things ever existed. Apparently they did not. Dalton points were spread by nomadic hunters and gatherers in the Early Preceramic tradition, not by fairly settled collectors of mollusks in the Late Preceramic tradition.

As another test, midden shell should include *Busycon* and *Melongena* shells in greater numbers than they occur in nature, for mollusk-gatherers collected these large gastropods even if relying more heavily on oysters. In contrast, natural beds of dead oysters, dredged up for fill, should be poor in gastropod shells, for it is only the living bed that has a rich fauna. Dredgings with Dalton points are made up of oysters to the virtual exclusion of other mollusks.

Mollusks also provide an illustration of the point that a useful archeological insight may result from some casual observation on faunal remains. This happened at the Hickory Hammock Site, on the mainland of Levy County, Florida, not far from the Cedar Keys. In the general vicinity are several hillocks, most of them obviously natural. The largest of them, relatively steep and superficially mound-like, might have been man-made in part, for it is bordered by depressions suggestive of borrow pits. Amateurs had dug a number of holes into the top of the large hillock, but no sherds, charcoal, or bone scrap appeared in their diggings. About 50 yards away, at the edge of the saltmarsh, tidal fluctuations had exposed a small amount of midden shell with a few sherds.

About 100 yards from the high hillock, I found an occupation level with sherds, artifacts of marine shell, a scattering of unmodified shells, and charcoal. The level was but five to six inches below the present ground surface. About 225 square feet of it were troweled through.

This procedure yielded 278 sherds. Of these, 152 were of the type called Tampa Complicated Stamped; nine others were probably this same type, although the design was indistinct; and 20 sherds, all small, could have been called Swift Creek Complicated Stamped, Late Variety, although their design more likely represented aberrant impressions on Tampa Complicated Stamped vessels. There were 77 plain sherds tempered with fine-grained sand; some of them might have been complicated stamped sherds from which the design had been obliterated. Nine of the plain sand-tempered sherds were marked externally with small, irregular dents, the appearance of which suggested that the vessel before drying had rested upon, or had been handled with, a wad of fabric or a mat of Spanish moss. One sand-tempered sherd had a thickened and heightened rim, and bore traces of dark red paint on the interior surface. Another sand-tempered sherd had two parallel, fine-line incisions below the rim. Finally, there were 18 Pasco (limestone-tempered) sherds, all plain except one with a single fine-line incision. The ceramic assemblage was that of the Weedon Island Period.

The sherds were accompanied by 138 items of marine shell. Of these, 46 were *Melongena* shells from which had been removed some part of the spire and some part of the outer whorl. Twenty items were the more familiar shell hammers and picks, neatly perforated and lip-notched for hafting. Of these 20 tools, seven were *Melongena,* the others *Busycon.* There were 35 stylus-like implements made from the columella of a *Melongena* (or perhaps a *Busycon* columella in a few cases). Of these styli, 28 were bipointed; the proximal end (proximal with reference to an intact shell) had been worked into a small, sharp point, the distal end into a blunt point, a spatula, a probe-like tip, or a chisel-like one. There were 30 broken-away pieces of shell wall, with at least a portion of the break ground down to leave a sharp edge; one of these specimens had been worked into a projection resembling the tip of a knife. One small *Busycon* had been altered by removal of a distal portion of the outer whorl, to expose the columella which had then been worked into a point. Three small, subtriangular implements, with all the edges ground sharp, were made from pieces of *Venus* shells. There were two broken-off *Melongena* tips, the beak ground into a point and a part of the broken edges ground down. Finally, there was a small, chisel-like tool made from the wall of a *Busycon.*

The sherds and shell artifacts threw a surprising new light on certain aspects of complicated stamping. Most prehistoric Southeastern styles of pottery decoration—cord marking, fabric marking, cord impressing, shell stamping, plain and dentate rocker stamping, red slipping, zoned red slipping, excision, negative painting, certain kinds of incision, punctation, brushing, and others—did not originate in the Southeast, but instead reached there by diffusion from other regions. Begging the question of ultimate origin, most of the styles reached the United States from lands farther south. Complicated stamping, however, stands out as a Southeastern development without close, obvious counterparts elsewhere. Check stamping and a rectilinear complicated stamping had continued into historic times, and had been described ethnographically: the potter impressed the vessel, while it was still wet and soft, with a wooden paddle into which a grid or other pattern of grooves had been cut. It was therefore reasonable to suppose that all complicated stamping had been produced by impressions of a paddle that had been carved elaborately. Some prehistoric complicated stamped designs, such as linked diamonds, lined blocks, and nested triangles, were rectilinear, while others combined rectilinear and curvilinear elements. One of these combinations, the filfot cross, probably was of symbolic import. Especially puzzling are curvilinear designs, usually involving a central boss and a series of spirals or concentric circles. Multiple, somewhat overlapping impressions of a curvilinear stamp produced decorations that were complex but exceedingly attractive.

W. H. Holmes, a pioneer student of American Indian pottery, thought that the motifs of curvilinear complicated stamping were significantly similar to West Indian woodcarvings. Another view held that wooden implements, used for stamping a pattern on human skin in order to guide a tattooist, were the prototypes of wooden paddles used to stamp pottery. I believe this view was stimulated by drawings of early historic Timucua Indians of Florida; the Timucua leaders were depicted as having been tattooed with zones of curvilinear designs. I had been impressed with wooden billets used by New Guinea potters to beat clay into a uniform consistency; often, a billet bore curvilinear carvings, which were impressed upon the clay roll at each blow. It would take no great mental leap to decide to make these impressions on the surface of the vessel and leave them there, and I wondered if North American curvilinear complicated stamping was a decorative technique inspired by the patterns that are impressed when clay is beaten with a carved billet. In any event, this kind of stamping seemed somehow to have been an outgrowth of the woodcarver's art. But the Hickory Hammock Site gave reason to question this interpretation.

I mentioned finding 45 *Melongena* shells from which part of the spire and part of the outer whorl had been removed. One of these implements was almost in contact with a sherd of Tampa Complicated Stamped, and about three inches away was a bipointed stylus made from a *Melongena* columella. The exposed whorls of the cut shell duplicated, in reverse, the designs on the sherd. Experiment revealed that the shell, impressed into modeling clay, produced a close counterpart of the complicated stamped sherd; and a near-perfect copy could be produced by minor modifications with the stylus. The cut-shell impression, into modeling clay, left a central boss from which a ridge extended in spiral fashion. The larger end of the stylus was used to separate the boss from the ridge. Close examination of the sherd showed that it had once been treated in the same fashion; at one point, the boss had not been completely separated, and a trace of the spiral design remained. The smaller, more sharply pointed end of the stylus was useful in picking off tiny, displaced particles of clay.

On the experimental impression, the design was bolder than on the sherd. However, the design on the original pottery vessel probably was smoothed over to a slight degree before firing. In the Central Gulf Coast region of Florida, curvilinear complicated stamped designs commonly were smoothed over. I believe the sherd had been decorated by stamping with the actual *Melongena* shell that accompanied it.

The artifact assemblage from the excavated part of the Hickory Hammock Site was a highly specialized one, consisting mainly of (1) sherds from complicated stamped vessels, (2) modified shell-wall fragments suitable for scraping the interior and smoothing the exterior of pottery vessels, (3) cut *Melongena* shells suitable for impressing Tampa Complicated Stamped designs, and (4) stylus-like columella tools suitable for improving such designs. Also, (5) fires had been present, as shown by charcoal; and (6) a wad of fabric or a mat of Spanish moss had been used to handle some vessels while they were still soft. I was led to wonder if the nearby tidal stream yielded an additional ingredient necessary for the production of Tampa Complicated Stamped pottery: clay. Collecting a few pounds of the sticky material that formed the bottom of the stream, I found that it could be stamped with a cut *Melongena* shell and fired. It was not necessary to add tempering, for the clay already contained an ideal amount of sand; any more sand would have left it too "short." Evidently, the excavated portion of the Hickory Hammock Site was the work area of a potter, or perhaps several of them, who used shell implements to scrape, smooth, stamp, and otherwise finish some Tampa Complicated Stamped vessels.

A puzzling detail of certain complicated stamped designs becomes explicable if it was produced not by the intentional carving of a wooden paddle or other stamping tool, but by the natural arrangement of whorls within a cut shell. In many parts of Florida and Georgia, one encounters concentric and spiral designs in which the central boss often bears a tiny, near-invisible dimple. It is unlikely that Indians over a wide area saw fit to reproduce this vague marking, in reverse, on stamping tools. The situation is clearer when it is realized that a cut *Melongena* or *Busycon* shell, used as a stamp, automatically produces this dimple, which persists unless subsequently erased or eroded away.

Some complicated stamped design units, on Swift Creek Complicated Stamped (both early and late varieties) vessels, look improbable as artistic conceptions of primitive carvers. The existence of certain off-balance designs, with a strange combination of symmetry and asymmetry, becomes intelligible when it is realized that they probably were produced by (or perhaps copied from, in some cases) the impressions of a cut shell into soft clay.

The recognition of "cut-shell stamping" permits assessment of a major theme in Southeastern pottery decoration. Check stamping, quite likely done with a carved wooden paddle, is older than complicated stamping. In Florida and Georgia, Deptford types exhibit both regular and linear check stamping. Before these types had gone out of fashion, certain complicated stamped types appeared in the Southeast. Some Florida workers have held that the appearance of the types marked the beginning of a new period, called Santa Rosa–Swift Creek. Period names aside, the point is that complicated stamped types were added to the Deptford ceramic inventory. Both stylistically and stratigraphically, the earliest complicated stamped type may be New River Complicated Stamped, which was concentrated on the Gulf coast near the base of the Florida Panhandle. At any rate, it is the earliest curvilinear complicated stamped pottery. It included a check stamp, plus a complicated stamp consisting of concentric circles, interlocked whorls, lobate forms, or rayed elements. Some sherds of New River Complicated Stamped look as though all the components of the design had been carved into a wooden stamping tool, but in many cases the circles, whorls, etc. were separately stamped upon the checked background. I believe that some of the whorls and apparently concentric designs were produced by cut-shell stamping, perhaps with some slight subsequent modification by a modeling stylus. In New River Complicated Stamped sherds with probable cut-shell stamping, the check stamped areas are much reduced in favor of the concentric or whorled designs. A little further reduction of the check stamped areas would result in designs about like those on Tampa Complicated Stamped and some Swift Creek Complicated Stamped.

The basic idea of New River Complicated Stamped was also carried over into the Weedon Island Period, as Old Bay Complicated Stamped. The latter type was check stamped, but was over-stamped at scattered spots on the vessel with a spiral, dot-in-circle, lozenge, or crossed simple stamping. The spiral is in my opinion the unmodified impression of a cut shell, either a *Melongena* or a small *Busycon*.

In cut-shell stamping, I am inclined to see one more instance of Mesoamerican influence in the Southeast. The gastropod shell, and the spiral that symbolized it, were of great significance in Mesoamerica. Quetzalcóatl, the Mexican god of wind and learning, was often depicted as wearing a "wind breastplate" made from a section of a gastropod shell. In western Mexico, an entire shell symbolized the soul or life; the wearing of it was portrayed by many figurines. More importantly in the present connection, certain Mesoamerican symbols, including several that related to the gastropod shell, were transferred to the Florida Gulf coast, where they began to appear as motifs on Southeastern pottery. David S. Phelps (1968) pointed out that Maya symbols, including glyphs, appear on Santa Rosa–Swift Creek pottery. They are concentrated on Crystal River Incised, Crystal River Negative Painted, Crystal River Zoned Red, Basin Bayou Incised, and Alligator Bayou Stamped types. Phelps thought that additional study would permit recognition of Mesoamerican symbols on the Swift Creek Complicated Stamped type.

Among Mesoamerican symbols found on Southeastern pottery, Phelps recognized the Spiral. A Maya main glyph and infix, it meant water. It was used as a symbol in the eyes of bird and serpent deities of earth, rain, and primeval water. Its shape was derived from the interior spiral of a gastropod shell. Also recognizable was the Conch Shell symbol. It represented a primeval body of water in which the earth serpent deity dwelt, and connoted both water and the underworld. The Shell Section symbol was the cross-section of a gastropod, having a scalloped exterior around a central spiral. It was a basic water symbol. The Abstract Bone and Shell combination of symbols was associated primarily with death and the underworld, but could be extended to sacrifice, offerings, or other matters involving the underworld deities.

Southeastern pottery was commonly decorated by impressing the vessel with something that left a pattern. From Mesoamerica there arrived the new idea that vessels might bear shell symbols. Cut-shell stamping incorporated the new idea into the old technique of pottery decoration. Possibly, in time, cut-shell impressions were duplicated on wooden stamps. Curvilinear complicated stamping, derived originally from cut-shell impressions, spread from the Florida Gulf coast. Meanwhile, rectilinear complicated stamping had developed elsewhere, for reasons that need not be considered here.

Thus, knowledge of molluscan anatomy has combined with other and more strictly archeological knowledge to open up a new pathway of research into an important style of Southeastern pottery decoration.

Returning now to the paper of Meighan et al., those authors discussed rupestrian art, including both carvings and paintings on rocks and cave walls. This is almost the only kind of art that throws much light on the ecology of hunting and gathering cultures. In the Old World, it includes portrayals of animals, hunting implements, and subsistence activities. In the New World, however, it usually consists of symbols that cannot be interpreted with any assurance. Much rupestrian art is hard to date, although there are some exceptions. Beyond the hunting and gathering stage, prehistoric peoples in both the Old World and the New turned out representational art in fired clay, stone, copper, and other materials. Figurines, sculptures, and castings often portray wild or domestic animals and plants, as well as many cultural activities.

From a study of hunting and gathering cultures, Meighan et al. concluded that no environment was so limited as to offer only one possible way of existence within it. I take this to mean that the environment offers a series of possible life-ways, while the culture determines which way is accepted and which rejected. It was also concluded that technology may be fairly constant in spite of considerable variety in ecological adaptations. Here, I would emphasize that the reference must be to technology of a kind that leaves obvious material traces in the archeological record. Two prehistoric hunting and gathering societies, pursuing different ecological courses, probably differed in such manufactures as traps, nets, weirs, cordage, basketry, wooden weapons, digging implements, and devices for preparing and storing foods. Probably, too, they differed in ideas that were not expressed artifactually: ideas about division of labor, food taboos, hunting techniques, and others. With rare exceptions, the archeologist can examine only those artifacts that are in stone, shell, bone, or some other fairly long-lasting material; these may give an undue impression of cultural homogeneity among ecologically diverse peoples. All the more reason, of course, to look beyond the artifacts at the environment of their makers.

As Meighan et al. noted, such classificatory terms as Hunting-Gathering Culture or Archaic Stage can be misleading when they are defined solely on the basis of artifacts; a certain sameness in these productions may mask a considerable degree of cultural diversity. Or to put the matter a bit differently, cultures would not be classified in quite the same way if attention were given not just to artifacts but also to the ecological adaptations of their makers. This point is very important, and should be enlarged upon.

If ecological adaptations were more diverse than imperishable artifactual productions, then a culture classification based on artifacts could be subdivided on ecological grounds. On the other hand, two societies were culturally related if they had artifact assemblages in common, even though they might occupy different environments. In archeological practice, artifacts and ecological considerations are curiously tangled in some current classificatory schemes.

In the first volume of his review of North American archeology, Gordon R. Willey (1966) employed the concept of a "major cultural tradition." Each such tradition had considerable temporal and spatial distribution; each was "characterized by a definite patterning of subsistence practices, technology, and ecological adaptation" (p. 4). Each probably had an ideological pattern, the nature of which might or might not be readily discernible. In the eastern United States, there was a chronological sequence of four major cultural traditions (ignoring possible manifestations of a pre-projectile point culture). These four were called Big-Game Hunting, Archaic, Woodland, and Mississippian.

The Big-Game Hunting tradition "was primarily adapted to, and developed in, a grasslands environment of the late Pleistocene" (Willey 1966:37). This I question. The big-game animals that were hunted were components of the Rancholabrean fauna. Quite a bit of plant remains have been recovered from Rancho La Brea, the type site of this fauna. These remains show the region to have been occupied by two different floras, one typifying the cool, moist conditions of the late Pleistocene, the other indicative of a warmer, drier climatic regimen. Neither flora was grassland. In the United States, there is no palynological or other evidence of widespread grassland in late Pleistocene times. I have argued for temporary eastward extension of the grassland and its fauna in the Pleistocene, but only during episodes of deglaciation when the climate was warmer and drier than it is now. Such episodes antedate the arrival of man in the New World, as far as is known. During the latter part of the fourth glaciation, with the climate cooler and rainier than at present, grassland should have been more restricted than it is today.

At any rate, the greater part of the Rancholabrean fauna was not limited to grassland. I see no reason why the big-game hunters should have restricted themselves to this type of vegetation, when their prey abounded in other types as well. At the driest time of year, grassland may carry a blaze and so be suitable for fire-drives; but more important to the hunters, probably, was the existence of cliffs, ravines, limestone chimneys, and boggy lake shores or creek bottoms—places where stampeding beasts were abruptly halted.

The Big-Game Hunting tradition has been regarded as a grassland adaptation partly because it happened to be discovered and most intensively studied in the Southwest. Sandia Cave, Blackwater Draw near Clovis, Folsom, Lindenmeier—these are the sites that first molded our impression of the tradition. It is easy to forget that more Sandia Cave projectile points have been found in the Southeast than in the Southwest. The Atlantic seaboard has produced far more Clovis points than have ever been found in the Southwest. Divers, hunting for fossils on the bottom of the Santa Fe River and other streams of the Suwannee drainage in Florida, have recovered over 800 Suwannee points. The Folsom and the Cumberland points are respectively western and eastern derivatives of the Clovis, and should have been approximately contemporaneous; but Cumberland points outnumber Folsom by a factor of several hundred.

I suggest that the Big-Game Hunting tradition, as manifested by the artifact complexes that include Clovis, Suwannee, and Simpson points, involved pursuit of the Rancholabrean beasts wherever they could be brought to bay, sometimes in grassland but often not. It is only the very last part of this tradition, as manifested by Folsom points and the Plano assemblage, that was strongly adapted to grassland. This part was essentially Recent, post-Rancholabrean, even though one or two Rancholabrean bison species persisted to be hunted by bearers of the tradition. Eventually, the hunting techniques were transferred to pursuit of bison belonging to the modern species.

In the eastern United States, apparent kill-sites of the big-game hunters have rarely come to light outside Florida, but this situation is not surprising. In many parts of the country, fossilization is a rare accident. In general, a mammal's bones will simply decay, not fossilize, unless they chance somehow to be covered up soon after the animal's death. Some environmental conditions, among them acidic soils, rainforest vegetation, and mountainous topography, militate against fossilization. Other conditions, such as erosion, can destroy fossils after they have formed. In consequence, there are only three really rich collecting grounds for Pleistocene mammals in the United States: peninsular Florida with its karst topography, southern California with its asphalt pits, and central Alaska with its frozen muck beds. Only one of these three, peninsular Florida, lies east of the Rockies, where the Big-Game Hunting tradition was concentrated. Preservation of Pleistocene mammal bones, in clear association with Paleo-Indian projectile points, would be a rare accident indeed in parts of the country where fossilization was improbable. Thus, I attach little significance to the absence of Pleistocene mammal remains from so many sites or localities that yield Paleo-Indian points, and think that the distribution of the Big-Game Hunting tradition was coextensive with Clovis points.

The Archaic major cultural tradition covered "cultures of the eastern North American woodland and river valleys in which subsistence was based on small-game hunting, fishing, and wild-plant collecting" (p. 60). Some workers have substituted the term "Preceramic" for "Archaic," partly because the latter had been used by different authors to mean different things. The term "Preceramic" also has a drawback, for in parts of Georgia and Florida, fiber-tempered pottery was added to the late preceramic artifact inventory without evidence of any other culture change. More importantly, whatever the tradition is called, it is too broadly conceived. Its definition has been refined by recognition of Early and Late subdivisions of the Preceramic or Archaic, but further refinement is needed.

Early Preceramic sites and isolated projectile points are widely but thinly distributed in about the same fashion and places as the sites and points of the Big-Game Hunters. In contrast, Late Preceramic habitation sites are for the most riparian and coastal; they are shell middens, accumulated by peoples whose molluscan economy permitted small, fairly permanent settlements. The cultural change from Early Preceramic to Late involved a shift from what was basically an ancient way of life (semi-nomadic hunting and gathering of terrestrial organisms) to a new way (semi-settled hunting and gathering of aquatic organisms, especially mollusks which had previously been rejected). In the eastern United States, this new way did not develop gradually out of the old; it arose suddenly, accompanied by a flood of new artifact types and a change in the physical characteristics of various local populations.

The passage of Paleo-Indian culture into Early Preceramic was regarded as marking the passage of one major cultural tradition into another, but an even greater and more significant culture change was from Early Preceramic to Late Preceramic. Accordingly, the Early Preceramic way of life should be regarded as a distinctive major cultural tradition, bracketed between Paleo-Indian and late Preceramic.

The Woodland major cultural tradition was distinguished by "cord-marked and fabric-marked ceramics [as well as] by the construction of burial mounds and other earthworks and by at least the beginnings of agriculture (Willey 1966)." As noted previously, archeologists have misused the term "woodland" to designate what ecologists would call the eastern deciduous forest. The term was introduced into archeology long ago, to emphasize cultural adaptation to that forest. The definition of the Woodland tradition calls a certain question to mind.

Not until near the end of the Late Preceramic did rise of sea level, and so of water table, provide southern Florida with extensive fresh-water marshes and waterways. To judge from a few finds of fiber-tempered pottery, the first occupants of the Glades archeological subarea were culturally similar to their contemporaries farther north in the state. But around 400 B.C., a distinctive local tradition began in the Glades, and the distinctiveness was maintained into historic times. Its pottery was sand-tempered—at first plain but later decorated by incision, punctation, or tooling; cord-marking and fabric-marking were not adopted, nor was agriculture. But the extensive marshes and coastal shallows evidently provided a solid economic foundation; time could be spared for the construction not only of burial mounds but also of exceptionally large ceremonial earthworks, shellworks, and canals. By historic times, one Glades people, the Calusa, were exerting hegemony over the others; so the Glades social organization became more complex than the tribal. The vegetation of the Glades region was not the eastern hardwood forest; it included sawgrass marsh, mangrove swamp, and West Indian tropical forest. The Glades artifact assemblage reveals striking adaptation to the environment of southern Florida.

The question is whether a distinctive life-way, such as that of the Glades, can be regarded as having existed outside any major cultural tradition, or whether the definition of some such tradition should be extended to encompass variants such as Glades. When Woodland influences arrived in Florida, those peoples north of the Glades subarea took up a fairly typical Woodland way of life, while those in the Glades substituted coastal and riparian collecting for agriculture, and developed their own styles of pottery decoration, and their own technological adjustments to a distinctive environment. But the bearers of the Glades local tradition were trading pottery and other items with the more Woodland-like peoples farther north in the state. Just north of the Glades subarea, all the way across Florida, there was a sizeable zone of intermediacy between the Glades local tradition and the other local traditions that held sway just north of the Glades.

In my opinion, the definition of Woodland might well be extended to encompass cultural variants such as that of southern Florida, although of course it would be well to distinguish between typical and atypical manifestations.

Monographers can scarcely be blamed if their broad categories of culture occasionally prove a little less than satisfactory in local application, especially when the categories are defined partly on ecological grounds; for local workers have been remiss in providing basic data about the ecological relations of geographically restricted cultures. In the United States, very few sites have ever been investigated intensively with the idea of discovering a great deal about the ecology of the original occupants. Instead, the emphasis has been on artifacts. In many cases, ecology has been inferred from artifact typology, not from actual investigation. Such inference can go astray.

For example, the Tallahassee type of projectile point no doubt characterized either the last of the Paleo-Indian Period or the first of the Early Preceramic. The type is lanceolate, with basal and lateral grinding; although not fluted, it is basally thinned. Typologically, it is close to Florida Paleo-Indian projectile points such as Clovis, Suwannee, and Simpson, and accordingly it has been listed as a Paleo-Indian type. But when I originally described this point (1963), I took environmental considerations into account. The Clovis type had been found with remains of extinct animals at scattered localities from Arizona to Florida; the Simpson, a very rare type, had once been found with such remains; the Suwannee had many times been discovered on stream bottoms at what I regard as Paleo-Indian kill-sites. In contrast, the Tallahassee point has not turned up in any kind of association with extinct animals, nor is it concentrated in and around the great springs, flooded caverns, and spring runs. Indeed, the distribution of the Tallahassee point has no counterpart among the definitely Paleo-Indian points of Florida. The Tallahassee type is concentrated and is fairly common along the Gulf lowlands of northern and central Florida, and is nearly or quite lacking from the comparatively high interior of the state where Paleo-Indian hunters frequented the vicinity of springs, caves, and streams. The Tallahassee was made by peoples whose way of life was not that of the Florida Paleo-Indian. The point has two characteristics that ally it to Early Preceramic types: the outline of the blade is angulate, and the edge of the blade is serrate. All in all, the Tallahassee appears to be among the first of the Early Preceramic points, not the last of the Paleo-Indian points.

Of course, typology and ecology are both important in culture classification. Needed now is a series of regional classifications using both typological and ecological criteria, distinguishing carefully between the two, and dispensing with the older terminology wherever it is ambiguous. When sufficient regional classifications have accumulated, they may be compared and correlated with one another.

So much, then, for directions taken by environmental archeology. No doubt many other directions will be taken even while the book is in press. Indeed, I may have overlooked some extant studies in the field. But enough of review. I wish to devote the next chapter to methods whereby environmental studies can be used to illuminate archeological problems. I believe these methods will prove novel to most archeologists, and perhaps useful to some.

CHAPTER TEN

Four Archeological Problems

The first problem relates to passage from the Late Archaic way of life to the Woodland. In Florida, the passage took place during what has been called the Transitional Period, roughly 1000 to 400 B.C. Ceramically, it was marked by a transfer of certain designs from the terminal Archaic fiber-tempered pottery (Orange Incised) to chalky (St. Johns Incised) vessels. Another marker was the Norwood series of pottery types, tempered with a variable mixture of sand and fiber. Also characteristic were steatite vessels imported from farther north, and mat impressions on the bottom of St. Johns Incised (rarely Orange) vessels. In Florida, many Late Archaic sites that had been occupied for millennia were abandoned soon after the arrival of Transitional pottery, and were reoccupied only after a lapse of about 2,000 years.

The Florida Transitional was a period during which Late Archaic ideas were phased out in favor of Woodland. It has generally been supposed that, in this state, the revolution in life-ways was purely a cultural matter, reflecting the arrival of new culture trait-complexes. The question I propound has not been asked before: Was some of this revolution brought about by environmental changes of so profound a nature that the Indians perforce changed some of their ways? The question is important; there is much current interest in determining the fashion whereby various peoples, including the North American Indians, reached a Neolithic level of culture. Passage from Archaic to Woodland was, in Old World terms, passage from Mesolithic to Neolithic.

There is reason to think that a cultural revolution might correspond with an environmental change. In Florida, the Paleo-Indian Period ended when the Pleistocene did, and when the Rancholabrean fauna was reduced to the Recent one. The Early Preceramic Period corresponded quite well with the Anathermal, the Late Preceramic with the comparatively warm, dry Altithermal. It was near the beginning of the Medithermal that the first fiber-tempered pottery was made in Florida, harbinger of many cultural changes soon to come. While the Transitional Period did not begin as soon as the Medithermal did, it began when that climatic episode had gotten well under way and had brought about environmental conditions markedly different from the warm, dry Altithermal ones under which the Late Archaic peoples had lived. The Transitional then continued through the first part of the Medithermal, during which the climate became progressively cooler and rainier; and when this early Medithermal trend reversed, the Transitional ended.

Around the end of the Transitional, the Florida climate should have been cooler and rainier than it had been for several thousand years. Presumably, one would have to go back into the Anathermal, into the Early Preceramic Period, to find climatic conditions equalling those of the Medithermal low point. However, the climatic episodes called Anathermal, Altithermal, and Medithermal have been studied mainly in parts of the United States well removed from Florida. Very little work has been done on Recent climatic shifts in the latter state, and some people have chosen to guess that the effects of these shifts were very attenuated toward Florida.

So much, then, for the theoretical background. The next step is to review unusual archeofaunal and archeofloral occurrences in Florida sites. The best procedure would be to review all such occurrences, for all culture periods, and see if they cluster in any significant fashion.

There is no need to summarize occurrences of extinct Pleistocene species, for their ecological requirements remain a matter for speculation. It is evident from fossil deposits that a great many animals and plants, today characteristic of areas well to the north of Florida, ranged southward into that state during glacial times. Most of these species have since returned northward, by a distance of 100 to more than 1,000 miles. Quite a number of the northern species, including vertebrates, invertebrates, and plants, were able to persist in Florida, but only in the deep, cool, humid ravines of the Apalachicola drainage, where they exist as geographically isolated, relict populations. In most cases, neither paleontology nor biogeography will reveal just which glacial episode resulted in the invasion of Florida by essentially northern species, but evidence is growing that each glaciation wrought comparable climatic changes. The Florida Paleo-Indians probably were in contact not only with the Pleistocene megafauna but also with some smaller animals that have since moved northward. The turtle *Pseudemys scripta* is the only species that I could single out in this connection, but remains of small game are lacking from most Paleo-Indian sites.

Faunal remains are wholly lacking from Florida sites of the Early Preceramic Period. However, they are very abundant in sites of the Late Preceramic Period, and are well preserved in midden shell. There is very little evidence that the warm Altithermal climate of the Late Preceramic permitted tropical species to range farther north into Florida than they do today. Nor would such evidence be expected; the modern tropical biota of extreme southern Florida includes very few species of kinds that might have left remains in midden shell. Florida was never connected by land with the West Indies, and so the tropical element of the South Florida biota is made up of the limited number of species that could cross the Straits of Florida. In general, the seed-bearing plants have crossed this barrier far more often than the terrestrial and freshwater vertebrates, but plant remains are virtually unknown from the Late Preceramic middens of Florida.

In short, Florida is not a region that would provide much archeofaunal evidence of northwardly shifting ranges during a warm climatic episode. An extremely warm, dry episode might permit eastward extension of essentially western organisms along newly formed tongues of grassland or other dry situations. Such extensions took place during times of deglaciation, but those times probably were much warmer and drier (and surely longer lasting) than the Altithermal. On the other hand, Florida sites might reasonably be expected to provide archeofaunal evidence of a shift toward a cooler climate, one that permitted essentially northern species to range farther south than they do today.

If extralimital paleoclimatic studies are applicable to Florida, then that state had a comparatively cool, rainy episode that began near the end of the Late Preceramic, in other words around the beginning of what is called the Orange Period, when the local Indians first added fiber-tempered pottery to their ceramic inventory. The episode became progressively cooler and rainier all through the Transitional, which succeeded the Orange Period. At the end of the Transitional, the climatic trend was reversed; temperatures began to rise, rainfall to decrease. One might describe the cool, rainy episode as having extended from immediately pre-Transitional times to immediately post-Transitional. It is highly significant that almost all of Florida's unusual archeofaunal and archeofloral occurrences are clustered within the span of this episode. These occurrences may be reviewed species by species:

A fragmentary jaw of the muskrat, *Ondatra zibethica,* was found at Site J–5 near Sneads, Jackson County, Florida (Neill and Bullen 1955). It dates from the Transitional Period as shown by the associated ceramics. The species does not now occur very far below the Fall Line in extreme western Georgia; Site J–5 may be about 100 miles south of its present range. Irving Rouse (1951) stated that faunal remains from Locality 2 of the Vero Site, Indian River County, Florida, like those from the South Indian Field Site of Brevard County, included "muskrat." Rouse's reference actually was to the round-tailed water rat, *Neofiber alleni,* often miscalled muskrat. This rodent is a Floridian species whose mere presence is of no significance.

Margaret V. Houck (1951) stated that round-tailed water rats from the South Indian Field Site were larger than the modern ones. However, this species is made up of several populations differing among themselves in average size. The present-day water rats of Brevard County should average larger than those from, say, the southern tip of the Florida peninsula. Houck's contention cannot be evaluated unless one knows the provenience of the material used for comparison; this information was not given. Standard mammalogical measurements, such as cranial length or length of the molar tooth row, could not be given for the archeofaunal specimens because they were too fragmentary. To judge from Rouse, these water-rat remains, possibly larger than modern ones, came from Layer 3 along with an abundance of Orange Incised sherds and fragments of steatite vessels. This combination of artifacts implies a date near the beginning of the Transitional.

Houck also noted that white-tailed deer, *Odocoileus virginianus,* from South Indian Field averaged quite large, although she was careful to state that the species exhibits regional variation in size. Elsewhere, I have pointed out that considerable variation exists even from place to place in peninsular Florida. Thus, it is possible, but not certain, that the deer from South Indian Field averaged larger than modern ones from the same area. The supposedly larger deer remains were mostly from Layer 3, which, as noted, dates from near the beginning of the Transitional Period.

At South Indian Field, A. T. Anderson found a cache of seven beaver jaws, minus the incisors. This find evidently was the basis for Rouse's report of the beaver, *Castor canadensis,* at that locality. Rouse (1951) stated that the remains were from Layer 3, and so they date from near the beginning of the Transitional. Beaver remains were also found in Layer 3 of the Palmer-Taylor Site, Seminole County, Florida. This layer, which varied in thickness from 3.9 to 19.7 inches, yielded no pottery, but produced an expanded-head bone pin with an incised design like that on some fiber-tempered and some Transitional pottery. The site had first been dug into by Clarence B. Moore in the 1890s, and then by an "Excavators Club" whose members found the beaver remains; the locality had also seen a great deal of other disturbance. The "account of stratigraphy must be treated with reservation. . . . Layer 2 [above Layer 3] is notable for the number of pits which protruded from its base into underlying layers. . . . Orange Incised sherds were found in Layer 2" along with other sherd types thought intrusive from higher levels. Thus, while the beaver remains from the Palmer-Taylor Site could date from the Late Preceramic, they could also very well date from a time when Orange Incised ware was in use. The latter interpretation accords with the situation at South Indian Field, about 60 miles farther south in the same river drainage. Furthermore, the incised, expanded-head bone pin is not known from the Late Preceramic; it appears to be a marker for the time when Orange Incised pottery was in use.

Beaver remains were also found at the De Bary Creek Site in Volusia County, Florida, John M. Goggin (1952) listed this as the "Du Barry" Creek Site, but did not give an indication of its time period. Previously, I suggested that this site, a midden, was "perhaps of St. Johns II times," around 1000 A.D. I so stated because St. Johns Check Stamped pottery, a time marker for St. John II, had been found there. However, it is usual in this area to find St. Johns Check Stamped sherds in the uppermost level of a midden, lying "unconformably" over a much thicker deposit with Orange Incised and often the Transitional St. Johns Incised pottery. Unfortunately, the De Bary Creek midden was hauled away for road fill before its deeper levels were investigated. At any rate, the De Bary Creek beaver remains may well have been associated with Orange Incised pottery. The De Bary Creek Site, like the Palmer-Taylor one, is in the same river drainage as South

Indian Field, where beaver remains date from near the beginning of the Transitional.

Within historic times the beaver has ranged as far south as the Altamaha River of Georgia and the Apalachicola River of the Florida Panhandle. The South Indian Field find represents a 250-mile southward extension of the species' range. Since the find was a cache of jaws, it might have been artifactual, a trade item from elsewhere; but the Palmer-Taylor and De Bary Creek sites are also far south of the species' modern range.

O. P. Hay (1902) described bones of the great auk, *Pinguinus impennis*, from a midden now called the Cotten site, in Volusia County, Florida. John W. Griffin and Hale G. Smith (1954) found this midden to date from near the end of the Orange Period, with reoccupation centuries later in St. Johns II times. However, Ripley Bullen (1959) has reinterpreted certain of Griffin and Smith's data to show evidence of Transitional occupation also. A mat-impressed bottom sherd of St. Johns Plain pottery, a Transitional type, was found by Griffin and Smith about a third of the way down in their deepest test. One of the previously found auk bones was from the "lower two-thirds" of the midden, and another was from near the bottom. Apparently, the species was present at the Cotten site in the time span from immediately pre-Transitional into Transitional. One of the specimens was radiocarbon-dated at 1060 B.C. ± 200, according to Pierce Brodkorb (1960), who also noted the presence of this bird in the Summer Haven site, a coastal midden of St. Johns County, Florida. The Summer Haven specimen was associated with Orange Incised pottery, and was thought to date from about 1000 B.C.

In historic times, the great auk occasionally appeared as far south as the coast of the Carolinas, having followed schools of southwardly migrating fishes during the winter.

The common murre, *Uria aalge*, was found with Orange Incised pottery at the Summer Haven site. Today it ranges no farther south than New Jersey.

The Cotten site yielded remains of the alligator snapping-turtle, *Macroclemys temmincki*, according to W. S. Blatchley (1902), presumably in an Orange or a Transitional context. Identification was made by O. P. Hay, who was a leading authority on turtle remains. At present the species is confined to rivers of the Gulf drainage as far east as the Suwannee, which it follows upstream to Okefenokee Swamp. The Cotten site record represents a 145-mile southward extension of the species' range.

Blatchley also reported a mud-clam, possibly *Anodonta imbecilis,* from the Cotten site, presumably in a late Orange or Transitional context. The species now ranges eastward in Florida as far as the Suwannee River drainage. However, if the clam from the Cotten site was misidentified, and was actually *Anodonta cowperiana,* its presence in the midden would not be remarkable; the latter species is widely distributed in the peninsula at the present time. Griffin and Smith found some species of freshwater clam in their excavations at this site, but it was not identified with certainty.

The freshwater middens of the St. Johns River drainage are composed largely of the shells of two snails, *Vivipara georgiana* and *Pomacea paludosa.* Both of these snails were comparatively small in preceramic times, becoming large around the beginning of the Transitional Period. It is not known how long they stayed large; they were small again by St. Johns II times, when many of the middens were reoccupied. Thereafter, they continued small.

A few interesting specimens came from the Vero locality, Indian River County, and the Melbourne locality, Brevard County, Florida. The localities warrant a bit of discussion, for their nature was misunderstood by early paleontologists, and the early, incorrect interpretation of them has been more widely disseminated than the modern, correct one.

At Vero in 1915, and at Melbourne in the 1920s, Indian skeletal remains and artifacts (including pottery) were found along with the bones of certain extinct Pleistocene animals. In the absence of archeological sequences, and in the absence of modern techniques of stratigraphic analysis, it was held by some paleontologists that the localities revealed a contemporaneity of man with extinct animals. By a masterly stratigraphic analysis, Irving Rouse (1951) showed otherwise. Rouse's findings may be recapitulated briefly.

At Locality 2 of the Vero site, Stratum 2 is the Melbourne Formation, rich in the remains of Pleistocene animals, many of them extinct. The top of the Melbourne is eroded. Lying unconformably over the Melbourne is the Van Valkenburg or a temporal equivalent thereof, called Stratum 3. The surface of Stratum 3 is exposed today. The first Indians arrived at Vero not in Melbourne times but during the erosional interval that disfigured the surface of the Melbourne. They dug a burial pit into the surface of the Melbourne atop which they were living, thereby commingling Pleistocene material with their own remains. These Indians, or some immediate successors, also dug a basin-like pit through the Melbourne, bringing up more Pleistocene material in the dirt thus removed. These Indians departed; Stratum 3 began to build up.

Another group of Indians arrived. These later comers also dug a sizeable basin, which cut through the earlier burial and into the Melbourne, bringing Pleistocene fossils well up into Stratum 3. The locality was growing damper, and a muck bed began to accumulate. These later Indians were still there as the muck bed began to develop, for Edward W. Berry (1917) stated that he "did collect a number of bone implements and fragments of pottery with the plant fossils" from the Vero muck bed. The increasing dampness of the site may have led to its abandonment. The locality was a marsh in modern times, prior to the digging of a drainage canal.

The first comers to the site left a stemmed projectile point of flint, a simple bone point, an expanded-head bone pin, and a peg-topped bone pin. This is an assemblage typical of Archaic times, and especially of the Orange Period although in the latter case one would expect accompanying sherds. As a matter of fact, one sherd was said to have been found in Stratum 2; but Rouse could not locate it. The first occupation at Vero might therefore date from Late Preceramic times, but more likely from Orange. The later comers to Vero left sufficient material to identify their culture period as Malabar I' (in Rouse's terminology); this was immediately post-Transitional.

Bullen (1968) reinvestigated the site and found three sherds, of wares later than the fiber-tempered, on the contact plane between Stratum 2 and Stratum 3. The find revealed that, at this locality, the eroded surface of the Melbourne Formation was exposed even after Orange times, presumably into immediately post-Transitional times.

Thus, the number of Indian occupations at Vero is uncertain. There was some Archaic occupation, probably in the Orange Period but conceivably a bit earlier. Malabar I' was the only period clearly represented, and most of the cultural remains are of this age. In any event, the time span involved is approximately the one under consideration here, immediately pre-Transitional through immediately post-Transitional; and it is necessary to discuss animal and plant remains from Stratum 3 of the locality.

Animal remains from Stratum 3 are mostly those of modern species, and form an assemblage typical of Indian refuse. A few remains of extinct Pleistocene animals, found in Stratum 3, were brought up into that level from Stratum 2 by basin-digging Indians, and may be ignored. Also, various of the "extinct species" described from Stratum 3 have since proven to be identical with modern Florida ones. Examples are the "extinct deer, *Odocoileus sellardsi,*" which is not distinguishable from the Florida white-tailed deer, *Odocoileus virginianus;* the "extinct gray fox, *Urocyon seminolensis,*" which is the modern gray fox, *Urocyon cinereoargenteus;* the "extinct gull, *Larus vero,*" which is the modern yellow-crowned night heron, *Nyctanassa violacea;* the "extinct heron, *Ardea sellardsi,*" which is the modern wild turkey, *Meleagris gallopavo;* and the "extinct teal, *Querquedula floridana,*" which is the modern hooded merganser, *Lophodytes cucullatus.*

With misidentifications and Pleistocene intrusions out of the way, we need concern ourselves with but two animal species from Stratum 3. One of these is a red fox. It was originally thought to be identical with the modern red fox, *Vulpes vulpes,* but was later described as an extinct species, *Vulpes palmaria.* It is known from the Melbourne Formation, and may have been a robust Pleistocene ancestor of the modern red fox. Its remains in Stratum 3 probably were intrusive from Stratum 2.

A somewhat different problem is presented by remains of an "extinct coyote, *Canis riviveronis,*" from Stratum 3 at Vero. It is now believed to be the modern coyote, *Canis latrans.* The Vero specimen was not found actually in the site, but in a nearby bed that had been disturbed by stream action. No doubt the specimen was intrusive from Stratum 2, where the species definitely occurred. However, at the Melbourne Golf Course locality there was found an upper jaw fragment of this coyote, worked by man. The dorsal surface of the bone had been cut and polished at the level of the root-tip of the canine tooth, and the bone had been cut squarely off posteriorly at right angles to the dorsal border. The Golf Course locality also yielded three carved and polished jaw bones of the modern white-tailed deer. It is not known whether the deer and coyote bone artifacts were found together.

Rouse analyzed the incomplete data provided by the original excavators of the Golf Course site. The situation there is much like that at Vero. Stratum 2 is the Melbourne Formation, rich in the remains of Pleistocene animals, some of them extinct. The top of the Melbourne is eroded and shows evidence of having been an old land surface. Lying unconformably over the Melbourne is the Van Valkenburg, Stratum 3, the top of which forms the present land surface. The first comers to the site arrived not during Melbourne times but during the erosional interval. They left material on the contact plane between Stratum 2 and Stratum 3. Fragmentary human remains were found either on the contact plane or in the upper six inches of Stratum 2 (a level marked everywhere by numerous vertical dark streaks, evidently the remains of old roots). Artifacts were found lying on the contact plane; these included sherds which were not saved but which were all undecorated. As at South Indian Field, the Indians had dug numerous basins into Stratum 2.

Rouse advanced two alternative explanations of the situation at the Golf Course site. There might have been two occupations, the first Archaic and the second dating from the Malabar I' Period; or there may have been but one occupation, in the Orange Period. The former idea seemed more likely because residence on the contact plane was thought to imply occupation no later than the end of the Orange Period; while a collection of sherds, all of them plain, suggested the Malabar I' Period with its characteristic St. Johns Plain pottery. However, during the first part of the Orange Period, only plain fiber-tempered vessels were made, and not all vessels were decorated during the last part; a small collection of sherds might by chance include only plain ones. But more importantly, Bullen showed that at the Vero site (hence inferentially at the Golf Course site), the eroded surface of the Melbourne Formation was still exposed after Orange times; and it nows seems likely that there was but one occupation at the Golf Course site, in the Malabar I' Period.

In spite of the vagueness of the data, it is clear that material from Stratum 3, including the contact plane, falls within the time span under consideration in the present account. Making use of all available data, it seems most likely that the coyote jaw from the Golf Course site, whatever its actual age, was worked during the Malabar I' Period.

Pleistocene bone beds of the Florida west coast (Pinellas and Sarasota counties), temporally equivalent to the Melbourne Formation and containing much the same group of extinct animals, have yielded remains of the aforesaid coyote. The Golf Course locality produced non-artifactual coyote remains at first assigned either to Stratum 2 or the contact plane, but now definitely assigned to Stratum 2. The coyote has not been found in any Florida archeological context—except at the Golf Course site, where the Indians had dug basins into the highly fossiliferous Melbourne Formation which lay beneath their feet. It is therefore concluded that basin-digging Indians of the Malabar I' Period unearthed a Pleistocene coyote jaw, and worked it as they might the jaws of animals with which they were contemporary.

Thus, the vertebrate remains of Vero and Melbourne are not of much importance in the present study. Plant remains from the Vero muck bed are interesting, however. These were identified by Berry or for him by specialists.

The plants from the muck bed, Stratum 3, date at least in part from the Malabar I' Period, for artifacts of this period were found in the deposit. However, some remains could very well date from a somewhat earlier period, because it is not known exactly when the muck bed began to form, and there is some uncertainty as to what Indian occupation preceded the development of this bed. Rather surely, the bed dates from within the time span of immediately pre-Transitional through immediately post-Transitional; it may well have begun to form in the Transitional. Unfortunately, although the bed occupied a good part of Stratum 3, no record was kept of the levels at which the various plant species were found within the deposit.

Berry thought the Vero plants included a considerable number of species not known from the region in modern times. However, progress of botanical collecting has extended the known range of some of these species to the Vero vicinity. I see nothing remarkable about the presence in the muck bed of such plants as the bald cypress, pond apple, water-lettuce, Chapman oak, water-shield, or the wild grape *Vitis coriacea*. From this bed, Berry reported some species of *Zizyphus*, a genus that includes the European jujube-tree. A *Zizyphus*, said by Berry to be identical with the Vero one, had been reported from the late Pleistocene (Talbot Formation) of New Jersey. As the Vero *Zizyphus* was represented by but a single stone, I suspect that this stone, if correctly identified, was intrusive into Stratum 3 like certain Pleistocene animal remains.

The bed yielded a *Viburnum* which seemed close to the arrowwood, *Viburnum dentatum*, "but may not be identical with it." Arrowwood is said to reach Florida today, but only in the Panhandle region. However, other species of *Viburnum* now occur in the peninsula, and the uncertainty of the identification prohibits the attribution of much significance to the Vero specimens. Berry also reported a *Benzoin*, species uncertain, from Vero. The two Southeastern species of this genus, called spice bushes, are today seldom found farther south than the Panhandle. However, identification was made only on the basis of immature fruits, and I am not sure that one can rule out identification as *Tamala*, a related genus with representatives in the Florida peninsula. Finally, Berry reported corkwood, *Leitneria floridana*, from the muck bed, on the basis of winter buds. These buds are very characteristic, and the identification is probably correct. This tree has been reported in modern times from as far south as the lower Altamaha in Georgia, and the vicinity of Apalachicola, Franklin County, in the Florida Panhandle.

Thus the muck bed provides somewhat tenuous evidence that a few plants, now ranging not much farther south than the Florida Panhandle, occurred at Vero in Transitional times, or perhaps a little sooner or a little later.

Although agriculture was a part of the Woodland major cultural tradition, for a long while it remained a minor pursuit in Florida, where the Indians continued to accumulate shell middens. Sites with well-preserved, abundant faunal remains are numerous for Florida local archeological periods within the Woodland time span. However, these remains include nothing noteworthy until one reaches the St. Johns II Period. Then, some northern faunal elements appear briefly in sites of the east coast. Green Mound, actually a midden in Volusia County, Florida, yielded bones of the razor-billed auk, *Alca torda;* brant, *Branta bernicla;* glaucous gull, *Larus hyperboreus;* and great black-backed gull, *Larus marinus.* Today, the first of these winters southward to New Jersey, the second to North Carolina, the third usually to New Jersey although rarely to North Carolina and Texas, the fourth usually to Virginia although rarely to Florida. Radiocarbon dates indicate that the northern species existed at Green Mound in the period 900–950 A.D.

I have already mentioned the possibility that the beaver was present at the De Bary Creek Site, Volusia County, in St. Johns II times.

Before bringing the discussion up into historic times, I want to dispose of a few minor archeofaunal occurrences. A West Indian seal, *Monachus tropicalis,* was reported by Rouse from Layer 3 at South Indian Field. Historic Florida records are from the Dry Tortugas, Key West, and Cape Florida (Monroe and Dade counties). However, in modern times the species has been recorded on the Texas coast, showing it to be tolerant of conditions that obtain north of the latitude of South Indian Field. Elsewhere, I have described the relentless pursuit of this animal in early historic times, resulting in its near-extinction. It was probably decimated before historic records accumulated on the northern periphery of its range. It is known from Stratum 2 at Melbourne, and possibly from South Carolina in an unidentified horizon.

Little significance attaches to archeological finds of the queen conch, *Strombus gigas,* at Cedar Keys, Levy County, Florida, although the species does not presently range so far north along the Gulf coast of Florida. Gulf coast shells passed far northward as trade items, far into the United States; they have been found even in Archaic sites of New York, Ohio, and Kentucky. Celts, made from the shell of the queen conch, are found in many sites well north of that mollusk's present range. However, these sites lack other evidence of the queen conch's presence, and the celts are to be regarded as trade items.

A West Indian top-shell, *Livona pica,* existed on the lower coasts of Florida in the Glades II and Glades III periods (around 300 to 850 A.D.) The species might not occur in the state today. It is a mollusk of rocky shores, which are not often encountered along the present Florida coastline. Continued rise of sea level, the coastal deposition of muck and sediments, and the coastal growth of saltmarsh and mangrove swamp may have severely reduced the habitat of the species. Predation by the Indians may also have hastened the extirpation of this ecologically restricted organism. Dead specimens have been found on beaches at Charlotte Harbor, Lee County, Florida, suggesting that the disappearance of the species from Florida waters has been completed only in historic times. One cannot assume that *Livona* first appeared in southern Florida in Glades II times; sites of earlier times are rare in the Glades archeological subarea.

The mottled top-shell, queen conch, and wolf seal are the only species to have been found in some archeological context farther north than their present respective ranges. The finds do not suggest actual movement of species northward.

In the Panhandle and along the central Gulf coast of Florida, the Woodland major cultural tradition gave way to the Mississippian around 1300 A.D. No doubt agriculture became more important throughout most of the state north of the Glades archeological subarea. Nevertheless, there was still considerable reliance on mollusks, and many sites acquired enough shell debris to permit preservation of faunal remains. These remains include nothing of interest in the present connection, and we must go well into historical times for observations possibly indicative of shifting ranges.

In the latter eighteenth century, the naturalist William Bartram (1791) mentioned a bird that he called the "painted vulture," supposedly found from Florida to the Carolinas. His description of its coloration suggests the king vulture, *Sarcorhamphus papa,* an inhabitant of the New World tropics from southern Mexico southward. However, he stated that it had shorter wings than the turkey vulture, *Cathartes aura;* and the statement is not applicable to the king vulture, a gigantic bird. Bartram's description of the "painted vulture's" coloration was clear and concise, a bit different from his usual flowery, romantic style; perhaps it was added later. Apparently, what Bartram actually saw was something he called the "royal standard." This was the calumet of the Creek and Seminole Indians, a ceremonial pipestem hung with the tail feathers of an eagle. The "standard" he saw was pure white. The tail feathers of the king vulture are black, those of the adult bald eagle white.

Apart from Bartramian dubieties, there is only one instance of shifting geographic range in historic Florida (ignoring, of course, the extirpation or extermination of various species by civilized man). The early Spanish explorers—De Soto in the 1540s, De Luna in the 1550s, Pardo in the 1560s—saw no bison in Florida. At that time, the species may not have ranged south or east of the Tennessee River. By the 1670s, however, it was common in the Florida Panhandle, and by early 1700s in northeastern Florida also. By the latter 1700s it may have reached Tampa Bay, but historical, toponymic, and archeological records are concentrated farther north in the state. Its decline in the Southeast, noticeable by the 1770s, is not important here, but an explanation should be offered for its sudden irruption into that region in the seventeenth century.

It will be recalled that about 1300 A.D., advanced agriculture began to spread into northern Florida, with resultant clearing of more forest than ever before. Next came the Europeans, with intensive agriculture, animal husbandry, and more effective farming tools. By the latter 1600s, the forest cover, from Louisiana eastward through northern Florida into the Carolinas, had been riddled and reticulated by clearings, cultivated and abandoned fields, and the scars of repeated burning. Several accounts of expeditions in and near northern Florida, made between the late 1600s and the late 1700s, mention the presence of both bison and wild cattle. Evidently, this part of the Southeast had been opened up by the activities of man, to a point where it would support cattle herds in a state of nature; hence it would support bison as well. In the Southeast (as elsewhere), the bison was described as a grazer rather than a browser. It extended its range southeastward as grassy situations multiplied in a land that had formerly been almost blanketed by forests.

Thus, since the end of the Pleistocene, there are only two times toward which our attention is directed. A small group of northern species were in Florida during the span 900–1300 A.D., perhaps clustering near 1000 A.D. More important in the present connection, a larger and more diverse group of northern species were in Florida during the approximate span 2000–400 B.C. Except for the great auk and common murre, which are marine, this larger group is made up of species that inhabit fresh waters or the associated marshes, swamps, and humid forests. The supposedly oversized deer, water rat, and freshwater snails are from this span also. In many a mammal species, the largest individuals inhabit the coldest part of the range, while the smallest inhabit the warmest part. The large size of the two snails might reflect heavier rainfall; these mollusks build their shells from dissolved limestone, the concentration of which might be greater at times of increased runoff. With or without the deer, water rat, and snails, the ecological picture is one of a notably cool, rainy period, during which there was an expansion of freshwater habitats and a southward movement of some northerly animals and plants.

The presence of the northern intrusives cannot be accounted for by rise of water table solely as a result of rising sea level; by the end of the period that concerns us, the sea had still not quite risen to its present stand. Nor would mere rise of water table, unaccompanied by cooling, affect sea-birds that move southward in the winter, well off shore. Expansion of freshwater and associated situations, unaccompanied by cooling, would scarcely have brought the northern species southward; in general, in their present respective ranges they exist where such situations are less widespread than in Florida. On the other hand, the drop of temperature during the period of northern intrusives was by no means as extreme as it was in glacial times; if it had been, a much larger number of northern species would have entered Florida.

The temporal distribution of the northern intrusives (and of the putatively oversized mammals and snails) corresponds well to the early segment of the Medithermal, during which the climate became progressively cooler and rainier. This early Medithermal affected much of the northern hemisphere, and altered many uncivilized cultures. For example, Central European lakes, which had reached a low stage, suddenly began to rise, while temperatures began to fall; the local populations were driven to warmer and drier localities, and agriculture became impossible at higher altitudes where crops had formerly grown. Similar histories have been traced for dwellers around lakes in northern Africa, as well as in western and central Asia.

In Florida, the period of the northern intrusives—the early segment of the Medithermal—corresponds well to a time span that began when pottery was first added to the Archaic inventory, and that ended soon after the Archaic had been phased out. I do not question the view that a profound cultural change in the Southeast was made possible by the arrival of new ideas: fiber-tempered pottery from northwestern South America, paddle-malleated pottery perhaps from Siberia, the polished stone celt perhaps from Mesoamerica, and so on. But it is important to search for aspects of this cultural change that might have been forced or encouraged by a climatic shift.

It will be recalled that the unusually cool and wet period, the early Medithermal, had been preceded by the unusually warm and dry Altithermal, during which the Archaic Indians had become adapted to life on river banks and coastal lagoons. But, in Florida at least, bands of Indians must have been forced to abandon the drowning middens as the water table rose in consequence of both increased precipitation and a rising sea-level. Evidently, large tracts of lowland were evacuated. For example, in the Northern St. Johns archeological sub-area, the most heavily populated region of the state during Archaic times, many sites yield evidence of continuous occupation from Late Preceramic through Orange and often into the Transitional Period; yet not one site has been reported to yield evidence of continuous occupation into the next period, St. Johns I. It cannot be argued that the Indians were moving to high ground in order to farm, for early Woodland agriculture was exceedingly minor or even nonexistent in Florida. The Indians must have been moving into unfamiliar localities, perhaps altering the style of clothing and housing in adjustment to the changed environment, surely subsisting by different techniques and upon different plants and animals, coming upon a few strange plants and animals newly arrived from the north, and quite likely encountering other bands of displaced Indians with whom to effect a cross-fertilization of ideas.

Indians underwent abrupt and profound cultural changes, closely paralleling the Transitional changes of Florida, in Mississippi, Louisiana, Alabama, and Tennessee. Indeed, an abrupt change from the Archaic to the very different Woodland way of life was characteristic of the eastern United States generally. If the revolutionary new ideas had arrived earlier, before the end of the Altithermal, they might never have become popular; indeed, they might soon have flickered out. But as it happened, they arrived when the Indians, after 5,000 years of adaptation to an environment warmer and drier than the present one, were suddenly confronted with an environment cooler and rainier than the present one. As the result of a climatic shift, the time was ripe for cultural change.

This situation may explain a circumstance that has long puzzled the archeologists: the apparent ability of a few groups of people, the bearers of new ideas, speedily to revolutionize the culture of eastern North America. Once again I am led to suggest that a culture declines and vanishes when a sizeable percentage of its bearers find it unsatisfactory, unrewarding. Among uncivilized peoples, the ones who are in intimate contact with the natural environment, a climatic shift can speedily negate the advantages of a long-established way of life. The Indians of the eastern United States were fortunate in that when the Archaic way became intolerable, a few immigrants arrived bearing knowledge of a better way.

The next problem I want to attack relates to an apparent discrepancy between ethnohistory and linguistics on the one hand, archeology on the other. In early historic times, the Glades archeological subarea was occupied by the Calusa and their subordinates. Around 1545—the exact date is uncertain—a Spanish youth named Hernando d'Escalante Fontaneda was shipwrecked on the Florida Keys, and taken captive by the Calusa. After perhaps 17 years residence among them, he was rescued and taken back to Spain, where he wrote a brief account of his experiences. In his account (True, ed. 1945), he provided a few Calusa phrases or toponyms, with imprecise translations. This is virtually the only linguistic material that has come down to us from the Calusa, and it is inadequate to identify the affiliation of their language.

Fontaneda's memoir languished for about 280 years in the Spanish archives, when it was discovered by Buckingham Smith, a lawyer and diplomat with an interest in history and philology. Smith naively supposed that Peter Perkins Pitchlynn, an elderly mixed-blood Choctaw from Mississippi, could diagnose the affiliation of any Southeastern Indian language. Accordingly, Smith brought Fontaneda's Calusa phrases to the attention of Pitchlynn, who not surprisingly said they sounded something like Choctaw. But ransacking the whole Choctaw language, Pitchlynn was unable to provide more than one or two Choctaw phrases that had even fairly close counterparts, phonetically and semantically, in the Calusa material. A. S. Gatschet (1877) also tried to identify Calusa, but compared it only with Spanish, Timucua (itself poorly known), and Creek.

Next, the eminent ethnographer John R. Swanton (1922) decided that Calusa really did sound something like Choctaw, and he tentatively classified the South Florida language as Muskhogean. After the Calusa had vanished from Florida, a group of Mikasuki Seminole joined the Spaniards at fishing *ranchos* along the central and lower coasts of the Florida peninsula. Although it is now clear from traditional, primary historical and linguistic data that these "Spanish Indians" were Seminole, Swanton held them to have been a Calusa remnant; and he used his misinterpretation of the situation to bolster his contention that the Calusa spoke a Muskhogean language akin to Choctaw. Fontaneda wrote that one Calusa settlement was called *Guarugunbe,* which meant "the town of weeping." The sound of "r" does not exist in Muskhogean, but Swanton got around this difficulty by suggesting that the settlement had been occupied by Arawak Indians from Cuba! Fontaneda gave *Certepe* as a Calusa phrase or title meaning "chief and great lord," and called the South Florida Indians not Calusa but *Carlos,* meaning "a fierce people." These occurrences of "r" were not explained away.

There the matter stands: the Calusa language is listed as Muskhogean in the literature relating to historic Indians of the Southeast. But now for the archeological aspects of the subject.

Near the end of Transitional times, around 400 B.C., Indians of the Glades archeological subarea began what has been called the Glades local tradition. It was the most highly distinctive of the Florida traditions, reflecting adaptation to the tropical and near-tropical environments of southern Florida, and a very sparing, selective acceptance of ideas from farther north. The Glades tradition had lasted for about 1,900 years when it emerged into the light of history; its historical bearers were the Calusa and their subordinates. Although the Glades way of life had not been static, it had maintained its general cultural configurations (which a local tradition, by definition, must do). There is no evidence that the Glades archeological subarea was taken over in late prehistoric times by Muskhogeans, as happened in the Florida Panhandle and some areas farther north. To judge from the archeological evidence, any Muskhogean affiliation of Calusa must have been tenuous: the Calusa were descendants of a people who had been in the Glades subarea since 400 B.C. or earlier, while the Muskhogeans entered the Southeast from somewhere farther west around 1300 A.D.

Thus, the archeological interpretation of the situation was in conflict with the non-archeological. Swanton once granted, "It is exasperating to reflect that if we had only ten or twenty bona fide words from the Calusa language we could probably classify it definitely." It occurred to me that it might be possible to recover some Calusa words along with their precise meanings. The line of reasoning was as follows:

The Seminole are not among those peoples who rarely borrow foreign words. Both of the Seminole languages include Spanish loan-words, as I have noted in chapters 2 and 3. From 1812 through 1858, the Seminole were under frequent attack by American troops, however, and for decades thereafter they frowned on the use of English words; even so, they adopted a few such words into both their languages. In modern times, a few more English words have been borrowed; they are dropped casually into conversations otherwise carried on in Creek or Mikasuki. Loan-words identified by me in the two Seminole languages relate mostly to the edible plants, man-made items, and concepts that were introduced to the Seminole by other peoples. When collecting linguistic material from the Seminole, I was impressed by the comprehensiveness and precision of their vocabulary relating to plants and animals; I mentioned this in Chapter 9. When the Seminole arrived in southern Florida, they encountered a striking assemblage of plants and animals that did not exist in the old Seminole homeland of Georgia and Alabama. Where did they obtain names for these organisms?

The early Seminole knew of the Calusa, and called one of their South Florida villages Caloosahatchee, "river of the Calusa." The Creek raids of the early 1700s, although directed principally against the missionized Timucua and Apalachee of North Florida, extended also into the far-southern part of the state, and did not come to an end when the missionized villages were destroyed. An eighteenth-century writer may have been correct in saying that the Seminole helped extirpate the Calusa, 80 families of whom departed for Havana in 1763. The modern Seminole have retained traditions of encounters with remnant groups of Florida aborigines. Billie Stewart, a medicine man of the Creek-speaking Seminole, recorded more than 200 songs for the ethnomusicologist Frances Densmore, and claimed that seven of them were from the Calusa. According to Stewart, the Seminole and the Calusa once lived near each other, attended each others' dances, and learned each others' songs. Later, however, they became enemies, and the Seminole defeated the Calusa.

Since the Seminole (1) were not averse to borrowing words, (2) used a precise, comprehensive vocabulary for plants and animals, and (3) could have been in contact with the Calusa who once dominated South Florida, it seemed possible that Calusa names for the characteristic South Florida organisms had been borrowed into one or both of the Seminole languages. Accordingly, I listed some of the most conspicuous plants (wild and domestic), plant associations, and animals that characterize peninsular or extreme southern Florida. Then I began to collect the Seminole names for these organisms, hoping in this way to acquire a list of words that could not be immediately identified as of Creek or Mikasuki origin. Such a list just might happen to have revealing similarities to some known Indian language.

In presenting the result of this study, it is not necessary to give the actual Creek and Mikasuki words; they can be rendered accurately only in phonetic symbols. It will suffice here to summarize the findings. Unless otherwise stated, it may be assumed that the Creek-speaking and the Mikasuki-speaking Seminole formed or acquired a name in the same fashion, and that a loan-word has been somewhat altered to conform with Creek and Mikasuki speech patterns.

Rice and the orange are called by Spanish loan-words. The borrowed word for orange, coupled with the Seminole for "large," designates the grapefruit; coupled with the Seminole word for "sour," it designates the sour orange, which still exists about old homesteads and village sites. The avocado is called by an English loan-word based on the fruit's alternative name, alligator-pear. A Haitian word, *kasabi*, passed into Spanish as *casabe* and into French as *cassave*, then into English as "cassava," finally into Seminole as *kasawi*.

In some cases, the Seminole transferred a name from a Georgia-Alabama organism to a peninsular Florida one. Thus, the name for a Smilax, one that bears starchy tubers, was transferred to the Zamia or coontie plant, which also has a starchy, tuberous root stock. The name for Arundinaria, a small cane widespread in the Southeast, was transferred to the giant bamboos that are planted ornamentally in South Florida. When the Seminole moved out of the range of the beaver and into that of the manatee, they transferred the name for the first of these animals to the second. Patches of tropical hardwood forest are called by the same name that had been used farther north for temperate hardwood forest, both mesic and hydric.

Many Floridian organisms were simply given a descriptive name in Creek and Mikasuki. The flamingo is a "red bird," the caracara a "variegated vulture," the Florida burrowing owl a "digging owl." The roseate spoonbill is called by the name of the white ibis, plus the modifier "red." Baur's mud-turtle is "striped longitudinally," and the American crocodile is an "alligator with a long, sharp nose." The papaya is "fruiting plant," the strangler fig "yielding chewing-gum," the cabbage palm "big palmetto." The bromeliads or airplants are "large Spanish moss," an appropriate description since they are indeed larger relatives of the Spanish moss. The black mangrove is "black wood," the mango a "sweet berry," the sugarcane "sweet bite," the royal palm "leaves fanning out." When the Seminole moved out of the range of the muskrat and into that of the round-tailed water rat, they did not transfer the name but called the latter animal by a phrase meaning "water rat." The guava is a "cultivated wood," in other words a cultivated woody plant, but often it is simply called "cultivated." As mentioned in chapter 3, the sand pine and rosemary association is described by a phrase roughly translatable as "go elsewhere."

Without lengthening the list, it may be said that the Seminole names for South Florida organisms were disappointingly easy to identify as Creek and Mikasuki transfers and descriptive circumlocutions, plus a few Spanish and English loan words. Only one name was puzzling, that for the banana: *wilendalo* in Creek and *wilendani* in Mikasuki. This is not a descriptive expression. Perhaps the name was derived from Spanish *platano*, influenced by English "plantain." It may also have been influenced by *wilana*, the Creek name for a sweet-scented herb of the Georgia and Alabama Piedmont. In any event, the banana presumably was introduced into Florida in historic times, so the Calusa name for it (if any) probably would not have been borrowed.

Thus, the problem of Calusa linguistic affiliation goes unanswered. Yet, I wanted to include it for several reasons. It makes the point that although in scientific research a trail may not lead to the hoped-for goal, the scenery is always interesting. The study has at least shown how the Seminole obtained names for the organisms they encountered in peninsular Florida. It has cleared up one point of toponymy: the Echashotee River lies far outside the beaver's range but has been noted for an abundance of manatee; it bears a name that means "manatee home," not "beaver home" as a toponymist once had it. The study has also shown how knowledge of plant and animal distribution might be useful to those who are interested in prehistoric migrations, especially as reflected in vocabulary. The absence of the hoped-for Calusa loan words suggests that the Seminole and the Calusa were not in contact with each other, except perhaps on the battlefield. Attention has been drawn to the considerable amount of special pleading that had been resorted to by those who tried to place the Calusa language as Muskhogean.

Finally, the study may stimulate someone to marshal the evidence that would refute my interpretation of the situation, which is as follows: In Late Archaic times, Indians making Orange Incised pottery were concentrated in the Northern St. Johns archeological subarea, but were also present in the Glades. By the end of Transitional times, the two subareas were becoming culturally different as a result of divergence from a common base. The long St. Johns local tradition began in one subarea; the equally long Glades local tradition began in the other. While both traditions changed with time, neither was ever abruptly revolutionized in a fashion that would suggest a take-over by an invading people. In other words, the early historic inhabitants of the Northern St. Johns—the Eastern Timucua—probably were of common ancestry with the Calusa, the two having branched from a single stock in the Orange Period. It is probably significant that the phonetics of the Timucua and the Calusa (and of some minor peninsular tribes allied to one or the other of these) included the sound of "r." This sound is otherwise of rare occurrence in Southeastern languages.

The next problem relates to prehistoric voyages between the Old World and the New. Archeologically acceptable proof of such voyages will come only from artifactual material excavated and reported meticulously, in the fashion of work at Valdivia, Ecuador (Meggers et al. 1965). I do not set out here to prove, through environmental studies, that any particular voyage was made. Rather, I draw attention to an overlooked approach that might prove useful to those who debate the topic of transoceanic culture contact. If several specialists made use of this approach, it might sometimes be possible to pinpoint the terminus of a prehistoric voyage.

Anthropologists, investigating biogeographical evidence of transoceanic voyages, have mostly confined their interest to domestic plants, but the distribution of other organisms, carried unintentionally by man, may yield data of equal or even greater significance. I say greater because the taxonomy and origin of domesticated plants have, in some cases, been almost hopelessly confused by man's long-continued horticultural efforts, and any argument based on the distribution of such plants must be extremely tentative. Unintentionally transported organisms include the parasites of man, both internal and external; the parasites of domestic animals and plants; algae, molds, and fungi; insects, spiders, and other arthropods; earthworms, roundworms, and other soil-inhabiting invertebrates; weed seeds and fern spores; and marine life such as barnacles, tunicates, and shipworms. And when man travels about in the tropics, he often carries with him certain small lizards called geckos, with which the present study has primarily to deal.

No doubt some other groups of organisms would yield more anthropologically useful information than the geckos; the present discussion is mostly confined to these reptiles because I am especially familiar with them. Before describing the transoceanic spread of geckos, it is desirable to present certain rules useful in interpreting the distribution of undomesticated organisms.

The identical plant or animal species does not evolve in two different places. If a species occurs in both the Old World and the New, yet is not readily disseminated interhemispherically by natural means, it was probably spread by man; and if it cannot live in the colder regions, it was probably carried across the ocean in the warmer latitudes rather than across Bering Strait. A distribution of this kind, perhaps attributable to man, should evoke two questions from the anthropologist: In which direction was the organism carried, and could it have been carried by historic rather than prehistoric voyagers?

It is usually possible to determine the direction in which an undomesticated species crossed the ocean. In its homeland, the organism is apt to occupy a comparatively extensive range, and to occur both coastally and in the interior. It may have diverged into several genetically different subspecies or geographic races, and it may be closely related to other species in the same region (species with which it had a common ancestry in past ages). In the country of introduction, however, the organism is apt to occur only at scattered localities, or at just one locality; it may be confined to the coast. It may have diverged from its parent population, but it is not apt to have produced a complex of genetically different races; and it may stand out as an isolated biotic element, with no close relatives in the surrounding region. While in theory no one of these criteria is infallible, taken together they are quite useful. Other criteria may prove useful in special cases. Of course, a good fossil record can provide indisputable evidence as to region of origin; but small organisms, of the kind that might accompany man, in most cases are not well known paleontologically.

When two populations of a single species come to be separated by a barrier such as an ocean, each goes its own evolutionary way; through the rigors of natural selection, the two populations diverge. The rate of divergence varies according to species and to circumstance, so one can offer only a rough estimate of the length of time needed to result in a given degree of divergence. Among small reptiles, with which this study is primarily concerned, a distinct subspecies might develop in 3,000 years, perhaps even 2,000; for various taxonomically recognized subspecies are confined to islands or other sharply delimited areas that have been in existence for just a few millennia. These figures are a minimum, however, and most reptilian subspecies have probably taken more than 3,000 years to develop. In other words, a reptilian population might evolve into a distinct subspecies in a few thousand years, or it might fail to evolve significant taxonomic differences even in a considerably longer time. At any rate, a reptilian subspecies could not have developed in the relatively short time that has elapsed since historic voyages were first made between the Old World and the New. Workers in other fields might be able to give better estimates of evolutionary rates in the organisms they study.

It may be asked why geckos, of all animals, might have been carried about by early voyagers. The majority of geckos are small, nocturnal lizards of the tropics. Shy and inoffensive, they spend the day hiding in some crack or crevice, and venture forth at dusk to prey upon small insects. Most of them are protectively colored, and lightning-like of motion. In nature they may live in clusters of dead leaves, beneath the leaf-axils of palm or banana trees, beneath the loosened bark of rotting trees and logs, or under stones and ground litter. However, some of them seem virtually to have abandoned all natural habitats, and now usually dwell with man. They probably occur about every village in the tropics, especially where pole-and-thatch huts are used. In the thatching they find abundant insect food, shelter from climatic rigors, and some freedom from predation and competition. However, they can also exist in cities, around buildings, walls, and other constructions.

Geckos, and certain other small lizards called skinks, commonly venture onto beaches and take up residence in native canoes, especially but not exclusively those with thatched cabins. Several herpetologists and biogeographers have reported finding geckos and skinks in beached canoes. In the Hawaiian islands, one investigator found the lizards laying eggs in the canoes, and thought it would be impossible to provision and launch a large canoe without including both adult geckos and their eggs. Another investigator found the lizards actually being transported from island to island in native craft. I examined the thatched cabins of native vessels in parts of New

Guinea, the Moluccas, and the Philippines, always finding geckos as well as numerous small insects and spiders upon which the reptiles might prey. But stowaway lizards are not limited to the simpler kinds of water craft; some of the geckos, at least, can be transported by cargo ships of modern design.

Herpetologists have long since fallen back upon the voyages of primitive man to explain certain peculiarities of lizard distribution in Polynesia and some other areas. For example, they have agreed that various species of lizards must have been transported to the Hawaiian Islands by Polynesian man in prehistoric times, and have shown why certain geckos and skinks are not likely to have reached those islands on drifting logs or in historic ships.

One herpetologist concluded that a gecko and a skink reached Easter Island not from the nearer islands to the westward but from the Hawaiian region; that these lizards probably were carried by man from central Polynesia first to Hawaii and thence to Easter Island. Certain lizards are believed to have been carried about in Melanesia, or in Indonesia, by primitive voyagers; and some aspects of reptile distribution along the shores of the Mediterranean, North Africa, and the Middle East seem to reflect the early development of shipping lanes in these areas. American Indians have been credited with the establishment of two edible, South American reptiles (an iguana and a red-footed tortoise) on West Indian islands from which these species were originally lacking.

Students of gecko distribution have long been puzzled by the existence of certain Old World species on the coasts of the New World. Until recently, anthropologists themselves had not considered the possibility of transoceanic voyages in prehistoric times; and so herpetogeographers have had to assume that the reptiles drifted over on logs or else were introduced by shipping in historic times. Both of these hypotheses have been unsatisfactory in certain instances. Of course, gecko distribution cannot provide conclusive evidence of prehistoric seafaring. However, if prehistoric man voyaged from Indo-China to Mexico as Gordon F. Ekholm (1953) suggested, or from northwestern Africa to the New World tropics as Thor Heyerdahl and Carroll Quigley postulated, he almost surely brought geckos with him. If an Indo-Chinese gecko, of a kind associated with man, also occurs on the Mexican west coast, or if a northwest African one also inhabits some Caribbean region, then the circumstance at least merits scrutiny.

An interesting reptile is Brook's gecko, *Hemidactylus brooki,* of Old

World origin. It is found in Asia, from India and Ceylon to Assam and Burma; also in Africa, from Sudan to Tanzania, and from Senegal to Angola. Somehow, it has reached two widely separated parts of the New World: the Greater Antilles (Puerto Rico, Hispaniola, Cuba) and northwestern South America (northern Colombia southward almost into Ecuador). Herpetologists once had to suppose that the species arrived in the New World from the west coast of Africa in the days of the slave trade. However, the Greater Antillean population turned out to be one distinct subspecies, the Colombian a second. The direction of evolution seems clear: the Colombian subspecies was derived from the Antillean, the latter from a West African one. So great a degree of evolutionary divergence could not have taken place since the days of the slave trade.

Another Afro-American lizard is the house gecko, *Hemidactylus mabouia,* a native of the Old World. It ranges from South Africa northward to Liberia and Ethiopia; it is also present on Madagascar. In the New World, it ranges coastally from Georgetown, Guyana, to Montevideo, Uruguay, and follows the Amazon inland to the headwaters in Ecuador and Peru. It also inhabits most islands of the Lesser Antilles, and has two isolated colonies in the Greater Antilles (Mona Island near Puerto Rico, and Guantanamo, Cuba). In Africa this species often occurs about buildings, although living also in rock crevices and beneath loosened bark of rotting trees. In the New World it is found about buildings, stone fences, and walls, or on the trunks of trees in gardens and along city streets. For a time it was thought to have no "natural" habitat outside Africa, but then it was found to inhabit a huge South American agave, where it hides between the bases of the closely appressed central leaves. This agave is a native of South America, and is occupied by the house gecko wherever the latter exists. No doubt many New World colonies of this African lizard resulted from introduction in historic times; but it seems just a little unlikely that the house gecko would consistently occupy such a specialized ecological niche if all the New World colonies were of recent origin. On the other hand, the taxonomic identity of New World specimens with Old World ones suggests that the transoceanic migration did not take place at any remote time, geologically speaking.

The bridled gecko, *Hemidactylus frenatus,* is widespread in the Philippines, southern Asia, and the East Indies; it seems to be native to that Oriental region. It has also reached West Africa, Madagascar, the Seychelles, Mauritius, St. Helena, New Guinea, and tropical Australia; but outside the Orient, its distribution is spotty, with widely separated colonies in coastal regions. In the New World, it is well established at Acapulco, on the Pacific coast of Mexico. Herpetologists have suggested that the lizard was brought to Mexico on the Manila Galleons, which annually from 1565 to 1815 made the long voyage between Manila and Acapulco. The species also occurs at Champerico, on the Pacific coast of Guatemala. No explanation of its presence here has been offered. New World specimens have not been studied for evidence of evolutionary divergence from Old World ones.

Garnot's gecko, *Hemidactylus garnoti*, ranges from India to China, thence south and east to various islands of the East Indies and Oceania; it has reached New Caledonia and Hawaii. Its recent appearance in Miami is of no significance; that city is a center of the pet trade, and a good many foreign frogs, lizards, and birds have escaped or been liberated there. However, Garnot's gecko was first made known to science in 1835 on the basis of a specimen from Tacna, a short distance inland from the Pacific coast of Peru. The supposed Peruvian occurrence has not subsequently been confirmed.

The Mediterranean gecko, *Hemidactylus turcicus*, is of Old World origin. It is found from the Pakistani province of Sind and Iran west to the borders of the Red Sea, thence into Egypt and westward around the Mediterranean basin to Morocco and the Canary Islands, and southward through Ethiopia into northern Kenya. Throughout this region the lizard has evolved into several geographic races. One of them ranges from Sind to the Red Sea, thence across North Africa to Morocco, and south into Ethiopia. This one has been transported to the New World, occurring at scattered localities along the east coast of Mexico (records from the states of Tamaulipas, Veracruz, Tabasco, Campeche, and Yucatán). It had already reached Louisiana by the early nineteenth century, for John James Audubon found a specimen in New Orleans and painted an identifiable picture of it. Records for Chile, Cuba, Texas, and Florida (Key West and Miami) probably reflect introduction by modern shipping. The Gainesville, Florida, population was introduced deliberately by amateur herpetologists about a decade ago. An assumption has been made that the New World colonies are all taxonomically identical with an Old World one, but geographic variation in this species has not been intensively studied. Specimens from Progreso, on the Yucatán coast, were once thought to represent a distinct species from *turcicus*. Their coloration was described as greenish, whereas that of *turcicus* is whitish, pinkish, or grayish; so perhaps the species has been in Yucatán long enough to have evolved a slight difference from the Old World parent population.

The African and Madagascan gecko genus *Lygodactylus* is said to have a representative in the Brazilian states of Bahia and Mato Grosso, but the occurrence has not been described in detail. The stump-toed gecko, *Peropus mutilatus,* is native to an area from Southeast Asia to New Guinea and some islands of Oceania. It has been found at localities on the Pacific coast of Mexico: San Blas and Tepic in Nayarit, Presidio and Mazatlan in Sinaloa. The gecko genus *Tarentola* includes five Old World species, collectively ranging from southern Europe southward to Saudi Arabia, the Canary and Cape Verde islands, Cameroon, and Sudan. It has a lone New World species, *Tarentola americana,* with one subspecies in Cuba and another in the Bahamas. Remains of this species have been found in a Cuban cave deposit possibly of pre-Columbian age, and in a Bahaman fossil bed assigned to the late Pleistocene.

Turning now to skinks, the snake-eyed skink, *Ablepharus boutoni,* is widely distributed from southern Asia to Africa, Australia, and Polynesia. Within this vast area, it has diverged into about 30 subspecies, only one of which concerns us here. This one, *Ablepharus boutoni poecilopleurus,* carries the distribution of the species eastward from Melanesia far into Polynesia (including Hawaii). It is a very small skink, a predator on mosquitos, beach fleas, and other small organisms, which it catches with remarkable agility. Although not confined to coasts, it is common on beaches and is known to enter native vessels. Somehow, it has crossed the tropical Pacific. It was first made known to science from a specimen collected on Pisacona Island, Peru. There have been subsequent reports of it on islands off the Peruvian and Ecuadorian coast, and on the adjoining mainland. The azure-tailed emo, *Emoia cyanura,* is a skink distributed from the East Indies eastward far into Polynesia. Like *Ablepharus,* it can live both coastally and interiorly, and has reached Hawaii. It has nearly crossed the Pacific, having been found on Clipperton Island, about 700 miles southwest of the Mexican coast. Clipperton is a rock three miles in diameter.

A few comments on sea-snakes, family Hydrophidae, may be given. The family includes about 50 species, concentrated in the tropical western Pacific. The yellow-bellied sea-snake, *Pelamis platurus,* ranges from Indonesian waters westward to Madagascan, southward to Tasmanian, northward to Siberian, and eastward to Hawaiian. It also inhabits tropical waters along the Pacific coast of the New World, from Sonora and Baja California, Mexico, to Ecuador or beyond. At one time, herpetologists thought it might have arrived in the New World as a stowaway in the hold of a Spanish ship, but a search of history revealed otherwise: the species was noted as abundant in Coasta Rican waters just six years after Balboa's discovery of the Pacific, and before trans-Pacific voyages were made by Europeans. Some kind of hydrophid, not *Pelamis platurus*, occurs along the Pacific coast of Colombia; it might be the Indonesian sea snake, *Laticauda colubrina*, which was recently reported off the Pacific coast of Nicaragua and Chiapas.

From what has been said, it is evident that some locality records of transoceanic reptiles will not throw much light on the possibility of voyages by prehistoric man. However, it seemed well to mention all records, for they give an idea of the considerations that are involved in the interpretation of the distribution patterns.

Tarentola probably crossed the Atlantic before man ever did. *Hemidactylus brooki* could have arrived with prehistoric voyagers, or at an earlier date without the aid of man. *Hemidactylus mabouia* and *Hemidactylus turcicus* may well have been transported by both prehistoric and historic man. The three trans-Atlantic hemidactyls are all lacking from Jamaica, which was a principal port of entry for slave ships; hence, the presence of these three in the New World is not attributable to the slave trade. *Ablepharus boutoni* and *Emoia cyanura*, if not *Peropus mutilatus* and *Hemidactylus garnoti* as well, may have accompanied prehistoric voyagers across the Pacific. *Hemidactylus frenatus* is perhaps an introduction of fairly early historic times. *Pelamydrus* probably arrived under its own power, following the Black Current, the West Wind Current, and the California Current. If the *Lygodactylus* is a distinct species, it probably arrived before man. The *Laticauda* presumably is a recent arrival, since it was not noticed until lately.

The foregoing explanations of distribution patterns are tentative. But as I remarked at the outset, studies on the lizards should be supplemented by those on other transoceanic organisms. If, say, Polynesian or Melanesian seafarers brought *Ablepharus* to islands in the Golfo de Quayaquil, then those islands should have at least a few other organisms transplanted from the opposite side of the Pacific, and one or two of these organisms might provide better evidence of transoceanic voyages than does *Ablepharus*. With attention focused on these islands, a search would then be made for their archeological sites.

The transoceanic reptiles provide a few other useful ideas. The direction of disperal has been from the Old World to the New, not the reverse. South America and the Caribbean islands have many native species of geckos, skinks, and other lizards, but there is no evidence that any of them made a transoceanic crossing in the days before modern shipping. Among geckos, a principal direction of transoceanic dispersal has been from northwestern Africa to the Caribbean and South America. The Canary and Cape Verde islands lie along the dispersal route. Even if it be argued that the various African geckos drifted across the ocean on logs, still their distribution reveals the approximate position of a trans-Atlantic route. The distribution shows, too, that this route can be followed across the ocean with remarkable rapidity. Trans-Pacific dispersal of lizard species apparently has been accomplished along a Counter Current route. Another trans-Pacific route, Black Current to West Wind Current to California Current, is no longer than the Counter Current one, but passes too far north to have carried many tropical organisms from one hemisphere to the other.

As a final benefit from an excursion into herpetogeography, attention is called to a body of literature which, being classified as biological, may have escaped archeological notice. This literature includes studies on winds, currents, natural rafts, rates and directions of drift as shown by actual experimentation—material that should be of considerable interest to those archeologists who admit the possibility of transoceanic voyages in prehistoric times. I have no doubt that certain biologists, specializing in something other than herpetology, could supplement my remarks on the transoceanic dispersal of organisms. Perhaps they will be stimulated to do so, once they are aware of the interesting archeological questions involved.

The fourth problem has a dual nature, being both archeological and ecological. On the one hand it relates to the collapse of the Maya civilization, on the other hand to the effect of Maya agriculture on tropical forest soils.

Large and small expanses of savanna are scattered over the New World tropics, from Veracruz in Mexico to the Amazon in South America. Usually, they exist as sharply defined areas set in a matrix of tropical rainforest or some other kind of forest. Conflicting theories have been offered to account for the existence of these savannas. Their origin has variously been ascribed to insufficient rainfall, alternating wet and dry periods, leaching, chemical deficiency of the soil, porosity of the soil, poor subsoil drainage, fires, the activities of man, or combinations of these factors. Of human activities, *milpa* agriculture has most often been singled out as having converted forest to grassland.

Expanses of savana exist in Belize (British Honduras) and the Guatemalan department of El Petén. Archeologists have been interested in these expanses, for they occupy sizeable parts of the region in which the Maya civilization developed. In certain aboriginal times, this region was much more heavily populated than it is today. British Honduras, which measures only 174 by 168 miles, supported a population of at least a million people when the Maya civilization was at its peak. However, the Maya abandoned El Petén and Belize, and they moved northward to begin anew in southern Mexico. The evidence indicates that the depopulation was comparatively rapid and virtually complete. Conflicting theories have been advanced in an effort to explain why the Maya, having been so successful in their homeland, then abandoned it. One theory has held that *milpa* agriculture converted forest to savanna, a type of vegetation that could not be farmed by Mayan methods. With their agricultural foundation intolerably eroded by this conversion, the Maya left for southern Mexico where the forest was still untouched.

The Mayan technological and intellectual accomplishments were possible partly because a thriving agricultural economy freed some of the population for non-subsistence activities. The Maya centers of El Petén and British Honduras were supported basically by *milpa* agriculture in the surrounding areas. Large patches of forest were cut down, and near the end of the dry season they were burned. Trees, brush, and leafy debris were burned to ashes, and the soil, thus enriched, was planted with a digging stick. The first year, the harvest was rich, but it fell off rapidly thereafter. Accordingly, the *milpero* would let the exhausted patch lie fallow, and clear a new patch elsewhere. In Yacatán, the present-day Maya farm a field for only two consecutive years, and then allow it to lie fallow for about ten, at the end of which time it is burned and planted again. Therefore the average farmer keeps six *milpas:* one in corn, and five others in various stages of regrowth. In rich country, six 10-acre plots may suffice to support a Maya family of average size; but in poor country a total of 1,000 acres may be needed, and the *milpero* may farm land miles away from his home. Comparable practices among the ancient Maya, carried on for centuries, may have depleted the soil to a point where it would no longer support forest but only grassland. So goes the aforesaid theory, which invokes human agency to explain the existence of certain savannas.

S. G. Morley, a leading student of the Maya, once wrote, ". . . by the Eighth Century A.D., after a thousand years of heavy occupation, the Petén–British Honduras area had been converted from a heavily forested area to vast man-made savannas. The forests were replaced by grasslands. . . ." C. Wythe Cooke, (1931) so well known for his studies on the geology of Florida, held that numerous lakes, around which the Maya built their settlements, gradually filled with silt in consequence of erosion from nearby deforested uplands; later studies by W. R. Bullard have tended to bear out those of Cook. Of course, the silting up of lakes with soil from nearby deforested areas does not necessarily mean that these areas were destined to be taken over by savanna; but the situation at least reveals that the Maya were playing havoc with the local ecology. Sherburne F. Cook (1949), working in the area of Indian civilizations in central Mexico, found that "the land is poorest in condition in those areas which formerly supported large populations. . . . Conversely, . . . where destruction is worst, a dense population once existed." Soil deterioration in central Mexico is not savannization in Belize and El Petén; nevertheless, the situation reveals that prehistoric Indians, carrying on *milpa* agriculture, altered the local soils in at least some parts of Mesoamerica.

It is sometimes held that Maya agricultural practices could not have been responsible for the creation of savannas, because the sites are in forest. It is true that archeological attention has been directed chiefly toward the more spectacular Maya ruins, which are concentrated in what are now the most heavily forested parts of Belize and El Petén. However, a majority of the sites were not cities but rather ceremonial centers whose builders lived elsewhere. And the real point is not where they lived but where they farmed. One might contend that *milpa* agriculture produced no savanna in those parts of the region that now lack grasslands and that are heavily forested; but if Maya farming converted forest to savanna, then the course of ecological succession might have restored the forest at many localities in the thousand years that have elapsed since the Maya left.

Much of eastern Belize is covered with an intricate mosaic of savanna and low, scrubby vegetation. It is this area from which Maya sites are supposed to be lacking. However, road-building and other activities of modern man are disclosing more and more sites there. Only one of them, Altun Ha, has been described in the literature, but there are many small habitation sites with utilitarian pottery and flint work. And there are quite a few unreported coastal sites on the eastern edge of the country's most thinly forested section.

J. S. Beard (1953) made a comprehensive study of New World savanna, and concluded that it was natural vegetation developing on highly mature or very young soils with unfavorable drainage and intermittent perched water tables. In these soils, an alternation of waterlogging with desiccation was the most important factor determining the nature of the plant association. Fires were frequent in savanna, but were not necessary for its maintenance. Beard held that his conclusions were applicable to all New World savanna, but his field work was concentrated in Guyana. Perhaps, then, Alexander G. Ruthven (1916) was right when he suggested that different savannas might have different origins; for some ecologists have reached conclusions at variance with those of Beard.

Thus, Gerardo Budowski (1960) found that savanna vegetation resulted from a sequence of human activities: a forest patch would be cleared, burned, farmed for about two years, and then abandoned. Fires, mostly started by man, would then sweep across the overgrown field almost annually, militating against the return of forest but favoring the establishment of grasses; for the seedlings of forest trees are killed by fire, whereas grasses will quickly sprout again after the blaze has passed. The sequence will alter the soil and its drainage, but all its effects are reversible; if the patch is shielded from human activities long enough, forest will eventually return to it. Budowski held that his conclusions were applicable to all New World savanna, but his field work was concentrated in Venezuela.

Savanna vegetation is widespread in the Old World tropics, and so is *milpa* agriculture (under some other name such as *ladang, kaingin,* slash-and-burn, shifting, or swidden agriculture). Workers in Asia and Africa have rather generally regarded savanna as the result of swidden agriculture followed by repeated burning and sometimes grazing.

It seems fair to say that the origin of the Petén–Belize savanna is still problematical. The specific question that I hope to answer may be phrased as follows: Are these particular savannas, in the old Maya country, to be regarded as natural, ancient, far older than the Maya civilization; or were they produced in aboriginal times? An answer to this question should be of interest not just in archeology and ecology, but also in the economic sphere. The principal industry of Belize is logging from the hardwood forest, and the supply of trees has already grown scarce. If *milpa* agriculture (which continues today) converts forests to savanna, then some sort of economic planning for the future is in order. Indeed, all tropical countries would do well to determine the extent to which the forest expanses are dwindling in consequence of swidden agriculture.

It seemed to me that the ecology of reptiles and amphibians could possibly throw light on savanna origins in El Petén and Belize. Many of these organisms are confined to one or a few plant associations, and within the association may be further confined to some microhabitat. Tropical herpetozoa, especially, tend to be very restricted ecologically. If the Petén–Belize savannas are natural and ancient, they should have a characteristic savanna herpetofauna, with some species that rarely or never invade the forest. But if the savannas were produced by the Maya a thousand or so years ago—a very short while ago in evolutionary terms—their herpetofauna should be much reduced, consisting only of those forest species that are also able to tolerate savanna conditions.

At the outset of the project, I published a statement of the problem and of the approach I hoped would solve it (Neill and Allen 1959). Eventually, there became available to me the herpetological material and relevant ecological data amassed by ten expeditions to Belize and nearby regions. I accompanied six of these expeditions; I visited most parts of that country, and also entered adjoining parts of Guatemala and Mexico. These trips were planned to carry us into all the principal animal habitats of the region, and to permit a look at the environs of Maya sites. In addition, I examined herpetological specimens in various museum collections, obtained useful information from inhabitants of Belize who were familiar with the local ecology and herpetozoa, and of course studied the pertinent literature. It became evident that, contrary to published statements, the herpetofauna of Belize was not merely a spillover from nearby parts of Guatemala; we encountered species, taxonomic relationships, and herpetozoan habits, the existence of which would not have been anticipated from the Guatemalan literature.

Over a period of six years, we published thirteen papers stemming from our trips. These collectively included some itineraries, a map and gazetteer of Belize, classification and photographs of animal habitats, description of new species and subspecies, taxonomic revisions, notes on herpetozoan habits, range extensions, a revised herpetological checklist for the country, and bibliographies. I describe this work in some detail because it brings out an important point: a project in the field of environmental archeology can dovetail neatly into biological projects. Our investigations had several stated objectives, most of them herpetological; but it was evident from the start that our herpetological data might throw light on savanna origins, hence on the possibility that the Maya had converted much of their old country from forest to grassland.

My conclusions about savanna origins have not previously been published. We found 2 species of salamanders, 13 of frogs, 21 of lizards, 25 of snakes, and 2 of turtles, all characteristic of the rainforest or the quasi-rainforest. Two species of frogs, 10 of lizards, and 5 of snakes were able to exist in both forest and savanna. Most of these, however, appeared to be essentially of the savanna or of open situations generally. That is to say, within the forest they were actually characteristic of man-made clearings, road shoulders, and deforested river or lake banks; they could not be regarded as forest-adapted species. Seven species of frogs, 6 of lizards, 14 of snakes, and 2 of turtles were savanna-adapted, and did not invade the forest. Various coastal situations may seem physically wet, but they are physiologically dry from the standpoint of invasion by terrestrial and arboreal organisms; for salt water has a drying effect on the tissues of these organisms. It was not surprising, therefore, to find that the littoral and supratidal herpetofauna included none of the forest-adapted species. It included a few of the savanna-adapted ones, plus 5 lizard species largely confined to mangrove swamp, strand, or some other haline situation.

I omit from this list a few species of amphibians and reptiles for which our data were insufficient to warrant a statement about habitat. I omit, also, some freshwater turtles, sea-turtles, and crocodilians, the occurrence of which is more or less independent of terrestrial vegetation. It is worth noting, however, that one of the crocodilians is (or was, before hide-hunting) typical of the *aguadas*, small lakes and ponds in the savanna.

In some parts of the New World tropics, there are savannas that probably were man-made, for they harbor only some ecologically tolerant herpetozoan invaders from the forest assemblage. However, this is not the case in Belize. Of the amphibian and reptile species inhabiting that country, a little less than half are forest-limited. There is a long list of species that are adapted for life outside the forest, usually in savanna. I would regard the savannas of El Petén and Belize as natural, ancient, far older than the Maya civilization. It might be argued that the savanna component of the local herpetofauna evolved in natural savannas elsewhere, then moved into Maya country after the Indians had converted much of its forest to grassland. However, the argument is unappealing, for several reasons. To begin with, it is hard to say where those natural savannas might have been. Second, if savannas can form naturally not far outside the Maya country, why not inside? Third, quite a few species of organisms (not just herpetozoa) are represented by one subspecies at the base of the

Yucatán Peninsula—that is, in El Petén and Belize—but by a different subspecies farther toward the tip of the peninsula. In other words, these species have been in place a long enough time to have developed subspecific differences, evolutionary adaptations to the local environment; and they probably could not have done this in the comparatively short while that has elapsed since the Maya departed. Fourth, some species or subspecies do not range any great distance out of the savanna region that is under discussion. Presumably, they have had a long evolutionary history in the region where we now find them.

Archeologists might abandon the idea that the Maya entered a continuously forested region, gradually converted much of its forest to savanna, and departed because the growth of savanna intolerably reduced the forest expanse that was available for *milpa* agriculture. This opinion, derived from herpetological studies, should of course be checked from other directions. One obvious direction would involve the identification and interpretation of faunal remains from Maya sites. On the average, amphibians and reptiles are exceptionally good indicators of ecological conditions, but some mammals, birds, freshwater fishes, and mollusks are good, too. A sizeable collection of faunal remains should reveal much about the habitats from which the animals were originally garnered by the Indians. For example, the remains from Uaxactun, in El Petén, suggest to me that the Indians were hunting mostly in forest, but also in savanna—this in spite of the fact that the immediate vicinity of Uaxactun is now forested.

Another approach would be through palynology. Some work has in fact been done along this line. Analysis of pollen from borings revealed that El Petén had more grassland in pre-Maya times than it did later. At one Petén locality, the earliest inhabitants, who were few in number, raised corn in savanna, not forest. This was some time prior to 840 B.C. Fires were frequent during this period. Between 840 B.C. and 660 A.D., the locality remained in savanna, but the pollen count included more and more of a cornfield weed, its presence reflecting intensive agriculture. Fires were frequent only in the early part of this period. After 660 A.D., agriculture declined and the locality was taken over by forest, of a kind present there today. These studies, and some others, support my contention that the savannas of the old Maya country are natural, their origin far antedating the arrival of man.

Epilogue

A science of man is badly needed, and seems to be in the making. By the definition of a science, it will progress through use of the scientific method. Sociology, beginning to proceed scientifically, and to hybridize freely with other fields, may play a central role in a science of man; but anthropology is forging ahead, also. True, the prospects are dim for one branch of anthropology, namely ethnology, for the rapid spread of modern civilization presages the speedy disappearance of those cultures that have traditionally been studied from the ethnological standpoint. But other branches of anthropology hold much promise.

Archeology is beginning to use the scientific method, admittedly over the opposition of the Old Guard. It is beginning to interact with certain other disciplines, producing paleoanthropology in one temporal direction, historic site and industrial archeology in another. Its possibilities for further hybridization are numerous. As I have tried to show, there are conceivable interactions between archeology and ethnology, linguistics, toponymy, physical anthropology, economic geography, history, sociology, psychology, and others. And of course there are numerous interdisciplinary bridges that might link archeology with the natural sciences, from zoology and botany through chemistry and physics to astronomy and geology. Some of these bridges already exist; witness environmental archeology, dating techniques, chemical archeology, and some aspects of paleoanthropology.

The Florida archeologist Ripley P. Bullen once said to me, "There is one way in which any archeological problem can be solved: keep digging." I have not forgotten this dictum, but I have wanted to provide an insight into other ways whereby some archeological problems might be attacked. I have taken a stand on regional or broader problems, not to solve them beyond peradventure but to show new directions from which they might be approached.

Some studies, involving archeology and other disciplines, are important if only because they guide our thinking about man, his relationship to the environment, perhaps even his destiny. Thus, paleoanthropology should be promulgated widely. It is vital to realize that man's characteristics are in some part the evolutionary response to factors of the natural environment; to continental drift, which affected the early history of the primates; to the spread or decline of forest and grassland; to climatic shifts; to episodes of glaciation and deglaciation. The human eye, adapted for keen vision by day but not by night; the human's weak sense of smell; certain dietary predilections; the upright posture and bipedal gait; the opposable thumb; some basic urges, for food, shelter, sexual experience, companionship, recognition, dominance—these evolved in response to environmental factors, long before the hominid line had produced anything that might be called human.

Today we are told, correctly, that modern man is on the verge of wiping out a great variety of wildlife. In this connection, it is important to understand what archeologists, paleontologists, and paleoecologists have jointly revealed regarding the disappearance of so many giant beasts at the end of the Pleistocene. It is now clear that this wholesale extinction resulted from the spread of Paleolithic man, with his specialized techniques for the hunting of big game. True, the disappearance of the Pleistocene giants coincided with the retreat of the last glaciation, and with a shift toward a warmer climate; but all these beasts had withstood previous episodes of deglaciation and glaciation, previous shifts toward warmer or colder climate. And of course the smaller beasts, which did not often command the attention of the Paleolithic hunters, were unaffected by the course of geologic and climatic events.

Drastic alteration of the world's ecology began not in the Space Age, not with the Industrial Revolution or with the spread of Neolithic agriculture. It began when bands of Paleolithic hunters, armed with flint-tipped spears, wandered to most parts of the world, spelling doom for mammoth elephant, mastodon, giant ground sloth, giant bison, and many another nightmare beast.

It is important, too, to note the great variety of religions that have existed down through archeological time, each no doubt regarded by its bearers as the only true one, none especially congruent with factuality, some used more than others as a tool of state.

And it may be well, especially in these days of a so-called "cultural revolution," to consider the suggestions that a culture declines primarily because a majority of its bearers find it unsatisfactory; because its rewards are not commensurate with its demands.

Bibliography

The bibliography is made up of articles mentioned in the text, plus other papers that were useful to me although I did not have occasion to cite them directly. Even as augmented, the bibliography is quite selective; the literature of environmental archeology alone is extensive enough to warrant a separate volume.

Needless to say, most readers of this book will have at least an interest in, if not a professional involvement with, the field of archeology. For such readers, strictly archeological bibliographies are numerous, and are readily available. But it may not be so easy to unearth the literature of the various para-archeological disciplines that especially concern me here. And so I have weighted the present bibliography in favor of those ethnological, linguistic, toponymic, economic, ecological, geographic, sociological, psychological, philosophical, and biological studies that conceivably could interact with archeology (*sensu stricto*) in the currently emerging—and desperately needed—science of man.

Abbott, R. Tucker. 1954. *American Seashells*. Princeton, N.J.: D. Van Nostrand.

Ackernecht, E. H. 1953. "Paleopathology." In A. L. Kroeber, ed. *Anthropology Today, an Encyclopedic Inventory*, pp. 120–26. Chicago: Univ. Chicago Press.

Adams, R. McC. 1968. "Archeological Research Strategies: Past and Present." *Science* 160:1187–92.

Ager, D. V. 1963. *Paleoecology*. New York: McGraw-Hill.

Allibone, T. E. et al., organizers. 1970. *The Impact of the Natural Sciences on Archaeology: a Symposium.* London: Oxford University Press.

Anderson, J. E. 1963. *The Human Skeleton, a Manual for Archaeologists.* Ottawa: National Museum of Canada, Dept. of Northern Affairs and Natural Resources.

Anderson, K. M. 1969. "Ethnographic Analogy and Archeological Interpretation." *Science* 163:133–38.

Anonymous. 1930. A Connexão Linguistica Basco-Americana. São Paulo.

Antevs, Ernst. 1945. "Correlation of Wisconsin Glacial Maxima." *American Journal of Science* 243-A:1–39.

―― 1948. "The Great Basin, with Emphasis on Glacial and Postglacial Times, III. Climatic Changes and Pre-White Man." *University of Utah Bull.* 38 (20):168–91.

―― 1953a. "Geochronology of the Deglacial and Neothermal Ages." *Journal of Geology* 61 (3):195–230.

―― 1953b. "Artifacts with Mammoth Remains, Naco, Arizona. II. Age of the Clovis Fluted Points with the Naco Mammoth." *American Antiquity* 19 (3):15–17.

Arieti, Silvano. 1956. "Some Basic Problems Common to Anthropology and Modern Psychiatry." *American Anthropologist* 58 (1):26–39.

Arnold, J. R., and W. F. Libby. 1951. "Radiocarbon Dates." *Science* 113:111–20.

Ascher, Robert. 1961. "Analogy in Archaeological Interpretation." *Southwestern Journal of Anthropology* 17:317–25.

―― 1962. "Ethnography for Archaeology: a Case from the Serai Indians." *Ethnology* 1:360–69.

Aveleyra Arroyo de Anda, Luis. 1964. "El Sacro de Tequixquiac." *Quadernos del Museo Nacional de Antropologia,* No. 2.

Baker, F. C. 1923. "The Use of Molluscan Shells by the Cahokia Mound-Builders." *Transactions Illinois Academy of Sciences* 16.

―― 1930. "The Use of Animal Life by the Mound-Building Indians of Illinois." *Ibid.* 22:41–64.

―― 1931. "Additional Notes on Animal Life Associated with the Mound Builders of Illinois." *Ibid.* 23:231–35.

―― 1937. "Pleistocene Land and Fresh-Water Mollusca as Indicators of Time and Ecological Conditions." In G. G. McCurdy, ed. *Early Man,* pp. 67–74. Philadelphia: Lippincott.

Banton, Michael. 1966. *Anthropological Approaches to the Study of Religion.* London: Travistock Monograph No. 3.

Bartram, William. 1791. *Travels through North and South Carolina, Georgia, East and West Florida, the Cherokee Country* [etc.]. Philadelphia.

―― 1909. "Observations on the Creek and Cherokee Indians." *Transactions of the American Ethnological Society* 3, pt. 1:1–81. (Facsimile reprint of 1853 edition.)

Bates, Marston. 1953. "Human Ecology." In A. L. Kroeber, ed., *Anthropology Today*, pp. 700–13. Chicago: University of Chicago Press.

Beadle, George, and Muriel Beadle. 1966. *The Language of Life*. Garden City, N.Y.: Doubleday and Co.

Beard. J. S. 1953. The Savanna Vegetation of Northern Tropical America. *Ecological Monographs*, 23 (2):149–215.

Bennett, W. C. 1946. "The Archaeology of the Central Andes." In J. H. Steward, ed., "Handbook of South American Indians. vol. 2. The Andean Civilizations," pp. 61–176. *Bureau American Ethnology Bull.* 143.

Berry, E. W. 1917. "The Fossil Plants from Vero, Florida." *Florida State Geological Survey, 9th Annual Report*, pp. 19–33.

Beverley, Robert. 1705. *The History and Present State of Viriginia* [etc.]. London.

Binford, L. R. 1967. Comment on "Major Aspects of the Interrelationship of Archaeology and Ethnology" by K. C. Chang. *Current Anthropology* 8:234–5.

—— 1968. "Archeological Perspectives." In S. R. Binford and L. R. Binford, eds., *New Perspectives in Archeology*, pp. 5–32. Chicago: Aldine.

Binford, S. R., and L. R. Binford. 1968. *New Perspectives in Archeology*. Chicago: Aldine.

Birket-Smith, Kaj. 1936. *The Eskimo*. New York: E. P. Dutton.

Blair, W. F. et al. 1957. *Vertebrates of the United States*. New York: McGraw-Hill Book Co., Inc.

Blanc, Alberto C. 1957. "A New Paleolithic Cultural Element, Probably of Ideological Significance: the Clay Pellets of the Cave of Basua (Savona)." *Quaternaria* 4:111–19.

Blatchley, W. S. 1902. *A Nature Wooing at Ormond by the Sea*. Indianapolis.

Bordes, François. 1968. *The Old Stone Age*. New York: McGraw-Hill.

Boyd, Mark F. 1949. Diego Peña's Expedition to Apalachee and Apalachicola in 1716. *Florida Historical Quarterly* 28 (1):1–27.

Boyd, Mark F., H. G. Smith, and J. W. Griffin. 1951. *Here They Once Stood: the Tragic End of the Apalachee Missions*. Gainesville: University of Florida Press.

Boyd, W. C. 1950. *Genetics and the Races of Man*. Boston: Little Brown.

—— 1953. "The Contributions of Genetics to Anthropology." In A. L. Kroeber, ed., *Anthropology Today*, pp. 488–506. Chicago: University of Chicago Press.

—— 1958. "Genetics and the Races of Man," In T. W. McKern, ed., *Readings in Physical Anthropology*, pp. 168–73. Englewood Cliffs, N. J.: Prentice-Hall.

Braidwood, R. J. 1960. "The Agricultural Revolution." *Scientific American* 203 (3):130–34, 136–38, 143–44, 146, 148.

Brodkorb, Pierce. 1957. "New Passerine Birds from the Pleistocene of Reddick, Florida." *Journal of Paleontology* 31 (1):129–38.

—— 1959. "The Pleistocene Avifauna of Arredondo, Florida." *Bull. Florida State Museum, Biological Sciences* 4 (9).

—— 1960. "Great Auk and Common Murre from a Florida Midden." *Auk* 77:342–43.

Broecker, W. S., M. Ewing and B. E. Heezen. 1960. "Evidence for an Abrupt Change in Climate Close to 11,000 Years Ago." *American Jour. Sci.* 258:429–48.

Brooks, C. E. P. 1951. Geological and Historical Aspects of Climate Change. In T. F. Malone, ed., *Compendium of Meteorology*, pp. 1004–8. Boston: American Meteorological Society.

Brues, A. M. 1958. "Skeletal Material from the Horton Site." *Bulletin Oklahoma Anthropological Society* 6:27–32.

—— 1959. "Skeletal Material from the Morris Site." *Ibid.* 7:63–70.

Budowski, Gerardo. 1960. "Tropical Savannas, a Sequence of Forest Felling and Repeated Burnings." *Boletin del Museo Ciencies Naturales*, tomos 6–7, no. 5.

Buettner-Janusch, John. 1967. *Origins of Man: Physical Anthropology.* New York: John Wiley and Sons, Inc.

Bullen, Adelaide D. 1964. "Skeletal Remains and Dental Pathology of the Savanne Suazey Site, Grenada, West Indies." In R. P. Bullen, The Archaeology of Grenada, West Indies. *Contributions Florida State Museum, Social Sciences,* no. 11:13–17.

Bullen, R. P. 1950a. "An Archaeological Survey of the Chattahoochee River Valley, in Florida." *Journal Washington Academy of Sciences* 40 (4):23–45.

—— 1950b. The Woodward Site. *Florida Anthropologist* 2 (3–4):49–64.

—— 1951. The Enigmatic Crystal Site. *American Antiquity* 17 (2):142–43.

—— 1955. "Stratigraphic Tests at Bluffton, Volusia County, Florida." *Florida Anthropologist* 8 (1):1–16.

—— 1958. "The Bolen Bluff Site on Payne's Prairie, Florida." *Contributions Florida State Museum, Social Sciences,* No. 4.

—— 1959. "The Transitional Period of Florida." *Southeastern Archaeological Conference Newsletter* 6:43–62.

—— 1966. "Stelae at the Crystal River Site, Florida." *American Antiquity* 31 (6):861–65.

—— 1968. *"A Guide to the Identification of Florida Projectile Point Types."* Florida State Museum, Gainesville.

Bullen, R. P. and H. K. Brooks. 1968. "Two Ancient Florida Dugout Canoes." *Quarterly Journal Florida Academy of Sciences* 30 (2):97–107.

Bullen, R. P. and F. W. Sleight. 1959. "Archaeological Investigations of the Castle Windy Midden, Florida." *William L. Bryant Foundation Amer. Studies, Report no. 1.*

Burrows, R. B. 1965. *Microscopic Diagnosis of the Parasites of Man.* New Haven: Yale University Press.

Byers, D. S. 1951. On the Interpretation of Faunal Remains. *American Antiquity* 16 (3):262–63.

Caley, E. R. 1971. "Archaeological Chemistry." In *Encyclopedia of Science and Technology* 1:560–62. McGraw-Hill, New York.

Callam, Hilary. 1970. *Ethology and Society: Toward an Anthropological View.* New York: Oxford University Press.

Candela, P. B. 1940a. "New Data on the Serology of the Anthropoid Apes." *American Journal Physical Anthropology* 27 (2).

—— 1940b. Serology of the Anthropoid Apes. *Ibid.,* no. 3.

Carnap, Rudolph. 1938. *Logical Foundation of the Unity of Science.* In O. Neurath, R. Carnap, and C. Morris, eds., *International Encyclopedia of Unified Science,* 1, pt. 1:42–66. University of Chicago Press, Chicago.

Carrel, Alexis. 1935. *Man, the Unknown.* Philadelphia: Harper and Brothers.

Carter, G. F. 1953. "Plants across the Pacific." In M. W. Smith, ed., "Asia and North America: Transpacific Contacts." *American Antiquity* 18 (2, pt. 2):62–71.

Casella, D. 1950. "La Frutta nella Pitture Pompeiana." *Raccolta di Studi per il Secondo Centenario degli Scavi di Pompeii,* pp. 355–86. Gaetano Maccharioli, Naples.

Casteel, R. W. 1972. "Some Archeological Uses of Fish Remains." *American Antiquity* 37 (3):404–19.

Ceram, C. W. 1967. *Gods, Graves, and Scholars: The Story of Archaeology.* New York: Knopf.

Chang. K. C. 1967. "Major Aspects of the Interrelationship of Archaeology and Ethnology." *Current Anthropology* 8:227–34.

Childe, V. G. 1951. *Man Makes Himself.* New York: New American Library.

—— 1954. *What Happened in History.* Baltimore: Penguin Books.

—— 1956. *Piecing Together the Past.* New York: Praeger.

—— 1958. *The Prehistory of European Society.* London: Penguin Books.

Christian, F. W. 1932. "Polynesian and Oceanic Elements in the Chimu and Inca Languages." *Journal of Polynesian Society* 41:144–56.

Clark, Eugenie. 1969. *The Lady and the Sharks.* New York: Harper and Row.

Clark, Grahame. 1946. "Seal-hunting in the Stone Age of North-western Europe. A Study in Economic Prehistory." *Proceedings Prehistory Society London,* n.s. vol. 12:12–48.

—— 1948. Fowling in Prehistoric Europe. *Antiquity* 2:116–30.

—— 1952. *Prehistoric Europe: the Economic Basis.* London: Methuen.

—— 1953. *An Economic Approach to Prehistory.* London: Oxford University Press.

—— 1957. *Archaeology and Society: Reconstructing the Prehistoric Past,* 2nd ed. Cambridge, Mass: Harvard University Press.

Clark, J. D. and F. C. Howell, eds. 1966. "Recent Studies in Paleoanthropology." *American Anthropologist* 66 (2, pts. 1–2).

Clarke, D. L. 1968. *Analytical Archaeology.* London: Methuen.

Clausen, C. J., H. K. Brooks and A. B. Wesolowsky. 1975. "Florida Spring Confirmed as 10,000 Year Old Early Man Site." *Florida Anthropological Soc. Pubs.,* no. 7.

Clements, F. E. 1945. "Historical Sketch of the Spiro Mound." *Contributions Museum American Indian, Heye Foundation,* 14.

Clifton, J. A., ed. 1968. *Introduction to Cultural Anthropology.* Boston: Houghton Mifflin.

Coe, M. D. and K. V. Flannery. 1967. "Early Cultures and Human Ecology in South Coastal Guatemala." *Smithsonian Contributions to Anthropology,* 3.

Colinvaux, P. A. 1964. The Environment of the Bering Land Bridge. *Ecological Monographs* 34 (3):297–329.

Comas, Juan. 1960. *Manual of Physical Anthropology.* Springfield, Ill.: Charles C. Thomas.

Conklin, H. C. 1959. "Ecological Interpretations and Plant Domestication." *American Antiquity* 25 (2):260–64.

Cook, O. F. 1909. "Vegetation Affected by Agriculture in Central America." *U.S. Bureau Plant Industry, Bull.* no. 145.

Cook, S. F. 1946. "A Reconsideration of Shellmounds with Respect to Population and Nutrition." *American Antiquity* 12 (1):50–53.

—— 1949. "Soil Erosion and Population in Central Mexico." *Ibero-Americana* 34:1–86.

Cook, S. F. and R. F. Heizer. 1953. "Archeological Dating by Chemical Means." *Southwestern Journal Anthropology* 9 (2):231–38.

Cook, S. F. and A. E. Treganza. 1950. "The Quantitative Investigation of Indian Mounds." *University California Publications American Archaeology and Ethnology* 40 (5).

Cooke, C. W. 1931. "Why the Maya Cities of the Petén District, Guatemala, Were Abandoned." *Journal Washington Academy Sciences* 21 (13):283–87.

Cornwall, I. W. 1956. *Bones for the Archaeologist.* New York: Macmillan.

—— 1958. *Soils for the Archaeologist.* New York: Macmillan.

Cotter, J. L. 1937. "The Occurrence of Flints and Extinct Animals in Pluvial Deposits near Clovis, New Mexico. Part IV." *Proceedings Academy Natural Sciences Philadelphia* 89.

—— 1938. "The Occurrence of Flints and Extinct Animals in Pluvial Deposits near Clovis, New Mexico. Part VI." *Ibid.,* 90, pp. 113–17.

Covarrubias, Miguel. 1957. *American Modern Art of Mexico and Central America.* New York: Alfred A. Knopf.

Cowgill, G. L. 1964. "The End of Classic Maya Culture: a Review of Recent Evidence." *Southwestern Journal of Anthropology* 20 (2):145–59.

Cowgill, U. M. 1961. "Soil Fertility and the Ancient Maya." *Transactions Connecticut Academy Arts and Sciences* 42:1–56.

Cowgill, U. M. and G. E. Hutchinson. 1963. "Ecological and Geochemical Archaeology in the Southern Maya Lowlands." *Southwestern Journal of Anthropology* 19:267–86.

Cowles, R. B. 1963. "Missiles, Clay Pots and Mortality Rates in Primitive Man." *American Naturalist* 97:29–37.

Crusoe, D. L. 1971. "A Study of Aboriginal Trade: a Petrographic Analysis of Certain Ceramic Types from Georgia and Florida." *Florida Anthropologist* 24 (1):31–43.

Cushing, E. J. and H. E. Wright, Jr., eds. 1967. *Quaternary Paleoecology*. New Haven: Yale University Press.

Daly, Patricia. 1969. "Approaches to Faunal Analysis in Archeology." *American Antiquity* 34 (2):146–53.

Dangel, Richard. 1930. "Quechua and Maori." *Mitt. Anthrop. Gesell. Wien* 60:343–51.

Daniel, Glyn. 1967. *The Origin and Growth of Archaeology*. New York: Crowell.

Darling, F. F. 1951. "The Ecological Approach to the Social Sciences." *American Scientist* 39 (2):244–54.

Dart, R. A. 1957. "The Osteodontokeratic Culture of *Australopithecus prometheus*." *Transvaal Museum Memoir* No. 10.

—— 1958. "The Minimal Bone-Breccia Content of Makapansgat and the Australopithecine Predatory Habit. *American Anthropologist*, 60 (5):923–31.

De Costa, John and C. N. Warren. 1967. "Paleolimnology and Prehistory." *American Antiquity* 32 (1):31–35.

Deevey, E. S., Jr. 1951. "Recent Textbooks of Human Ecology." *Ecology* 32 (2):347–50.

De Laet, S. J. 1957. *Archaeology and Its Problems*. New York: Praeger.

Denig. E. T. 1953. "Of the Crow Nation." *Bureau American Ethnology, Bull.* 151, paper 33.

Dethier, V. G. and Eliot Stellar. 1964. *Animal Behavior: Its Evolutionary and Neurological Basis*. Englewood Cliffs, N. J.: Prentice-Hall.

Deuel, Thorne. 1957. "The Modoc Shelter." *Illinois State Museum, Report of Investigations*, no. 7.

Dietz, E. F. 1957. "Phosphorus Accumulation in Soil of an Indian Habitation Site." *American Antiquity* 22 (4, pt. 1):405–9.

Dimbleby, G. W. 1967. *Plants and Archaeology*. New York: Humanities Press.

Dixon, J. E., Jr., J. R. Cann, and Colin Renfrew. 1968. "Obsidian and the Origins of Trade." *Scientific American* 64:38–46.

Dobzhansky, Theodosius. 1955. *Evolution, Genetics, and Man*. New York: Wiley.

—— 1962. *Mankind Evolving: The Evolution of the Human Species*. New Haven: Yale University Press.

Douglass, A. E. 1935. "Dating Pueblo Bonito and other ruins of the Southwest." *Nat. Geog. Soc., Pueblo Bonito Series*, No. 1.

—— 1936. "Climatic Cycles and Tree Ring Growth." *Carnegie Institution of Washington*, pub. no. 289.

—— 1942. "Checking the Date of Bluff Ruin, Forestdale: A Study in Technique." *Tree Ring Bulletin* 9 (2):2–7.

Doran, J. P. 1970. "Systems Theory, Computer Simulations and Archaeology." *World Archaeology* 1 (3):289–98.

Dorf, Erling. 1959. "Climatic Changes of the Past and Present." *Contributions Museum of Paleontology, Univ. Michigan* 13 (8).

Driver, H. E. 1961. *Indians of North America.* Chicago: University of Chicago Press.

Driver, H. E. and W. C. Massey. 1957. "Comparative Studies of North American Indians." *Trans. Amer. Philosophical Soc.,* n. s. 47 (2).

Drucker, Philip and R. F. Heizer. 1960. "A Study of the Milpa System of La Venta Island and Its Archaeological Implications." *Southwestern Journal of Anthropology* 16 (1):36–45.

DuBois, Cora. 1944. *The People of Alor.* Minneapolis: University of Minnesota Press.

Dumond, D. E. 1961. "Swidden Agriculture and the Rise of the Maya Civilization." *Southwestern Journal of Anthropology* 17 (4):301–16.

Durant, Will. 1954. *The Story of Philosophy.* New York: Affiliated.

Dyer, J. O. 1917. *The Lake Charles Atakapas (Cannibals), Period of 1817–1820.* Galveston, Texas.

Dyson, R. H., Jr., and E. Tooker. 1949. *The Palmer-Taylor Mound, Geneva, Florida.* Cambridge, Mass.

Easly, D. T., Jr. 1966. "Early Metallurgy in the New World." *Scientific American* 62:72–78, 81.

Edwards, W. E. 1954. "The Helen Blazes Site of Central Eastern Florida." Ph.D. dissertation, Columbia University, New York.

Eiseley, Loren. 1962. *The Immense Journey.* New York: Time Inc.

Eisman, Louis and Charles Tanzer. 1971. *Biology and Human Progress,* 4th ed. Englewood Cliffs, N.J.: Prentice-Hall.

Ekholm, G. F. 1950. "Is American Indian Culture Asiatic?" *Natural History* 59 (8):344–51, 382.

—— 1953. "A Possible Focus of Asiatic Influence in the Late Classic Cultures of Mesoamerica." *in* M. W. Smith, ed., "Asia and North America: Transpacific Contacts." *American Antiquity* 18 (3, pt.2):72–89.

Emiliani, Cesare. 1968. "The Pleistocene Epoch and the Evolution of Man." *Current Anthropology* 9 (1):27–47.

Enzie, F. D. and E. W. Price. 1956. "Internal Parasites of Dogs and Cats." *in Animal Diseases,* U. S. Dept. Agriculture Yearbook (1956), pp. 503–17.

Erdman, J. A., C. L. Douglas, and J. W. Marr. 1969. "Environment of Mesa Verde, Colorado." *Nat. Park Service Archaeological Research Series,* no. 7-B.

Evans, R. V. 1961. "Synthesis: Will o' the Wisp of New World Archaeology." *Southern Indian Studies* 13:3–20.

Eyre, S. R., ed. 1971. *World Vegetation Types.* New York: Columbia University Press.

Fairbanks, C. H. 1952. "Creek and Pre-Creek." In J. B. Griffin, ed., *Archeology of Eastern United States,* pp. 285–300. Univ. Chicago Press, Chicago.

—— 1956. "Archeology of the Funeral Mound, Ocmulgee National Monument, Georgia." *Nat. Park Service Archaeological Research Series,* No. 3.

—— 1964. "Underwater Historic Sites on St. Marks River." *Florida Anthropologist* 17 (2):44–49.

Fairbridge, R. W. 1958. "Dating the Latest Movements of the Quaternary Sea Level." *Trans. New York Academy Sciences*, ser. 2, 20:471–82.

—— 1960. "The Changing Level of the Sea. *Scientific American* 202(5):70-

Ferguson, G. E., C. W. Lingham, S. K. Love, and R. O. Vernon. 1947. "Springs of Florida." *Fla. Geol. Survey, Geol. Bull.* no. 31.

Ferrario, Benigno. 1933. "La Investigación lingüistica y el parentesco extracontinental de la lengua 'qhexwa.' " *Rev. Soc. Amigos Arqueol.* 7:89–120.

—— 1938. "Della possibile parentela fra le lingue 'altaiche' ed alcune americaine." *Tip. della R. Accademia dei lincei del Dott.* Rome.

Firth, Raymond. 1939. *Primitive Polynesian Economy.* London: Routledge.

—— 1956. *Human Types: an Introduction to Social Anthropology.* London: Thomas Nelson.

Fischer, Joseph. 1903. *The Discoveries of the Norsemen in America with Special Relation to their Early Cartographical Representation.* St. Louis: B. Herder.

Fitting, J. E. 1968. "Environmental Potential and the Postglacial Readaptation in Eastern North America." *American Antiquity* 33(4):441–45.

Flint, R. F. 1956. "New Radiocarbon Dates and Late-Pleistocene Stratigraphy." *American Journal Science* 254(5):265–87.

Follett, W. I. 1957. "Fish Remains from a Shellmound in Marin County, California." *American Antiquity* 23(1):68–71.

Fontana, B. L. 1965. "The Tale of a Nail: On the Ethnological Interpretation of Historic Artifacts." *Florida Anthropologist* 18(3, pt. 2):85–102.

Forbis, R. G. 1956. "Early Man and Fossil Bison." *Science* 123:327–28.

Ford, J. A. 1969. *A Comparison of Formative Cultures in the Americas: Diffusion or the Psychic Unity of Man.* Washington, D.C.: Smithsonian Institution Press.

Forde, C. D. 1949. *Habitat, Economy, and Society. A Geographical Introduction to Ethnology.* London: Methuen.

Fowke, Gerard. 1902. *Archaeological History of Ohio.* Clumbus.

Fowler, Melvin. 1953. "Radiocarbon Dates and Illinois Archaeology." *Journal Illinois State Archaeological Society* 4(1):28–32.

—— 1969. "Middle Mississippian Agricultural Fields." *American Antiquity* 34(4):365–75.

Fowler, Melvin and P. W. Parmelee. 1959. "Ecological Interpretation of Data on Archaeological Sites: The Modoc Rock Shelter." *Trans. Ill. State Acad. Sci.* 52(3–4):109–19.

Freeman, Howard, Sol Levine, and Leo Reeder, eds. 1972. *Handbook of Medical Sociology,* 2nd ed. Englewood Cliffs, N.J.: Prentice-Hall.

Freeman, L. G. 1968. "A Theoretical Framework for Interpreting Archeological Materials." In R. B. Lee and Irven De Vore, eds., *Man the Hunter,* pp. 262–67. Chicago: Aldine.

Freilich, Morris. 1967. "Ecology and Culture: Environmental Determinism and the Ecological Approach in Anthropology." *Anthropological Quarterly* 40(1):26–43.

Frenguelli, Joaquin. 1950. "The Present Status of the Theories Concerning Primitive Man in Argentina." In J. H. Steward, ed., *Handbook of South American Indians* 6:11–18. *Bureau American Ethnology Bull.* 143.

Fritz, J. M. and Fred Plog. 1970. "The Nature of Archaeological Explanation." *American Antiquity* 35(4):405–12.

Fry, G. F. and J. G. Moore. 1969. *Enterobius vermicularis:* 10,000-Year-Old Human Infection." *Science* 166:1620.

Funkhouser, W. D. 1938. "A Study of the Physical Anthropology and Pathology of the Osteological material from the Norris Basin." In W. S. Webb, "An Archaeological Survey of the Norris Basin in Eastern Tennessee." *Bureau American Ethnology Bull.* 118:225–52.

—— 1939. "A Study of the Physical Anthropology and Pathology of the Osteological Material from the Wheeler Basin." In W. S. Webb, "An Archaeological Survey of Wheeler Basin on the Tennessee River in Northern Alabama." *Ibid.*, 122:109–26.

Gagliano, S. M. 1967. "Kirk Serrated: An Early Archaic Index Point in Louisiana." *Florida Anthropologist* 20(1–2):3–9.

Gancedo, A. 1922. "El idioma japonés y sus afinidades con lenguas americanas." *Rev. Derecho Hist. Let.* 73:114–22.

Gardner, W. M. 1969. "An Example of the association of Archaeological Complexes with Tribal and Linguistic Grouping: The Fort Walton Complex of Northwest Florida." *Florida Anthropologist* 22(1–4):1–11.

Gatschet, A. S. 1877. "The Timucua Language." *Proc. American Phil. Soc.* 16:626–42.

—— 1884. "A Migration Legend of the Creek Indians, vol. 1. *Brinton's Library of Aboriginal American Literature,* no. 4.

—— 1888. "A Migration Legend of the Creek Indians, vol. 2. *Trans. Acad. Sci. St. Louis* 5(1–2).

Gebhard, P. H. 1949. "An Archaeological Survey of the Blowouts of Yuma County, Colorado. *American Antiquity* 15(2):132–43.

Gehlbach, F. R. and R. R. Miller. 1961. "Fishes From Archaeological Sites in Northern New Mexico." *Southwestern Naturalist* 6(1):2–8.

Geyl, P. 1957. *Debates with Historians.* New York: Meridian.

Gifford, E. W. 1916. "Composition of California Shellmounds." *Univ. Calif. Pubs. American Archaeology and Ethnology* 12(1).

Gilmore, R. M. 1947. "Report on a Collection of Mammal Bones from Archeologic Cave-Sites in Coahuila, Mexico." *Journal Mammalogy* 28(2):147–65.

—— 1949. "On the Identification and Value of Mammal Bones from Archeological Excavations." *Ibid.* 30(2):163–69.

Goff, J. H. 1957. "The Buffalo in Georgia." *Georgia Review* 11(1):19–28.

Goggin, J. M. 1947. "A Preliminary Definition of Archaeological Areas and Periods in Florida." *American Antiquity* 13(2):114–27.

—— 1948a. "Florida Archeology and Recent Ecological Changes." *Journal Washington Acad. Sci.* 38(7):225–33.

—— 1948b. "Some Pottery Types from Central Florida." *Gainesville Anthropological Assoc., Bull.* 1.

—— 1949a. "Cultural Traditions in Florida Prehistory." In J. W. Griffin, ed., *The Florida Indian and his Neighbors,* pp. 13–44. Rollins College: Winter Park, Fla.

—— 1949b. "A Florida Indian Trading Post, Circa 1763–1784." *Southern Indian Studies* 1(2):35–38.

—— 1950. "Florida Archeology—1950." *Florida Anthropologist* 3(1–2):9–20.

—— 1952. "Space and Time Perspective in Northern St. Johns Archeology, Florida." *Yale Univ. Pubs. Anthropology,* no. 47.

—— 1958. "Seminole Pottery." In *Prehistoric Pottery of the Eastern United States.* Ann Arbor: University of Michigan, Museum of Anthropology.

—— 1960. "Underwater Archeology: Its Nature and Limitations." *American Antiquity* 25(3):348–54.

—— 1962. "Recent Developments in Underwater Archeology." *Southeastern Archeological Conference, Newsletter* 8:77–88.

—— 1964. *Indian and Spanish Selected Writings.* Coral Gables: Univ. Miami Press.

Goggin, J. M., M. E. Goodwin, E. Hester, D. Prange, and R. Spangenberg. 1949. "An Historic Indian Burial, Alachua County, Florida." *Florida Anthropologist* 2(1–2):10–25.

Goggin, J. M. and F. H. Sommer, III. 1949. "Excavations on Upper Matecumbe Key, Florida." *Yale University Publications in Anthropology,* no. 41.

Goslin, R. M. "Animal Remains from Ohio Rock Shelters." *Ohio Journal Science* 5(6):358–62.

Greenberg, J. H. 1960. "The General Classification of Central and South American languages." In A. F. C. Wallace, ed., *Selected Papers, 5th International Congress of Anthropological and Ethnological Sciences,* pp. 791–94. Philadelphia: University Pennsylvania Press.

Greenman. E. F. 1960. "The North Atlantic and Early Man in the New World." *Michigan Archeologist* 6:19–39.

Griffin, J. B., ed. 1951. *Essays on Archeological Methods:* Proceedings of a Conference Held under the Auspices of the Viking Fund. Michigan University Museum of Anthropology, Anthropological Papers, no. 8. Ann Arbor: University of Michigan Press.

Griffin, J. B. 1960. "Climatic Change: A Contributory Cause of the Growth and Decline of Northern Hopewellian Culture." *Wisconsin Archeologist* 41(1):21–33.

Griffin, J. W. and H. G. Smith. 1954. "The Cotten Site: An Archaeological Site of Early Ceramic Times in Volusia County, Florida." *Florida State University Studies,* no. 16:27–59.

Guerra, F. 1972. *The Pre-Columbian Mind.* New York, Seminar Press.

Hammond, Norman. 1973. *South Asian Archaeology*. Park Ridge, New Jersey: Noyes Press.

Hamon, J. H. 1959. "Northern Birds from a Florida Indian Midden." *Auk* 76:533–34.

Hardman, Clark, Jr. 1971. "The Primitive Solar Observatory at Crystal River and Its Implications." *Florida Anthropologist* 24(4):135–68.

Hargrave, L. L. 1938. "A Plea for More Careful Preservation of All Biological Material from Prehistoric Sites." *Southwestern Lore* (December):47–51.

—— 1939. "Brid Bones from Abandoned Indian Dwellings in Arizona and Utah." *The Condor* 41:206–10.

Harpstead, D. D. 1971. "High-Lysine Corn." *Scientific American* (July):34–42.

Hawkes, Jacquetta. 1973. *First Great Civilizations*. New York: Alfred A. Knopf.

Hawley, A. H. 1950. *Human Ecology: A Theory of Community Structure*. New York: Ronald Press.

Hay, O. P. 1902. "On the Finding of the Bones of the Great Auk (*Plautus impennis*) in Florida." *Auk* 19:255–58.

Heizer, R. F. 1958. *A Guide to Archaeological Field Methods*, 3rd ed. Palo Alto: National Press.

Hibbard, C. W. 1960. "An Interpretation of Pliocene and Pleistocene Climates in North America." *Michigan Academy Arts, Sciences, and Letters, Annual Report*, 1959–60.

Hibben, F. C. 1941. "Evidences of Early Occupation in Sandia Cave, New Mexico, and other Sites in the Sandia-Manzano Region." *Smithsonian Miscellaneous Collections* 99(23). Washington, D.C.: Smithsonian Institution.

Hill, James N. 1970. "Broken K: A Prehistoric Society in Eastern Arizona." *Anthropological Papers University Arizona*, no. 18. Tucson.

Hole, Frank, K. V. Flannery and J. V. Neely. 1969. "Prehistory and Human Ecology of the Deh Luran Plain: An Early Village Sequence from Khuzistan, Iran." *Memoirs Museum Anthropology, University of Michigan*, no. 1. Ann Arbor.

Holmes, W. H. 1903. "Aboriginal Pottery of the Eastern United States." *Annual Report, Bureau of American Ethnology*, 20.

Hooton, Edwin. 1935. *Apes, Men and Morons*. Garden City, N.Y.: Doubleday, Doran.

Houck, Margaret V. 1951. "Animal Remains from South Indian Field." Appendix to V. M. Ferguson, Chronology at South Indian Field, Florida. *Yale University Publications in Anthropology*, no. 45, pp. 51–60.

Howard, Hildegarde. 1929. "The Avifauna of the Emeryville Shellmound." *Univeristy of California Publications in Zoology* 32(2).

Hrdlička, Aleš. 1940a. "Catalog of Human Crania in the United States National Museum Collections: Indians of the Gulf States." *Proc. U. S. National Museum* 87:315–464.

—— 1940.b. "Ritual Ablation of the Front Teeth in Siberia and America." *Smithsonian Miscellaneous Collections* 99(3).

Hurt, W. R. 1953. "A Comparative Study of the Preceramic Occupations of North America." *American Antiquity* 18(3):204–22.

Huxley, Julian et al., eds. 1957. *Evolution as a Process.* New York: Macmillan.

Imbelloni, Jose. 1928. L'idioma Kichua nel sistema linguístico dell' Oceano Pacifico. Rome: International Congress of Americanists, Session 22, vol.2:495–509.

Inkeles, Alex. 1964. *What Is Sociology? An Introduction to the Discipline and Profession.* Englewood Cliffs, N.J.: Prentice-Hall.

Jelinek, A. J. 1962. "An Index of Radiocarbon Dates Associated with Cultural Materials." *Current Anthropology* 3(5):451–77.

Johnson, Frederick. 1951. "Radiocarbon Dating." *Memoir Society American Archaeology* No. 8.

Kaplan. D. and R. A. Manners 1972. *Culture Theory.* Englewood Cliffs, N.J.: Prentice-Hall.

Keesing, F. M. 1962. "Cultural Anthropology: The Science of Custom." New York: Holt, Rinehart and Winston.

Kidder, A. V. 1947. *Artifacts of Uaxactun, Guatemala.* Washington, D.C.: Carnegie Institution, Publication 576.

Kluckholn, C. 1949. *Mirror For Man.* New York: McGraw-Hill.

Kroeber, A. L. 1939. "Cultural and Natural Areas of Native North America." *University California Publication American Archeology and Ethnology* 38.

—— ed. 1953. *Anthropology Today: An Encyclopedic Inventory.* Chicago, University Chicago Press.

—— and Clyde Kluckhohn. 1952. "Culture: A Critical Review of Concepts and Definitions." *Papers Peabody Museum American Archaeology and Ethnology* 47(1).

Kurtén, Björn. 1971. "Time and Hominid Brain Size." *Commentationes Biologicae* 36.

—— 1972. *Not From the Apes.* New York: Vantage Books.

—— 1976. *The Cave Bear Story: Life and Death of a Vanished Animal.* New York: Columbia University Press.

Larabee, Edward M. 1964. "Industrial Archaeology in Great Britain." *Florida Anthropologist* 17(2):82–93.

Laughlin, William S. (ed.). 1951. *The Physical Anthropology of the American Indian.* New York: The Viking Fund, Inc.

Lawson, John. 1714. *History of Carolina, Containing the Exact Description and Natural History of That Country.* London.

Lazarus, W. C. 1965. "Effects of Land Subsidence and Sea Level Changes on Elevation of Archaeological Sites on the Florida Gulf Coast." *Florida Anthropologist* 18(1):49–58.

Leone, J. 1972. *Contemporary Archaeology: A Guide to Theory and Contributions.* Carbondale: Southern Illinois University Press.

Libby, Willard F. 1955. *Radiocarbon Dating.* Chicago: University of Chicago Press.

Limprey, S. 1972. *Soil Science in Archaeology.* New York: Seminar Press.

Linton, Ralph. 1945. *The Science of Man and the World Crisis.* New York: Columbia University Press.

Longacre, W. A. ed. 1970. *Archaeology of Anthropology: A Case Study.* Tucson: University of Arizona Press.

Lutz, H. J. and R. F. Chandler. 1946. *Forest Soils.* New York: Wiley.

McDowell, Bart. 1970. "Gypsies, Wanderers of the World." Washington, D.C.: National Geographic Society.

McKern, T. W. and T. D. Stewart. 1957. "Skeletal Age Changes in Young American Males, Analyzed from the Standpoint of Age Identification." *Technical Report* EP-45, *Environmental Protection Research Division, Quartermaster Research and Development Center,* Washington, D.C.

McNeish, R. S. 1967. "A Summary of the Subsistence." In D. S. Byers, ed. *The Prehistory of the Tehuacán Valley: Vol. 1. Environment and Subsistence.* Austin: University of Texas Press.

MacWhite, Eoin. 1956. "On the Interpretation of Archeological Evidence in Historical and Sociological Terms." *American Anthropologist* 58(1):3–25.

Martin, P. S. n. d. "Pleistocene Ecology and Biogeography of North America." *American Association Advancement Science Pub.* no. 51.

Martin, P. S. 1971. "The Revolution in Archeology." *American Antiquity* 36:1–8.

Martin, P. S., G. I. Quimby, and D. Collier. 1947. *Indians Before Columbus.* Chicago: University of Chicago Press.

Martin, P. S. and F. W. Sharrock. 1964. "Pollen Analysis of Prehistoric Human Feces: A New Approach to Ethnobotany." *American Antiquity* 30(2, pt. 1):168–80.

Martin, P. S. and H. E. Wright. 1973. *Pleistocene Extinctions: the Search for a Cause.* New Haven: Yale University Press.

Mason, J. A. 1950. "The Languages of South American Indians." In J. H. Steward, ed., *Handbook of South American Indians* Vol. 6. Bureau of American Ethnology, Bulletin 143.

Mason, R. J. 1962. "The Paleo-Indian Tradition in Eastern North America." *Current Anthropology* (June):227–78.

Medawar, P. B. 1960. *The Future of Man.* New York: Basic Books.

Meggers, B. J. 1966. *Ecuador.* New York: Praeger.

Meggers, B. J., C. Evans and E. Estrada. 1965. "Early Formative Period of Coastal Ecuador: the Valdivia and Machalilla Phases." *Smithsonian Contributions to Anthroplogy* 1.

Meighan, C. W. et al. 1958. "Ecological Interpretation in Archeology." Part 1. *American Antiquity* 24(1):1–22. Part 2: *Ibid.* (2):131–50.

Metraux, Alfred. 1949. "Weapons." In Julian H. Steward, ed. *Handbook of South American Indians,* Vol. 5, *The Comparative Ethnology of South American Indians,* pp. 229–61. Washington, D.C.: Smithsonian Institution, Bureau of American Ethnology. Bulletin 143. (The two figures appear on pp. 235 and 236 respectively.)

Miller, Carl F. 1950. "Early Cultural Horizons in the Southeastern United States." *American Antiquity* 15(4):273–88.

Miller, R. R. 1955. "Fish Remains from Archaeological Sites in the Lower Colorado River Basin, Arizona." *Papers of Michigan Academy of Science, Arts and Letters* 40:125–36.

—— 1961. "Man and the Changing Fish Fauna of the American Southwest." *Ibid.* 46:

Mochon, M. J. 1972. "Language, History, and Prehistory: Mississippian Lexico-Reconstruction." *American Antiquity* 37(2):478–503.

Montagu, Ashley. 1960. *An Introduction to Physical Anthropology*, 3rd ed. Springfield, Ill.: Charles C. Thomas.

Mori, J. L. "Procedure for Establishing a Faunal Collection to Aid in Archeological Analysis." *American Antiquity* 35(3):387–89.

Murdock, G. P. et al. 1950. *Outline of Cultural Materials*, 3rd ed. New Haven: Human Relations Area Files, Inc.

Napier, John. 1967. "The Antiquity of Human Walking." *Scientific American* (April):56–66.

Neill, W. T. 1952. "Unusual Rattles from Silver Springs, Florida." *Florida Anthropologist* 5(3–4):33–34.

—— 1953. "Notes on the Supposed Association of Artifacts and Extinct Vertebrates in Flagler County, Florida." *American Antiquity* 19(2):170–71.

—— 1955a. "An Historic Indian Burial from Columbia County, Georgia." *Southern Indian Studies* 7:3–9.

—— 1955b. "The Identity of Florida's 'Spanish Indians.' " *Florida Anthropologist* 8(2):43–57.

—— 1957a. "Historical Biogeography of Present-day Florida." Bull. Florida State Museum of Biological Science 2(7).

—— 1957b. "The Rapid Mineralization of Organic Remains in Florida, and Its Bearing on Supposed Pleistocene Records." *Quarterly Jour. Fla. Acad. Sci.* 20(1):1–13.

—— 1958a. "The Site of Osceola's Village in Marion County, Florida." *Florida Historical Quarterly* 33(3–4):240–46.

—— 1958b. "A Stratified Early Site at Silver Springs, Florida. *Florida Anthropologist* 11(1):33–52.

—— 1962. "Hunters of the Glades." *Florida Wildlife* 15(8):10–13, 30.

—— 1963. "Three New Florida Projectile Types, Believed Early." *Florida Anthropologist* 14(4):99–104.

—— 1964a. "The Association of Suwannee Points and Extinct Animals in Florida." *Florida Anthropologist* 17(1):17–32.

—— 1964b. "Trilisa Pond; an Early Site in Marion County, Florida," *Florida Anthropologist* 17(4):187–200.

—— 1966. "Westo Bluff, a Site of the Old Quartz Culture in Georgia." *Florida Anthropologist* 19(1):1–10.

—— 1968a. "The Galphin Trading Post Site of Silver Bluff, South Carolina." *Florida Anthropologist* 21(2–3):42–54.

—— 1968b. "An Indian and Spanish Site on Tampa Bay, Florida." *Florida Anthropologist* 21(4):106–16.

—— 1968c. [Review of] G. W. Dimbleby, 1967. *Plants and Archeology.* New York: Humanities Press.

—— 1969. *The Geography of Life.* New York: Columbia University Press.

—— 1971. "A Florida Paleo-Indian Implement of Ground Stone." *Florida Anthropologist* 24(2):61–70.

—— 1973. *Twentieth-Century Indonesia.* New York: Columbia University Press.

—— 1976a. "Ecological Data Bearing on the Age of Kirk Serrated Points in Florida." *Florida Anthropologist* 29(4):153–59.

—— 1976b. "The Seminole Pumpkin." *Fla. Anthropologist* 29(3):129–32.

Neill, W. T. and Ross Allen, 1959. "Studies on the Amphibians and Reptiles of British Honduras." *Pubs. Research Division, Ross Allen's Reptile Institute* 2 (1).

Neill, W. T. and R. P. Bullen. 1955. "Muskrat Remains from a Prehistoric Indian Site in Jackson County, Florida." *Journal of Mammalogy* 36(1):138.

Neill, W. T., H. James Gut, and Pierce Brodkorb. 1956. "Animal Remains from Four Preceramic Sites in Florida." *American Antiquity* 21(4):383–95.

Neumann, G. K. 1952. "Archeology and Race in the American Indians." In J. B. Griffin, ed. *Archaeology of the Eastern United States*, pp. 13–34. Chicago: University of Chicago Press.

Olsen, S. J. 1958. "The Wakulla Cave." *Natural History* 67(7):396–98, 401–3.

Parmelee, P. W. 1956. "A Comparison of Past and Present Populations of Fresh-Water Mussels in Southern Illinois." *Ibid.* 49:184–92.

—— 1958a. "Evidence of the Fisher in Central Illinois." *Journal of Mammalogy* 39(1):153.

—— 1958b. "Marine Shells of Illinois Indian Sites." *Nautilus* (April): 71(14):132–39.

—— 1958c. "Remains of Rare and Extinct Birds from Illinois Indian Sites." *Auk* 75(2):169–76.

—— 1959. "Use of Mammalian Skulls and Mandibles by Prehistoric Indians of Illinois." *Trans. Ill. State Acad. Sci.* 52(3–4):85–95.

Parmelee, P. W. and D. F. Hoffmeister. 1957. "Archaeo-Zoological Evidence of the Spotted Skunk in Illinois." *Journal of Mammalogy* 38(2):261.

Parmelee, P. W. et al. 1969. "Pleistocene and Recent Vertebrate Faunas from Crankshaft Cave, Missouri." *Report Investigations* No. 14. *Illinois State Museum.*

Parsons, Talcott. 1966. *Societies: Evolutionary and Comparative Perspectives.* Englewood Cliffs, N.J.: Prentice-Hall.

Patterson, C. C. 1971. "Native Copper, Silver, and Gold Accessible to Early Metallurgists." *American Antiquity* 36(3):286–321.

Phelps, D. S. 1968. "Mesoamerican Glyph Motifs on Southeastern Pottery." *International Congress Americanists.* (Mimeographed).

Piggott, Stuart. 1965. *Approach to Archaeology.* New York, McGraw-Hill Book Co.

Pizzi, Tulio and Hugo Schenone. 1954. "Finding of *Trichuris trichiura* Eggs in the Intestinal Content of an Archeologic Body of an Inca." *Boletin Chileno de Parasitologia* 9(3):63–75.

Quimby, G. I. 1954. "Cultural and Natural Areas Before Kroeber." *American Antiquity* 19(4):317–31.

Quinn, J. A. 1950. *Human Ecology.* New York: Prentice-Hall.

Renfrew, Colin. 1971. "Carbon 14 and the Prehistory of Europe." *Scientific American* (Oct.):63–70, 72.

Renfrew, J. M. 1973. *Palaeoethnobotany: The Prehistoric Food Plants of the Near East and Europe.* New York, Columbia University Press.

Riley, C. L. et al. 1971. *Man Across the Sea: Problems of Pre-Columbian Contact.* Austin: University of Texas Press.

Rivet, Paul. 1925. "Les Melaneso-polynesiens et les Australiens en Amererique." *Anthropos* 20:51–54.

Rouse, Irving. 1951. "A Survey of Indian River Archeology, Florida." *Yale University Publications in Anthropology,* no. 44.

—— 1960. "The Entry of Man into the West Indies." *Ibid.,* No. 61.

Royal, W. and E. Clark. 1960. "Natural Preservation of Human Brain, Warm Mineral Springs, Florida." *American Antiquity* 26(2):285–87.

Sampson, John. 1926. *The Dialect of the Gypsies of Wales.* London: Oxford University Press.

Sapir, Edward. 1916. *Time Perspective in Aboriginal American Culture.* Geological Survey Memoir 90, Anthropological Series no. 13.

Sears, W. H. 1967. "The Tierra Verde Burial Mound." *Florida Anthropologist* 20(1–2):23–73.

Smith, H. G. 1965. "Archaeological Excavations at Santa Rosa Pensacola. *Florida Dept. Anthropology, Notes Anthropology* 10.

Smith, M. W., ed. 1953. "Asia and North America: Transpacific Contacts." *American Antiquity* 18 (3, pt. 2).

Snow, Charles E. 1941. "Anthropological Studies at Moundville." Alabama Museum of Natural History, Museum Paper 5. University, Ala.

—— 1943. "Two Prehistoric Indian Dwarf Skeletons from Moundville." Alabama Museum of Natural History, Mus. Paper 21.

—— 1962. "Indian Burials from St. Petersburg, Florida." *Contributions Florida State Museum, Social Sciences* no. 8.

Solheim, W. G. 1972 "An Earlier Agricultural Revolution." *Scientific American* (April): 34–41.

Sorenson, J. L. n.d. "The Significance of an Apparent Relationship between the Ancient Near East and Mesoamerica," pp. 1–42 (mimeographed).

Steward, J. H., ed. 1946–50. Handbook of South American Indians. 6 vols. *Bureau American Ethnology Bulletin* 143.

Swanton, J. R. 1911. "Indian Tribes of the Lower Mississippi Valley and Adjacent Coast of the Gulf of Mexico." U.S. Bureau of American Ethnology, Series Bulletin No. 43.

—— 1922. *Early History of the Creek Indians and Their Neighbors.* (Reprinted 1971.) New York: Johnson Reprint.

—— 1942. *Source Material on the History and Ethnology of the Caddo Indians.* Reprinted. New York: Scholarly Reprints, Inc. n.d.

—— 1946. "Indians of the Southeastern United States." *Bureau of American Ethnology Bulletin* no. 137. Reprinted. Westport, Conn.: Greenwood Publications. n.d.

—— 1952. *Indian Tribes of North America.* Reprinted 1968. New York: Scholarly Reprints, Inc.

Swadesh, Morris. 1964. "Linguistic Overview." In J. D. Jennings and E. Norback, eds., *Prehistoric Man in the New World,* pp. 527–58. Chicago: University of Chicago Press.

Swadesh, Morris et al. 1954. "Symposium: Time Depths of American Linguistic Groupings." *American Anthropologist* 56:387–94.

Tarling, Don and Maureen Tarling. 1971. *Continental Drift.* Garden City, N.Y.: Doubleday and Co.

Taylor, W. W. 1948. "A Study of Archeology." *American Anthropologist* 50 (3, pt. 2).

—— ed. 1957. "The Identification of Non-artifactual Archaeological Materials." National Academy Sciences, Pub. 565.

Thomas, D. H., 1969, "Great Basin Hunting Patterns: A Quantitative Method for Treating Faunal Remains." *American Antiquity* 34(4):392–401.

Thomas, W. L., ed. 1956. *Man's Role in Changing the Face of the Earth.* Chicago: University of Chicago Press.

Tobias, P. V. 1965. Early Man in East Africa. *Science* 149:22–33.

Trigger, B. G. 1968. *Beyond History: The Methods of Prehistory.* New York: Holt, Rinehart and Winston, Inc.

True, D. O., ed. 1945. *Memoir Respecting Florida.* By Hernando d'Escalante Fontaneda. Translated from the Spanish with notes by Buckingham Smith. Washington: 1854. Reprinted with revisions by The University of Miami and the Historical Association of Southern Florida. Miscellaneous publications, no. 1.

Tyler, S. A., ed. 1969. *Cognitive Anthropology.* New York: Holt, Rinehart and Winston, Inc.

Watson, P. J., S. A. LeBlanc, and C. L. Redman. 1971. *Explanation in Archeology: an Explicitly Scientific Approach.* New York, Columbia University Press.

Waters, J. H. 1962. "Animals Used as Food by Late Archaic and Woodland Cultural Groups in New England." *Science* 137(3526):283–84.

Weaver, W. G. Jr. and J. S. Robertson. 1967. "A Re-evaluation of Fossil Turtles of the *Chrysemys scripta* Group." *Tulane Studies in Geology* 5(2):53–66.

Weigel, P. H. 1958. "Great Auk Remains from a Florida Shell Midden." *Auk* 75:215–16.

Whittlsey, Derwent. 1941. "Geography and Its Influence on History." *Bulletin Wagner Free Institute Science* 16(2):5–14.

White, T. E.. 1955. "Observations on the Butchering Techniques of Some Aboriginal Peoples, nos. 7, 8, and 9. *American Antiquity* 11(2):170–78.

Whyte, L. L. 1948. *The Next Development in Man.* New York: Holt.

Willey, G. R. 1949. "Archeology of the Florida Gulf Coast." *Smithsonian Miscellaneous Collections* 113.

—— 1966. *An Introduction to American Archeology.* Vol. 1, North and Middle America. 1971. *Ibid.* Vol. 2, *South America.* Englewood Cliffs, N.J., Prentice-Hall, Inc.

Willey, G. R. and Philip Phillips. 1958. *Method and Theory in American Archaeology.* Chicago: University of Chicago Press.

Williams, Stephen and John M. Goggin. 1956. "The Long-nosed God Mask in Eastern United States." *Missouri Archeologist* 18(3):3–72.

Williams, T. R. 1967. *Field Methods in the Study of Culture.* New York: Holt.

Wilson, Logan, and W. L. Kolb. 1949. *Sociological Analysis: An Introductory Text and Case Book.* New York: Harcourt.

Wing, E. S. 1963. "Vertebrates from the Jungerman and Goodman Sites Near the East Coast of Florida." *Central Florida State Museum of Social Science* 10:51–60.

Wissler, Clark. 1938. *The American Indian.* 3rd ed. New York: Oxford University Press.

Wormington, H. M. 1949. *Ancient Man in North America.* Denver: Museum of Natural History.

—— 1958. *Ancient Man in North America,* 4th ed. *Denver Museum Natural History, Popular Series* no. 4.

Wright, H. E. 1961. "Late Pleistocene Climate of Europe: A Review." *Geological Society America Bulletin* 72:933–84.

Wyman, Jeffries. 1875. *Fresh Water Shell Mounds of the St. John's River, Florida.* Reprinted 1972. AMS Press, n.p.

Yarnell, R. A. 1964. "Aboriginal Relationships Between Culture and Plant Life in the Upper Great Lakes Region." *Museum of Anthropology, University of Michigan Anthropological Papers No. 23.*

Index

Ablation of teeth, ritual, 93–94
Agriculture, *milpa,* 286–88; origins of, 197–99
Algonquian languages, 53
Altithermal climatic stage, 207
Anathermal climatic stage, 207
Antevs, Ernst, 174–75
Anthropology, 3, 9–10; physical, 14–15, 77–80; urban, 10
Archaic Major Cultural Tradition, 253–56
Archeobotany, 189–93
Archeology, environmental, 155–57, 187; industrial, 4; regional differences in, 31–32
Archeology and astronomy, 154–55; and economics, 136–39; and ethnography, 34–37; and history, 143–46; and human geography, 142–43; and psychology, 149–51; and sociology, 145–46; and toponymy, 58–66
Armadillo scutes, 219, fig. 35
Arthritis, 95–96
Astronomy, 154–55
Auk, 262
Australopithecus, 122–26

Bahía culture, 56
Banana, 211
Bartram, William, 269–70
Bates, Marston, 17–18
Bayshore Homes site, 81–83
Beadle, George W., 29–30
Beads, wampum, 47–49, fig. 8
Beard, J. S., 288–89

Belize (British Honduras), 287–91, figs. 48–52
Berry, Edward W., 264, 267–68
Big Circle Mounds, 155, fig. 28
Big-Game Hunting Tradition, 251–53
Big Midden site, 147–48, 201
Bison, 184–85
Blanc, Alberto C., 132–33
Blatchley, W. S., 262–63
Blood group systems, 107–8
Bluffton site, 169–70
Bon Terra Farm site, 205
Botany, 15–16, 189–90
Bottle-gourd, 209
British Honduras (Belize), 287–91, figs. 48–52
Bromeliads, 277, fig. 43
Brown's Valley Man, fig. 20
Bullen, Adelaide K., ix, 92–93
Bullen, Ripley P., ix, 60, 154, 262, 264, 293
Business, 147–48
Butchering techniques, 235–36

Calibration of radiocarbon dates, 177–78
Calusa Indians, 273–75
Caries, dental, 81–83
Carrel, Alexis, 19–20
Cavern site, 173–74
Cemeteries, prehistoric, 230–31
Chemistry, archaeological, 186–87
Circumcision, 88, fig. 15
Civilization, Mayan, 286–88; modern, fig. 2
Climatic stages, 207–8
Cochineal insects, 213